Prima Games
A Division of Random House, Inc.

3000 Lava Ridge Court
Roseville, CA 95661
1-800-733-3000
www.primagames.com

Created by **Kaizen Media Group**
Producer: Howard Grossman
Author: Keats Hanson
Designer: Ivor Forgevhen

007 EVERYTHING OR NOTHING
PRIMA'S OFFICIAL STRATEGY GUIDE

INTRO

INTRODUCTION

BACKGROUND: EVERYTHING OR NOTHING

The world's greatest secret agent returns in the latest and greatest interactive adventure from EA Games: *James Bond 007: Everything or Nothing*. This game delivers the ultimate cinematic gaming experience. It features the voice talents and likenesses of top stars such as Willem Dafoe, Shannon Elizabeth, Heidi Klum, and Mya, as well as those of the original cast members from the current James Bond movies, including M (Judi Dench), Q (John Cleese), and of course, James himself (Pierce Brosnan). Top all of this off with a slew of new vehicles, slick gadgets, exotic locales, and a "jaw-dropping" return of a familiar old enemy—*Everything or Nothing* it is certainly the most exciting Bond adventure so far.

Prima's Official Strategy Guide will take you through the game, showing you how to progress through each level just as Bond would—with savvy, daring, and the kind of genius only 007 could whip up. The walkthrough (which covers the Xbox, GameCube, and PlayStation 2 versions of the game) will take you step-by-step through missions that span four continents—from the Valley of the Kings in Egypt to the French Quarter in New Orleans.

AND NOW FOR THE STORY...

The biggest development in technology is small—very small—and it's missing. At Oxford University's Department of Microtechnology, prototype nanorobots have been stolen, and project scientist Dr. Katya Nadanova has disappeared. The nanobots are equipped with an organic compound that can eat away metal, providing the key ingredient in Nikolai Diavolo's plan to seize control of his native Russia and return it to its former glory as a bastion of hardline anti-Westernism.

Diavolo is more than merely a former KGB officer disillusioned by the westernization of his homeland. The prodigy of 007's nemesis Max Zorin, Diavolo was groomed to carry Zorin's plans to their natural conclusion: world domination.

Another agent, 003, was sent to investigate a mysterious mining operation and is now missing. His last known contact was American geologist Serena St. Germaine, and Bond is sent to locate her in Peru. While there, he discovers that 003 had contacted her in regards to her research on the anomalous platinum levels in the surrounding mountains. Investigating with St. Germaine, Bond is astonished to see Agent 003 undergoing a brutal interrogation at the hands of a mysterious stranger (Diavolo). Bond listens as 003 whispers his dying words: "You must get to New Orleans...stop Diavolo...."

Bond arrives in New Orleans while the city is preparing for Mardi Gras. He has plans to meet with Mya Starling, an undercover NSA agent who is assigned to keep an eye on a Russian colonel. Mya is discovered by Arkady Yayakov, the club's owner, before Bond reaches the club. Yayakov and his right-hand man, Jean Le Rouge, have lethal plans for her. To save Mya, Bond must race through the club and the nearby cemetery to a crematorium.

The following morning 007 receives orders to head to a plantation in the bayou, where he learns that Dr. Nadanova has modified the nanobot technology for Diavolo's sinister plans. Bond destroys the facility, and sees Jaws escaping toward New Orleans with a tanker full of the improved nanobot technology. He must stop Jaws before the villain unleashes the nanobots on the steel-supported city of New Orleans. If Jaws succeeds, the Big Easy will dissolve into the Mississippi River, and millions will be killed.

At the Q-Lab, Bond learns that platinum is the only metal that the nanobots won't destroy. He surmises that this bizarre chain of events must tie directly to Serena's research in Peru.

Will the world be made safe for democracy once again? That's up to you....

GAMEPLAY

GAME SCREEN: STATUS DISPLAY

While you're playing *Everything or Nothing*, the bottom of the game screen will indicate everything you need to know regarding your status. Here's how it breaks down, moving from left to right on the game screen.

1 POWER MODE INDICATOR

This "glowing Bond" icon flashes onscreen after you dispatch multiple enemies with hand-to-hand combat. In Power mode, your hand-to-hand attacks cause more damage (you'll see some new animations as well), and you will take less damage from enemies.

2 HEALTH METER

This is the most vital indicator—it shows how close you are to dying. It will flash red when you sustain damage. If you have vibration enabled on your controller, it will pulse like a rapid heartbeat when you are critically low on health.

3 BATTERY METER

This will tell you how much power you have left for using gadgets such as the Nano Suit and the RC car. Some gadgets (such as flares and the Q Cloak) will recharge— you'll see your meter build slowly or quickly depending on the gadget.

4 WEAPON/AMMO STATUS

The weapon or gadget currently equipped will be listed here, in the box on the lower line. The upper line has two numbers separated by a dash. The left number indicates how many bullets are in the weapon equipped. When that number goes to zero, you'll need to reload (you'll actually see an animation of Bond reloading the weapon). The number on the right indicates how many extra rounds are available to reload.

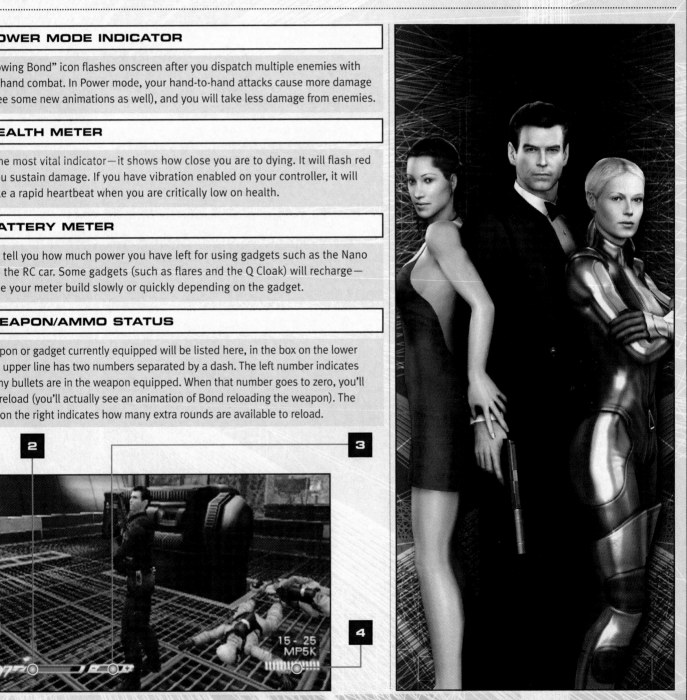

BOND MANEUVERS: CONTROLS/MOVES

While playing as Bond, you have a wealth of moves at your disposal. Some are obvious (walking around, firing a weapon, looking around, or performing an action), but a few moves are worth pointing out.

1 MOVEMENT/ROLLING

Thanks to analog control, Bond can walk, jog, or run depending on how far you push the analog stick. While moving, you can also roll, which is useful for dodging enemy fire. Since you can roll while crouched, it's also good to roll when moving from behind one box to another.

2 CROUCHING

Not only can you crouch behind items for cover, you can move while crouching. Although you move slower as a result, you'll make less noise and be able to sneak up behind enemies. Crouching while moving is essential for missions in which you need to avoid detection.

> **TIP**
>
> You can roll down stairs, but not up. (Bond is good, but he can't defy gravity.)

3 PUNCHING

Bond can punch with either hand, and pull off combos depending on the combinations pressed. Sometimes during hand-to-hand combat, the game will go into slow motion when you pull off a cool combo. Some combat moves are location-dependent: If you use stealth while crouching behind an enemy, you'll execute a choke hold. If you are near a wall, you'll be able to slam your enemy against it while fighting. It is best to mix up punch combos—if you use a specific move too often, enemies will learn to counter it. It's important to note that enemies will not fire at you while you're directly engaged in combat (they won't risk the chance of shooting their allies).

4 THROW/COUNTER ATTTACKS

When both punch buttons are pressed simultaneously during hand-to-hand combat, a throw will be executed. When the left punch and action buttons are pressed simultaneously, you will counter an enemy's attack. You can even counter armed foes—you'll parry their gunshot or grab their weapon, for instance.

> **TIP**
>
> Additional moves are covered in the sections ahead. Bond has a lot of tricks up his sleeve, so be sure to master them all!

BEFORE YOU START

INTRO

AGENT RANK: DIFFICULTY LEVELS

Everything or Nothing has three difficulty levels, which roughly equate to easy, medium, and hard.

1 OPERATIVE

In this easy mode, you complete only the core mission objectives. Enemies are less challenging, as well. This is the perfect setting for beginning players or for those who want to get a feel for the level before attempting it at Agent difficulty. You will find fewer enemies in some missions, and enemies will react more slowly, fire with less accuracy, and cause less damage. Also, there will be additional armor vests. You get a 1x score multiplier bonus upon completing a mission (in other words, your score is unaffected).

2 AGENT

This is the default difficulty, and standard mission objectives apply. Enemies are at regular strength. Those who have played previous 007 games should be able to handle this level of difficulty. You get a 1.5x score multiplier bonus upon completing a mission.

3 OO AGENT

This is the level reserved for expert players who probably have defeated the missions previously on Agent difficulty and are looking for a challenge worthy of 007 himself. While standard mission objectives apply, enemies will be a bit more formidable: They cause more damage, take more hits to dispatch, and shoot with better accuracy. In addition, there will be additional enemies in some levels, and fewer armor vest locations. In some levels (notably the vehicle missions), you will begin with less ammo and weaponry. You get a 2x score multiplier bonus upon completing a mission.

HOW TO USE THIS STRATEGY GUIDE

This strategy guide is optimized for Agent difficulty; gameplay changes at oo Agent difficulty are noted where appropriate. In addition, some of the armor vest locations noted in the walkthrough may not be available at oo Agent difficulty—and additional armor vests may be found at Operative difficulty. At the end of each walkthrough, you'll find tips on how to achieve the optional platinum objective at oo Agent difficulty. Since there are fewer objectives at the Operative difficulty level, you can ignore portions of the walkthrough that deal with non-core objectives if you are playing on that setting.

MAP LEGEND

The maps throughout this guide are labeled to provide all the crucial details of your missions. Refer to the following legend for icon meanings.

Armor Vest	Battery	Bond Moment	Key Item	Map Connection

Q Spider Path Entrance	Rappel Point	Switch	Security Camera	Shortcut/Secret Path
			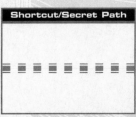	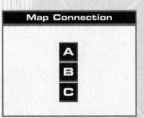

CAST OF CHARACTERS

One of the things the Bond franchise is best known for is its outrageously cool characters. *Everything or Nothing* maintains the series's commitment to providing intriguing characters to go along with all that Bond-style action. From the ubiquitous Q and M, to the ever-so-seductive "Bond Babes," to the disgruntled goons bent on world domination and/or destruction, *Everything or Nothing* has 'em all.

JAMES BOND

Agent 007 is MI6's most valuable (and most notorious) agent, and he has a long resume full of world-saving feats. Thanks to his impeccable style, irresistible charm, and unparalleled combat and driving skills, he's the spy who's called to action when no one else can handle the job.

Actor

Pierce Brosnan

M

As the director of MI6, M oversees 007's missions and is the key source for mission objectives and advice. At times, M is at odds with Bond's rather cavalier and unorthodox methods.

Actor

Judi Dench

Q

Q heads the division of MI6 responsible for developing cutting-edge spy gadgets, vehicles, and weaponry necessary for oo agents to complete their missions. A skilled inventor of covert equipment, Q is often irritated with 007's lack of respect for his creations.

Actor

John Cleese

MISS NAGAI

Miss Nagai assists Q in developing cutting-edge technology for the oo agents of MI6. A British citizen raised overseas, she returned to the United Kingdom to research nanotechnology at Oxford University. Her exotic looks prove to be quite a distraction for 007.

Actor

Misaki Ito

Actor

Willem Defoe

NIKOLAI DIAVOLO

Diavolo is a product of the cold and merciless Max Zorin, Bond's nemesis from A View to a Kill. A former KGB agent, Diavolo attempted a revolt in the former Soviet Union when he became disillusioned by the westernization of his homeland. A failed attempt by the KGB to end Diavolo's life sent him into seclusion; now, several years later, he has returned. Armed with a powerful nanotechnology arsenal, he has a score to settle—both with the western world and with 007.

Actor

Shannon Elizabeth

SERENA ST. GERMAINE

Serena is a beautiful and intelligent geologist. She was investigating anomalous platinum levels in a small South American village when she was swept up into 007's world of danger and intrigue—be it as a skilled helicopter pilot or a beautiful distraction.

Actor

Heidi Klum

KATYA NADANOVA

Seductive and menacing, Katya Nadanova is Diavolo's "Girl Friday." A brilliant scientist and a deadly assassin, Katya enables Diavolo to gain control of deadly nanotechnology. She continues to cause problems for 007 in all of the game's exotic locales: Egypt, New Orleans, South America, and Moscow.

Actor

Mya

MYA STARLING

As the NSA's primary agent in New Orleans, Mya assists James Bond in his quest to prevent Diavolo from fulfilling his evil plans. She works undercover as a singer in a nefarious nightclub connected to Diavolo, and she soon finds herself in the line of fire as she helps 007 gather information. Their symbiotic relationship is memorable...for many reasons.

Actor

Richard Kiel

JAWS

One of Bond's most fearsome enemies returns! Boasting superhuman strength and size—as well as a metal-filled mouth powerful enough to crush anything it clamps onto—this hit man will to stop at nothing to defeat his nemesis once and for all.

GENERAL STRATEGY

TACTICS: NAVIGATION

To complete many of the game's mission objectives, you'll have to perform tasks related to inanimate objects, such as finding switches or rappel points. That's where Bond Sense comes in.

BOND SENSE

When Bond Sense is activated, the screen turns blue and time slows to a crawl ❶. This gives you time to look around your environment to see not only combat targets, but also items and objective points. If you zoom in on a specific object (using the fire button), Bond Sense will give you more information on that item— whether it's throwable, whether it's an objective, whether it's shootable, whether it's a threat, etc. If you're stuck at a location and don't have a clue what to do next, Bond Sense will help target possible points of interest. If you lock on to an object while Bond Sense is active, you will remain locked on when Bond Sense is inactive—a vital skill if you want to shoot security cameras, steam vents and other inanimate objects.

NAV TIP A

When using Thermovision, not only can you see enemies (in bright colors), but **you can also see the outlines of items such as weapons and armor vests** ❷. Make sure you explore darkened areas carefully so you don't miss any key items.

NAV TIP C

In darkened areas that require Thermovision, **use Bond Sense to get a cleaner picture of the environment** ❸a and ❸b. This will help you locate hidden items and identify doors and passageways.

NAV TIP D

Lost while driving? Look for a blue dot on the GPS map in the upper left. This is usually where your objective lies. **An arrow will indicate your position relative to the objective** ❹. In most missions, you can also **switch to a full-screen map that you can keep onscreen while driving** ❺.

NAV TIP E

While using the Nano Suit, you can walk or jog ❻, but if you make any sudden turns or run, the suit will deactivate, exposing you to full view and alerting enemies to your presence. In general, crouch while moving with the Nano Suit to ensure stealth. Also keep monitoring your battery level— once it's down to zero, the suit will deactivate.

NAV TIP F

Having trouble seeing things onscreen, especially in dark areas of the game? It might be your TV. Fortunately, the game supplies a brightness-adjustment screen that'll help optimize your vision; access it from the Options menu.

NAV TIP B

When in a vehicle, note that there is no health replenishment—pilot your vehicle with care.

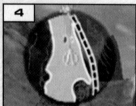

TACTICS: COMBAT

Everything or Nothing employs an intricate combat system that allows Bond to dispatch enemies in a variety of ways: with weapons, with hand-to-hand combat, and even with stealth. Be aware, however, that the enemies are sharp. They will react to your actions. For instance, if you make it a habit to charge enemies and engage in hand-to-hand combat, enemies will begin to retreat while firing at you. Likewise, if you hide after they've spotted you, they'll remain at alert status and search for you. Enemies will often work as a team to fight you—one foe may stand back and fire while the other engages you in hand-to-hand combat. To top it all off, enemies will remember what you did on previous missions and adjust their tactics accordingly! You'll have to choose your strategy carefully to succeed—and mix things up when necessary. The following combat strategies apply to all missions.

SHOOTING AND LOCKING ON

This is the most fundamental tactic in the game. **By pressing the target-lock button, you will select the best target in your field of vision** . When multiple enemies are onscreen, press the target-lock button again to cycle through available targets.

The lock-on viewfinder will change color: Red means that you are at close range to a target, orange means you're at medium range, and yellow means you're at long range—your aiming accuracy will improve the closer you are to a target. Green means that the target has been neutralized, and gray indicates that a target is behind cover and can't be hit. You can fine-tune your aim after locking on to a target: Move the view control up or down. **You'll see a red dot moving inside the lock-on viewfinder—that's your aim point** . This is useful for hitting someone who's hiding behind a wall: Move the target to aim at an exposed body part, such as an arm or a head.

USING COVER

You won't survive long unless you learn to use walls and crates as cover. When you're trying to reach a safe area, roll. Bond is harder to hit when he's rolling. While behind cover, you will be able to lock on and shoot enemies that are in view. **You can crouch behind low-standing obstacles such as short walls, boxes, and couches** . **You can hide behind walls or other flat obstacles that are taller than Bond (with the exception of some doors) and at least as wide as him to shield his entire body** ⑩. While behind cover, 007 is greatly protected from enemy fire, even while shooting at targets. Don't want to stay behind cover in one spot for too long—enemies will try to rush your position, or they will flush you out with rockets or grenades.

BOND SENSE

Bond Sense is also useful in combat: When in a target-rich environment, you'll want to see what you're up against. Bond Sense gives you the time to select which target you want to focus on first. Usually, you'll engage Bond Sense to target an inanimate object, such as a fuel barrel, that's next to an enemy. Other times, you'll want to lock on to a specific soldier in a crowd, such as one who has a rocket launcher instead of a gun.

Bond Sense can also be used to discover the status of a specific enemy. Once you have a target selected, press the **fire button to get information** ⑪—you will usually get a description of the enemy and its health condition, and find out whether it's been alerted to your presence.

Be warned: Enemies will still fire at you when you have Bond Sense activated, so don't use it for too long.

ADDITIONAL COMBAT TIPS

COMBAT TIP A

Bond can disarm enemies by attacking them from the front. However, if you use a certain hand-to-hand move many times, enemies will begin to anticipate that attack—mix things up when fighting.

COMBAT TIP B

Having trouble locking on to an enemy in the distance? You probably need to switch to a weapon with that can shoot farther! In general, weapons such as the rocket launcher and rifles have longer range than pistols.

COMBAT TIP C

Having trouble locking on to enemies that are in plain view while you're in wall-cover mode? Adjust the camera angle slightly to get a clearer line of sight to the target, then try again.

COMBAT TIP D

Make it a habit to reload your weapon when idle. The animation delay for reloading during a fierce firefight could cost you some health.

COMBAT TIP E

When in a vehicle, be patient with missiles to improve efficiency. The longer you're locked on to a target, the more accurate the missile is likely to be.

COMBAT TIP F

Shooting at explosive fuel barrels to eliminate troops ⑫ will improve your ammo efficiency immensely. Not to mention, it's kinda fun watching things blow up!

COMBAT TIP G

You can fire bullets through wooden crates to attack guards ⑬. Crates are breakable when fired upon—some may even contain extra ammo or weapons. This is a classic opportunity to kill two birds with one stone (or bullet).

COMBAT TIP H

Darting into a hallway then running back behind cover may lure out enemies hiding behind walls or crates. If you have any extra Q Spiders, you can actually send one toward an enemy or have it scout an area—this also may lure enemies out ⑭.

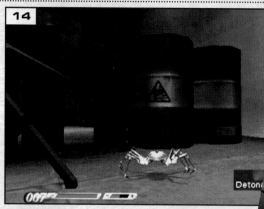

COMBAT TIP I

Crouching while moving is essential for avoiding detection and performing stealth attacks ⑮. Enemies will often hear you walking up to them if you are not crouching.

TACTICS: SCORING

When you complete a mission, you will get a score based on several factors and broken down into various categories:

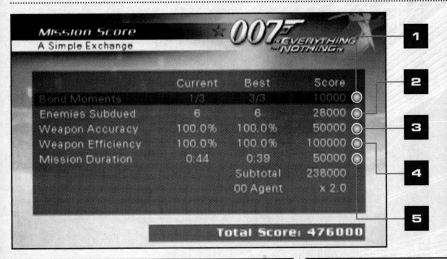

1 BOND MOMENTS

The more Bond Moments you achieve in the mission, the higher your score.

2 ENEMIES SUBDUED

The more enemies you dispatch in a mission, the higher your score. However, Bond earns even higher scores for eliminating foes using nonlethal methods (such as hand-to-hand combat and sleeper darts) or stealth takedowns. To reach the Gold Target score (especially late in the game), it is essential to use these non–weapon-based methods to complete mission objectives and boost your score.

3 WEAPON ACCURACY

The greater the percentage of shots that hit their target, the higher the score. Ideally, you want to shoot targets at close range and be fully locked on before firing.

4 WEAPON EFFICIENCY

The fewer rounds you use to dispatch foes, the higher your score. Using heavy one-shot weapons (such as the AT-420 rocket launcher, SPAS 12 shotgun, and Desert Eagle) to dispatch foes can really boost this part of the score, while semiautomatic weapons generally will hurt your score. Taking shots to explode fuel barrels near enemies will also increase efficiency—especially when you can take out multiple foes with just a single shot!

5 MISSION DURATION

The level will give you a target time for completing the level, then penalize you for any extra seconds you spend to complete it. Don't expect to get a good score here until you know a mission inside and out.

BRONZE, GOLD, AND PLATINUM 007

All of the above scores are added together, then multiplied depending on the difficulty level: x1 for Operative, x1.5 for Agent and x2 for oo Agent. Your final score plays a role in determining whether you will receive a bronze, gold, or platinum 007.

BRONZE

A Bronze 007 is awarded for merely completing a mission without meeting the gold 007 target score listed on the mission select screen. Earning bronze unlocks the next mission.

GOLD

A Gold 007 is awarded if you complete the mission and beat the target score listed on the Mission Select screen. Gold rewards will unlock extras in the game, such as vehicle upgrades, concept art goodies, new outfits for certain characters, and much more. In addition, earning gold will unlock an optional platinum challenge at oo Agent difficulty (but only after you complete that mission at oo Agent difficulty first). In later levels, you will have to play at oo Agent difficulty to generate a high enough score to earn gold.

PLATINUM

A Platinum 007 is awarded if you complete the optional platinum objective after you've completed the mission with a gold-level score. You can achieve the Gold 007 in the same attempt or a previous one. You must play on oo Agent difficulty to achieve platinum—and you can't use any cheats! Earning platinum 007s will unlock in-game cheat codes.

INTRO

WEAPONS

AK-74

Total Rounds before Reloading: 20

This machine gun is a favorite of paramilitary groups because of its raw power, ruggedness, and easy maintenance. It's loud but effective, although slightly less potent than the SIG 552.

AT-420

Total Rounds before Reloading: 4

This rocket launcher device is a bit unwieldy but very potent. It has the capability of penetrating armor, so it's most useful against larger targets such as jets and armored vehicles. It can also be used effectively against enemy troops—you can take out multiple targets thanks to its blast radius. However, don't use it at close range, or you'll sustain damage from the blast!

DESERT EAGLE

Total Rounds before Reloading: 6

The Desert Eagle is a powerful handgun because of its ability to neutralize an enemy with a single shot—which helps improve weapon accuracy and scoring efficiency.

DRAGUNOV

Total Rounds before Reloading: 5

This single-shot sniper rifle is equipped with a crosshair scope with zooming capability. When using the Dragunov at long range, there will be a short delay from when the shot is taken to impact. Keep that time gap in mind when aiming.

MP5K

Total Rounds before Reloading: 15

This submachine gun is compact but effective at quickly dispersing bullets. It is most accurate when shot in short bursts, and has a somewhat limited effective range.

P99

Total Rounds before Reloading: 10

The P99 pistol is the standard weapon that you'll start with for most missions. You can dispatch foes with multiple shots, but it's not well suited for heavy firefight situations. On some missions, a silencer option will be available for the P99.

SIG 552

Total Rounds before Reloading: 30

This semiautomatic rifle is surprisingly powerful—thanks to its large-caliber bullets, a well-aimed short burst can knock down an enemy soldier. It also has a long range, which is a plus when locking on to distant targets.

SLEEPER DART

Total Rounds before Reloading: 5

This weapon carries a cartridge of five darts; however, there is a lag time between shots, basically making it a single-shot device. Despite its very limited range, it is ideal for stealth missions, in which avoiding detection is paramount.

SPAS 12

Total Rounds before Reloading: 8

This powerful shotgun is a good weapon because of its knockdown capability. At close range, a single shot has the power to incapacitate an enemy immediately.

VEHICLES

The only thing cooler than James Bond himself are the various vehicles he pilots to complete his missions. Here are some of the most important vehicles found in the game.

PORSCHE CAYENNE TURBO

Porsche's latest SUV is the perfect vehicle for any off-road excursion. In addition to its impressive performance, Q-Lab has added a formidable arsenal to help 007 out of sticky situations. The Cayenne has also been modified to accept a recently developed Q-Cloak gadget that renders the vehicle invisible for short periods of time. As a result of its impressive abilities, this is the vehicle of choice for agents in rougher parts of the world.

Levels: Train Chase, Serena St. Germaine

WEAPONS
- Missiles
- Machine Gun
- Q Cloak
- RC Car

WEAPONS UPGRADES
- Cluster Bombs
- Improved Machine Gun

TRIUMPH DAYTONA 600

Powerful and lightweight, the Daytona 600 is the perfect vehicle for oo agents who need to get somewhere in a hurry. Q's biggest achievement on this vehicle was to fit a side-firing flamethrower for close-quarters battle. This, along with forward-firing rockets, makes the Q-Bike one of the most lethal and nimble vehicles in the MI6 garage.

Levels: A Show of Force, The Pontchartrain Bridge, The High Road

WEAPONS
- Rockets
- Shotgun
- Flamethrower

WEAPONS UPGRADES
- Double Rockets Shot
- Stronger Flamethrower

ASTON MARTIN V12 VANQUISH

The Vanquish is no stranger to MI6 assignments, having seen service in numerous countries. Combining power and agility, the Vanquish is a match for almost anything on the road. The addition of the acid slick and electro-magnet gadgets enhances its already formidable arsenal. Unfortunately for Q, he has become far too accustomed to repairing this vehicle as a result of 007's exuberance in the field.

Levels: Mardi Gras Mayhem, Battle in the Big Easy

WEAPONS
- Missiles
- Machine Gun
- Acid Slick
- RC Car
- Electro-Magnet

WEAPONS UPGRADES
- Double Missile Shot
- Improved Machine Gun

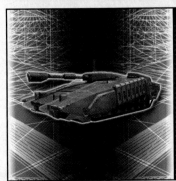

PLATINUM TANK

This vehicle doesn't come from Q Branch but is no less sophisticated than one of Q's creations. All exterior surfaces of the tank are made of platinum, which is impervious to Diavolo's nanotech weapons. This is important because nano shells are one of the primary weapons on this vehicle. The nano shells will lock on to almost any type of metal and completely eat it away, making it an extremely destructive piece of technology. What better way to bring down Diavolo's army than with one of his own weapons...

Levels: The Platinum War

WEAPONS
- Tank Cannon
- Nano Shells
- Plasma Gun

WEAPONS UPGRADES
- Stronger Tank Cannon

GADGETS

FRAG GRENADE

It's the latest in stealth munitions from Q's laboratory: A small coin that delivers a surprisingly large explosion. This weapon (disguised as a coin) is great for hitting targets stubbornly stuck behind walls or boxes. It can be thrown in a general direction without aiming, but it's more effective when locked on to a specific target. Despite its small size, its blast can be strong enough to injure multiple foes.

STROBE GRENADE

Q delivers yet another amazing feat of engineering with this coin-sized device. This weapon is similar to the Frag Grenade, but instead of damaging foes, it stuns them with a bright flash of light. It's a great tool to use to get past a crowd of enemies. It is also a vital tool in missions where ammunition limits are in place (notably in several Platinum 007 objectives for certain missions)—use of the Strobe Grenade does not count toward your ammo limit!

EMP GRENADE

The final variation on the coin-sized grenade design, the EMP does not damage enemies, but its electromagnetic-pulse blast will knock out devices within its blast radius such as security cameras and Nano Suits. This device is also extremely useful for deactivating Nano Suits worn by enemy soldiers in the final missions of the game.

NANO SUIT

The technology used in the Porsche Cayenne's Q-Cloak gets implemented in a new stealth device that'll prove very useful to Bond. Like the Q-Cloak, the Nano Suit maps a picture of the surroundings and "paints" it onto Bond's body—effectively making him invisible to enemy forces. While not a weapon per se, the Nano Suit will help Bond move past guards and security cameras undetected. It's a great aid when performing stealth attacks. Its drawbacks: It uses up battery power quickly, and it is deactivated when you perform quick movements such as firing a weapon or running. Smart use of the Nano Suit may help Bond complete several Platinum 007 optional objectives—especially those limited by time or ammunition constraints.

THERMOVISION

More of a weapon aid than a weapon, Thermovision allows Bond to see heat signatures in dark environments—cool objects such as walls and inanimate objects show up in shades of purple or blue, while people (such as Bond as well as enemy soldiers) show up in shades of orange and red. This feature makes Thermovision invaluable during combat in low- or no-light situations. It can also be used to detect enemies wearing Nano Suits, since their bodies emit heat even when camouflaged. However, because the device detects heat in any form, explosions and fires can create a distraction in Bond's field of vision.

RAPPEL

The versatile rappel allows you to run up and down walls. Look for smooth ledges to ascend, then walk toward the wall to climb. To rappel down any structure, just jump off a smooth wall face. Once on a wall, Bond also has the ability to switch directions at any time.

Q SPIDER (AND VARIANTS)

The Q Spider is a small remote-control device that lets Bond explore small areas and passageways too large for people. It's invaluable for finding secret areas; however, it will self-destruct if it falls from a high ledge (which can hurt enemies nearby). Variants on the Q Spider give the device greater offensive potential: explosive capability, Sleeper Darts, and even a cloaking feature. These latter models are useful for scouting out hostile areas and dispatching enemies from a safe distance. The latter models are useful for scouting out hostile areas and dispatching enemies from a safe distance. When Bond is in control of the Q Spider, he can choose to equip different variants as the situation warrants—for instance, he can use the Q Spider's sleeper dart function to disarm several foes, then detonate it to complete an objective. Multitasking with Q Spiders is an effective way to use them—especially in missions in which they are in short supply. The Q Spiders can be easily damaged—if detected, enemy soldiers will shoot at them—so care must be taken to ensure that they are not destroyed prematurely.

ICON	GADGET	HOW TO UNLOCK	DESCRIPTION
	Frag Grenade	Complete Ground Zero	A grenade disguised as a coin: It's good for dispatching enemies.
	Rappel	Complete Ground Zero	The versatile rappel allows you to run up and down walls. Look for smooth ledges to ascend, then walk toward the wall to climb.
	Q Spider	Complete Sand Storm	A small field-reconnaissance device. It cannot climb walls, but it can enter small areas or be used to scout ahead. It will self-destruct if it falls from a height, and enemies can shoot it to destroy it.
	Strobe Grenade	Complete Sand Storm	This grenade explodes with a flash, stunning any nearby enemies. Use it when you need to disable a group of enemies quickly.
	Sleeper Dart	Complete Sand Storm	This dart gun carries a fast-action toxin that will render anyone hit unconscious for a few hours. It has a limited range, however.
	Q Cloak	Complete Sand Storm	This upgrade to the Porsche Cayenne is a cloaking device that will render the car invisible to enemies temporarily. It has a limited battery life, so use it sparingly.
	RC Car	Complete Sand Storm	This upgrade to the Porsche Cayenne is a remote-control car that can be used to access smaller areas. Its laser is capable of destroying some targets, as well. It has a limited range and battery life, so move quickly while using it.
	Q Spider Explosive	Complete A Show of Force	This Q Spider upgrade adds an explosive function to the device. You can detonate it near enemies to dispatch them.
	EMP Grenade	Complete The Pontchartrain Bridge	This grenade works only on machines. An electromagnetic pulse will disable any electronic device (such as a security camera) within its blast radius. The grenade has to be aimed at its target and manually detonated near the device to work effectively.
	Network Tap	Complete Diavolo's Plan	Shoot a special dart at a Network Tap-capable device (such as a tank or enemy cannon) to take control of that weapon.
	Q Spider Dart	Complete Diavolo's Plan	This Q Spider upgrade adds the Sleeper Dart function to the unit. With it, you can subdue enemies while remaining completely undetected.
	Q Spider Nano	Complete Diavolo's Plan	Similar to Bond's Nano Suit, this Q Spider upgrade makes the unit invisible as long as it doesn't move too quickly.

MISSION 1

GOLD TARGET

Score 75,000 points to unlock the Platinum objective.

PLATINUM TARGET

Complete the level at oo Agent difficulty with 500 or fewer damage points.

STARTING WEAPONS	
	RAPPEL
	P99
	SIG 552
	MP5K

ACQUIRED WEAPONS	
	SPAS 12
	AT-420

GROUND ZERO

GROUND ZERO: MAP 01

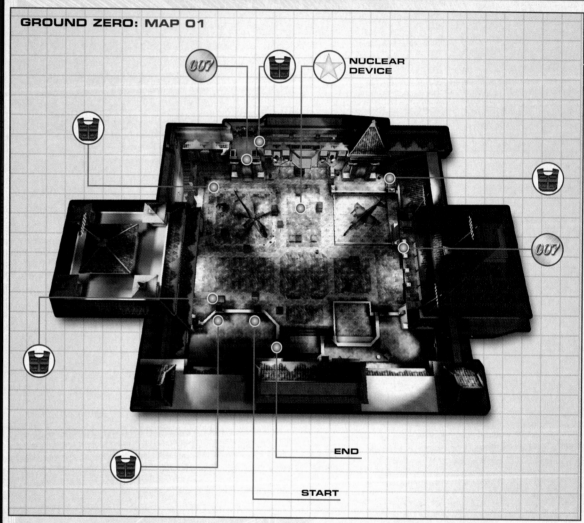

007 · NUCLEAR DEVICE · 007 · END · START

START:
MISSION BRIEFING

In true movie style, the game starts with an exciting introductory action level, which will help teach you combat skills and familiarize you with the new third-person gameplay environment. The level begins with you witnessing a $100 million transaction for a nuclear device—it's your mission to retrieve that device by any means necessary.

OBJECTIVE 1:
RETRIEVE NUCLEAR DEVICE

You begin Ground Zero in the middle of a fierce fire-fight. You will be shown some basic combat tech-

niques, including how to lean against walls, aim at enemies, and fire a weapon. When the level begins, quickly eliminate as many enemy targets as possible, **leaning back against the lighted column in front of you ❶**. From that spot, **move left to find an armor vest in the corner ❷**. Dart from column to column to find optimal firing angles and to avoid being outflanked. Use Bond Sense to find fuel barrels dispersed throughout the courtyard—blow them up to take out any enemies nearby.

Once a number of soldiers have been dispatched, a departing hover jet will blow open a new path into the square. A nuclear device (which looks like a small silver briefcase) lies in the middle of the square. Take out

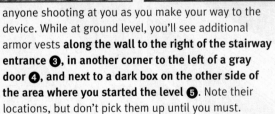

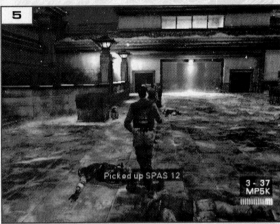

MISSION 1

007 SCENE 1
BOND MOMENT

After destroying the hover jet, use the rappel to get to ground level instead of taking the stairs.

OBJECTIVE 3: DESTROY THE HOVER JET

Armed with the AT-420, run down a set of short steps to trigger a cinema scene of the hover jet. **Lean back against the right corner wall for cover ❼**, then aim at the hover jet and fire. Get in as many shots as possible, but duck back behind the walls when incoming missiles appear. It will take three to five shots to destroy the jet, depending on the difficulty level you've chosen. Do not stand in the open: This will make you a prime target for the hover jet's missiles.

anyone shooting at you as you make your way to the device. While at ground level, you'll see additional armor vests **along the wall to the right of the stairway entrance ❸, in another corner to the left of a gray door ❹, and next to a dark box on the other side of the area where you started the level ❺**. Note their locations, but don't pick them up until you must.

OBJECTIVE 2: OBTAIN A ROCKET LAUNCHER

After you retrieve the device, a rocket-launching soldier will appear on a balcony above you. He is your greatest threat, so **eliminate him first ❻**. Look for an entryway that leads to stairs. A guard will try to surprise you— make him regret that decision. Then head up the stairs to find a control console that houses some rocket launchers as well as an armor vest.

SCENE 2
BOND MOMENT

When the antitank gun pops out of the ground (after you reach ground level once the two armored personnel carriers are destroyed), eliminate at least one enemy soldier (rappelling down from the wall near the gun) before he untethers and reaches ground level.

OBJECTIVE 4: ESCAPE TO THE LANDING ZONE

Once the hover jet flies off, two armored personnel carriers will roll in. Use the AT-420 to disable both vehicles—two shots each should do the trick. Stand on the balcony to **get a clear shot of the APC on the left as it rises to ground level** ⑧, then lean against the same wall that you used for cover against the hover jet to take out the APC on the right. Stay on the second level, darting from wall to wall to target any remaining small-arms fire.

Rappel down the opening across from the control console to earn a Bond Moment ⑨. Rappel down the opening across from the control console. An antitank gun will pop out of the ground shortly afterward. **Take cover behind boxes nearby** ⑩ and duck behind

them to avoid the antitank fire. **To earn a Bond Moment, immediately focus your attention to the left of the gun (adjust the camera view if necessary and use Bond Sense to give you time to aim) to neutralize the enemies that rappel from the upper level** ⑪. Once that's completed, **use two AT-420 missiles to take out the big gun** ⑫.

Defeat any remaining hostile soldiers and complete the level by reaching the broken rubble created by the errant hover jet missile that was launched after shooting down the hover jet.

EXTRA OBJECTIVE: EARN PLATINUM 007

To earn a platinum (once the objective is unlocked), you must take 500 or fewer points of damage before finishing the level at 00 Agent difficulty. The key is to move slowly, darting from cover to cover. Shoot from behind boxes and walls whenever possible—do not run into the open until all enemy fire has subsided. In some cases, you can wait behind cover for the soldiers to approach you. The only time you will need to be exposed to gunfire is while you're on the balcony when the two armored personnel carriers appear—you can shoot rockets at the APC on the left, then quickly run for cover once it's disabled to take out the APC to the right. Since time is not a factor, and since you do not need to earn any Bond Moments to achieve this Platinum objective, a slow-but-safe approach to knocking out enemies is best.

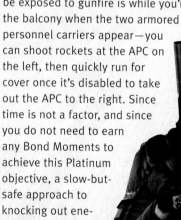

MI6 TRAINING

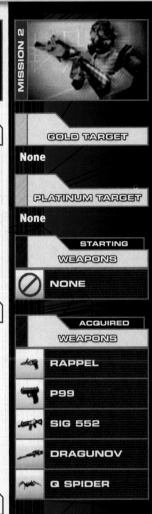

MISSION 2

GOLD TARGET	
None	

PLATINUM TARGET	
None	

STARTING WEAPONS	
⊘	NONE

ACQUIRED WEAPONS	
	RAPPEL
	P99
	SIG 552
	DRAGUNOV
	Q SPIDER

START: MISSION BRIEFING

The MI6 training simulator is essentially a tutorial mission that will help you learn combat techniques, use gadgets and employ Bond Sense. The objectives are broken down into categories; after completing one objective, follow the blue arrows to the next one. This level has only one difficulty setting (Agent).

OBJECTIVE 1: COMBAT: HAND-TO-HAND

The tutorial starts with unarmed soldiers rushing toward you one at a time. The hand-to-hand combat system is simple on the surface but has surprising depth depending on the button sequences used. Essentially, two buttons correspond to a left punch and a right punch. Repeated pressing of one or the other can trigger another combat move, such as a kick. Press both punch buttons to throw an enemy; to counter an attack, press the right punch plus the action button as an enemy throws a punch at you.

OBJECTIVE 2: GADGET: RAPPEL

Arm the rappel device, then **lock on to the ledge at the high wall to your right ❶** and shoot. Climb toward the wall to pull yourself up.

OBJECTIVE 3: COMBAT: CROUCHING

Crouching lets Bond hide behind low obstacles such as boxes—a key skill to avoid enemy detection and fire. While crouched, you can move (just at a slower pace), lock onto enemies, and fire. Defeat all the enemies that appear to move on—if you're having trouble hitting the target in the middle, fine-tune your aim to shoot an exposed target such as your enemy's head.

OBJECTIVE 4: BOND SENSE: TARGETING OBJECTS

Bond Sense is how you can target an inanimate object such as a box. When Bond Sense is triggered, the screen turns blue and everything moves in slow motion. **Any relevant targets will be highlighted by a blinking red cursor ❷**. While using Bond Sense, you can lock onto an inanimate target, then shoot it. To complete this objective, destroy all three floating yellow objects.

OBJECTIVE 5: COMBAT: WALL COVER

This essential skill keeps you safe from enemy fire and lets you peek around corners before rushing into an open area. While the skill is activated, you can move left and right freely along the wall's edge (using the control pad). There are two ways to disable wall cover mode: Move away from the wall with the control stick or press the wall cover button again.

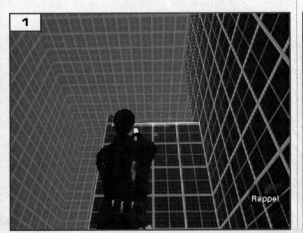

Rappel

5 - 35
P99

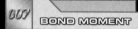

007 BOND MOMENT

There are no Bond Moments in this level.

DID YOU KNOW?

Leave the Q Spider idle onscreen for a little while to view some extra animations of the device patiently waiting for your next command.

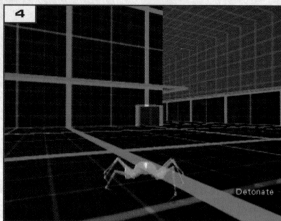

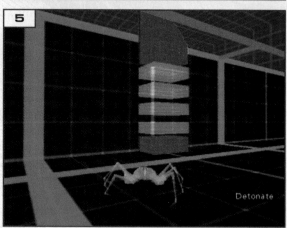

OBJECTIVE 6: COMBAT: SNIPER RIFLE

Basic weapons training continues. Some points worth noting: First, you can crouch and still use the sniper rifle effectively. Second, you'll notice that the target scope shakes ever so slightly. To complete this objective, ignore the enemies: **Zoom in and aim for the flashing red target ❸**.

OBJECTIVE 7: GADGET: Q SPIDER

The Q Spider is yet another innovative new gadget from Q's R&D laboratory. It is a remote-control mechanical spider capable of navigating spaces too small (or too dangerous) for any person. Once it's activated, the perspective switches to that of the Q Spider. To finish the level, **find a small red-highlighted hole nearby ❹** and navigate through the little narrow maze. Exit the maze to find **a flashing red column ❺**, and detonate the Q Spider once you're next to it. Run to the area where the red column was, then look for **a door switch nearby ❻**. Open the door and enter to complete the level.

COMBAT: SNIPER RIFLE

GADGET: Q SPIDER

A LONG WAY DOWN

A LONG WAY DOWN: MAP 01

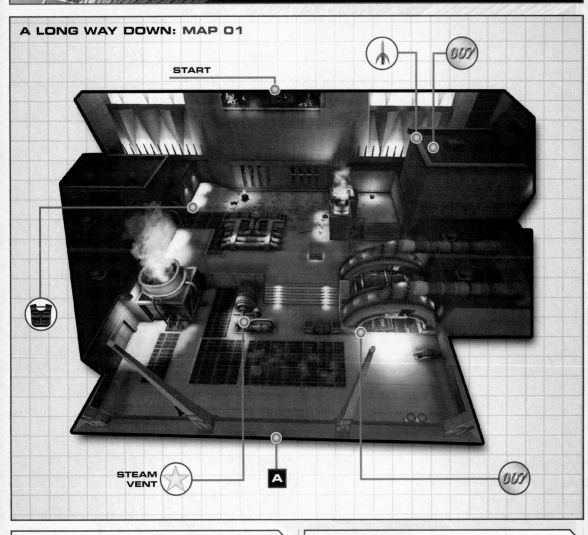

START

007

007

STEAM VENT ★

A

MISSION 3

GOLD TARGET

Score 90,000 points to unlock the Platinum objective.

PLATINUM TARGET

Complete the mission at oo Agent difficulty in 3:30 or less.

STARTING WEAPONS

- RAPPEL
- THERMOVISION
- GRENADE (1)
- P99 w/Silencer
- MPK5

ACQUIRED WEAPONS

- DRAGUNOV
- DESERT EAGLE
- AT-420

START: MISSION BRIEFING

Oxford scientist Katya Nadanova has been kidnapped while demonstrating top-secret nanobot technology. MI6 has tracked her to a nanotech facility. Your mission: to secure Nadanova and destroy the nanobot prototypes so they don't fall into the wrong hands.

In this mission, you will rappel down the exterior of the facility to find Nadanova. The level starts with you rappelling—do so as quickly as possible. Avoid flames, as they will cause damage.

OBJECTIVE 1: FIND DOCTOR NADANOVA

At the start, look right. **In a corner behind a barrel is armor ❶**. Note its location, but retrieve it only after neutralizing all the enemies on this level—but before dropping the explosive into the vent. First, **head left and look up to find a rappel point ❷ (use Bond Sense)**. If you're spotted, you'll find a soldier with a Dragunov up there.

SCENE 1
BOND MOMENT

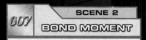

After rappelling at the very start of the level, head left and use Bond Sense. Look up to find a secret ledge to rappel to. Climb up the wall to retrieve a Dragunov sniper rifle.

SCENE 2
BOND MOMENT

From the rappel point on the roof, rappel and move left over a short stairway. Pass a small control console on your right and look for a steam valve nearby, underneath the half-tube-shaped tunnel. With soldiers standing over the steam vents nearby, open the valve to let loose some steam on them.

If not, you'll just find the rifle. Either way, take the rifle for a Bond Moment. You can use the rifle for here, or head back down to find a guard at a control console to your left. Neutralize him fast, then look for **a steam vent to the left of the console at the end of a tunnel ❸.** Press the action button in front of that vent: If any enemies are stunned by the resulting blast of steam, you'll earn a Bond Moment.

OBJECTIVE 2:
DROP EXPLOSIVE INTO VENT

Stand next to the vent ❹ and press the action button to trigger a cinema scene that leads to the next objective.

OBJECTIVE 3:
RAPPEL OFF THE BUILDING EDGE

Immediately after the cinema scene, more guards will appear. Rather than engage, rappel down the building (look for an opening created by the explosion). Move as far right as possible. You'll reach a small square ledge, and two enemy rappellers will come down to meet you. Defeat them, then continue falling to the right. **You'll find a hidden area that features an armor vest ❺.**

ALTERNATE ROUTE

You can opt to rappel straight down, which eventually leads to an exploding platform. However, this route may expose you to extra enemy fire without benefit of cover, which isn't an ideal situation. Rappelling all the way to the left bypasses a Bond Moment but is much faster (see the Extra Objective for more details). See the map on the next page to gain perspective on this alternate route.

A LONG WAY DOWN: MAP 02

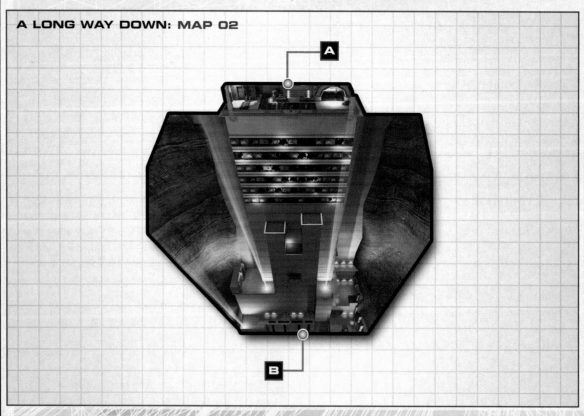

A LONG WAY DOWN: MAP 03 (ALTERNATE)

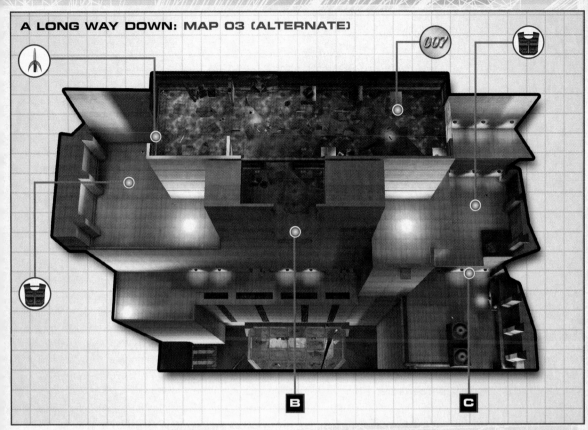

SCENE 3
BOND MOMENT

In the small burned-out room where you break a shattered window to reveal two rappelling enemies, look for a nearby table to flip over for cover.

SCENE 4
BOND MOMENT

Upon reaching the level with the flame vents blocking your path, look for another steam valve near the vent switch. Trigger this valve while enemies are standing atop the steam vents to immobilize your foes temporarily.

From the point where that armor vest was, look up to find an opening to rappel to. This leads to a small burned-out room. On the way up, watch out for a soldier coming down to greet you: While rappelling upward, dispatch him before he reaches you. Terminate all the enemies in this level, and look for an AT-420 rocket launcher as well as **a table to flip over to earn a Bond Moment** ❻. Using the table as cover, **look for a window that will break to reveal two rappelling enemies** ❼. Defeat them before they surprise you, then rappel through the opening they appeared in. Once below (you should be standing next to their fallen bodies), rappel once again to reach **another isolated area with armor** ❽.

OBJECTIVE 4:
SHUT OFF FLAME VENTS

With your armor replenished, rappel to a level where flame vents are activated, blocking your path downward. Look immediately left to activate **a steam valve to disorient enemies and earn a Bond Moment** ❾. Charge toward them and take them out: Look for the **flame valve switch nearby, and press the action button to turn off the flames** ❿. Then take cover behind this wall near the switch ⓫: This is an excellent spot to camp out and let enemy forces advance toward you. Pick them all off before moving ahead (the most notable target, in addi-

SCENE 5
BOND MOMENT

Near that second steam valve is a large burned-out room. Use Bond Sense to find several weak ceiling points. Shoot the ceiling when soldiers run underneath—incapacitate at least one enemy using this method.

11

12 B

13

tion to the extra rappellers, is a rocket-wielding soldier—roll to avoid his missiles, then take him down with a powerful weapon such as the Desert Eagle or AT-420).

With the flames off and the coast clear, move to a large burned-out room where more enemies lurk. Crouch behind any boxes nearby to avoid enemy fire, then use Bond Sense to **target weaknesses in the ceiling** 🄬 that you can use to fall on enemies' heads to earn a Bond Moment. As you move through the room, watch out for additional rappellers that will drop into the holes in the ceiling. Also look for another **armor next to a cracked fallen column** 🄭. Once all enemies are taken care of, head to the ledge where the flames were, then rappel

A LONG WAY DOWN: MAP 04

END

FLAME VENT ★

down to finish the mission. A cinema scene afterward will reveal Nadanova's whereabouts.

EXTRA OBJECTIVE: EARN PLATINUM 007

To earn platinum (once the objective is unlocked), you must complete the mission in less than 3:30. It's possible to complete this objective with more than a minute to spare, so preserving health is more vital than time management.

At the start of the mission, eliminate all the enemies before dropping an explosive in the vent, using the steam vent (the one you used to earn a Bond Moment) and fuel barrels to silence enemies quickly. Once all the enemies on the level are dispatched, grab the armor vest (behind a fuel barrel) to recharge your health. Quickly run back to the steam vent, drop the charge, then rappel down in a hurry, **moving as far left as possible** ❶. While heading down the building, target and eliminate any nearby enemies. By going left, you avoid a whole level of combat, and you will be able to rappel down to a hidden area that contains an additional armor vest.

You should have full health before rappelling down to the level with the flame vents. Once there, run to the steam vent to stun enemy soldiers. Fire on the remaining soldier who's not stunned (hiding behind the box), then take out the rest. Turn off the flame vents, then get ready to take cover! A swarm of rappellers will advance toward your position, but your high-priority target will be a rocket-launching soldier who'll run into the open. It is imperative that you take him out without getting hit by a rocket. To do this, **stay to the right of the wall, then lean back against it to target incoming enemies** ❷. If you creep too far left along this wall, you might get hit by a rocket, so keep right. Once the influx of attackers dies down, get ready to run out and engage the rocket-launching soldier. Roll to avoid his attack, then take him out quickly before he gets a chance to fire again. Also target any remaining rappellers firing at you.

At this point, you should have at least half your health with about a minute to spare. Run into the burned-out room, but instead of fighting, keep running to the flame-vent ledge and rappel down.

P1

P2

TRAIN CHASE

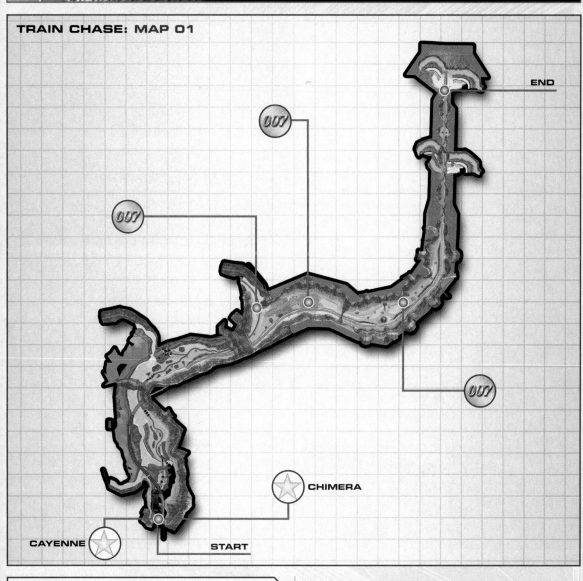

TRAIN CHASE: MAP 01

GOLD TARGET

Score 150,000 points to unlock a Platinum objective.

PLATINUM TARGET

Complete the mission in 2:15 or less.

STARTING WEAPONS

⊘ NONE

ACQUIRED WEAPONS

MISSILES
MACHINE GUN
MISSILES

START: MISSION BRIEFING

You are now in hot pursuit of Doctor Nadanova, who has been kidnapped and is being held in a speeding train. Your mission: to find a vehicle and catch up to the train.

You have two ways to complete this mission. At the start of the level, head left to reach the Porsche Cayenne, or head right to reach the motorcycle. The motorcycle is faster but more difficult to control. In addition, you'll sustain serious damage (up to half of

your health) to the motorcycle if you hit anything head-on at high speed, such as a wall or parked enemy truck. For those beginning the level, the Cayenne is the best bet, but at oo Agent difficulty (and for the Platinum objective), the motorcycle is the only way to go (more details in the Extra Objective section).

OBJECTIVE 1a: CATCH UP TO TRAIN (CAYENNE OPTION)

If you want to drive the Cayenne, run left at the start of the mission and uncloak the Cayenne. Jump in and

MISSION 4

SCENE 1
007 BOND MOMENT

Blow up the helicopter hovering before the temple area. To get to the helicopter via the Cayenne, look for a hidden path to the left just after the first long tunnel you enter. This leads to a ramp that eventually will take you to a path with enemy motorcyclists on it. The helicopter lies at the end of that path. Using the motorcycle, when you reach a fork in the road with motorcyclists on the left and trucks on the right (the enemy outpost area), go left and follow the motorcyclists.

SCENE 2
007 BOND MOMENT

At the temple area when columns begin to fall, look for a ramp to jump. If on the motorcycle, look for a pillar and action-slide underneath it.

1

2

drive through the burning warehouse. **Shoot a missile to blow through the main gate ➊** of the compound. Follow the road and take out any enemies along the way. After driving through a long tunnel, look left to find an **alternate path ➋**. Make sure you're driving fast enough to make the jump across a chasm on that path, which leads to the enemy outpost and two enemy motorcyclists. Use the machine gun to take care of them. Continue down this path to reach a large stone tunnel. **At the end of this tunnel is a helicopter that will rise to greet you ➌**. Return the greeting with a missile to trigger a cinema scene and earn a Bond Moment.

Drive into the temple area immediately after the cinema scene. When you reach an area with falling columns, stay left and **take the ramp to jump over the fallen columns and earn a Bond Moment ➍**. Upon exiting the temple, take out one more enemy truck and drive through the canyon toward the train. Avoid any incoming missiles from the train (you can gauge the missile trajectories and steer away from the expected blast points). **Look for a large foot of a broken statue—to the right of that foot is a jump leading to the train tracks ➎**. Take the jump to earn a Bond Moment.

3 **B**

4 **B**

5 **B**

6

ALTERNATE ROUTE

It is possible to continue on the lower path instead, but since you have a limited time to destroy the train's defenses and get onto the train, it's almost a requirement to take the ramp onto the train tracks.

OBJECTIVE 1b: GET UNDERNEATH THE TRAIN (CHIMERA OPTION)

At the start of the mission, run to the right to find a Chimera motorbike. Jump on the bike and take a ramp that leads to the warehouse interior. Drive through two sets of glass windows to get back outside onto a path that leads to the train tracks. **Avoid the train's missiles and rock debris by staying to the right of the tracks ➏**. The train will fire a missile that will destroy the bridge—and you'll drop to a lower level. Take out the helicopter harassing you with missiles, then **jump a bridge to land smack-dab in an enemy outpost with motorcyclists to the left and missile trucks to the right ➐**. While it may be slightly faster to head right, you should head left and follow the enemy motorcycles. This is the path that leads to the long stone tunnel and the helicopter that, if destroyed, will earn you a Bond Moment.

7

After that point, drive into the temple area. When you reach the area with the falling pillars, **press the gadget button to action-slide underneath the fallen pillar and earn a Bond Moment 8**.

OBJECTIVE 2:
GET UNDERNEATH THE TRAIN

Whether driving the Cayenne or the Chimera, the rest of the mission is the same for both vehicles. Once on the tracks, stay in between them and target the gun and two rocket henchmen on the back (at oo Agent difficulty, two enemy motorcyclists will join the party as well). **Use missiles to take out all the target points on the train 9.** Once destroyed, drive up directly behind the train as closely as possible (but watch out for the flames from the train if critically low on health). Eventually, a trench will appear between the tracks. Drive underneath the train to complete the mission.

EXTRA OBJECTIVE:
EARN PLATINUM 007

To earn platinum (once the objective is unlocked), you must complete the mission in less than 2:15—which is

actually 2:00 if you subtract the 10 seconds it should take to get Bond to the Chimera motorcycle. The Chimera is the only way to go—it's a faster vehicle, and it carries more missiles—which is a must at oo Agent difficulty.

The strategies for this objective are obvious: Don't lose control of the bike, and don't run into anything. For the sake of the end of the level, it's best to outrun enemies rather than waste missiles—as a rule, just shoot enemies that are directly ahead of you. Don't worry about getting hit by machine gun fire—missiles are your only big worry.

The strategy for the Chimera still applies, but when you reach the enemy outpost with motorcyclists to the left and missile trucks to the right, **you might prefer to go right and drive straight through the flat desert area 1** instead of heading left. This is the better option for three reasons: First, the wider flat area is much easier to drive through than the winding path the enemy motorcycles take. Next, it may save you a second or two—not much, but every second counts. Finally, you'll probably take some damage hitting the ground after destroying the helicopter for a Bond Moment, so avoiding it altogether may save health.

If you do go right, make sure to pass through the temple area as a time-saving shortcut—if you decide to take the ramp instead of sliding underneath the pillar, make sure you're angled pointing right—if you're angled pointing left on the ramp, you'll hit the wall in a most nasty way. After the temple area, taking the ramp by the statue's foot is an absolute necessity to save time.

Once on the train tracks, let loose your missile supply. Don't be gun-shy, because the sooner you defeat the train, the sooner you can drive up to it. It is possible to complete this objective with about 10 seconds to spare—even if you hit something once—so don't be so quick to restart if you make a mistake along the way.

SCENE 3
BOND MOMENT

After the temple area, keep your eyes peeled for a statue that marks the location of a ramp. Take the jump onto the train tracks.

DID YOU KNOW?

At the start of the mission while driving the motorcycle, if you gain enough speed when hitting the first ramp, you can land on the roof of the warehouse. Once on the roof, you'll crash back down through some skylights—so there isn't any real advantage to getting up there. Still, it's a flashy way to start off!

GOLD TARGET

Score 125,000 points to unlock the Platinum objective.

PLATINUM TARGET

Complete the mission without taking any damage.

STARTING WEAPONS

 THERMOVISION

 P99 w/Silencer

 GRENADE (1)

ACQUIRED WEAPONS

 DESERT EAGLE

 SIG 552

SCENE 1
007 BOND MOMENT

Use stealth to dispatch enemies and avoid detection in the first train car (see walkthrough for details).

AN OLD FRIEND

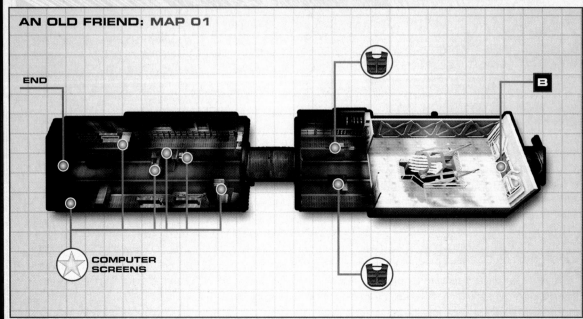

AN OLD FRIEND: MAP 01

END

B

★ COMPUTER SCREENS

START: MISSION BRIEFING PART 01

Once you make it onto the train, you must make your way through the cars to find Doctor Nadanova. Stealth is paramount in this level—the longer you can remain undetected through the train, the more Bond Moments you'll earn.

OBJECTIVE 1: DESTROY 6 MISSILE LAUNCH COMPUTERS

This objective can be completed in the first car—even though missile launch computers can be found throughout the entire train. When the mission begins, wait for the guard in the middle and the guard on the right to turn around. Once all three guards are facing away from you, **crouch and creep up to the guard on the left to perform a stealth attack ❶**. Once done, immediately do a stealth attack on the middle guard and crouch behind the computer. When the third guard

senses something is amiss and runs toward you to investigate, use the silenced P99 to drop him—just make sure the third guard doesn't trigger the alarm (the yellow box on a crate in the back of the car).

With all enemies silenced, **target and destroy six of the seven computer screens in that car with the silenced P99 ❷**: two where the guards were standing, two in the middle of the car, two next to the exit, and one to the right of where you begin the mission. (Note: There are more computers to destroy in train cars ahead should you miss one.) If you can dispatch all the enemies in this train car without raising the alarm, you'll earn a Bond Moment upon exiting.

AN OLD FRIEND: MAP 02

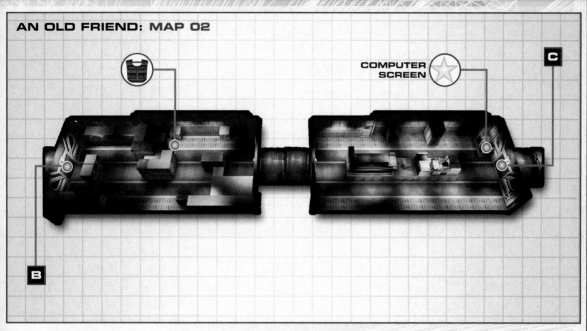

MISSION 5

SCENE 2
007 BOND MOMENT

Use stealth to dispatch enemies and avoid detection in the second train car (see walkthrough for details).

SCENE 3
007 BOND MOMENT

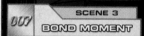

Use stealth to dispatch enemies and avoid detection in the third train car (see walkthrough for details).

The second train car is a bit trickier in terms of stealth. Enter the second train car crouching, and moving slowly, then quickly stealth-attack the first guard closest to the door as the other guard turns away. Make a note of the two armor vests behind each counter (Note: The vests do not appear at oo Agent difficulty), then steadily move towards the other guard as he goes on his patrol. **Creep very close to the walls to remain undetected ❸**. As Bond gets close enough, perform a stealth attack. Eliminate the enemies in this room while undetected to earn a Bond Moment upon exiting the car.

Only two guards patrol the third car. When you enter, don't immediately stealth-attack the first guard you see—the other guard will hear if you attack the first one too close to the middle of the train car. Instead, **stay crouched behind the boxes at the start ❹**, and wait for the guard to return. The moment he turns around to walk back, **creep behind him and perform a stealth attack as soon as possible ❺**—you must perform it before the guard has a chance to turn right so the other guard isn't alarmed! If done correctly, **you can hide behind some boxes ❻** and wait for the other guard to turn his back on you. Immediately creep up behind him and perform a stealth attack. **Then look for an armor vest in the middle of the car ❼**. Dispatch both guards without alerting them to your presence to earn a Bond Moment upon exiting the car.

MISSION 5

SCENE 4

007 BOND MOMENT

Use stealth to dispatch enemies and avoid detection in the fourth train car (see walk-through for details).

AN OLD FRIEND: MAP 02

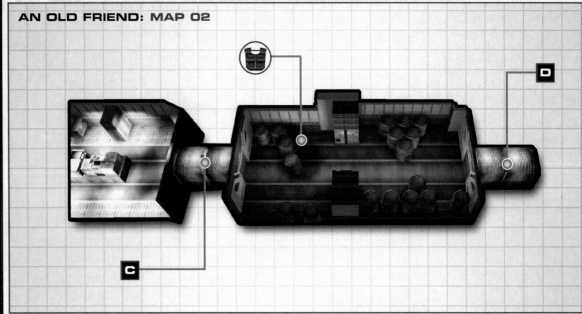

In the fourth car, crouch and creep up the left side. **Once the patrolling guard makes it more than halfway across the train car, stealth-attack him** **8**. (Note: If you attack this guard too soon, the patrolling guard on the other side of train car will hear you.) Then **stealth-attack the stationary guard behind the console** **9** and quickly creep back to the car entrance to **wait for the other guard to turn his back to you** **10**. When he begins walking away, do a stealth attack—using stealth in this car earns you the fourth and final Bond Moment upon exiting the car.

The fifth train car has very little lighting, so use your Thermovision. Forget about stealth: Dispatch the first guard to the right upon entering the room, then **use a large cylindrical barrel nearby as cover** **11**. Eliminate the other guards as they pop into the middle of the train car. Stay behind cover until the coast is clear, then use **Thermovision to find an armor vest in a darkened area of the car** **12**.

MISSION BRIEFING: PART 02

After making it through all five cars, be prepared to meet an old "friend"—Jaws! This hulking hitman will greet you rudely, so get ready for a big fight!

OBJECTIVE 2: DEFEAT JAWS

Use the columns of electricity to shock Jaws into submission—there's no need to attack right away. When Jaws throws a steel column at you, roll opposite the direction you're facing to avoid the column (if you're facing left, for instance, quickly turn 180 degrees and roll right), or **use the pillars behind you as cover** **13**. Use a three-punch combination to knock Jaws back a few steps. Adjust your position so

AN OLD FRIEND: MAP 04

D

BOSS

13

Jaws

14

Jaws

007

you **knock him toward the electric current** 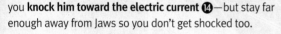—but stay far enough away from Jaws so you don't get shocked too.

After one or two shocks (depending on the difficulty level), Jaws may start to charge at you after being shocked. Position yourself so that you are in between Jaws and a column of electricity—when he charges, roll or run to one side to avoid him. If positioned properly, Jaws will charge right into the electricity.

EXTRA OBJECTIVE: EARN PLATINUM 007

To earn platinum (once the objective is unlocked), you must complete the mission without taking any damage. If you weren't using stealth before to knock out enemies, you better start! Once the guards are alerted, you will surely get hit at some point in the mission. The mission's walkthrough strategy still applies (including the fight with Jaws), but

there are more things to watch out for. First, if you remain hidden too long behind cover, a guard may throw a grenade (all the more reason to use stealth). Second, watch out for stray bullets from fallen enemies (yes, you can still get hit by bullets from their guns even after they are dispatched).

Using stealth in the first, third, and fourth cars is mandatory. It's very difficult to achieve stealth in the second car after you disable the stationary guard because an additional patroller is placed at oo Agent difficulty. However, you can crouch behind one of the countertop consoles, using it as cover to pick off any remaining foes. In the fifth car, immediately dispatch the guard on the right before he can shoot at you, then quickly take cover behind the large barrel as the remaining guards rush toward you. Stay behind cover at all times, moving only to entice a guard into venturing into the open.

MISSION 6

GOLD TARGET

Score 160,000 points to unlock the Platinum objective.

PLATINUM TARGET

Destroy the general's secret base in less than 45 seconds.

STARTING WEAPONS

 MISSILES

 BOMBS

 FLARES

ACQUIRED WEAPONS

 NONE

SCENE 1
007 BOND MOMENT

When you reach a wooden bridge with enemy missile trucks on it, destroy the bridge so the trucks fall into the canyon.

SAND STORM

SAND STORM: MAP 01

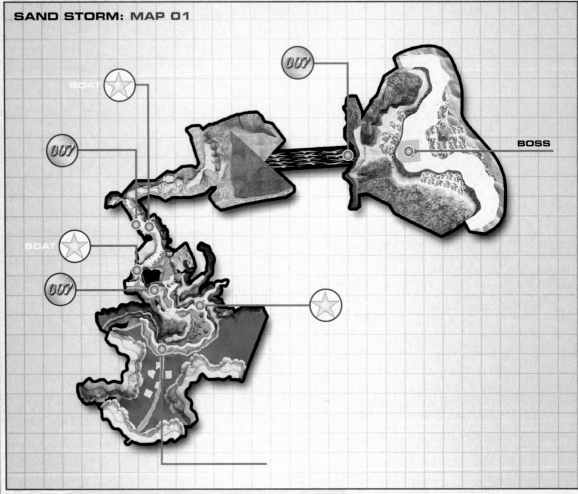

START:
MISSION BRIEFING PART 01

Your first taste of flying in Everything or Nothing begins as you and just-rescued Doctor Nadanova chase another helicopter through river canyons and an Egyptian pyramid.

OBJECTIVE 1: CATCH UP TO THE GENERAL'S HELICOPTER

As the mission begins, fly through the canyon following the river. The **first enemy boat is on the river just past the large rock spires ❶**. It's faster to take the boats out with bombs, but missiles can be used as well. Follow the river, using flares along the way to prevent missiles from hitting your helicopter. When you reach a

large waterfall, turn left to find two jeeps parked on a wooden bridge. **Destroy the bridge to earn a Bond Moment ❷. Pass another wooden bridge on your left to find a second boat to attack ❸**. Afterward, fly through a large stone gate to find a helicopter waiting. Destroy that helicopter before it has a chance to shoot back at you (or at any tall stone structures that might crash on top of you). Avoid any falling rocks or structures at all costs.

Just after this point will be **the third and final enemy boat 4**—if you destroyed all three boats to this point, you'll earn a Bond Moment. Right after the boat, watch out for the enemy helicopter shooting at the land bridges. Avoid the falling debris, and you'll eventually catch up to the general's helicopter.

OBJECTIVE 2: ELIMINATE THE GENERAL

Actually, you won't be able to eliminate the general just yet—instead, save your missiles and follow him through a pyramid. Maneuver quickly and/or use a flare to avoid the general's missiles. When you reach **an area with flames shooting out of the walls 5**, avoid getting hit by any of them to earn a Bond Moment. The best tactic is to stay near the ceiling and move just slightly left or right to avoid any flames.

OBJECTIVE 3: DESTROY THE GENERAL'S BASE

After you fly through the pyramid, the general's secret base will rise from the water. Deploy flares or strafe to avoid any incoming fire, then quickly **use missiles on the three glowing shield generators 6**—it may be help to hover briefly to aim at each generator effectively. With the three generators destroyed, avoid the general's missiles and **target your firepower on the remaining base structure 7**—destroy it to complete the mission. After completing this mission, an MI6 interlude cinema will be unlocked.

EXTRA OBJECTIVE: EARN PLATINUM 007

To earn platinum (once the objective is unlocked), you must destroy the general's secret base in less than 45 seconds. The key is to have full health by the time you reach the secret base—so you can focus on destroying the base rather than on monitoring your health. To preserve health through the level, make it a habit to shoot off a flare once per second—it may seem like overkill, but it will help keep you from getting hit by missiles. Avoid the boats and concentrate on the jeeps and helicopters, using as few missiles as possible to destroy enemies. Do not get hit by any falling rocks or debris—hover in place and wait if you must, rather than try to fly quickly under them. Also avoid the flames in the pyramid by using the same tactics you used to earn a Bond Moment there.

It's possible to reach the secret base with 85 percent or more of your health intact—you'll be in good shape to earn platinum. Keep firing off flares, but focus on shooting missiles rapidly rather than fancy flying footwork. If you can destroy the three shield generators in 25 seconds or less, you'll have plenty of time to destroy the rest of the base.

SCENE 2
BOND MOMENT

Destroy all three enemy missile boats.

SCENE 3
BOND MOMENT

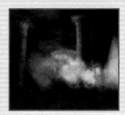

When in the temple area where the flames shoot out of the walls, avoid any damage from the flames.

007 EVERYTHING OR NOTHING

GOLD TARGET

Score 150,000 points to unlock the Platinum objective.

PLATINUM TARGET

Reach the bottom of the fortress in less than 1:55.

STARTING WEAPONS

 MISSILES

 MACHINE GUN

 Q CLOAK

 RC CAR

ACQUIRED WEAPONS

 NONE

Note: The Porsche Cayenne can utilize cluster bombs as a weapons upgrade once you've completed this mission. See the Vehicles section at the beginning of the book for additional details.

SERENA ST. GERMAINE

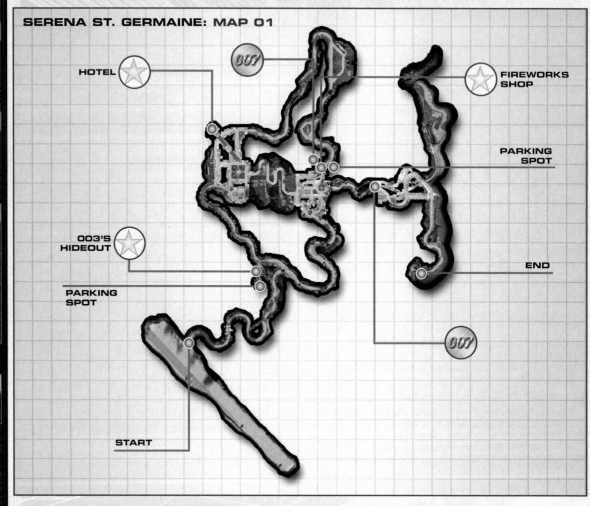

SERENA ST. GERMAINE: MAP 01

HOTEL

007

FIREWORKS SHOP

PARKING SPOT

003'S HIDEOUT

PARKING SPOT

END

007

START

START: MISSION BRIEFING

You will be flown off to Puerto Viejo in Peru to discover the whereabouts of Agent 003. You will take your trusty Porsche Cayenne to navigate through the village, as well as employ some neat new gadgets.

OBJECTIVE 1: INTERCEPT THE PATROL JEEP

At the start of the mission, a jeep will witness your arrival and try to report your presence. **Follow the jeep and destroy it as quickly as possible ❶.** (Note: At oo Agent difficulty, the jeep will take a shortcut to the right, so get ready to follow it taking that route. In addition, missiles will be less

effective unless at close range and directly behind the jeep.)

OBJECTIVE 2: LOCATE AND ENTER 003's HIDEOUT

Keep following the road until you see **a narrow road branching off to the left ❷**. This leads to 003's hideout: When a cinema scene reveals its location, drive

over the metal bridge, look for a place to park, and exit the car. Go inside the hideout to take a phone call.

OBJECTIVE 3: AVOID ENEMY PATROLS

A countdown will begin when you jump back in the Porsche (4:00 at Agent difficulty, 3:10 at 00 Agent difficulty), which is your signal to get moving. Get back in the Cayenne, drive back up the metal ramp and head left, then make a hard right to return to the main road that leads to the village.

OBJECTIVE 4: GET TO THE HOTEL AMERICANO

As you near the village, Q will inform you that enemy patrols will be on the lookout for you. Fortunately, your GPS map (in the upper-left corner of your screen) will pinpoint their locations in orange, so you'll know where they are. **Upon reaching the village entrance, brake and wait for a patrol sentry to drive past ❸**, then turn right. When you reach a **grassy open circle with a fountain in the middle, activate the Q Cloak and turn left ❹**. You will see a long winding road in the distance, and a cinema scene will kick in. Turn right at the T-intersection and follow the road until you see **a hidden location by the fireworks shop where you can park your car ❺**. Use the RC car to drive up the ramp next to the fireworks building, then **look for a grate to shoot with a laser ❻**. Drive into the fireworks building and target the laser on the crates to create an eye-catching diversion, which will earn you a Bond Moment.

With the patrols now distracted, turn off your Q Cloak and drive right past the patrols (they won't bother you thanks to the distraction) to find **the entrance to the long and winding road ❼**—use your full-screen map if you're lost. Follow this road uphill, then activate your Q Cloak when you reach the top (or simply avoid any patrol jeeps). Use the map to find the front of the hotel, where a cinema scene will kick in. With the Q Cloak activated, you can even take **a diagonal shortcut through an alleyway ❽** that leads directly to the hotel.

MISSION 7

SCENE 1
007 BOND MOMENT

Use the RC car to explode the fireworks shop in the village.

SCENE 2
007 BOND MOMENT

While en route to the mountain fortress, when you reach a point in the road blocked by two jeeps, look for and take a shortcut to the left that leads to a sunken alleyway.

OBJECTIVE 5: REACH THE BASE OF THE MOUNTAIN FORTRESS

After picking up Serena, follow her directions to the fortress. Enemy detection is no longer an issue, so get ready to use up the Cayenne's weapon arsenal. Drive back down the long and winding road. At the bottom, dispatch the enemy jeep ahead, then quickly veer left and right to return to the **a grassy open circle with a fountain in the middle ❾**. Drive around the fountain but go straight to get to another winding roadway. This will lead to a roadblock with two jeeps—instead of driving into them, **steer left to find a sunken alleyway, which will trigger a Bond Moment ❿**. Drive through the alley until you see a tank ahead, then make a hard left. Take out the remaining jeeps until you reach a cinema scene featuring a tank. **Look for an opening to the left created by the tank's destruction, and drive off the cliff ⓫**. Make sure you have enough speed to jump over the chasm, then drive up the hill to reach the road again. Just before reaching the fortress, **hang a left and smash through a yellow barrier ⓬** to complete the mission.

EXTRA OBJECTIVE: EARN PLATINUM 007

To earn platinum (once the objective is unlocked), you must reach the base of the mountain fortress in less than 1:55 after picking up Serena St. Germaine. The walkthrough points out the optimal route.

The key to completing this objective? Preserve as much health as possible before reaching Serena. At the start of the mission, you must get directly behind the jeep as quickly as possible and shoot missiles at short range (the missiles will miss if shot from far away or if you are not directly behind the jeep). Don't run into anything that may damage the Cayenne, and use the Q Cloak to avoid detection whenever possible. It is vital to have at least 75 percent health by the time you reach Serena.

When the actual challenge begins, turn right to take a diagonal shortcut through the alleyway. Activate the Q Cloak before emerging from the alleyway, then head as far as possible down the long and winding road until the Q Cloak runs out. Continue on the path described previously (including the Bond Moment shortcut)—it'll take driving skill and some practice to nail this objective.

VEHICLE: PORSCHE CAYENNE TURBO

VERTIGO

VERTIGO: MAP 01

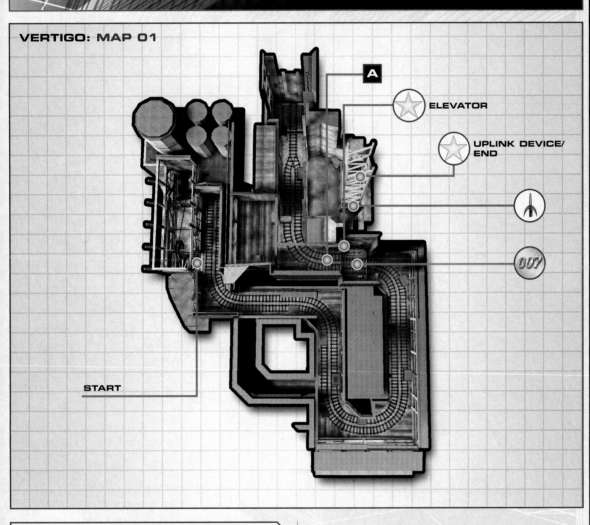

A

ELEVATOR

UPLINK DEVICE/
END

007

START

GOLD TARGET

Score 150,000 points to unlock the Platinum objective.

PLATINUM TARGET

Complete the mission in 4:00 or less.

STARTING WEAPONS

RAPPEL	
THERMOVISION	
Q SPIDER	
STROBE	
SLEEPER DART	
P99 w/Silencer	

ACQUIRED WEAPONS

AK-74	
AT-420	
MP5K	

START: MISSION BRIEFING

Your search for any sign of missing Agent 003 continues as you split up with Serena to make your way through this mountain fortress. During this mission, you will make liberal use of the rappel as you make your way to the top of the cliff. This is the first mission in which you'll be able to put your Q Spider to good use. Because of the backtracking in this level, it may be wise to bypass some armor vests for later use.

OBJECTIVE 1: GET TO THE TOP OF THE CLIFF

When the mission begins, exit the elevator and crouch. Take a left turn and follow the train tracks, hide behind mine carts and wait for a guard to appear. **Once he turns his back, creep up behind him and perform a stealth attack ❶**. Continue following the train tracks, using the mine carts for cover and repeating this process for the remaining guards. If you can dispatch all the guards on this level without raising the alarm, you'll earn a Bond Moment. **Look for a rappel point at the end of the mine tracks ❷**, then head up.

1

2

MISSION 8

007 SCENE 1
BOND MOMENT

Use stealth attacks to avoid detection through the area where you start the mission.

3

3 - 0
Silenced P99

4 **5**

6

Rappel

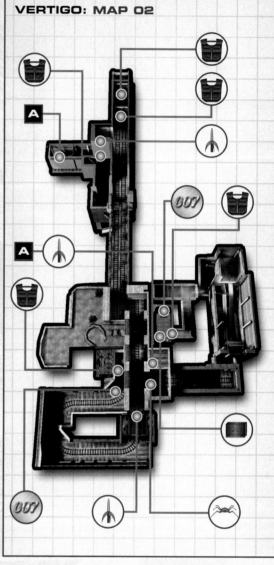

VERTIGO: MAP 02

A

A

007

007

007

At the top of the rappel point, get ready to pull out heavier firepower (such as the AK-74) to dispatch the enemy guards that appear. **Run to the corner to the right, and lean back against the wall for cover** ❸. Target the remaining guards from this point as well as any that rappel down. Once the coast is clear, make note of **an elevator area** ❹—you'll be backtracking to this point later—as well as a rappel point upward where the mine tracks dead-end. Pull yourself up with the rappel to find an **armor vest between two stacks of crates** ❺, then look for **another rappel point** ❻.

After reaching the top, to the left of the rappel point is **yet another armor vest** ❼, but save it for later if you can. Turn right and quickly duck behind a mine cart—a rocket-firing soldier is at the end of the hallway. While crouched, **roll to the two mine carts that are side by side** ❽. Press the action button to cause the cart on

the right to move forward, and crouch behind it for cover. Eliminate the rocket-wielding guard at the end of the tracks.

7 **8**

TIP

It is possible to target and eliminate this guard without moving the carts! When you reach the two side-by-side carts, pull out the AK-74 and finesse your aim point on the target slightly upward to target the head. A short extra cinema scene will play if you can pull this off!

At the end of the corridor, look for a short passage to the left—dispatch the guards that pop up here. There will also be a rappel point downward into a darkened mine shaft. Use Thermovision to navigate through this area and locate enemy targets. **At the end of this hallway is an AT-420 that, when acquired, will earn you a Bond Moment ⑨.** An armor vest may be found here as well. Watch for enemies to pop out as you backtrack to the rappel point. Upon leaving the darkened mine shaft, **use a Q Spider and take it past the boarded-up passage-way ⑩** (Note: At oo Agent difficulty, you'll need to use Bond Sense to target the planks and create a hole for the Q Spider). Look for a small entryway on the left that leads to a maze of planks, which if successfully navigated, leads to a metal vent and **a locked armory area with various weapons, an armor vest, and a battery ⑪.** Open the sliding

armory door with the Q Spider to activate another Bond Moment. Take out the last of the guards to finish up.

SHORTCUT

It is possible to destroy the signal-jamming antenna before climbing up with the rappel. **Use Bond Sense to look through the window where the rocket-launching guard was ⑫ to target the fuel generator below the antenna. Blow it up to knock down the antenna.**

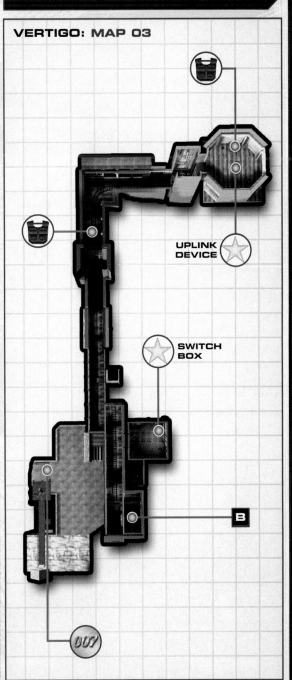

VERTIGO: MAP 03

UPLINK DEVICE

SWITCH BOX

B

007

MISSION 8

SCENE 2
BOND MOMENT

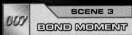

In the dark train tunnel when you first use Thermovision, reach the end. M will tell you that it may be a trap when you reach the end of the passageway. On the ground nearby will be a rocket launcher.

SCENE 3
BOND MOMENT

When you reach the enemy that carries a rocket launcher (where you have to push a train cart forward to get within range), look for a side alcove that appears walled off—but is accessible using a Q Spider. Navigate the spider through a hole and up a series of wooden planks to reach a supply room with armor, a battery, and weapons. Open the blue door nearby to surprise the guards and trigger a Bond Moment.

MISSION 8

SCENE 4
BOND MOMENT

After installing the control room uplink device, shoot the fuel storage below the jamming dish to take down both the jamming dish and the catwalk.

Back at the boarded-up passageway, look up to find another rappel point. Reach this next level to see **a large antenna with guards posted next to it ⑬** (if you haven't destroyed it already). Quickly run out to the opening, then **use Bond Sense to target the large fuel canisters below the antenna to earn a Bond Moment ⑭**. Then quickly run back behind wall cover to dispatch any remaining guards along the walkway.

As you head through the walkway, look right to find **the computer room the Q Spider discovered ⑮**—save the items in the armory if you can, though, because you'll be backtracking here later. Continue down the tunnel to the end of the tracks to find another rappel point upward.

At this level, **note the armor vest near the mine cart ⑯**. Of greater concern will be the guards—some of whom now have flak jackets. Since these guards are heavily armored, you might want to employ hand-to-hand combat to dispatch them (or take a head shot). Run to the end of the tracks to pull yourself up to the next level, which dead-ends at a room.

OBJECTIVE 2: RETRIEVE AGENT 003's UPLINK DEVICE

To the left, an armor vest is lying beside a table. You will encounter **two more guards with flak jackets, and a guard with an AK-74**—this time, the guard gets smart and flips a table for cover ⑰. Now would be a great time to use the AT-420 you found earlier: One shot will stun them all! **Retrieve 003's uplink device from the stack of crates on the right side of the room ⑱**.

OBJECTIVE 3: INSTALL THE CONTROL ROOM UPLINK DEVICE

To install the uplink device, rappel back to the level below. You will be greeted by an ambush of sorts, with guards as well as enemy rappellers appearing to attack you. Crouch behind any available cover, then take out the rappelling guards once they come down. Rappel to the next level, taking out enemies along the way. Return to the room that housed the large computers. Press the action button to **install the uplink device to the switch box at the back of the room ⑲**. Don't forget to pick up all the goodies in the armory room before leaving.

OBJECTIVE 4: DESTROY THE SIGNAL JAMMING ANENNA

Remember that signal-jamming dish you saw earlier in the mission? If you've already destroyed it, this objective will already be accomplished. If not, run out of the room and look for the guards on the catwalk near the signal-jamming dish. Use Bond Sense to find the generator next to the jamming dish (see screenshot 10). Target and destroy the generator to neutralize both the dish and the guards to earn a Bond Moment (if you haven't already).

OBJECTIVE 5: TAKE THE ELEVATOR TO THE CLIFF TOP

Get ready for a fierce firefight as you backtrack toward the elevator (see screenshot 4) you saw at the start of the mission. Rappel and return to the area where the rocket-launching soldier had been. Duck behind the mine cart at the end of the tracks and use heavy firepower to engage enemy forces. Guards will be waiting for you behind the numerous mine carts lining the wall. **At the end of the tunnel, a small room will be opened ⑳**, and from here a guard will attack. Shoot him to get him out of the way, and grab the armor vest in the room.

Rappel down the level where the elevator is: Guards in front of you as well as in the rafters will open fire. **Lean back against the stack of crates at the bottom of the rappel point for cover ㉑**, then shoot each of the guards to clear the way to the elevator. Press the action button in the elevator to proceed to the top of the cliff.

EXTRA OBJECTIVE: EARN PLATINUM 007

To earn platinum (once the objective is unlocked), you must complete the level in less than 4:00. Follow the walkthrough strategy but ignore all Bond Moments: Forget stealth, forget the area requiring Thermovision, and forget the Q Spider path. However, do destroy the signal-jamming uplink as soon as possible, using the shortcut previously mentioned.

MISSION 9

GOLD TARGET

Score 175,000 points to unlock the Platinum objective.

PLATINUM TARGET

Fire 10 rounds or fewer.

STARTING WEAPONS

- RAPPEL
- THERMOVISION
- Q SPIDER
- GRENADE
- STROBE
- SLEEPER DART
- P99 w/Silencer

ACQUIRED WEAPONS

- AK-74
- AT-420
- SIG 552
- DESERT EAGLE
- DRAGUNOV

THE RUINED TOWER

THE RUINED TOWER: MAP 01

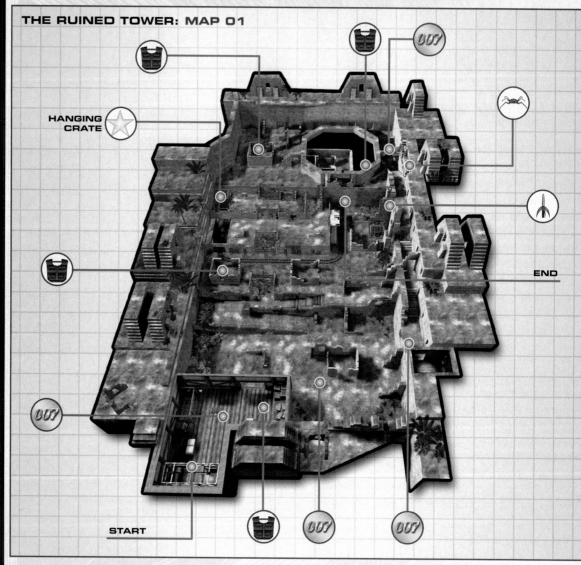

HANGING CRATE

007

END

START

START:
MISSION BRIEFING

Your search for missing Agent 003 continues: This time, you've reached a formidable ruined tower with plenty of locations for enemies to hide and ambush you. Skillful use of cover will ensure a successful mission. However, don't linger behind any cover for too long, because some soldiers will be armed with grenades to flush you out. Finesse aiming will also be necessary to hit enemies behind cover.

OBJECTIVE 1:
INFILTRATE THE RUIN

The level begins with you exiting the elevator. Quickly crouch behind the elevator wall for cover. When the guard closest to you turns his back, use a stealth attack to dispatch the guard, then **quickly crouch behind a crate with a wrench atop it ❶**. Grab the wrench, then wait for the other guard to investigate the fallen comrade. Target and throw the wrench at the other guard (or use the Sleeper Dart) before he ducks. Using stealth on both guards without being detected will earn you a Bond Moment. **Look for an armor vest**

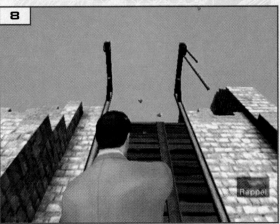

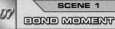

behind a metal crate ②. Crouch behind the **short walls next to the elevator room entrance ③** to see guards patrolling the area. Follow one of the guards and perform a stealth attack, then use the Sleeper Dart when the other guard comes to investigate. This will result in another Bond Moment.

Use Bond Sense to find a rappel point on a stone wall to the right of the warehouse exit ④. You may have seen a guard atop that point before. Use the rappel to get up the wall to earn a Bond Moment. Dispatch the guard in the room to find a Dragunov sniper rifle and another armor vest. **Using the short stone walls nearby for cover, crouch and equip the sniper rifle from your elevated position ⑤.** It is best to **aim for the AT-420–wielding guard tucked away in a room in the front of the fortress tower ⑥.** Take out any remaining visible targets with the Dragunov, then

rappel back down and head up the ramp leading to the higher levels of the fortress. As the ramp turns and heads back the other way, guards will pop up. Take cover by leaning up against any nearby wall corners, then take aim at the guards. Also keep an eye out for guards coming up the ramps behind you. There is an **armor vest nearby, in a broken room area ⑦** near the boarded-up mine cart exit point.

After following the ramps upward, **Bond will reach a second rappel point ⑧.** Before heading down the stairs to the left, **notice the small ledge on the right of the stairs ⑨.** Deploy a Q Spider and run it along this path to earn a Bond Moment. Use the spider to pick up an armor vest along the thin path ringing the ruined tower.

WARNING

Running the Q Spider along the edge may activate the appearance of enemies that will attack you (Bond, not the Q Spider). You may need to switch back to Bond if that occurs, then return to the Q Spider once the coast is clear again.

MISSION 9

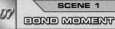

SCENE 1
BOND MOMENT

Use stealth attacks to dispatch the guards in the first room.

SCENE 2
BOND MOMENT

Use stealth attacks to dispatch the guards patrolling the outside of the elevator room.

SCENE 3
BOND MOMENT

Use the rappel to reach the top of the warehouse to find a Dragunov sniper rifle.

MISSION 9

10

11

13

14

SCENE 4
007 BOND MOMENT

After you ascend to the area to the right of the ruined tower, set down the Q Spider to find a narrow path cut into the side of the wall.

12

After using the Q Spider, head down the stairs and take cover: Guards will rappel down the wall in front of Bond. Eliminate them and move forward behind the back of the tower. Take corner cover along the left or right wall alcoves or crouch behind the small walls as the next wave of guards arrives. Look for another **armor vest sandwiched between two walls** 🔟. Afterward, look for **a passageway into the small room** 1️⃣1️⃣ where the rocket-launching soldier was at the start of the level. Find more ammo for the Dragunov sniper rifle. Get ready for rappelling guards to rush into the room—but stay out of the window opening, because another AT-420 guard will shoot at you from the top of the elevator room's roof. Exit this room and dispatch any guards still remaining.

To rid yourself of that pesky rocket-shooting guard, **camp behind a rocky structure near the room** 1️⃣2️⃣. As long as you're crouched, you won't get hit by the rockets. While crouched, set up the sniper scope, then pop up and quickly locate the target. If you see a rocket coming, just duck until it passes, then pop up again to seek and neutralize him with a well-aimed shot.

Once the area is cleared of enemies, **head down a short set of stairs and turn right** 1️⃣3️⃣. You'll find a hanging crate. Press the action button to drop the crate to open up a new path. Jump in the newly created hole, then press the action button to trigger the mine cart's brake system on the wall next to it. This will start the mine cart rolling and open up a way out of the tunnel.

Get ready for a quick firefight: There will be more guards waiting for you to roll out. Duck behind what cover you can find, and fight your way to where the mine cart comes to a rest. (If you left the armor vest nearby, now would be perfect time to grab it.)

WARNING

At oo Agent difficulty, watch out for a rocket-launching soldier that will pop up behind you. He is very hazardous to your health, so look for any large walls to shield yourself from him, and take him out as soon as possible.

When you reach the area where the mine cart crashed, watch out for enemy rappellers to the right. Once the coast is clear, **target the dynamite on the ground** 1️⃣4️⃣.

WARNING

Don't stand too close to the dynamite when you set it off, for obvious reasons.

This will blow open a door—go through the doorway to finish the mission.

EXTRA OBJECTIVE:
EARN PLATINUM 007

To earn platinum (once the objective is unlocked), you must fire 10 rounds or fewer. Using stealth and achieving the first three Bond Moments are essential at the beginning of this mission. You'll need to use the first Dragunov rifle you find to snipe five enemies from a safe point before proceeding, then use hand-to-hand combat for the rest. You'll need to grab the AT-420 for the end of the mission to clear the path quickly—and don't forget to save one bullet for the dynamite that blows open the door!

DEATH OF AN AGENT

DEATH OF AN AGENT: MAP 01

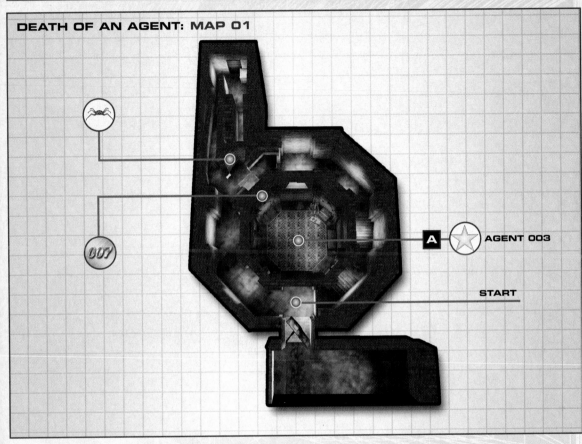

A — AGENT 003

START

GOLD TARGET

Score 200,000 points to unlock the Platinum objective.

PLATINUM TARGET

Complete the mission, taking 100 damage or less.

STARTING WEAPONS

	RAPPEL
	THERMOVISION
	Q SPIDER
	GRENADE
	STROBE
	SLEEPER DART
	P99 w/Silencer
	SIG 552

ACQUIRED WEAPONS

	AK-74
	SPAS 12
	DESERT EAGLE
	AT-420

START: MISSION BRIEFING PART 01

You've finally found where agent 003 is being held—but he may not have much longer to live. You must get to him quickly!

OBJECTIVE 1: GET TO 003 BEFORE HE DIES

After the cinema of Diavolo shooting 003 finishes, you must rescue the fallen agent fast. But instead of rushing into battle, deploy a Q Spider. **Use the Q Spider to find a hole in the wall ahead ❶**. Have the Q Spider follow that path, crossing a wooden plank before falling on unsuspecting guards to earn a Bond Moment. This method is much safer and more efficient for your score (as well as your health).

Once done, move along the right side of the wall to shield yourself from any possible enemy fire

(although there should be none if you used the Q Spider). Crouch and creep down the stairs and take out any remaining guards (you can use stealth attacks for extra points if they don't detect you).

OBJECTIVE 2: FIND ANOTHER WAY OFF THE CLIFF

When you get to the bottom of the stairs, a cinema will kick in. After that, get ready to attack guards that will rush into the room. Dispatch them quickly, then head out the way they came in. Use the wooden boxes nearby for cover, then peer around the corner to see **a staircase and an enemy guard ❷**. Drop him, then go down the long staircase and hide behind the entryway at the bottom to find another enemy lurking behind a wall. Fine-tune your aim to hit an exposed area of his body.

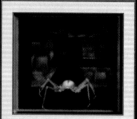

SCENE 1
BOND MOMENT

At the start of the mission, deploy a Q Spider. Take it down the hallway to find a spider hole. Navigate that hole upward, then have the Q Spider fall to detonate over unsuspecting guards.

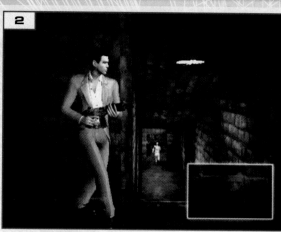

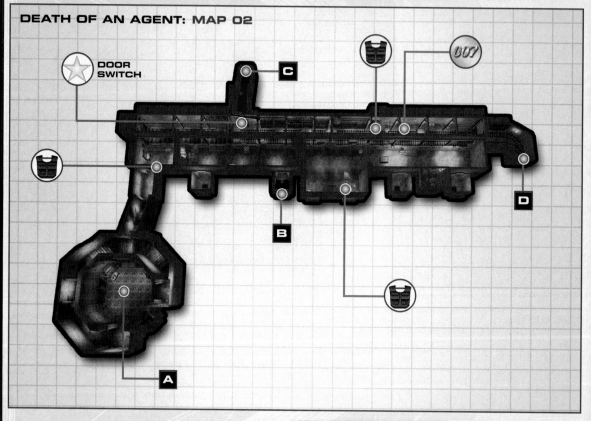

DEATH OF AN AGENT: MAP 02

DOOR SWITCH

C

007

B

A

D

You will then enter a long hallway. On the table is an armor vest in plain view, and ahead will be a gang of enemies firing on you. **Take cover to the right of the broken wall ❸.** Using Bond Sense, if you look carefully in the crowd, **you'll be able to see a fuel canister to target ❹.** Shoot it with a long-range gun such as the SIG 552 to explode the fuel canister. Once the guards in this area are cleared out, look for a short staircase nearby that leads to the rest of the long hallway. Near a tipped-over mine cart, look for **an armor vest behind a wooden crate ❺.**

4

Shootable

5

3 - 0
Desert Eagle

007

MISSION 10

007 | SCENE 2
BOND MOMENT

Find an AT-420 in an alcove in the catacombs.

DEATH OF AN AGENT: MAP 03

C

007

B

OBJECTIVE 3: LOCATE THE EXIT TO THE CATACOMBS

The only way out is down a hole ❻. Drop into it and activate Thermovision. Get ready to be flanked by enemies to the left and right. Take cover behind boxes or walls and wait for enemies to appear. Move slowly through this area

to ensure you don't get outflanked. At the start, you'll have two directions to explore. Head left initially to clear out that area, then head right. **Look for a two small alcoves along the way that have armor vests** ❼. Your goal is to reach **a long stone ramp upward flanked by a pair of statues** ❽. It'll be guarded, so be prepared to fight.

After reaching the top of the stairways, **press the action button by a switch nearby** ❾ to activate a door at the other end. Guards will emerge as a result, so quickly roll and crouch behind the mine carts for cover. You'll notice some heavy propane tanks, but regular bullets won't work. Instead, **use Bond Sense to target some slightly**

6

2 - 0
Desert Eagle

007

7

Desert Eagle

007

MISSION 10

007

SCENE 3

BOND MOMENT

After emerging from the catacombs and opening the exit doorway, look for some explosive crates in a nook along a wall, sandwiched between propane gas tanks. Shoot the crates to explode the tanks—take out at least three soldiers with this tactic to earn the Bond Moment.

DID YOU KNOW?

At Operative difficulty, it is possible to catch Serena before reaching the final Bond Moment locations.

---

hidden explosive crates 🔟 that will detonate all the tanks. If you take out at least three guards with this tactic, you'll earn a Bond Moment. Eliminate any remaining soldiers, then look for **an armor vest in a stone alcove alongside the mine cart tracks ⓫**. Exit through the opened doorway to complete the mission.

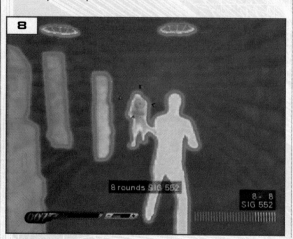

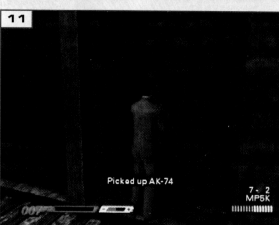

DEATH OF AN AGENT: MAP 04

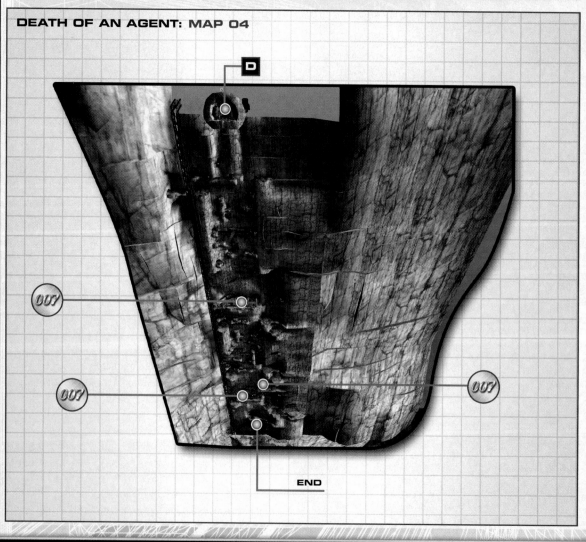

MISSION BRIEFING
PART 02

The good news is that you've found Serena. The bad news is that she's falling for you hard—but not in the way you'd prefer. Instead, she's being pushed out of a helicopter, and she'll be plunging to her untimely end unless you can save her!

OBJECTIVE 1:
CATCH SERENA

This is arguably the most exhilarating level of the game, but stay focused: Hitting a rock or object means serious damage or mission failure. If you aren't quick enough to reach Serena in time, you will fail as well. If you're feeling rushed, use Bond Sense to gain your bearings as well as acquire targets. If you hit any rocks or ledges head-on, the mission will end in failure. If you graze them, you will lose health, and you may not be able to catch up to Serena—so don't run into anything!

TIP

You don't have to follow Serena's exact route—she's more of a visual distraction than an actual guide to follow.

Before you reach the cliff face, make sure you're equipped with a strong knock-down weapon such as the Desert Eagle—you won't have time for multiple shots on enemies. When you reach the cliff face, a cinema will kick in. Immediately jump off the cliff. You will encounter the first guard on the ledge directly below. Avoid the ledge by moving to the left of it, and fire a few rounds at the guard. **Navigate between the two wooden walkways** and avoid the two enemy guards on either side along the way. As Bond moves past the two wooden walkways, there will be another wooden obstacle in the center. **Move Bond to the right to avoid the obstacle**, then shoot the guard on the ledge to the right. Avoid the wooden obstacle that explodes as you continue to fall.

Directly below the first exploding obstacle is a ledge with two rocket guards. Look for the guard standing next to crates full of TNT, then **activate Bond Sense to target the crates of TNT once you're in range**. Detonate the explosives to earn a Bond Moment. With that complete, quickly veer left to avoid hitting the ledge, then right to avoid another.

When you see a wide rock ledge with two AT-420-shooting guards, use Bond Sense to find a TNT crate behind the left guard—target and destroy that crate to dispatch the guard.

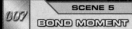

SCENE 5
007 BOND MOMENT

When you see a white propane tank on a ledge, squeeze between the small opening between a rock to the left and a wooden walkway to the right.

SCENE 6
007 BOND MOMENT

Shoot the white propane tank mentioned in the previous Bond Moment to eliminate a guard near-

Continue down the center of the cliff, shooting guards as you pass them. **As Bond passes a wooden walkway with a guard on the right of it, a metal overhang will be visible ⑮.** Right as you are about to pass the metal overhang, move left to avoid another ledge, and shoot the guard standing on it. After you pass that ledge, **look for a white propane tank between a rock cliff and a wooden walkway ⑯.** From this point, you can pull off two Bond Moments in rapid succession: First, fall between the cliff and the walkway—it's an extremely tight squeeze, but it's doable. This shortcut will earn you the first Bond Moment. Then **immediately use Bond Sense to target the propane tank on the ledge below ⑰.** Shoot it while veering hard left so you don't splatter on the ledge. Destroying the tanks (and the guards nearby) will result in another Bond Moment.

With that accomplished, move right to avoid a final ledge (with a guard atop it) right below. At this point, Serena should be in sight. Get close to her to trigger the mission-ending cinema.

ALTERNATE ROUTE

If you are too chicken to complete the shortcut Bond Moment, simply veer to the right of the wooden walkway, then veer hard left—you'll need to make the move as soon as possible to get all the way across.

EXTRA OBJECTIVE: EARN PLATINUM 007

To earn platinum (once the objective is unlocked), you must complete the first part of this mission having taken 100 points of damage or less. This will be a test of your skill and patience, because you must play the first half of the level almost flawlessly to pull this off. As a result, you must tread slowly and carefully—especially in the catacombs area—to make sure you don't miss any enemies who might snipe you from behind. When you get to the broken wall area (see screenshot 3), enemies will be able to hit you if you remain exposed for too long, so fire in short bursts and get behind cover quickly. While behind that wall, watch out for guards trying to outflank you on the left—they'll attempt to sneak behind you if you're not paying attention.

A SHOW OF FORCE

A SHOW OF FORCE: MAP 01

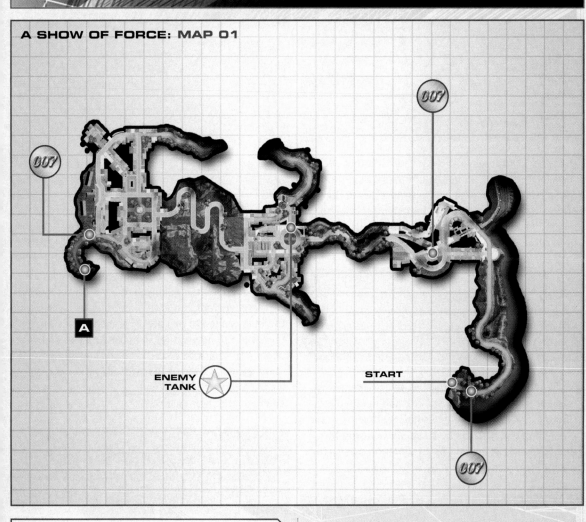

007

007

A

ENEMY TANK

START

007

MISSION 1.1

GOLD TARGET
Score 200,000 points to unlock the Platinum objective.

PLATINUM TARGET
Get from 003's hideout to the extraction point in 45 seconds or less.

STARTING WEAPONS
 TANK CANNON
 MACHINE GUN

ACQUIRED WEAPONS
 ROCKETS
SHOTGUN
FLAME-THROWER

SCENE 1 BOND MOMENT

Use the tank cannon to blow up the fortress gate at the very start of the mission.

START: MISSION BRIEFING

With Serena safely back on the ground, it's time to make a quick getaway in true Bond fashion: Commandeer a tank and wreak havoc on enemies (and villagers) in the process. Unfortunately, it's Serena at the wheel, so get ready for a bumpy but exciting ride.

OBJECTIVE 1: GET SERENA SAFELY TO 003's HIDEOUT

When the mission begins, use the tank cannon to **blow out the front gate of the fortress ❶** to earn a speedy Bond Moment, then dispatch several enemy jeeps that you encounter before veering through a bunch of trees. After returning to the road, look for a helicopter. Use

your machine gun to dispatch the helicopter—however, it is also possible to use the tank cannon if you can tar-

1 B

007 Tank Cannon 50

MISSION 11

SCENE 2
007 BOND MOMENT

Just before driving through the pottery store, use the tank cannon to blow up explosives next to two soldiers in the market square area.

SCENE 3
007 BOND MOMENT

Eliminate all gas station enemies with a single shot by targeting the gas pumps.

get it quickly. Your tank will eventually rumble into town and up a long ramp. **Look for enemy soldiers to target with the machine gun on both sides of the stairs—especially the rocket-launching soldiers ❷**, and target exploding fuel barrels to maximize your firepower.

TIP

When using the machine gun, you'll automatically aim at targets as long as you're pointed toward them in general. You can also use the regular automatic-aim button to zoom in on enemies.

At the top of the stairs will be two jeeps, use the machine gun to destroy them both and get ready to turn right. When you see two soldiers standing at the end of the alley, **use the tank cannon to target the fuel barrels next to them ❸**. Explode the barrels to earn a Bond Moment.

TIP

When it comes to the jeeps, you can use either the machine guns or tank cannons. However, the tank cannons can take out jeeps with a single shot. This might make them a better weapon than the machine gun when it comes to ammo efficiency, as well as quick enemy elimination.

Thanks to Serena's dubious tank-piloting skills, you'll drive straight through a pottery shop before returning to the roadway. Use the tank cannon or machine gun to attack the missile jeeps that appear, as well as some soldiers on the ground—**look for another fuel barrel near the soldiers to make quick work of them ❹**. After that point, look back with the tank cannon or machine gun to shake off a pursuing jeep.

After taking a winding path, you'll enter the square with the fountain, only to watch it get blown to bits by an enemy tank. Go around the fountain and use the tank cannon to dispatch the enemy tank. The tank will also be moving, so make sure you **aim your shots a little ahead of the tank so they don't fall short ❺**. With the tank dispatched, you might still have a pursuing jeep on your tail—take it out before you reach the next point.

TIP

The tank cannon has a reload lag time of several seconds between shots. Make sure you're aimed properly before firing.

With the enemy tank silenced, you'll reach **four rocket-firing soldiers atop an archway ❻**. Use the machine guns to neutralize the soldiers, or use the tank cannon to collapse the arch itself. You will then proceed straight up a hill with a helicopter in hot pursuit. **The helicopter will fly toward you from the rear in a linear fashion, so if you're already turned back to see the line it's taking, you can shoot it down with a single cannon shot ❼!** Otherwise, the machine gun does the job just as well.

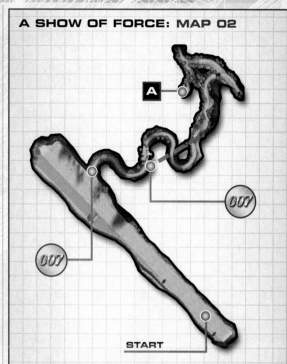

A SHOW OF FORCE: MAP 02

START

MISSION 11

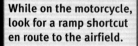

SCENE 4
BOND MOMENT

While on the motorcycle, look for a ramp shortcut en route to the airfield.

SCENE 5
BOND MOMENT

When you reach the roadblock in front of the airfield, look for a ramp on the right to jump over enemy forces.

When you reach the top of the hill, look for a jeep to drive out in front of you. Dispatch it with a tank cannon. Once the tank heads right toward a blue building, **look for another tank approaching from down the street 8**. Try to get a quick tank cannon shot on it before you drive past it. When you return through the market area back into the open, quickly knock out that tank and any remaining enemies with the tank cannon.

There'll be a lull in the action until you reach the gas station. Do not engage the enemies here. **Instead, target the gas pumps with the tank cannon 9**. This will trigger a chain reaction that'll knock out all the enemies nearby, and will result in a Bond Moment.

OBJECTIVE 2:
GET TO THE EXTRACTION POINT

After reaching 003's hideout location, get onto the Triumph Daytona motorcycle, head over the steel ramp, and turn right to return to the airport. You have 1:10 to get to the extraction point (45 seconds at oo Agent difficulty). Destroy any bikes and jeeps that pop up along the path. **Look out for a shortcut by a tree on your right just before a big bend in the road 10**. Taking this shortcut the whole way through will earn you a Bond Moment. Keep driving up the road. Just before reaching the airport landing strip, you'll find a makeshift roadblock greeting party. Rather than engage them in combat, **look for a trailer next to two enemies, and use it as a ramp over them onto the airport grounds to earn a Bond Moment 11**.

OBJECTIVE 3:
DRIVE INTO THE Q-PLANE

Once you reach the airport grounds, speed to the departing plane. Shoot anything in your way that might slow you down, because you will fail the mission if you miss your flight. Get close enough to the plane's rear hatch to trigger a mission-ending cinema scene.

Completing this mission will unlock another MI6 interlude cinema.

EXTRA OBJECTIVE:
EARN PLATINUM 007

To earn platinum (once the objective is unlocked), get from 003's hideout to the extraction point in 45 seconds or less using the Daytona Triumph. The key? Don't collide with anything head-on, and use all the Bond Moment shortcuts. Also, don't gun the acceleration on the Daytona Triumph right away, or else you won't be able to steer it properly when you go over the metal ramp at the start—and don't try to pop any wheelies, or you may lose control of the bike. When you reach the roadway, take out the jeep that appears as soon as possible, or else it'll block your way to the shortcut. Let off the acceleration a little at the tight left turn at the end so you don't rub the Triumph against the roadside cliffs.

007 EVERYTHING OR NOTHING

MISSION 12

GOLD TARGET

Score 200,000 points to unlock the Platinum objective.

PLATINUM TARGET

After talking on the phone to Mya, get to the van in less than 40 seconds.

STARTING WEAPONS

 MISSILES

 MACHINE GUN

 ELECTRO MAGNET

 ACID SLICK

ACQUIRED WEAPONS

🚫 NO WEAPONS

MARDI GRAS MAYHEM

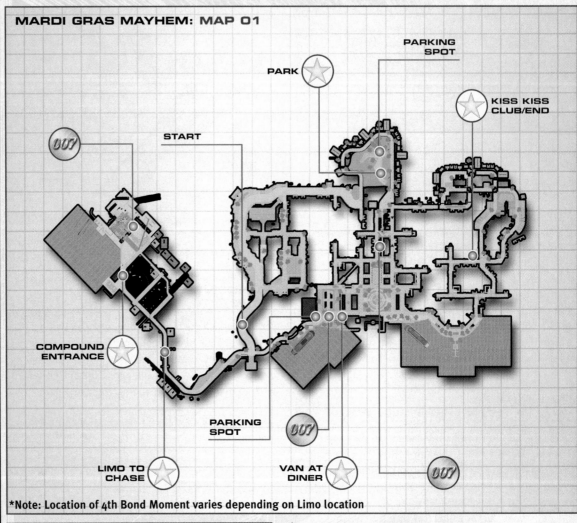

MARDI GRAS MAYHEM: MAP 01

PARKING SPOT

PARK

KISS KISS CLUB/END

007

START

COMPOUND ENTRANCE

PARKING SPOT

007

007

LIMO TO CHASE

VAN AT DINER

007

*Note: Location of 4th Bond Moment varies depending on Limo location

START: MISSION BRIEFING

This time, you'll get to tour the streets of New Orleans at night during Mardi Gras. Unfortunately, it's mostly business and no pleasure, as you take your Aston Martin Vanquish through town to rendezvous with NSA Agent Mya Starling. Hitting any objects will damage your car, so drive carefully. To park a vehicle, look for a glowing white "007" circle.

OBJECTIVE 1: RENDEZVOUS WITH THE NSA AGENT

As the mission begins, keep driving down the main road in the direction you are facing. Be careful of traffic: If you destroy any vehicle with weapons or a hard collision, the mission may end in failure. **At the end of the main street is a trolley station ❶**. Turn left and use the GPS map to get to the glowing objective marker: **A parking lot in front of a park ❷**. Turn right from the road you're on to park, then run to the entrance to the park and answer the phone ringing there.

OBJECTIVE 2: STEAL A TRANSPORT TRUCK

After hanging up the phone, you'll have 1:55 to find the van (1:10 at 00 Agent difficulty, 3:10 at Operative difficulty). Use the GPS map radar to help guide you. Gun the car in reverse to make a quick three-point turn out of the parking lot. Turn right to get back onto the road you were originally on. **When you see the flashing left-turn signal lights ahead, turn right onto a wide brick sidewalk ❸**. This leads to a ramp that will trigger a cinema scene and send you across into a building—this activates a Bond Moment. Upon exiting that building, **cut diagonally right through the green square with a horse statue in the middle ❹** and look for a road that leads to **the Gumbo Diner on your left ❺**. Park in the nearby parking lot so your car is facing the rear of the truck, then get out of the vehicle. **Look for a switch on the left-rear side of the truck to open the bay door ❻**, then return to the Aston Martin and pull the car into the back of the van to earn a Bond Moment. If you used the shortcut, you'll have plenty of time to spare.

OBJECTIVE 3: INFILTRATE THE COMPOUND

When you get into the van, bust a U-turn by **driving over the ramp entryway to the Gumbo Diner to return to the road ❼** that got you to the van. Take this long road all the way to the end. Go as fast as you can without hitting any traffic. A cinematic will kick in upon reaching the compound entrance.

OBJECTIVE 4: PLANT TRACKING DEVICES ON TRUCKS

Upon reaching the compound, **turn left to enter the van parking area ❽**. Park the van, then get out and open the van's bay door to get the Aston Martin ready for a quick getaway. **Walk to the rear wheel of the other van parked there ❾** to install the tracking device.

MISSION 12

SCENE 1
BOND MOMENT

After talking to Mya by phone, head toward the van. Look for a brick walkway that leads to a ramp that will send you over the Mardi Gras floats and into a building.

SCENE 2
BOND MOMENT

Reach the van with enough time to put the Vanquish in the back of the transport truck. You'll have to get out of the Vanquish and open the rear truck door (look for the switch on the rear-left corner of the van).

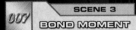
SCENE 3
BOND MOMENT

Leave the compound by using the Vanquish to drive into a large concrete pipe ramp. Make sure you have enough speed to crash into the building windows across from the compound to earn a Bond Moment.

Place Tracking Device

OBJECTIVE 5:
STOP THE HENCHMEN

After installing the device, you'll have 3:00 to catch up to (and annihilate) a limousine hoping to end Mya Starling's career prematurely. Get back into the Vanquish, and gun it quickly in reverse **to head right through the now-opened door** ⑩. Head right again and look for **a large concrete pipe to drive through** ⑪. Make sure you have enough speed through the pipe to crash into the building windows across from the compound to earn a Bond Moment.

TIP

If you forgot to pack the Vanquish with you in the van (or if you lose a life midway through the level), you've got a different challenge ahead. You'll have to chase the limo with the van (which is actually easier in some respects, because it can sustain more damage). It is still possible to catch up to the limo and ram it into oblivion. Forget the Bond Moment shortcut out of the compound—take the main gate out and follow the limo as normal. Ride up behind the limo to force it to crash into structures, or broadside your van into it to cause damage.

The timer won't turn off until you destroy the limo, so don't mess around here. Follow the limo closely, using the Electro Magnet weapon to slow the limo down. Watch out for any enemy jeeps that may appear, and dispatch them with missiles or the machine gun—if you have health to spare (or if you're driving the van), ignore them altogether. If you lose sight of the limo, use the GPS radar to find the limo and catch up. There are several shortcut points during the limo's path, which you can use to get ahead of it. First, when the limo enters the large underground garage, instead of following it, you can wait for it at the exit, **which leads to a large walkway ramp** ⑫—this may be a great place to employ an acid slick. Another minishortcut is by the Gumbo Diner: Look for a **building with gates to drive through** ⑬ when the limo drives around it. **If you can get right behind the limo as you reach a ramp near the Gumbo Diner** ⑭, the limo will be destroyed. However, if you can disable the limo beforehand by getting in front of it and using the acid slick, you will earn a Bond Moment.

007 **SCENE 4**
BOND MOMENT

Use an acid slick to stop the enemy limousine.

OBJECTIVE 6: GET TO THE CLUB

After catching up to the henchman, you'll have 1:30 to reach the Kiss Kiss Club. (Note: The actual route will vary depending on where you finally disable the limo, but in general, you want to return to the long road that the Gumbo Diner was on, and which led to the compound.) **Rather than go toward the compound, go in the other direction** ⓯. **This long road will end in a T-intersection** ⓰. Turn right and then left from this point. At the intersection, **make a quick left to see a parking spot that marks the entrance to the club and the end of this mission** ⓱.

TIP

If you're having trouble getting to the club, **try turning on the full-screen map** ⓲—it'll show you the shortest path to the club.

EXTRA OBJECTIVE: EARN PLATINUM 007

To earn platinum (once the objective is unlocked), you must reach the van in less than 40 seconds after talking to Mya—you'll need perfect timing to pull this off. The walkthrough (with the Bond Moment shortcut) outlines the fastest route. Some final tips that'll help: First, mastering the reverse three-point turn is key for getting out of the parking lot quickly. Second, jam on the buttons to try and skip the Bond Moment cinema. Third, hit the brakes hard upon reaching the Gumbo Diner so you don't overshoot the parking spot. Finally, don't hit any cars or walls head-on, and be sure to cut corners tight to take the shortest route!

TIP

The challenge ends once you reach the diner, so don't worry if you think you've run out of time. Your best bet is to check the pause screen to verify that you've completed this challenge (there should be a green check mark next to the objective).

007 EVERYTHING OR NOTHING

MISSION 13

GOLD TARGET

Score 225,000 in mission to unlock the Platinum objective.

PLATINUM TARGET

Complete the mission without using any ammunition.

STARTING WEAPONS

 RAPPEL

THERMOVISION

Q SPIDER

NANO SUIT

STROBE

GRENADE

SLEEPER DART

P99 w/Silencer

ACQUIRED WEAPONS

MP5K

DESERT EAGLE

SPAS 12

KISS KISS CLUB

KISS KISS CLUB MAP 01

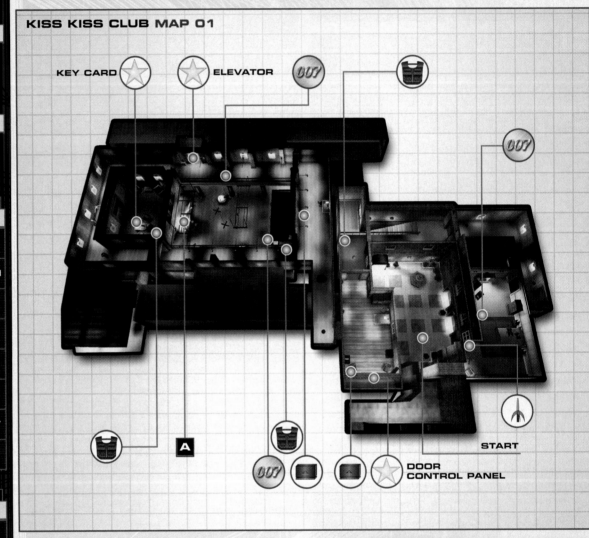

KEY CARD • ELEVATOR • 007 • 007 • 007 • A • 007 • DOOR CONTROL PANEL • START

START: MISSION BRIEFING

You've reached the Kiss Kiss Club—now all you'll have to do is get inside this intimate jazz nightclub and rendezvous with Mya Starling. Unfortunately, you don't have an invitation, so you'll have to find another way in...

OBJECTIVE 1: ENTER THE KISS KISS CLUB

Ignore the front door. **Use Bond Sense to locate a window rappel point to your right ❶** as the mission begins. Upon entering, give the woman inside the room a back massage to earn a Bond Moment. Exit the room.

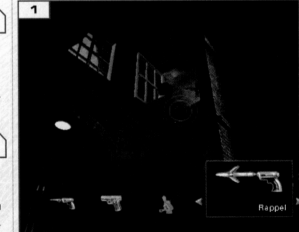

1

Rappel

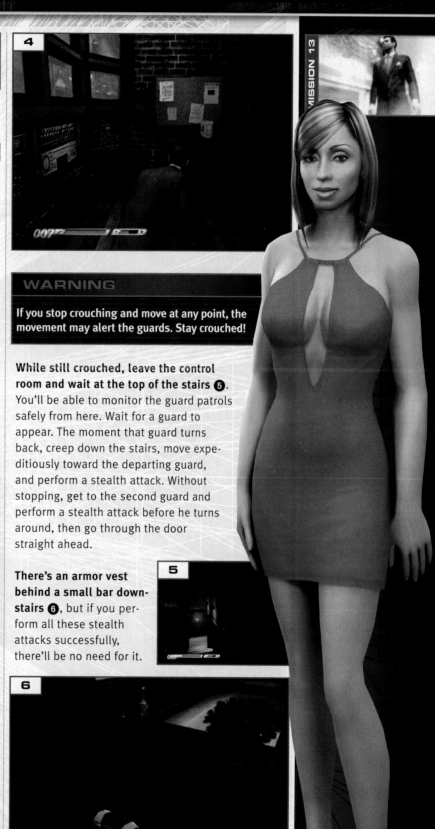

MISSION 13

WARNING

If you don't give the woman a back massage, she will alert the guards to your presence!

OBJECTIVE 2: FIND MYA BEFORE HER SONG ENDS

Although you can enter the club with guns blazing, that option is definitely more hazardous to your health. It's best to dispatch all enemies using stealth attacks so you don't alert the guards. When M informs you of this objective, hide behind a corner to peer around a door. **Wait for a guard to go through the door and look at a picture ②**. Crouch and get behind him to perform a stealth attack. Stay crouched and immediately go through the door to see some stairs. Don't go down just yet—head left to see a security monitor control room. Go straight to the closest guard and stealth-attack him before he turns around, then head to the guard by the monitors and perform another stealth attack. Look for **a switch in front of the control panel and activate it to open the club door below ③**, and look for **a battery to your right as well ④**.

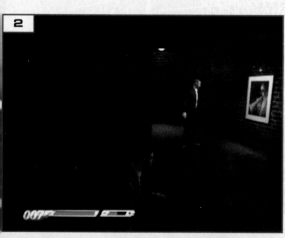

007

✕ Open door

007

While still crouched, leave the control room and wait at the top of the stairs ⑤. You'll be able to monitor the guard patrols safely from here. Wait for a guard to appear. The moment that guard turns back, creep down the stairs, move expeditiously toward the departing guard, and perform a stealth attack. Without stopping, get to the second guard and perform a stealth attack before he turns around, then go through the door straight ahead.

There's an armor vest behind a small bar downstairs ⑥, but if you perform all these stealth attacks successfully, there'll be no need for it.

WARNING

If you stop crouching and move at any point, the movement may alert the guards. Stay crouched!

MISSION 13

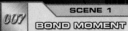

SCENE 1
BOND MOMENT

In the first room you enter, take care of the woman lying down on the massage bed.

SCENE 2
BOND MOMENT

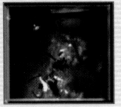

When behind the bar, head left and look for a switch that will bring the lights down on enemies.

KISS KISS CLUB MAP 02

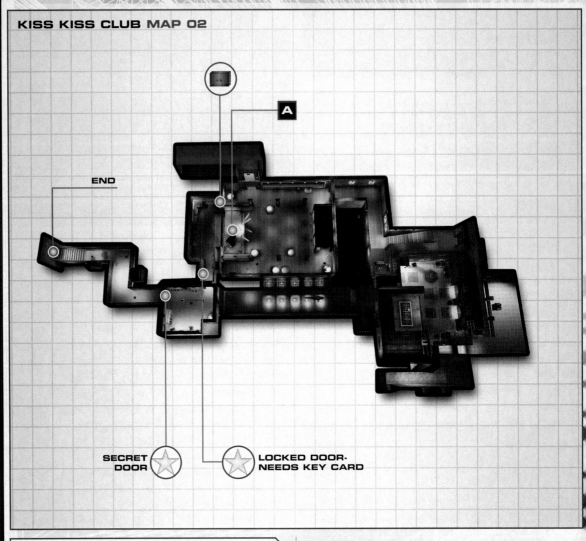

A

END

SECRET DOOR

LOCKED DOOR- NEEDS KEY CARD

OBJECTIVE 3: RETRIEVE THE SECURITY ACCESS CARD

A cinema scene will play upon your entering the stage area. You'll find yourself behind the bar. Immediately head left and you'll automatically get a SPAS 12 shotgun, as well as **a switch that will bring** the lights down—if you take out any enemies with this tactic, you'll earn a Bond Moment **7**. Make note of an armor vest on a table to the left of that switch **8**, then remain behind the bar to dispatch the enemies on the floor. Adjust your aim point upward to hit any enemies hiding behind tables.

7 B

OBJECTIVE COMPLETE:
Mya found

8

9 B

10

11

MISSION 13

Once the floor is cleared, venture from behind the bar to find more henchmen on the balcony above. Use the SPAS 12 to quickly disable them and **send them crashing to the floor ❾**—you'll earn a Bond Moment by sending to the ground the guard who's closest to the elevator.

Use the elevator to get upstairs ❿. Head for the nearest corner (the one away from the open bar area). Dispatch any enemies along the way as you make your way to a **double door that leads to an office ⓫.** Eliminate the guard inside and make note of an armor vest in that room. **On the desk in that room is the security keycard ⓬.** On the **balcony across from the office is a battery on the floor ⓭**; you might want to grab it.

Return to the elevator, watching out for any guards that will appear once you reach the elevator doors. Go downstairs to see a gang of henchmen converge on you. If you're quick enough, you can go back up **the elevator and dispatch the henchmen easily from the balcony ⓮.** Otherwise, get ready for a very difficult hand-to-hand combat fight. Arm yourself with a crowbar to help even the odds.

With the keycard found, **go behind the stage. To the right is another battery atop a box ⓯,** and to the left is **a door with a keycard switch ⓰.**

Looking for a quick escape? If you have enough battery power, you can activate the Nano Suit before opening the keycard door and bypass all the guards along the way to reach the end of the level—it's hardly sporting, but if you're low on health or don't want to use ammo, it might be a good idea.

Open the door with the keycard by pressing the action button, then get ready to gun down the thugs in the dressing room. Once dispatched, look for a **cleverly disguised brick sliding door ⓱** that leads to a secret exit. Continue down this path, dispatching any enemies along the way until you reach the exit at the end of this passage.

EXTRA OBJECTIVE: EARN PLATINUM 007

To earn platinum (once the objective is unlocked), you must complete the mission without using any ammo. It'll be a big challenge, but it is possible to accomplish. First, use stealth attacks to get to the bar (see the walkthrough for details)—if the alarm is raised, get to the bar entrance before additional enemies pop up. When the bar fight begins, it's essential to get to the light control as soon as possible to knock out all three gunmen in front of the bar. Look for bottles or anything else you can hurl to dispatch any other guards. Otherwise, you'll have to resort to hand-to-hand combat, which will make things difficult. Make sure to get all the armor pickups, and collect as many batteries as you can find—the Nano Suit is a quick and effective solution to exiting the level quickly after retrieving the keycard.

007   SCENE 3 BOND MOMENT

During the bar fight, wait for two henchmen to get close to the balcony above. Shoot the enemy closest to the elevator so that he falls to the ground once dispatched.

12

15

16

17

13

14

MISSION 14

GOLD TARGET

None

PLATINUM TARGET

None

STARTING WEAPONS

- RAPPEL
- THERMOVISION
- Q SPIDER
- NANO SUIT
- GRENADE
- SLEEPER DART
- P99 w/Silencer
- MP5K

ACQUIRED WEAPONS

- DESERT EAGLE
- SIG 552
- SPAS 12

UNDERWORLD

UNDERWORLD MAP 01

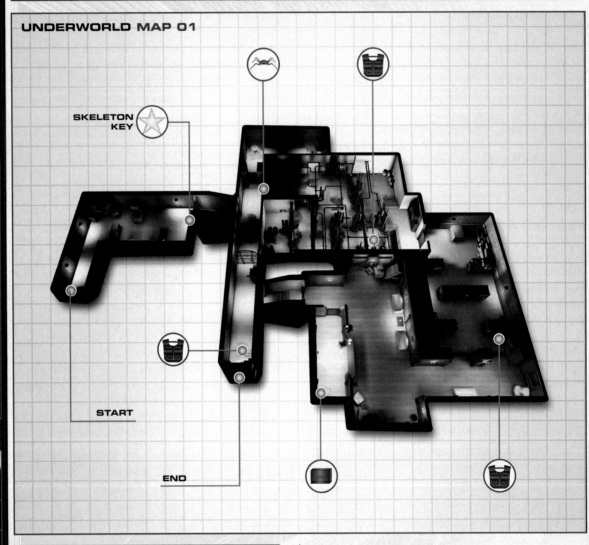

SKELETON KEY

START

END

START: MISSION BRIEFING

Unlocked via obtaining golds and completing The Kiss Kiss Club, Underworld is an optional combat level that you can play en route to rescuing Mya. This mission can be played on any difficulty setting.

OBJECTIVE 1: RESCUE MYA

Quietly dispatch the first enemy in the room, then **find a skeleton key hanging on the wall ❶**. Grab it, then head down the stairs. Open the exit door and wait for an enemy to rush in. Eliminate him via

hand-to-hand combat, then dispatch the remaining guard in the narrow hallway. Look for a **Q Spider hole in plain view ❷**. Use the Q Spider to go through the hole, then **detonate it in front of some fuel barrels ❸**—do it fast before the guard there steps on the spider! The resulting explosion will blow a hole in the wall.

ALTERNATE ROUTE

If you don't have or don't want to use a Q Spider, you can open the door to the left of the hole. However, this isn't the preferred option—you want to keep that door closed!

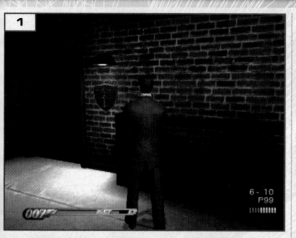

MISSION 14

007 BOND MOMENT

There are no Bond Moments in this level.

Stay behind wall cover and dispatch any enemies that appear **4**. Another **place to stay behind cover is a large pipe in front of the hole 5**. More henchmen will appear as you walk into the room with the pipes, so feel free to backtrack to one of these areas to avoid enemy fire. Look for **an armor vest in the pipe room, it's hidden by the maze of pipes next to the stairs to the exit 6**. If you blew a hole in the wall, you'll see the way to the vest easily. Using Bond Sense, target any **fuel barrels along the back edge of the pipe room to dispatch enemies efficiently 7**.

Take the stairs at the back of the pipe room. They lead to a box-storage area with more enemies to deal with. Use Bond Sense to **target the propane tanks and eliminate foes near them 8**. At the end of the storage area, look for an **armor vest behind**

a metal shelf **9**. Save the armor vest if you don't need it right away. Enter the hallway and silence any attacking enemies. Look for a **battery on a shelf behind the check-in counter 10**. Once behind the counter, get ready for more foes to appear; crouch behind the counter to take them out. Look out for any enemies that open the door to the check-in counter as well. When the coast is clear, turn left and open a door that leads to the narrow hallway you were in previously—but now you're on the on the other side of the gate. Watch out for a henchman and a gunner on the opposite side of the gate. Head left to find a **final armor vest and the level exit 11**.

007
EVERYTHING OR NOTHING

MISSION 15

GOLD TARGET

Score 275,000 points to unlock the Platinum objective.

PLATINUM TARGET

Complete the mission in 3:15 or less.

STARTING WEAPONS

RAPPEL	
THERMOVISION	
Q SPIDER	
SLEEPER DART	
P99	
SPAS 12	
DESERT EAGLE	
MP5K	

ACQUIRED WEAPONS

DRAGUNOV	

DEATH'S DOOR

DEATH'S DOOR: MAP 01

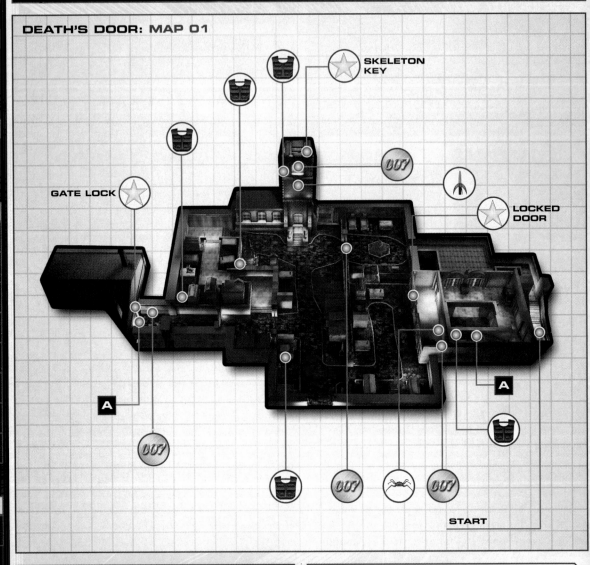

SKELETON KEY

GATE LOCK

007

LOCKED DOOR

A

A

007

007

007

START

1

10-10
SIG 552

007

START: MISSION BRIEFING PART 01

Your pursuit of Mya ends at a dark, foreboding cemetery as Yayakov hands Mya over to Jean Le Rouge, who whisks her away to the crematorium. You must make your way through the cemetery and infiltrate the crematorium before your hopes of saving her go up in flames.

OBJECTIVE 1: RETRIEVE SKELETON KEY FROM THE BELL TOWERS

Head down the corridor and turn left to go outside. Kill the first two guards before they can run to alert anyone else, and keep walking forward. The gate ahead is locked; turn left to find a group of guards streaming out the hotel, ready to attack. Dispatch them quickly. **Look for a Dragunov sniper rifle behind a tomb near the fountain ❶**. Once the front door of the hotel is busted open by guards, immediately dispatch them and run inside before you get hit by sniper fire. Then head into the hotel to find a locked door to the left—you'll need to find a skeleton key now.

Before leaving the hotel, crouch behind **some boxes in front of a boarded window ❷**. Next to that area is a spider hole in which you'll find armor—this triggers a Bond Moment as well. Stay behind the boxes and use Bond Sense to target and destroy the boarded-up window. **This will give you a clear view of a sniper on a far rooftop ❸**. Drop him before leaving the hotel.

Upon reaching the opened gate by the hotel, more enemies will stream out, as well as another sniper. Take out the enemies on the ground first, then quickly roll to **the location of an armor vest ❹** directly across from the open gate.

TIP

An effective alternate tactic at this point is to **crouch behind the small bush and equip the Dragunov ❺**. With the scope activated, stand up to see the sniper in the bell tower. Drop him with a single shot. However, note that while this method keeps you safe from the sniper, you won't be able to earn a Bond Moment later on.

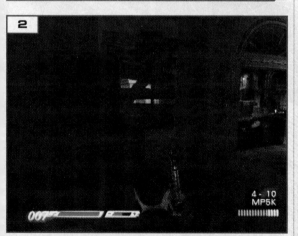
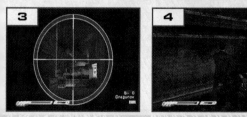

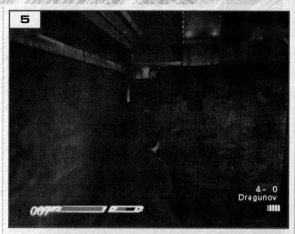

Move toward the bell tower: When you see more enemies appear, take cover and dispatch them. **Look for one enemy that runs toward the gate to the right near the large tree ❻**—eliminate him before he unlocks the gate to earn a Bond Moment.

SCENE 1
007 BOND MOMENT

Upon entering the hotel at the start of the level, head right to find a stack of boxes. Near the boxes is a Q Spider hole. Take the Q Spider in to find a small nook with an armor vest.

SCENE 2
007 BOND MOMENT

When you see the set of enemies that appears when you reach the bell tower, look for one who tries to unlock a gate between the bell tower and the hotel. Dispatch the guard before he unlocks the gate.

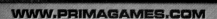

MISSION 15

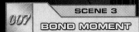

SCENE 3
BOND MOMENT

Eliminate the guard in the bell tower using your trusty hand-to-hand combat.

Rappel

Look for a rappel point to reach the top of the bell tower **7**. Once at the top of the rappel point, use hand-to-hand combat to neutralize the sniper in the tower. Subduing the guard in this manner results in another Bond Moment.

Look for the skeleton key hanging on the back wall **8**.

3 - 0
Dragunov

You'll find armor and more sniper rifle ammo up here—so use the Dragunov to silence anyone still shooting at you before heading back down. Heading down will trigger a cinema, and you will be unable to head back up again—so make sure you've done as much as you can from this vantage point before leaving.

DEATH'S DOOR: MAP 02

SHOOT GATE LOCK
FROM BALCONY

A

9

10

MISSION 15

box will unlock the large wooden gate. Do this in a hurry, because more enemies will appear—dart back into the hotel if the enemy fire is too heavy to take, then crouch and slowly creep back out.

OBJECTIVE 4: INFILTRATE THE CREMATORIUM

After opening the gate, descend the stairs and head toward the gate, dispatching any guards along the way (or running past them if you're in a hurry). You'll have to wind around the locked gates and pass the bell tower to reach **a small cemetery area up a flight of stairs** 12. Pick up any armor you might have saved for later, and look for one more **armor vest and** 13, then follow along the path to the now-opened gate to complete this mission.

11

Shootable Objective

12

13

OBJECTIVE 2: INFILTRATE THE HOTEL

The bell tower will be destroyed once you rappel (hope you got the armor up there already!), so make your way back to the hotel, using the crypts as cover and neutralizing any guards in your path. You'll find an **armor vest hidden behind a tall monument in front of the bell tower** 9—but save it for later if you can.

Return to the hotel and open the once-locked door. Once inside, activate Thermovision. Look for a surprise ambush as you head up the stairs to the second floor—dispatch these foes without delay. At the back of the second floor, there's **an armor vest** 10. Collect them then look for a balcony door on the right.

OBJECTIVE 3: DESTROY THE SECURITY BOX TO OPEN A GATE

Turn off Thermovision upon heading outside, then quickly crouch. You'll find a sniper rifle up there (in case you're out of ammo). **Use Bond Sense to locate a security box to fire at across the cemetery** 11; destroying the

MISSION 15

007 | SCENE 4
BOND MOMENT

While atop the hotel balcony, use the sniper rifle to find and destroy a security box on the crematorium wall (across the cemetery) to open the gate to the crematorium.

DID YOU KNOW?

It's so cold in this level, you can see Bond's breath frost up!

DEATH'S DOOR: MAP 03

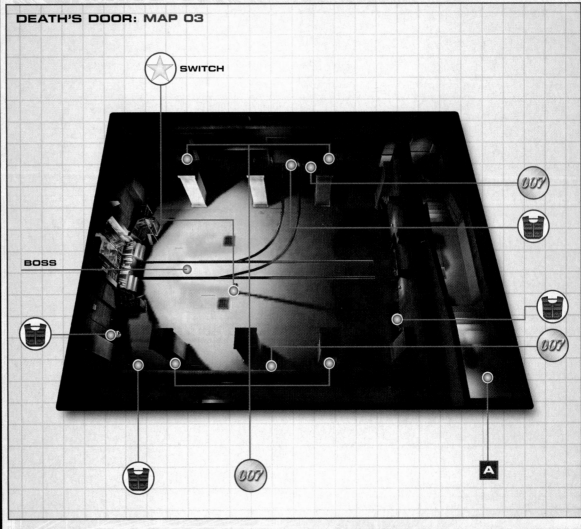

SWITCH

BOSS

007

A

MISSION BRIEFING PART 02

Now you're in the crematorium to face Jean Le Rouge. You know you've got to stop him, but you've also got to rescue Mya before she's toast! He will be an intimidating foe, but you can confuse him into submission with lots of movement and a few Bond-worthy tricks.

OBJECTIVE 1: DEFEAT JEAN LE ROUGE AND RESCUE MYA

It's actually two objectives, but you'll need to complete both simultaneously—you can't do one and not the other. First, make sure **the switch in the middle leading Mya toward the furnace ⓮** remains off at all times. Turn it off by pressing the action button when next to the switch as soon as you can after Le Rouge activates it. Listen for audio clues from Mya—she'll tell you if it's on, or look at the box to see whether it's lit green.

14

Jean Le Rouge

You'll find armor vests along the perimeter of this area, as well as more powerful weaponry—save the armor until needed, but pick up the heavy weapons as soon as possible.

You can earn two Bond Moments while fighting this boss. **When Le Rouge stands near a fuel barrel, use Bond Sense to target the barrel 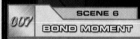**—if he takes damage, you'll earn a Bond Moment. **Use Bond Sense to look for ceiling and wall gas vent switches **—shoot a switch when Le Rouge is standing near it to damage him and earn a second Bond Moment.

WARNING

Do not stand next to any untargeted fuel barrels or switches yourself: Le Rouge is smart enough to use them against you!

Do not attempt to engage Le Rouge in hand-to-hand combat. Use the six pillars around the room for cover, but don't stand motionless—if you do, Le Rouge will target you with devastating missile darts. The key to survival is to prevent Le Rouge from getting a bead on you: **While crouched behind a wall, slide repeatedly left and right behind it to confuse his targeting ability 17**—you'll know if you're doing it right if he begins to jump back and forth into the open, trying to fol-

low your movement. You can even sneak in a shot (but not more than one) if he's in the open, but immediately slide away from the wall corner in case he decides to shoot a missile dart at you. You'll be safe from his darts as long as you're hiding behind the farthest point away from the pillar corner he aims at (if you're next to the corner, you will get hit).

Keep rolling and running while in the open if you think Le Rouge has you in his sights. He is most vulnerable when he runs out to activate the switch—**equip your heaviest weapon (the SIG 552 is best) and empty your magazine into him as he stands in front of the switch 18**. Don't forget to turn off the switch again immediately afterward!

After you give Le Rouge more than 50 percent damage, guards will rush to his aid. Find cover out of Le Rouge's line of sight, and take out the guards first—they'll drop ammo, which will help you finish your mission. When Le Rouge gets even lower in health, he'll start shooting triple darts. Still, once you master the art of moving left and right while leaning back against a pillar, he won't be able to hit you accurately, and you will ultimately defeat him.

EXTRA OBJECTIVE: EARN PLATINUM 007

To earn platinum (once the objective is unlocked), complete the mission in less than 3:15. Remember all those armor locations pointed out in the walk-through? Those become vital to your success. Make sure the gate's unlocked (don't perform that Bond Moment) between the hotel and bell tower so you have a more direct route to the end of the level.

SCENE 5
007 BOND MOMENT

While fighting Le Rouge, use Bond Sense to target the fuel barrels in the room. If Le Rouge takes damage from the explosion, you'll earn a Bond Moment. You'll have two chances to earn this Bond Moment (two sets of fuel barrels).

SCENE 6
007 BOND MOMENT

While fighting Le Rouge, use Bond Sense to target the gas-vent switches in the room on the wall and ceiling. If Le Rouge takes damage from the flames, you'll earn a Bond Moment. There are four switches to target: two in the ceiling and two on the back walls.

007 EVERYTHING OR NOTHING

MISSION 16

BATTLE IN THE BIG EASY

GOLD TARGET

Score 250,000 points to unlock the Platinum objective.

PLATINUM TARGET

Get from Bond's hideout to Diavolo's compound in less than 55 seconds.

STARTING WEAPONS

- SMOKE SCREEN

ACQUIRED WEAPONS

- MACHINE GUN
- MISSILES
- ELECTRO MAGNET
- RC CAR w/Laser
- ACID SLICK

BATTLE IN THE BIG EASY: MAP 01

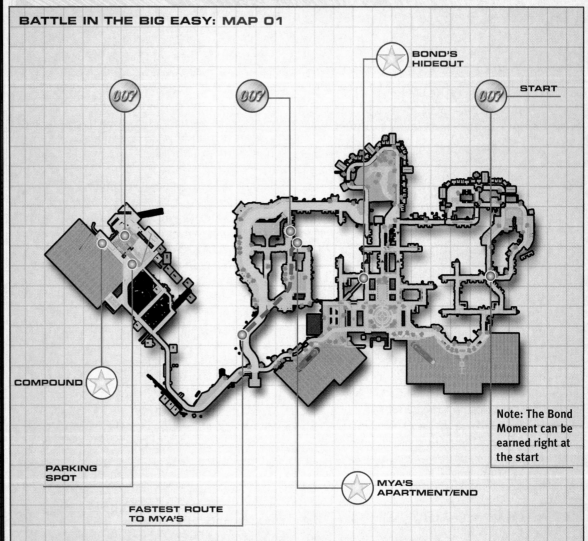

- 007
- 007 — BOND'S HIDEOUT
- 007 — START
- COMPOUND
- PARKING SPOT
- FASTEST ROUTE TO MYA'S
- MYA'S APARTMENT/END

Note: The Bond Moment can be earned right at the start

Smoke Screen

007

START: MISSION BRIEFING

You've just rescued Mya from a fiery end, but you're not in the clear just yet. You'll be pursued by Yayakov's henchmen through the streets of New Orleans as you try to destroy his compound/warehouse. **Turning on the large GPS map** ❶ may be extremely helpful your first time through this mission.

OBJECTIVE 1: TAKE MYA TO BOND'S LAIR

As the mission begins, drive straight ahead. You'll be pursued by an enemy car—use the smoke screen on him to earn a Bond Moment. You'll quickly approach a roadblock: **You can literally cut corners by driving through the windows to the right of the roadblock** ❷.

OBJECTIVE 2: ALLOW MYA TO DEFUSE THE BOMB

Immediately take a left turn ❸ to get on a long road—you'll quickly realize that this is the same road you took to get to the Kiss Kiss Club (in the Mardi Gras Mayhem mission)—but now you're going the other direction! Concentrate on driving.

You must keep your speed up so the bomb in your limo does not explode—don't run into anything! Use the smoke screen liberally to shake off any pursuers. When you reach the central area of the city, you can take **one of several side streets** ❹ to reach Bond's lair, which will be marked on the GPS map with a blue dot. Make sure you don't have any guards on your tail, or else you won't be able to reach the compound. (NOTE: AT oo Agent difficulty, you'll have to drive longer to defuse the bomb.

It's best to head past the French Quarter area and make **a right at the trolley station** ❺, then drive downtown to shake off enemy cars. Once the bomb is defused, by the time you backtrack to the French Quarter the coast should be clear).

OBJECTIVE 3: DESTROY THE COMPOUND

Finally, you'll get to even the odds by taking the Aston Martin Vanquish out for a spin. Upon leaving, prepare your missiles for **an enemy car that will try to block the lair exit** ❻. Quickly turn left then left again to head toward **a dirt ramp** ❼. Jump the ramp, then quickly destroy the enemy car that appears. You'll see the Gumbo Diner and recognize the road that leads to the compound. Dispatch any enemy cars that pop up as you drive toward the compound's open gate—use an acid slick when necessary to shake off any tailgating enemies.

SCENE 1 — BOND MOMENT

Use the smoke screen on an enemy car—you can earn this Bond Moment right at the start of the mission.

VEHICLE: ASTON MARTIN V12 VANQUISH

SCENE 2
007 BOND MOMENT

Use only one RC car to destroy the compound.

SCENE 3
007 BOND MOMENT

Get to Mya's apartment quickly.

OBJECTIVE 4: LOCATE THE ACCESS POINT FOR THE RC CARS

Once in the compound, look for **a place to park and deploy your RC car ⑧**. The RC car has a limited battery life, so you don't want to spend too much time driving it. Nearby will be **an open vent shaft you can drive the RC car into ⑨**. Follow the vent until a cinema is activated. Then use **the laser to shoot a steam vent above two henchmen ⑩**.

WARNING

If you don't shoot the vent, the henchmen will shoot your RC car and destroy it once it falls down.

OBJECTIVE 5: USE A LASER ON THE FUEL ACCESS PANEL

With the henchmen cleared, drop the RC car to the metal-grated floor. Immediately turn left, then left again at the next T intersection. This will take you on a route that rings the perimeter of the compound's interior and **ultimately leads to a ramp ⑪**. You may be low on battery power, so immediately look for **the large generator while you're airborne, and target it**

with your laser ⑫. If you use only one RC car in the process, you'll earn a Bond Moment.

OBJECTIVE 6: DELIVER MYA TO HER APARTMENT

With the compound destroyed, all you have to do is drop Mya off home. Unfortunately, some enemies will be left to stop you. The large GPS map may be helpful for pinpointing the shortest route to Mya's apartment. If you're worried about health, shoot cars before driving past them—they do damage if they're tailing you (use the acid slick in that case). However, if you can return Mya to her apartment quickly and complete the mission without wasting any time, you will earn a Bond Moment.

EXTRA OBJECTIVE: EARN PLATINUM 007

To earn platinum, you must get from Bond's hideout to Diavolo's compound in less than 55 seconds. The route described in the walkthrough is the most direct. Don't hit anything along the road that might slow you down (especially any enemy cars that might pop up). Ease off the acceleration button (feather-tap it) so you don't lose control on turns, and you should be OK.

FADED SPLENDOR

FADED SPLENDOR: MAP 01

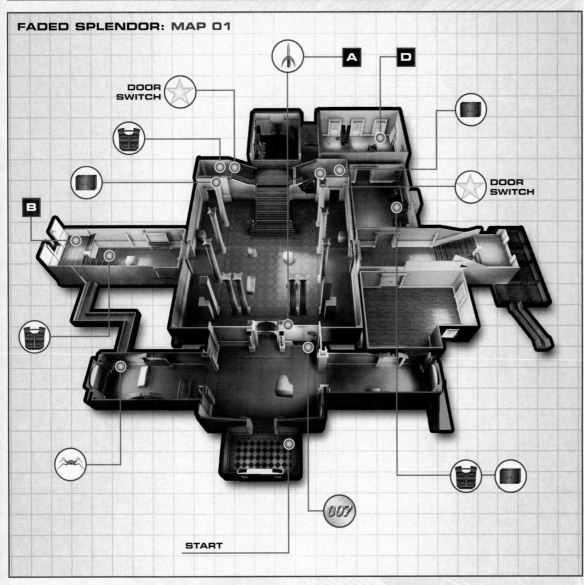

DOOR SWITCH

B

A

D

DOOR SWITCH

007

START

GOLD TARGET

Score 300,000 points to unlock the Platinum objective.

PLATINUM TARGET

Complete the mission, taking 100 damage or less.

STARTING WEAPONS

	RAPPEL
	THERMOVISION
	Q SPIDER
	NANO SUIT
	GRENADE
	STROBE
	SLEEPER DART
	P99 w/Silencer

ACQUIRED WEAPONS

	MP5K
	SIG 552
	SPAS 12
	DRAGUNOV

START: MISSION BRIEFING

Remember the tracking devices you placed on the vans in the Mardi Gras Mayhem mission? Well, that helped MI6 track Yayakov to an old plantation on the outskirts of the city. It's your job now to infiltrate the plantation and find out what Yayakov's up to.

OBJECTIVE 1: FIND YAYAKOV'S LAIR

The mission begins with you by a corner near the mansion entrance. Look for a Dragunov sniper rifle to your right, but creep slowly to get it, or the guards will hear you. Activate your Nano Suit, then creep left into a hallway. The Nano Suit will keep you from alerting the sniper on the second floor. **Hide behind a couch deep in the corner ❶** and turn off your Nano Suit to save batteries. Wait for a guard to pass by, and when his back is fully turned, employ a stealth attack on him.

SCENE 1
BOND MOMENT

At the start of the mission, use stealth attacks to dispatch all the enemies on the ground level without alerting the sniper on the upper level.

10 - 10
P99

3 - 0
Sleeper Dart

Now return to the couch and wait for the second patrolling guard to return to the central room. Immediately cross the central room by crouching and hugging the wall directly underneath the sniper so he doesn't spot you. Follow the second guard into the hallway he patrols. Dispatch him with a stealth attack,

then stay crouched and turn back to the central room. Hug the wall as tightly as you can (to avoid detection by the sniper above) to **hide behind the planks blocking the two rooms ②**. An alerted but confused guard will be looking for you—shoot him with a Sleeper Dart.

FADED SPLENDOR: MAP 02

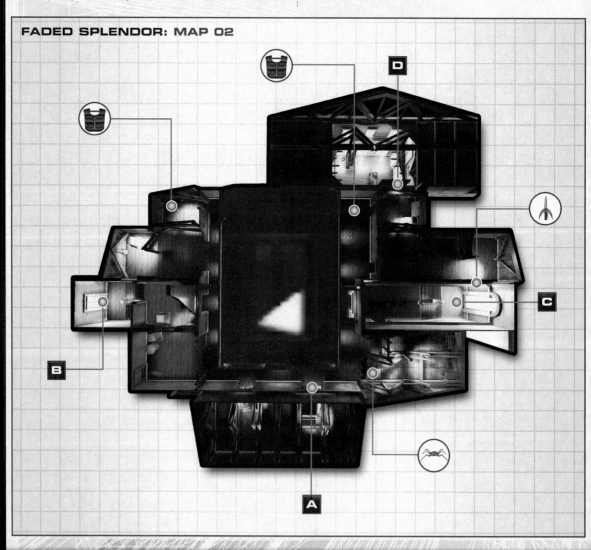

3

Rappel

4

5

Detonate

6

10 - 8
SIG 882

Keep hugging the wall, and look up in the central room to find a rappel point **3**. Head up, armed with the sleeper dart. At the top, immediately turn left to subdue the sniper perched there with a Sleeper Dart. Using stealth to this point will earn you a Bond Moment.

ALTERNATE ROUTE

Interested in an option Q Spider path? At the area where you used a stealth attack on the first guard, head left to find a **Q Spider hole at the end of the hallway 4**. This leads to an armor vest—grab it if necessary—as well as **a guard standing in front of a doorway 5**. You can take him out by exploding the Q Spider near him.

Navigate left to where the sniper was to find several guards. Take cover to dispatch them. Once this level is cleared, look for **a room with a hole in the floor and a**

7

5 - 16
SIG 552
007

8

Detonate

9

Detonate

staircase **6**. But don't go down just yet—to the right is **a small alcove with an armor vest 7**.

Now backtrack to the rappel point and head right. Look for an opening for you **Q Spider to fit through 8**. Follow the wooden planks down to the first level. **You'll see a guard near a doorway at the end of the Q Spider path 9**—detonate the Q Spider to dispatch him.

MISSION 8

MISSION 8

SCENE 2
BOND MOMENT

Shoot down the chandelier in the large ballroom so it crashes down on several gunmen.

Return to the stairs and head down to the middle level. Take care of the guard that jumps out of the room on the left. Move toward the railing to see more guards at the lower level. **Use Bond Sense to aim at the chandelier above them ❿**, then send it crashing down on top of them for a Bond Moment.

10 B

11 - 0
SIG 552

TIP

A SAFER OPTION? When the enemies at the lower level of the ballroom appear, it's possible to backtrack to the attic quickly, where the sniper stood at the beginning of the mission. You'll find a broken-open window, from which you can target the chandelier with the sniper rifle (you may not be able to hit it using Bond Sense because of the odd angle.) This might be a good idea if you're trying to limit how much damage you take.

Head downstairs to find **a small room that contains a battery and a door switch on the wall ⓫**. Immediately take wall cover to look into the ballroom area ⓬, and look for henchmen to rush into the room. Adjust your aim point slightly upward to hit the targets hiding behind the tables. When the coast is clear, you'll find the second door switch in a similar room on the other side of the grand staircase—this area contains **a battery and another armor vest ⓭**. Trigger the switch to

FADED SPLENDOR: MAP 03

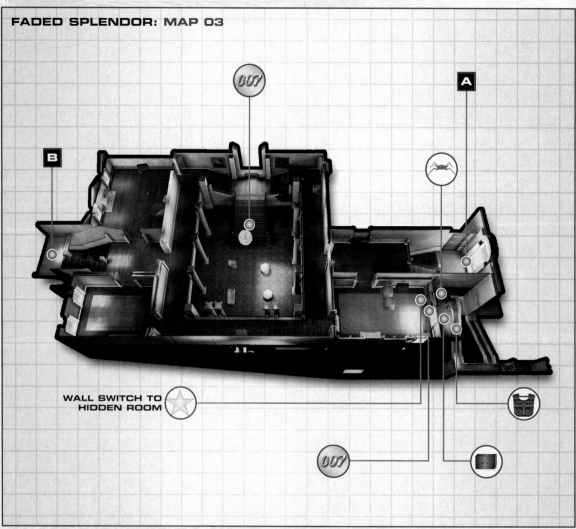

WALL SWITCH TO
HIDDEN ROOM

MISSION 8

SCENE 3

007 **BOND MOMENT**

Find a hidden weapons cache in the room on the second level. The room is blocked at one entrance by a fallen door and has artwork laying against a wall (the door switch is near that artwork).

reveal more enemies approaching your position, **use wall cover in the room to dispatch as many enemies as you can see** 14, then quickly rush to the nearest column **to take out the snipers on the second floor balcony** 15 and any remaining foes.

Return to the second floor, but do not run down the open balcony area. Instead, get to a room with red walls on the second floor. **Take wall cover near a desk in the room and look down to see two enemies hiding behind a fallen door** 16. Take them out to get into that

room—but quickly hide behind some draped boxes to **dispatch enemies that will rush into the room after you** 17. In this room, look for some artwork propped up against a wall. **In the corner is a wall switch** 18 that

19

opens up a weapons cache filled with ammo, armor and batteries—and results in a Bond Moment upon discovery. Inside this weapons cache room is a Q Spider hole that leads to the first-floor computer control room. You can eliminate the guards here by detonating the Q Spider.

Leave that room and head right to find a staircase and a rappel point—however, watch out for **a sniper atop the rappel point 19**.

ALTERNATE ROUTE

Down the stairs past the rappel point is **a computer control room that houses a battery and armor vest 20** (you may have seen it already with the Q Spider). It is possible to visit this room after rappelling down to the computer room next to it—but the door will lock behind you.

Quickly head up and dispatch him with hand-to-hand combat (he has a vest on), then **take cover behind the wood plank walls as more enemies rush in 21**. Look for **an armor vest in the room at the end of this area 22**, then continue to **find a large opening to rappel down 23**. Rappel quickly and **crouch behind the closest computer console 24**. This will send in guards, but your top-priority target should be **the soldier behind the desk to the left 25**, because he has a penchant for throwing grenades to flush you out of your position. Clear out all enemies, then run into the computer control room directly ahead to end the mission.

EXTRA OBJECTIVE: EARN PLATINUM 007

To earn platinum (once the objective is unlocked), you must complete the mission, taking 100 points of damage or less. Using stealth at the start of the mission for the first Bond Moment will help, as well as taking advantage of all the Q Spider paths to eliminate foes. Take your time, don't rush into the open unless the coast is clear, and always use cover during combat. Sniping the chandelier from the attic (see the walkthrough for details) with the sniper rifle may help you dispatch the enemies below without exposing yourself to enemy fire. However, don't stay behind cover in a single spot for too long—some foes can and will throw grenades at you to flush you out.

MACHINERY OF EVIL

THE MACHINERY OF EVIL: MAP 01

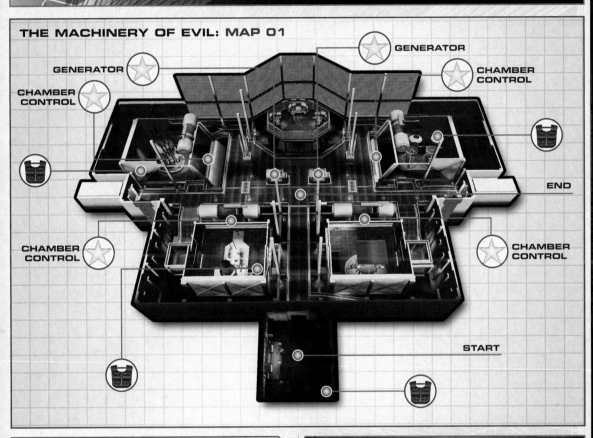

GENERATOR

GENERATOR

CHAMBER CONTROL

CHAMBER CONTROL

CHAMBER CONTROL

CHAMBER CONTROL

END

CHAMBER CONTROL

START

GOLD TARGET

Score 300,000 points to unlock the Platinum objective.

PLATINUM TARGET

Complete the mission using 10 rounds of ammo or fewer.

STARTING WEAPONS

	THERMOVISION
	Q SPIDER
	NANO SUIT
	GRENADE
	DRAGUNOV
	SLEEPER DART
	P99
	SPAS 12
	MP5K
	SIG 552

ACQUIRED WEAPONS

	AT-420

START: MISSION BRIEFING

Well, you've found out what Yayakov's been up to—and the news is not good. He's busy producing swarms of nanorobots that will eat into the levees surrounding New Orleans to flood the city. You must stop Yayakov before his sinister plan comes to fruition.

OBJECTIVE 1: DESTROY ALL FOUR PROCESSING CHAMBERS

When this mission gets under way, look for an armor vest behind you, and a SPAS 12 by the doorway leading to the control center. Walk through the door to the right of that SPAS 12.

TIP

The following walkthrough shows one way of progressing to each chamber. However, it is possible to do the chambers in a different order (such as doing the third chamber first).

After a cinema finishes, move down the pathway and immediately turn left to dispatch the first guard that appears. Run toward **a safe point ❶** where you can crouch to avoid cover and eliminate the remaining guards. Immediately to the right of that safe point is **the first processing chamber entrance ❷**.

SCENE 1
BOND MOMENT

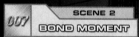

Find a rocket launcher downstairs behind two red glowing pipes. To get to the AT-420, use Bond Sense to target and shoot one of the pipes.

SCENE 2
BOND MOMENT

Send a Q Spider into the third processing chamber from the small hole by the ramp in the lower level.

5

6

7 B

8 B

Once inside, watch out for **the electric current shooting into the wall** ❸, blocking your path to the control panel. Wait for the current to stop, then quickly dart across before it starts again. **Grab the armor vest and the weapon near the control panel** ❹, then press the action button to overload the generator. Get out of the room quickly before it explodes (you have less than 15 seconds), and return to the safe point (see screenshot 1).

Dispatch all enemies in sight from that safe point (use hand-to-hand combat when they venture too close, then reestablish your hiding position). With the coast clear, head to the northwest corner of the room. Down the stairs is the **entrance to the second processing chamber** ❺. In the second chamber is **an armor vest and additional ammo near to the control panel** ❻. Press the action button in front of the panel to activate it, then head downstairs to the lower level—a stream of electricity will block the path back up.

Once downstairs, immediately turn left to find **two glowing red beams** ❼. Use Bond Sense to target the

beams until one explodes. In that crevice is an AT-420, the discovery of which will earn you a Bond Moment.

WARNING

Do not destroy both red beams, as it will allow enemies to loop back behind your position if you're using wall cover nearby.

Dispatch all the guards in this lower area, using cover at all times. Look for three guards stationed at the end of a short hallway. Using Bond Sense, look for **a steam vent switch behind them** ❽. Shoot the switch to stun the guards, after which you can easily dispatch them. Employing this tactic will earn you another Bond Moment. There is also another armor vest to find in another corner of the room, on the other side of the glowing red beams mentioned earlier.

While downstairs, look for a ramp downward. You may notice **a hole in the floor at the bottom of the**

THE MACHINERY OF EVIL: MAP 02

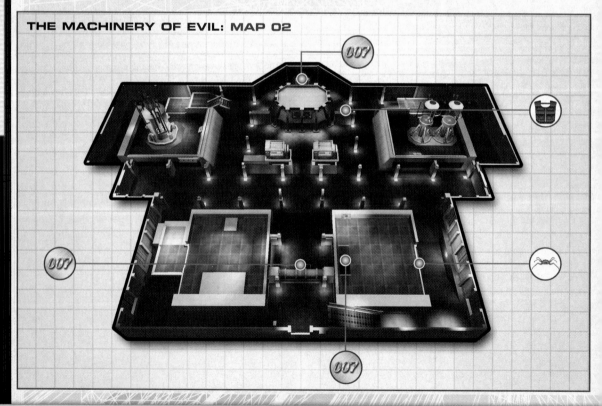

ramp **9**—this is a Q Spider hole. Find a safe place away from any possible guards (such as the nook where the AT-420 was), crouch and send a Q Spider out to the hole.

WARNING

You'll have to switch back to Bond occasionally from the Q Spider to make sure no guards are in his immediate area and that he's not under attack.

Inside the hole is a small elevator that will take the Q Spider up to the third chamber. Leave that elevator and take a metal vent up to the interior of the chamber to earn a Bond Moment. Send the Q Spider to the cracked-open door and explode to open a way into the chamber.

ALTERNATE ROUTE

If you are in a hurry or are trying to complete the extra platinum objective, head up to the top level and **send a Q Spider right up to the slightly cracked-open front door of the third chamber 10.** Explode the Q Spider right in front of the crack to jar the door open. You can also opt to shoot the door open by using Bond Sense to target the broken control panel behind the slightly opened door.

Whichever option you prefer, note that the ramp with the Q Spider leads back up to the computer control room—but this time guards may be inside. Dispatch the guards and **don't forget about the armor vest that was there originally 11.**

Now go to the fourth and final chamber in the room, which is located at the northeast corner. **Look for the entrance down a short set of stairs 12.** Inside is yet **another armor vest worth grabbing 13,** as well

as the control panel. Press the action button to overload this fourth chamber, then get out. Eliminate any remaining enemies, retreating to **another similar safe point 14** nearby if necessary.

OBJECTIVE 2: DESTROY BOTH GENERATORS

The final task is easy once the coast is clear. Approach the two generators in the middle of the room, and grab **the flashlights on the two tables across the generators 15. Throw a flashlight into the generator to disable it 16.** Do this twice to bid farewell to Yayakov and complete the mission.

EXTRA OBJECTIVE: EARN PLATINUM 007

To earn platinum (once the objective is unlocked), you must complete the mission using 10 rounds of ammo or less—so get ready for lots of hand-to-hand combat. You'll have a lot of options in terms of how to use the ammo, but in general, stick to a heavy weapon (such as the SPAS 12), and never use any semiautomatic guns. Enemies will automatically replenish as you dispatch them, so don't waste time eliminating foes unless they're directly in your path. Use your Nano Suit while running in the open—but turn it off once you're in the chambers. Another option to consider: Take one ammo shot with the SPAS 12 to get the AT-420, then use the rocket launcher to take out enemies in bulk downstairs—but forget about the other Bond Moments. Note the wrenches on the tables across from the generators that you can throw at enemies, and use the flashlights on the table to disable the generators.

SCENE 3
BOND MOMENT

At the lower level of the facility, look for a steam vent behind three soldiers. Shoot a switch on the vent to stun the three soldiers temporarily.

MISSION 19

STARTING
WEAPONS

 ROCKETS

 FLAME-THROWER

 SHOTGUN

ACQUIRED
WEAPONS

 NONE

SCENE 1
BOND MOMENT

Jump over the barbed-wire fence at the start of the mission.

DID YOU KNOW?

This mission is actually based on a real-life toll bridge that spans Lake Pontchartrain! Completed in 1956, the 24-mile-long bridge (it's actually two parallel bridges) is the longest in the world!

THE PONTCHARTRAIN BRIDGE

THE PONTCHARTRAIN BRIDGE: MAP 01

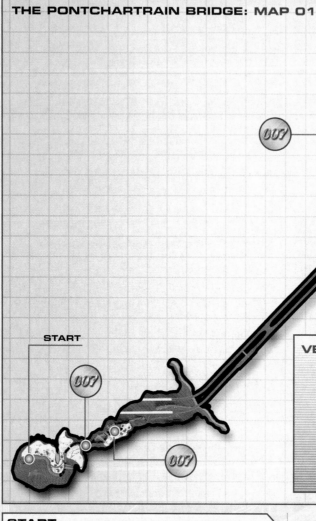

START

VEHICLE: TRIUMPH DAYTONA 600

START:
MISSION BRIEFING

You may have stopped Yayakov for good, but an old friend—Jaws—will reintroduce himself to you in a most nasty way. He'll stop at nothing to take the already-produced nanorobots to destroy New Orleans, and it'll be up to you to stop him before he can reach the city.

OBJECTIVE 1:
DISABLE JAW'S TANKER

Leave the plantation area immediately **by taking the left wooden-bridge path at the very start of the mission ❶**. This will help you generate enough speed to

cut across the water and use the bank to jump over the gate without breaking through it ❷ to earn a Bond Moment. You'll have to generate enough speed to pull off this move. There'll be a fork in the road immediately afterward: Stay left to see a **shack coming up on your right, with four henchmen firing machine guns ❸**. Send a rocket into the shack for a satisfying explosion and a second Bond Moment.

Drive through the tunnel and up onto the highway bridge. Dodge through the traffic to reach a tollbooth. Stay in the middle lane and **line yourself up with a flipped-over pickup ❹**. This will send you smashing through the billboard. (You can also drive on the right through a tollgate, but you will suffer a little damage as a result.) Shortly after the tollbooth, enemy bikes will pull in front of you. Drive up close and take them out with your flamethrower or missiles (but in general, save your missiles for the larger vehicles).

Avoid the cars at all costs—a direct head-on collision will cause lots of damage and possibly end the mission. It may help to use very small movements on the control stick to weave through traffic. It also may help to drive on the shoulders if you see tight traffic ahead—the speed bumps will naturally slow you down a little. After several sets of enemy bikes, look for a road construction zone. Stay in the left lane and look for **a jump that will take you over to the other side of the bridge ❺**. A successful jump will earn you a Bond Moment—but get ready to swerve to the shoulder to avoid oncoming traffic upon landing.

If you are feeling truly adventurous, you can stay and drive into oncoming traffic—but for the sake of health, it's best **to cross back over to the right side of the bridge at the first or second crossover point ❻**. If you choose the first point, two vehicles will attack you—use the missiles to dispatch them. Waiting for the second crossover point may save you a little time as long as you don't collide with oncoming traffic.

Once you get close enough to Jaws, a cinema will show his truck smashing into a gas tanker, and you'll get a Bond Moment. After that cinema, drive straight for the jack-knifed tanker and hit **the gadget button to slide underneath the tanker ❼**.

TIP

During the slow-motion cinema, you can select your flamethrower and roast the enemy motorcyclist flying over the top of you.

After the tanker explodes, catch up to Jaws by dispatching two vans with henchmen dropping barrels out the back. Avoid the barrels: Upon explosion, they will cause a fire slick that will damage you if you drive through (you might be able to avoid damage by popping a wheelie, however). Destroy the vans with missiles, and when you reach Jaws, **burn the back four tires on his truck ❽**. Use the flamethrower to take out one side, then slow down a little to get back behind the truck. Speed up again to use the flamethrower on the rear tires on the other side. Don't linger too long next to Jaws, because he will try to pin you along the shoulder. Try to complete this task quickly before Jaws attempts evasive maneuvers and before you run out of bridge. Q will inform you how many miles you have left.

Completing this level will unlock the third MI6 Interlude cinema.

EXTRA OBJECTIVE: EARN PLATINUM 007

To earn platinum (once the objective is unlocked), you must complete the mission in 3:10 or less. There's no real secret to this other than to not run into anything; if you do, you'll receive both a health and time penalty. Avoiding collisions is a very difficult task once the "tunnel vision" effect kicks in when you reach a certain speed. The walkthrough strategy still applies—although you may opt to stay on the right side of the road rather than execute the construction ramp Bond Moment. In addition, you may want to skip the second Bond Moment (the path that leads to the shack) and take the left path that leads to the highway sooner—this will help you build speed.

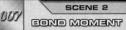

Use a rocket to destroy the shack with machine gunners in front.

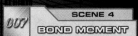

After entering the toll-bridge area, use a ramp to jump over a blocked-off roadway that's under construction to reach the other side of the bridge.

Once you reach Jaws, slide under the yellow fuel tanker. A cinematic sequence will cut in if you're successful.

A SIMPLE EXCHANGE

GOLD TARGET

Score 325,000 points to unlock the Platinum objective.

PLATINUM TARGET

Complete the level in 40 seconds or less.

STARTING WEAPONS

	THERMOVISION
	Q SPIDER
	NANO SUIT
	EMP
	STROBE
	GRENADE
	SLEEP DART
	P99 w/Silencer

ACQUIRED WEAPONS

	DESERT EAGLE

START: MISSION BRIEFING

You'll return to Peru to try and meet Diavolo and see what scheme he's plotting with regard to Dr. Nadanova's nanobots. Unfortunately, he hasn't sent you an invitation. The only way to meet Diavolo is to win one of his exclusively run rally car races—so you'll have to sneak into the hotel and steal a race car driver's outfit. It won't be as easy as you think: This hotel will be swarming with security, and you won't be able to go in with guns blazing. Stealth will be the key.

OBJECTIVE 1: ENSURE THERE ARE NO CASUALTIES / DON'T RAISE THE ALARM

These are objective "rules" that will have to be followed throughout the mission. It's best not to engage in any shooting (other than your Sleeper Dart), and to avoid detection at all costs, using the Nano Suit whenever necessary. In addition, you can disable the cameras with an EMP grenade—just make sure no guards are around to hear the noise—or you can just watch the cameras carefully and sneak past when they're not pointed at you.

"No casualties" is a bit misleading, because you can use stealth attacks to dispatch enemies (apparently, stealth attacks are nonlethal in this mission) as long as you

A SIMPLE EXCHANGE: MAP 01

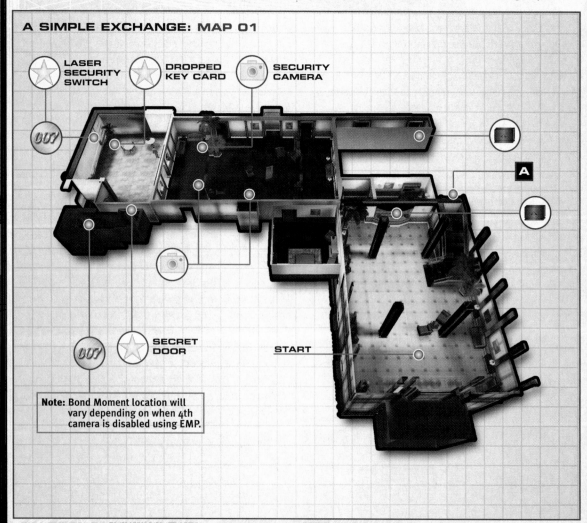

LASER SECURITY SWITCH

DROPPED KEY CARD

SECURITY CAMERA

A

SECRET DOOR

START

Note: Bond Moment location will vary depending on when 4th camera is disabled using EMP.

don't alert any other guards in the process. You'll want to remain crouching through the whole mission.

Most importantly, do not get spotted by any cameras—that triggers the appearance of more guards. If you see a camera icon on your screen, you can still salvage the mission by remaining hidden—but it'll be much more difficult. Now that you know the ground rules, it's time to begin the mission.

OBJECTIVE 2: DISABLE SECURITY LASERS

You begin the mission in the lobby to see a guard walking away from you. Forget about the stairs for the moment: Crouch and move closer to him slowly, then use a stealth attack to subdue him. **Look behind the front check-in counter for a battery ❶**.

Activate the Nano Suit and quickly head across the first floor to find **a guard patrolling an outdoor patio ❷**. Get behind him and perform a stealth attack, then deactivate your Nano Suit to save battery life. (This should take care of all the enemy patrols on this level as long as you aren't detected by cameras.) Look for **a red panel on the wall ❸**, and press the action button to deactivate the lasers—this will earn you a Bond Moment.

While at the outdoor patio, look for a cabinet **in a corner ❹**. Press the action button in front of it to slide the cabinet, **revealing a hidden room with Sleeper Dart ammo ❺**. You'll earn a Bond Moment.

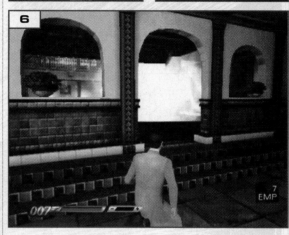

From the outdoor patio, you can deactivate two first floor cameras near the patio with **EMP grenades ❻**. Make sure you have a good throwing angle, then press the action button to detonate the EMP once it's near the camera—you must detonate it manually or the EMP will bounce to the floor. A third camera can be disabled by throwing an **EMP grenade from behind a column ❼** after the first two cameras are knocked out. With the first-floor cameras disabled, head to a dead-end hallway opposite the outdoor patio **to find a battery at the end ❽**.

Now that the lasers are disabled, move on to the second floor. **Stop at the foot of the stairs so you are just out of range of the camera on the second floor ❾**. Throw an EMP grenade at it (you'll earn a Bond Moment), then stay in place and activate your Nano Suit. A guard will rush in to investigate the explosion—when he turns his back, perform a stealth attack on him. From the foot of

007 SCENE 1 BOND MOMENT

Disable the laser security on the second floor.

007 SCENE 2 BOND MOMENT

Find the secret room by the outdoor patio by moving the brown cabinet that hides its entrance.

MISSION 20

SCENE 3
BOND MOMENT

Disable at least four security cameras using the EMP grenades. Make sure to detonate the EMPs manually so that they explode right next to the camera!

A SIMPLE EXCHANGE: MAP 02

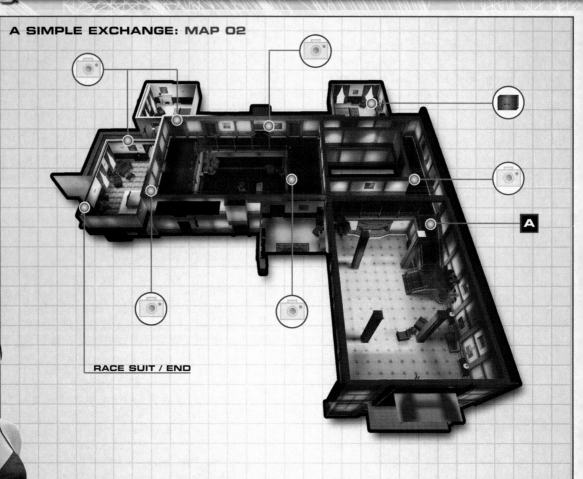

RACE SUIT / END

A

the stairs, go straight. When the hallway turns left, look for an unlocked door on the right side. **In this bedroom is another battery** ❿.

Leave the bedroom, then stop before entering the second-floor balcony to look for **a camera on the right wall** ⓫.

Use an EMP grenade to disable this camera, then activate your Nano Suit to head down the hall to the last door on the right—this leads to **a bedroom with an outdoor walkway** ⓬. A camera is monitoring this route, so keep the Nano Suit activated and walk across. Runto the door with the race suit hanging on it to complete the mission.

EXTRA OBJECTIVE: EARN PLATINUM 007

To earn platinum (once the objective is unlocked), complete the mission in 40 seconds. It sounds impossible, but it's actually easy once you get the route down. At no point should you stop moving—forget about cameras, stealth, or picking up items or Bond Moments. From the start, run right at the first guard and shoot him with the Sleeper Dart. Then immediately run to the outdoor patio, and shoot the guard there quickly with a Sleeper Dart before he can react. Without stopping, run to the switch on the wall to deactivate the laser barrier—you should have about 24 seconds left after the Bond Moment animation plays. Quickly engage Bond Sense to equip the Nano Suit, then run right back to the stairs, shooting anyone in your way with the Sleeper Dart (the Nano Suit will make it a little tougher for enemies to engage you). Take a direct route to the room with the outdoor walkway (the same path as in the walkthrough, but without the detour for the battery in the bedroom). If you're lucky, you'll make it to the bedroom without getting hit or being blocked by an enemy—and you'll make it to the suit with less than a second to spare!

RED LINE

MISSION 21

RED LINE: MAP 01

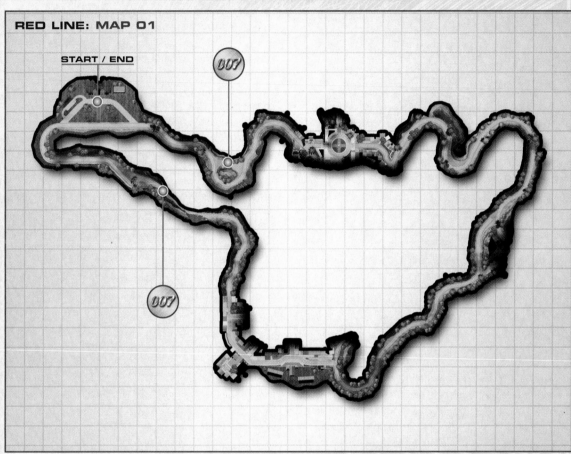

START / END

GOLD TARGET

Score 350,000 points to unlock the Platinum objective.

PLATINUM TARGET

Complete the race in less than 4:50.

STARTING WEAPONS

RALLY CAR (No Weapons)

ACQUIRED WEAPONS

NONE

SCENE 1 BOND MOMENT

After the first turn to start the race, look for and take two small jumps on the road.

START: MISSION BRIEFING

Not only do you have to be the world's greatest secret agent, but now you have to prove that you're a world-class race driver to boot. You must place first in this race mission, taking advantage of any shortcuts you can find.

OBJECTIVE 1: PLACE FIRST IN THE RACE

Upon starting the race, as you come around the first bend, watch out for explosive barrels placed on the right. If you don't hit them, one of the opponents will veer off and blow up (one less driver to worry about). Past this point is **a small jump next to a tree on the right side of the road** ❶. Take the jump to be lined up correctly for **another small jump on the left side of the road** ❷. Take both jumps to earn a Bond Moment.

You'll find more barrels on the left side of the road before you head into the upper village. Drive through the village and watch out for **a sharp right turn with more Barrels** ❸. You must slow down a bit here to avoid an explosive collision with the barrels. You now enter some twisty corners. Look out for more barrels on your right side, then proceed to the big drop-off onto the lower road that will wind alongside the ridge to your left. When you reach the lower village, **get ready for a sharp right turn** ❹. Follow the road around the fountain. You'll see more barrels up ahead to your left as you leave the village. After a left turn, you will reach a blind-turn shortcut.

SCENE 2

BOND MOMENT

Look for a hard-to-see shortcut as you return to the villa. You'll need to take a hard right turn to find it.

Look for a hay-bale arrow sitting at the entrance as a turn marker ❺. Make a hard right into the shortcut to earn a Bond Moment. If you can master this turn, you can pass a couple of cars at this point. Race back to the villa to finish a lap. The total number of laps you'll need to complete will vary depending on difficulty level (two at Operative difficulty, three at Agent and oo Agent).

EXTRA OBJECTIVE: EARN PLATINUM 007

To earn a platinum (once the objective is unlocked), complete the race in less than 4:50. Naturally, this will put you in first place (with a huge lead) by the end of the race. Unfortunately, you won't have any gadgets at your disposal to aid you this time—only pure driving skill will get you through. Obviously, hit the brakes before tight turns, feather the acceleration on long curves so you don't lose control, and don't hit anything that'll slow you down. You must use all the Bond Moments on every lap, and avoid extensive jostling with other cars; you'll lose time if they slide in front of your car. You should have at least 3:10 to 3:15 left on the clock after the first lap, and 1:40 to 1:35 by the end of the second lap. If you haven't hit these marks, restart the mission.

AMBUSHED!

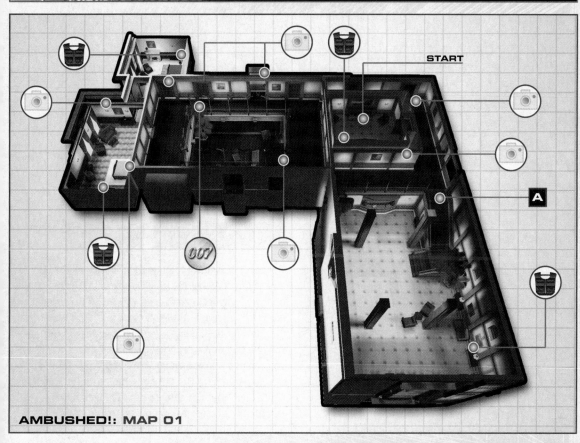

AMBUSHED!: MAP 01

GOLD TARGET

Score 350,000 points to unlock the Platinum objective.

PLATINUM TARGET

Complete the level using no ammo.

STARTING WEAPONS

🏃	THERMOVISION
🏃	NANO SUIT
⊙	EMP
⊙	STROBE
⊙	GRENADE

ACQUIRED WEAPONS

🔫	P99
🔫	AK-74
🔫	SPAS 12
🔫	AT-420

START:
MISSION BRIEFING

Diavolo invites the winner of the car race (the Red Line mission) to have dinner with him at the hotel—and the winner just happens to be you. Unfortunately, your meeting with Diavolo doesn't go exactly as you hoped—thanks to his less-than-friendly reception, you'll have to find Serena (who's being held by Diavolo's henchmen) and escape the hotel.

OBJECTIVE 1:
DESTROY THE FUSE BOX
TO OPEN SHUTTER

You begin the mission being held by one guard as another shoots at you. Use a punch combination to flip the first guard, then rush the second guard to dispatch him before he can shoot. More guards will rush in; you can use hand-to-hand combat to eliminate them. **Look for an armor vest next to the desk in the room ❶**. Use wall cover by the room entrance to see two cameras, **one to the left ❷(a) and one to the right ❷(b) just outside the room entrance.**

SCENE 1
BOND MOMENT

Disable the shutter switch on the outdoor patio wall from the outdoor second-floor balcony by shooting it or throwing an item at it.

3

4

Use the P99 (dropped by one of the fallen enemies) to take out the cameras on either side of the wall. Disable cameras as you see them so that fewer guards rush at you. If you hear an alarm sound, that means you've been detected.

When the coast is clear, exit the room, turning left to avoid the hotel staircase. Go down that hallway back to the second-floor balcony area, disabling all four cameras along the balcony—**you can use the throwable items atop the drawers ❸ to knock out the cameras and save ammo in the process.** You will even be able **to disable a camera on the first floor from the second floor ❹**. Use Bond Sense to make sure you have all the cameras knocked out (they will no longer appear as shootable targets). Also make note of **an armor vest in each alcove on the second level ❺(a) and ❺(b).**

5a

5b

6

7a

7b

Your goal is to reach the last door on **the right at the end of this hallway ❻**, which leads to the room and outdoor walkway (the area where you found the racecar outfit in A Simple Exchange). More guards will emerge from this room—dispatch them and go inside. **In each of the two bedrooms connected by the outdoor walkway, you'll find two more armor vests ❼(a) and ❼(b)**, each one by a bed. Stand in the bedroom as far back as possible to **knock out the camera near the walkway ❽, then dispatch the henchman below on the outdoor patio with a weapon ❾**. Finally, use Bond Sense to **find the security shutter switch on the wall below ❿**, then shoot it to deactivate it—this will earn you a Bond Moment if the alarm has not been raised.

AMBUSHED!: MAP 02

Note: Locked door requires keycard found in "A Simple Exchange" mission.

SHUTTER SWITCH

SECRET DOOR

SERENA / END

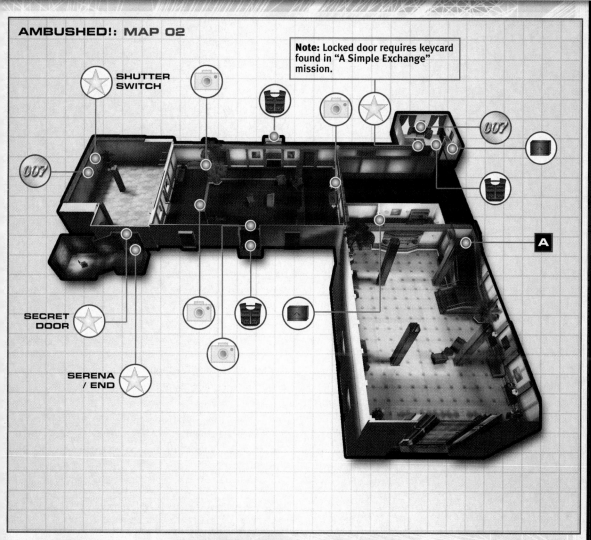

A

MISSION 22

SCENE 2
BOND MOMENT

Throw an enemy from the second-floor balcony. You will need to lure an enemy toward the balcony railing to pull this off.

8

9

10 B

OBJECTIVE 2: FIND SERENA

Unfortunately, destroying that switch will earn you a lot of attention by bringing out a gang of thugs onto the second floor—including **a rocket-launching soldier** ⑪. Make him a high-priority target, rolling forward to dodge his missiles. Dispose of as many foes as possible by using hand-to-hand combat to save ammo. If you can manage to toss a guard over the rail, you will earn a Bond Moment. (Note: This may be possible only at oo Agent difficulty because there may not be enough guards to toss over at other difficulty settings.)

11 B

DID YOU KNOW?

Leave Bond idle for a couple of moments to see some extra idle animations, such as him checking his shoes.

Run down to the first-floor lobby and make way for an ambush as more guards appear. Your best bet is to **hide behind a pillar near the lobby entrance ⑫**. If you want to use the AT-420, target the guard in the middle of lobby so the ensuing explosion takes out multiple foes. **Atop one of the drawers in the entrance lobby is an armor vest ⑬**.

Once all the foes are dispatched, run past the check-in counter, but don't rush into the large room yet. **Use wall cover and look for a camera to the left ⑭**, as well as enemies that will drop from the second floor. Remain hidden until the enemies run just past your position, then dispatch them with hand-to-hand combat. Disable the remaining cameras on this floor by shooting or throwing objects at them once the coast is clear—use Bond Sense to make sure they're all disabled.

Run to the outdoor patio area, and look for the cabinet that **hides the entrance to a secret room ⑮**. Slide the cabinet aside using the action button, then enter to complete the level.

EXTRA OBJECTIVE: EARN PLATINUM 007

To earn platinum (once the objective is unlocked), complete the mission without using any ammo. It's actually easier than it sounds, because it's best to dispatch foes using hand-to-hand combat in this mission for points purposes (to earn a gold 007)—so you should be well-prepared for the task to begin with. Although you should try to avoid camera detection whenever possible (you can throw objects to disable them), you'll mostly need to roll and run—dispatching guards along the way. The key is to pick up an item in the hallway, such as a bottle, to throw at the security shutter switch. On the way to the first floor, try to dispatch any carrying shotguns and rockets first, because those will do the most damage to you. Your goal, after the switch is disabled, should be to run downstairs (picking up armor vests as needed along the way) to reach the entrance to the secret room before you run out of health. Avoid getting caught in a crossfire or being surrounded—and keep rolling to prevent enemies from targeting you effectively. Finally, don't forget to use a strobe grenade if you're in a jam—it does not use up ammo!

THE HIGH ROAD

THE HIGH ROAD: MAP 01

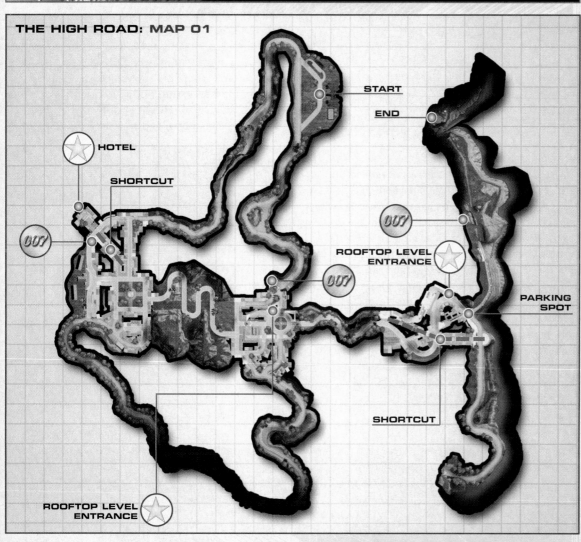

HOTEL

SHORTCUT

007

007

START

END

007

ROOFTOP LEVEL
ENTRANCE

PARKING
SPOT

SHORTCUT

ROOFTOP LEVEL
ENTRANCE

GOLD TARGET

Score 300,000 points to
unlock the Platinum
objective.

PLATINUM TARGET

After reaching the
demolished mine
entrance, get to the
mine in less than 1:20

STARTING WEAPONS

RALLY CAR
(No Weapons)

ACQUIRED WEAPONS

ROCKETS

FLAMETHROWER

SHOTGUN

START:
MISSION BRIEFING

Your escape from the hotel will be hampered by tanks
and jeeps surrounding your Porsche Cayenne.
Fortunately, you have a second option—your race car.
You and Serena will have to "race" to the hotel with
enemy forces in hot pursuit.

OBJECTIVE 1:
DELIVER SERENA TO THE HOTEL
AND ACQUIRE THE Q-BIKE

The race car has no weaponry, but it can do damage.
When the mission begins, **use the car to ram into enemy
motorcyclists as you take the road into the city** ❶.

1

Take the jump at the fire-works shop to bypass the first roadblock.

Upon getting the Q-Bike, jump the ramp on the right at the hotel to reach the roof and bypass the roadblock.

When you reach the fireworks shop, you'll see a tank roadblock—**take the stairway ramp to the right of the roadblock to bypass them ②** and earn a Bond Moment. Continue ahead to **the long, winding uphill road ③**, which you'll need to take to get to the hotel. Run over or sideswipe all enemy motorcycles you encounter while on this road. At the top will be another roadblock—this time **run over the yellow barrier between the enemy vehicles to get past ④**. A diagonal shortcut to the hotel can be found by driving through an alley way sandwiched between **a white building to the left and a blue building to the right ⑤**—look at the GPS map to see where the shortcut entrance is. Look for a parking spot to drive through at the end of that alleyway next to the hotel to complete this objective.

OBJECTIVE 2: ARRIVE AT THE MINE ENTRANCE

Armed with the upgraded Triumph Daytona 600 (also known as the Q-Bike), you'll be confronted with a roadblock. **Immediately head right to take a stairway ramp ⑥** that will earn you a Bond Moment if you can reach the roof on the other side. Return down the long, winding road, **dispatching motorcycles with your flamethrower ⑦**. Cross through the grassy area with the fountain to reach **a second winding road ⑧**. (**Note:** At oo Agent difficulty, there will be a tougher roadblock—you'll need to use missiles to dispatch a jeep and get through.)

After navigating that road, look left for **a shortcut through an alley ⑨** that will take you all the way to the coastal road (it's the same shortcut as the Bond Moment in the Serena St. Germaine mission). When you reach the coastal road, turn left and look for **a glowing parking spot ⑩** in front of the mine entrance.

OBJECTIVE 3: FIND SECRET ACCESS TO THE MIND ROUTE

Unfortunately, the mine entrance has been blocked off, so you'll need to find another way in. From your parking spot, drive ahead and **look right for a hidden archway opening** ⑪—this leads to a back alley of sorts, filled with ramps. The key is to make sure you have enough speed going through **a narrow winding portion with stone walls on both sides** ⑫ to make a jump at the end—otherwise, you'll fall back down to street level. **DON'T WORRY:** If you fall, there's another ground-level opening in the square that will get you back up ⑬.

MISSION 23

Follow the path (despite all the distractions, it's pretty linear) and hit the ramps with speed—but don't run into anything head-on, or you'll take lots of damage. You will reach a second winding portion that will lead to another set of rooftops—**but this time you have two paths, left and right** ⑭. Either one is OK, but make sure you have enough speed through this area or else you'll miss the final roof jump and will have to backtrack from the starting access point. Use the shotgun to dispatch any enemies firing from the roof.

You'll eventually make it to the **top of the mine-entrance perimeter wall** ⑮, which is really two routes in one. You might be tempted to take the right path (the raised wall). This leads to a treacherous drive alongside a cliff—but the safer route is the lower-left path that leads to a broken bridge. Past that point is a **water slide that leads to a narrow opening** ⑯. Press

and hold the gadget button to slide underneath the opening to earn a Bond Moment, then speed your way over one last jump to complete the mission.

EXTRA OBJECTIVE: EARN PLATINUM 007

To earn a platinum (once the objective is unlocked), you must get to the mine in less than 1:20 after reaching the demolished mine entrance. You'll need to hit lots of rooftop jumps and keep speed through the narrow winding areas to make this time. Obviously, you cannot fall down from the rooftop level at any point. If you follow the path described by the walkthrough above, you can beat this time limit with nearly 10 seconds to spare.

007 EVERYTHING OR NOTHING

MISSION 24

GOLD TARGET

Score 375,000 points to unlock the Platinum objective.

PLATINUM TARGET

Complete the mission in 3:10 or less.

STARTING WEAPONS

- EMP

ACQUIRED WEAPONS

- RAPPEL
- SLEEPER DART
- P99
- DESERT EAGLE
- MP5K
- DRAGUNOV
- AT-420
- AK-74

DIAVOLO'S PLAN

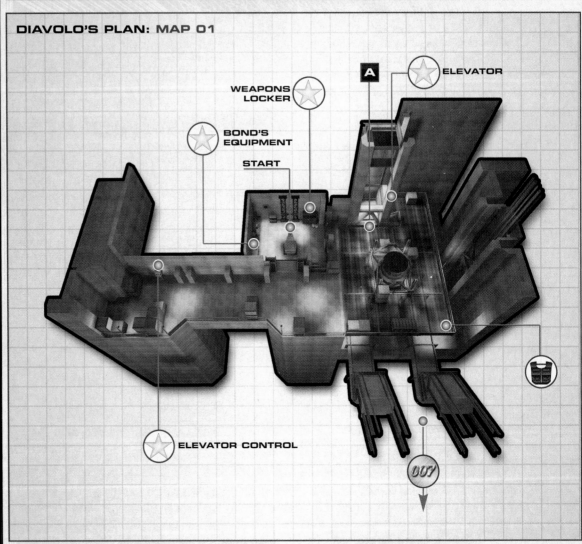

DIAVOLO'S PLAN: MAP 01

WEAPONS LOCKER

BOND'S EQUIPMENT

START

A

ELEVATOR

ELEVATOR CONTROL

007

START: MISSION BRIEFING

While infiltrating Diavolo's platinum mine, you are captured by the seductive Dr. Nadanova. As a result, you now face imminent death at the end of a mining drill—you must find a way to escape before Diavolo can execute his ultimate plan.

OBJECTIVE 1: ESCAPE

Bond starts the mission on the wrong end of a drill bit. **Immediately enter Bond Sense to equip your EMP grenade and trigger it to escape ❶.**

OBJECTIVE 2: RETRIEVE YOUR RAPPEL

Look for your gear on a nearby table—take your rappel to satisfy the objective requirement. Next, wait for a guard to open the door to the locked room that holds you. Use your hand-to-hand skills to dispatch him, then quickly take his weapon and his key to the gun cabinet. Wait for the rest of the guards to rush into the room, and dispatch them. For the locked gun cabinet, you can use your key or use Bond Sense to **target the propane tanks next to it ❷**. Take the weapons inside the cabinet—the cache will include a sniper rifle.

OBJECTIVE 3: DESTROY BOTH EXHAUST GEAR SYSTEM

Stay in the drill room, crouching behind an open window ❸. Equip the sniper rifle, then quickly stand up to eliminate the guards patrolling the catwalks across the chasm—**target the fuel barrels next to them to earn a Bond Moment ❹**.

With that threat eliminated, leave the room and take a right out of the drill room. **When you reach a control panel, press the action button to activate an elevator on the other side of the drill room ❺.**

BOND MOMENT

Shoot the propane tanks near a guard across the chasm.

DIAVOLO'S PLAN: MAP 02

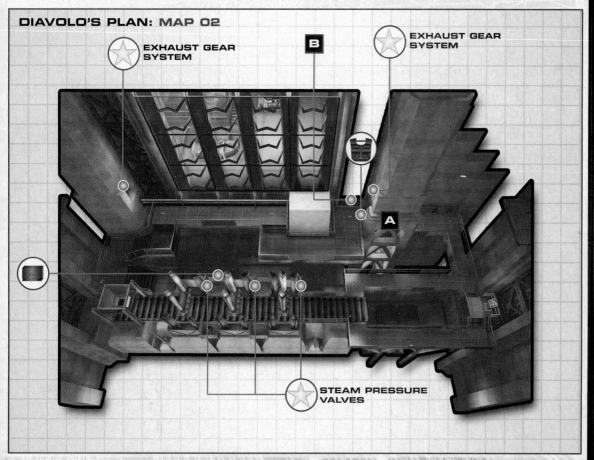

EXHAUST GEAR SYSTEM

B

EXHAUST GEAR SYSTEM

A

STEAM PRESSURE VALVES

MISSION 24

This will trigger the appearance of more enemies, so take cover immediately behind the closest metal boxes and dispatch all that appear—roll from box to box to advance to the elevator. Before reaching the elevator, **look for an armor vest at a corner point atop the metal grating 6**.

Once in the elevator, look for a switch on the back wall to go up. More guards will be waiting for you—and reinforcements will appear across the gorge. Crouch behind **the covered metal walkway areas (not the areas with gaps) for protection 7**, and use a long-range weapon such as the sniper rifle or AK-74 to take care of the guards across the chasm—**there'll be another fuel barrel to target across the chasm 8**.

On this level will be a rather intimidating conveyor belt—deactivate its hammer presses by **using Bond Sense to shoot the steam pressure valves on the upper right 9**. Look for **a battery in a niche along the conveyor belt 10**. This should stop the presses (Note: You can actually walk into the belt and shoot them to save a little time.) Past the conveyor belt, head up some stairs, and **take cover behind a covered metal walkway area 11** to take care of some rappelling guards looking to greet you rudely. On the walkway the guards landed on, look up and left to find **the first exhaust gear system 12**. On the floor nearby will be a wrench: Pick it up and throw it at the gears. You'll find the **second exhaust gear system on the other side of the walkway, to the right of another wrench and armor vest 13**. Throw the wrench into the gears again, then look up to find a rappel point.

DIAVOLO'S PLAN: MAP 03

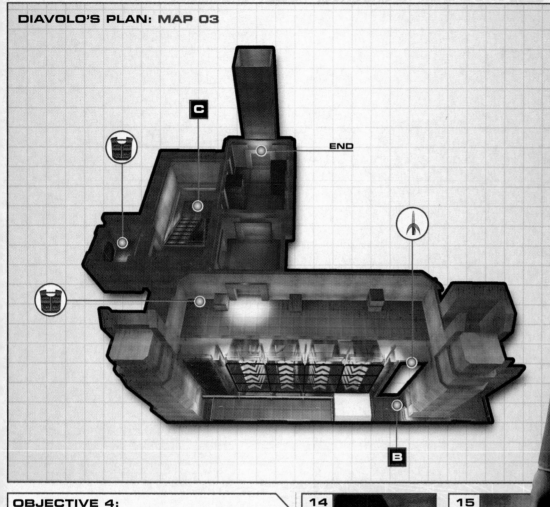

MISSION 24

END

C

B

OBJECTIVE 4:
ACTIVATE THE OVERRIDE SWITCH
IN THE CONTROL CENTER

Disabling the gear systems will activate a timer count-down of 3:30. Immediately use your rappel to reach the top and face additional rappelling guards—your best spot for cover is **a metal box along the outside railing** 14. Look for **another armor vest in a corner** 15, near an open doorway. You'll immediately see a door blocked with lasers—remember this door, because you'll be backtracking to it later to complete the mission.

To the right is a doorway that leads to stairs and **a room with a sniper rifle and armor vest** 16—but watch out for the door behind a corner in that room. Eliminate all enemies as you head down the stairs. Make note of another armor vest underneath the stairs—save it for later if you can.

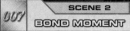
SCENE 2

BOND MOMENT

Use the Q Spider to retrieve an armor vest under the stairs in the control room (it's near the console with the override switch).

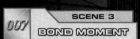
SCENE 3
BOND MOMENT

Use the Q Spider to destroy the exposed security laser panel to enter the room containing AT-420 rocket launchers. The room is immediately across from the console with the override switch, and the actual panel is just to the right inside the entryway to that room.

DIAVOLO'S PLAN: MAP 04

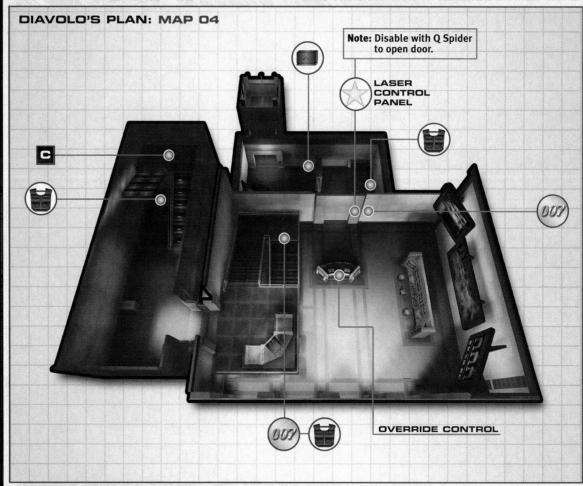

Note: Disable with Q Spider to open door.

LASER CONTROL PANEL

C

007

007

OVERRIDE CONTROL

17 B

18 B

The next doorway to the control room will be guarded on the other side by many enemies—rush in and eliminate all the threats as quickly as possible—the clock will be ticking. If you need an armor pickup badly, look underneath the staircase in this room—there'll be **an armor vest that you can grab with the Q Spider to earn a Bond Moment 17**.

Look in the middle of the room to find a console that houses the override control. Press the action button to override it. Crouch behind the console and quickly deploy a Q Spider to enter the room guarded by lasers. Turn immediately right to find the **exposed laser control panel, and panel and detonate the Q Spider immediately to deactivate the lasers 18**. This will earn you a Bond Moment. Don't wait too long to complete your task, or a guard may shoot the Q Spider.

Run into the room, eliminating any remaining guards. Pick up an armor vest, a battery, and AT-420 rocket launchers in the room, and quickly return up both sets of stairs. The door once guarded with lasers will be open. Clear out all the threats inside, then run into the elevator and call it immediately (there'll be a short time delay until the elevator appears) to complete the mission before time expires.

EXTRA OBJECTIVE: EARN PLATINUM 007

To earn platinum (once the objective is unlocked), complete this mission in 3:10 or less. There's no real secret other than speed, picking up armor vests along the way, and using cover only when necessary—the "shoot and charge" technique will work as long as you're not under heavy fire. To save a little time, enter the conveyor belt and shoot the vents along the way. Ignore all the Bond Moments to save time—however, the weapons cache in the drill room at the start is worth grabbing; it'll give you enough firepower to target any enemies across the chasm (use the AK-74 for that task).

THE PLATINUM WAR

THE PLATINUM WAR: MAP 01

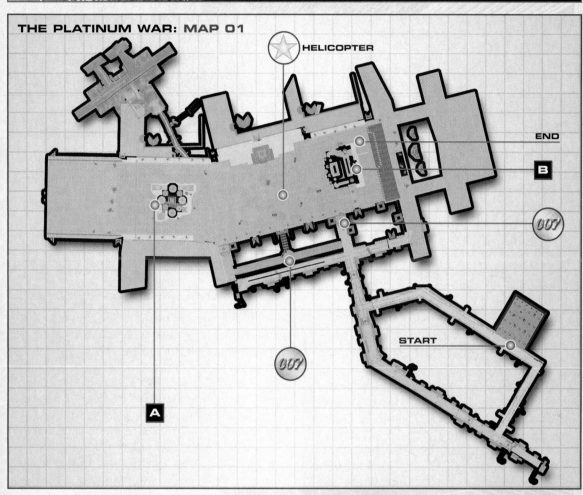

HELICOPTER

END

B

007

007

START

A

MISSION 25

GOLD TARGET

Score 400,000 points to unlock the Platinum objective.

PLATINUM TARGET

From the start of mission, neutralize the bomb in less than 2:15.

STARTING WEAPONS

 TANK CANNON

 NANO SHELLS

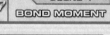 PLASMA GUN

ACQUIRED WEAPONS

⊘ NONE

SCENE 1
BOND MOMENT

007

After destroying the wall, look for a tank lying underneath an arch. Shoot a Nano Shell at the arch so it collapses and crushes the tank.

START: MISSION BRIEFING

Diavolo's army of platinum tanks has invaded Moscow and is advancing toward Red Square. The Russians are unable to stop him because his nanotechnology weapons are eating up their armored vehicles. You've got to find a way to stop him before he is able to release toxic gas into the Kremlin!

OBJECTIVE 1: NEUTRALIZE THE BOMB UNDER THE KREMLIN

Drive forward until you come to a wall blocking the street. Use the tank cannon to bring down the wall. Drive through the wall and turn right. Before you pass through the arch in front of you, select the Nano Shells weapon. **A target will come up on the arch ahead; a tank sits underneath ❶**. Once you're locked

HINT
Nano Shells can be used to destroy metal

007   Nano Shells

on to the arch above the tank (not the tank itself), fire a Nano Shell at the arch so it collapses on the tank for a Bond Moment.

MISSION 25

SCENE 2
BOND MOMENT

Immediately after the first Bond Moment, turn left to find a propane tanker on the street. Destroy the tanker to blow open an entrance into the building.

At the intersection, turn left and drive toward a propane truck. **Shoot the truck with the tank cannon or plasma gun**  to set off an explosion that will blow a hole in the side of the building for a Bond Moment. Enter through that hole and drive straight through into Red Square. Once you enter the square, look to the left and right for two tanks. Use the yellow walls on the side of the store exit as partial cover, then take out both tanks with the tank cannon.

TIP

When turning tightly, it's best to let off the accelerator, or the tank controls may get frustrating. Use the acceleration button only for moving forward quickly and making wider turns. The best way to fire effectively is to stop behind or near wall cover whenever possible, then turn the turret quickly to hit the target while stationary—don't drive toward a tank (at oo Agent level, you'll lose health fast). Aim just below the turret: You'll know you're hitting a tank if sparks fly from your shot. Press down on the tank-control stick to reset the cannon so it's pointing forward: This will help you maneuver much more easily.

With both tanks dispatched, **turn left toward a cathedral** ❸. Destroy the two tanks guarding the underground door entrance, then drive to the back of the building to find a door that leads underground. When the bomb is set, you'll have two minutes to get underground and disarm it. **Drive down the tunnel until it breaks into two paths** ❹. Take the left path, which leads down to an

open area. The bomb lies on an open walkway; **shoot the bomb with the Nano Shells** ❺ to neutralize it. (Note: On Agent oo difficulty, a tank will be guarding this room. Stop at the room entrance and target it quickly with your turret.)

OBJECTIVE 2: PREVENT TANKS FROM PENETRATING THE KREMLIN WALL

From this point, you'll have two minutes to get back to the surface and stop the tanks. **Backtrack to the T-intersection and turn left into a tunnel you haven't been through yet** ❻. Down this tunnel is an open room with three large green metal pillars and a tank. (Note: On oo Agent difficulty, two tanks guard this room—drive to a spot where the stationary tank on the right can't get a clear shot at you, such as behind **a stone pillar next to the three large green pillars** ❼, then target the tank entering the room first. Once that tank is taken care of, you can merely rotate to shoot Nano Shells at the pillars, then drive far around the pillars to the left of where the green columns were to avoid the other tank altogether.) Dispatch the tanks, then **shoot Nano Shells at the three large green pillars** ❽.

Once that's completed, look for an exit tunnel that leads back to the surface. Destroy the tank guarding that entrance on the right, then turn left to head back into Red Square. As you turn the corner, one last tank might be waiting for you. Disable it immediately, then drive

THE PLATINUM WAR: MAP 02

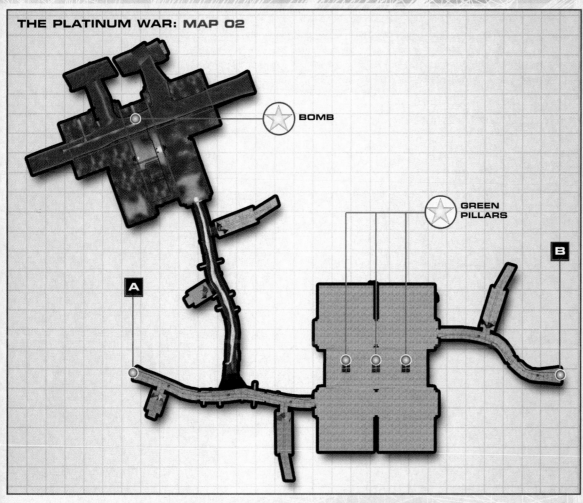

BOMB

GREEN PILLARS

A

B

DID YOU KNOW?

At the start of the mission, you can turn around to explore the tank warehouse area and another alleyway that ultimately leads to a deadly end. You'll surely fail the mission, but you'll wind up discovering an area that you might have otherwise overlooked.

VEHICLE: PLATINUM TANK

into the square to trigger a cinema scene. Look for a helicopter above that's carrying a statue of Diavolo (as well as tanks shooting at the wall—but ignore them). **Don't drive forward into Red Square. Stay on the hill to get a good angle for shooting the helicopter with a Nano Shell ❾.** This will complete the mission.

EXTRA OBJECTIVE: EARN PLATINUM 007

To earn platinum (once the objective is unlocked), you must neutralize the bomb in less than 2:15. This is actually plenty of time—the trick is to reach that point with enough health to finish the level. The walkthrough shows the optimal path; however, the only two tanks at which you should shoot to destroy are the ones directly in your path—the one blocking the entrance to the underground tunnel and the other in the room with the bomb. Quickly ignore the rest and keep moving so they can't get a good shot at you. By bypassing enemies, you should clinch the objective with time to spare—and hopefully with enough health to finish the level.

MISSION 26

GOLD TARGET

Score 300,000 points to unlock the Platinum objective.

PLATINUM TARGET

Complete the mission taking 100 damage or less.

STARTING WEAPONS

RAPPEL	
THERMOVISION	
Q SPIDER	
NANO SUIT	
NETWORK TAP	
EMP	
STROBE	
GRENADE	
SLEEPER DART	
P99 w/Silencer	

ACQUIRED WEAPONS

AT-420	
SIG 552	
DESERT EAGLE	
SPAS 12	

DANGEROUS DESCENT

DANGEROUS DESCENT: MAP 01

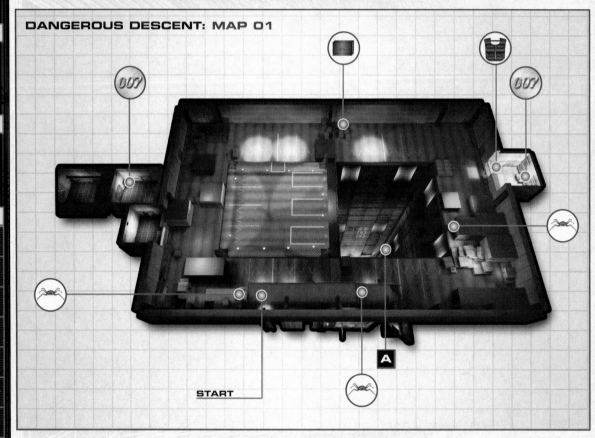

START: MISSION BRIEFING

Your search for Diavolo continues in a secret underground military base. Get ready for your toughest stretch of the game, as the enemies in this and future missions will be well armed and tougher to dispatch.

OBJECTIVE 1: REACTIVATE THE LIFT

When the mission first begins, you may be tempted to go town the open shaft—but don't. Instead, put your Q Spiders to good use. Crouch and send a spider underneath the railing nearby to navigate over some metal boxes. **A thin pillar and slanted board will lead to an open window ❶**. Once inside, look for an ajar door and **watch the guard in the room open a vault ❷**. Once he opens the door, eliminate the guard for a Bond Moment. Also destroy any nearby **crates with a picture of the AT-420 on it to get this rocket launcher weapon and ammo ❸**.

Detonate

Detonate

4

TIP

This first Bond Moment is required to obtain a Bond Moment in the final mission, "Everything or Nothing." Be sure to achieve it or you'll miss out at the end of the game!

Walk down the stairs to the edge of the open shaft. Use Bond Sense to target **a wooden crate in front of the large red storage container near the edge of the shaft** . This will clear the way for your Q Spider. First retrieve a **battery hidden behind boxes near the fence** ❺, then head back

5

6

7

8

to find a hole. Inside the room is **an armor vest in one corner and the security laser computer** ❻. Detonate the Q Spider in front of it to stop the beams from moving.

The lasers will still be dangerous to touch, however – so be careful when you finally decide to rappel down the shaft. **In addition, rocket turrets will come out of the wall** ❼. You can rappel straight down and bypass them without stopping, or you can use the AT-420 to dispatch them. Keep moving so you don't get hit by the turrets. (With the lasers disabled, you can head down the far right side, **momentarily slow rappelling so you land short of the laser at foot level** ❽, then go over it and keep moving down quickly as normal—you should avoid all damage with this pattern). Once you reach the platform at the bottom of the shaft, wait for it to stop moving.

TIP

To avoid early detection by enemies, it helps to crouch while navigating through this area. Never forgot how important the stealth factor is when filling the shoes of James Bond!

MISSION 26

007   SCENE 1
BOND MOMENT

At the start of the mission, take a Q Spider down a path atop metal boxes to reach a small window that leads into a room. Wait for the guard to open a large red vault door, then subdue him by detonating the Q Spider.

MISSION 26

007

SCENE 2
BOND MOMENT

Before rappelling down, disable the security lasers with a Q Spider bomb. To disable them, find a red flashing computer in a room accessible only by a small hole.

SCENE 3
BOND MOMENT

After rappelling down to the lower level, use the Q Spider to find a long narrow passageway that leads to the backs of three enemy guards hiding behind crates. Surprise the guards with a Q Spider detonation.

DANGEROUS DESCENT: MAP 02

Note: These two vests appear only after consoles have been activated.

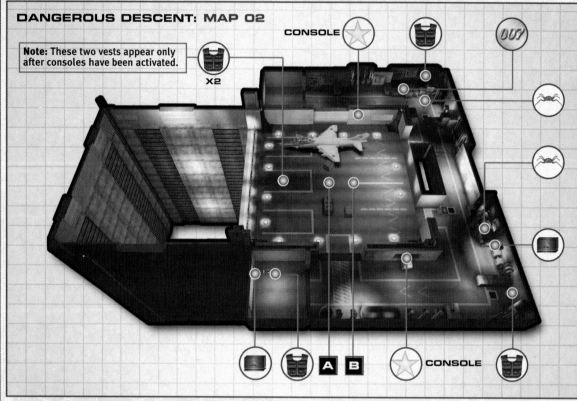

CONSOLE

x2

A B

CONSOLE

9

10

13

Sleeper Dart

Once the platform stops, three doors will open up. Go into **the door closest to the two weapon crates 9** and head towards **a console just below the window 10**. Crouch behind the console and send out **a Q Spider to find a hole underneath a large metal tank nearby 11**. There's a hole that leads to a small passageway: When you reach a T-intersection in that area, **head left to find a battery 12**, **then head the other direction down a much longer passageway 13**. Stop before you reach a vent fan: **Switch to Bond and turn the corner to target the floor vent 14**. Switch back to the Q Spider and **down the passageway, which leads to an armor vest 15**. Emerge from the hole to see **three enemy soldiers waiting for you 16**. Surprise them with a detonation to earn a Bond Moment.

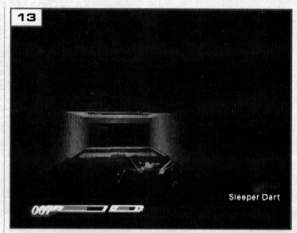

14

15 B

11

Sleeper Dart

12

Pickad up battery

Sleeper Dart

WARNING

While operating the Q Spider, make sure Bond is behind cover and that no enemies are coming up to attack. The last thing you need is someone sneaking up on you while your attention is elsewhere!

to fire at the controls on the right. You can opt to dispatch any rocket-firing enemies if necessary in case you're worried about taking damage. If you do get hit, make note of two armor vests in the middle of this area.

PART 2: MISSION BRIEFING

You've disabled the breaking mechanisms holding the floor elevator up, and it is now descending at a rapid pace. To make matters worse, Jaws has dropped in with his brand new flamethrower. You must act fast to defeat Jaws and avoid a crushing end.

OBJECTIVE 1: DISABLE JAWS' FLAMETHROWER

With the Bond Moment completed, activate the console: This will trigger the appearance of enemies. Take cover behind the closest wall to dispatch any remaining enemies. As you head towards the next console located underneath the other window, **look for an armor vest in a corner 17**. Head to the location where the Q Spider dispatched the enemy guards behind the crates and pick up their ammo. Immediately crouch behind cover as **a door will open at the end of the hallway, revealing more enemies 18**. Dispatch them, and when the coast is clear, **activate the switch on the second console nearby 19**.

After all of these guards have been dealt with, activate the second console. At this point, two of the three doors leading to the platform will close. The only door that remains open is the middle door. Make your way down the hall to this open door, using corner cover along the way—**tread carefully and quietly, because several rocket-launching soldiers will be lurking around the corners ahead 20**. Once the open doorway is reached, go past it to the first console—**in the garage where a rocket-launching soldier hides out will be a battery and armor vest 21**. Stock up on any leftover ammo on the ground, then exit the area to the middle of the platform.

After a short cinema, you will find yourself under attack. **Take out the four brake controls located at each corner of the shaft to escape 22** – use Bond Sense if you don't know where they are exactly. Take cover behind the metal boxes to get the brake controls on the left, and behind or beside the tail section of the damaged plane

When this battle begins, **pick up any weapons needed on the floor and find cover behind the nearest metal box 23**. Fire at Jaws every chance you get, and use flash grenades to stun him and get some easy shots on him. You'll need to roll to another box to hide behind when Jaws turns his flame towards you—**you'll know it's time to move when you see the box turning red hot 24**. Whenever Jaws takes a break and turns his back to you, shoot the flame pack on his back to cause extra damage. After doing some damage to Jaws, he will start spitting out flame salvos—stand in place until he fires at you, then immediately roll to one side or another to avoid them. Immediately fire at Jaws before the next salvo comes. If you spend too much time fighting Jaws, the mission will end in failure – so work as fast as you possibly can.

MISSION 26

DANGEROUS DESCENT: MAP 03

PLANE COCKPIT

A

B

END / BOSS

OBJECTIVE 2:
ENTER THE PLANE'S COCKPIT

Once you defeat Jaws and set him aflame, run to the plane cockpit to complete the mission.

EXTRA OBJECTIVE:
EARN PLATINUM 007

To earn a platinum (once the objective is unlocked), complete the mission taking 100 damage or less. The first big challenge is to make it to the bottom area without taking any damage from the lasers or rockets—the walkthrough describes a technique that may work for you. Dispatching the soldiers guarding the lower level isn't too difficult. First, run inside for cover immediately upon reaching the bottom so enemies can't fire at you from the

open doors. Second, find a safe spot to camp out and use the Q Spider sleeper dart and/or explosive function to scout ahead and dispatch enemies (including performing the third Bond Moment)—this will shield you from enemy fire. At all other times, take cover and make the rocket-launching enemies your top priority—you can use the AT-420 to take out these foes (and possibly anyone nearby) quickly.

The next "make or break" point is when you face the rocket-launching enemies to disable the brake controls. For safety reasons, it may be best to take immediate cover and take out several or all of enemies first before attempting to shoot the brake controls—it may be a waste of ammo, but it's worthwhile insurance from getting hit by a rocket.

RED UNDERGROUND

RED UNDERGROUND: MAP 01

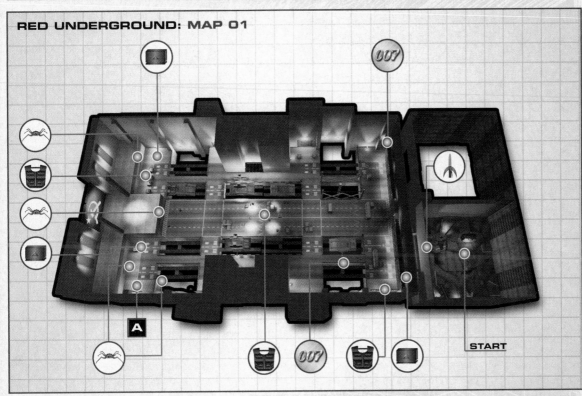

START

GOLD TARGET

Score 425,000 points to unlock the Platinum objective.

PLATINUM TARGET

Complete the mission firing 10 rounds or fewer.

STARTING WEAPONS

	RAPPEL
	THERMOVISION
	Q SPIDER
	NANO SUIT
	NETWORK TAP
	GRENADE
	STROBE
	EMP
	SLEEPER DART
	P99 w/Silencer

ACQUIRED WEAPONS

	SIG 552
	DESERT EAGLE
	AT-420
	SPAS 12

START: MISSION BRIEFING

Having escaped your most recent encounter with Jaws, you've fallen to the bottom of what appears to be a top-secret underground military fortress and command center. Unfortunately for you, the area is crawling with Diavolo's henchmen—some of which have Nano Suit cloaking technology (a new challenge you'll have to overcome)—so you'll need stealth in abundance and all the gadgets at your disposal to survive.

OBJECTIVE 1: EXIT SHAFT

This mission is unique because you can approach it from so many angles: You can go full firepower, rushing into battle; you can employ stealth and disable guards with your Q Spider sleeper darts; snipe targets with the Dragunov rifle; you can use the Network Tap to control a Nanotank—or do a combination.

You begin the mission in an elevator shaft, surrounded by flaming rubble and debris. **Run forward and rappel up to the ledge above you ❶**. As the bay doors open

take wall cover to the left and note **the guard at the catwalk across the way ❷**: You can dispatch him right off the bat for your first Bond Moment. **Run left at the catwalk to find a battery ❸**, then run back to the bay area behind wall cover. **Shoot the Network Tap at the Nano Tank below to earn another Bond Moment ❹**, and immediately target fuel barrels to take out the soldiers in the middle of the room—take out any remaining threats before disengaging the Network Tap.

SCENE 1
BOND MOMENT

Retrieve the Dragunov on the top catwalk at the start of the mission: Use a platform switch to get across the catwalk.

SCENE 2
BOND MOMENT

Dispatch the guard on the catwalk, who you can see immediately across the way as the bay doors open when the mission begins.

SCENE 3
BOND MOMENT

At the lower level, look for a guard underneath a tank suspended by a hydraulic lift. Use Bond Sense to target its hydraulic control, and shoot it so the tank falls on the guard.

TIP

If you're looking to preserve stealth and/or limit ammo, you can watch the patrols below. As long as the guards are turned away, they won't be able to see you on the catwalk—don't wait too long though, or else they will spot you eventually. You might want to use this method if you prefer using the Dragunov to dispatch enemies.

Head back out right to find a small platform on the catwalk. Activate the control on that platform with the action button to reach another catwalk—**at the end is a Dragunov sniper rifle to earn a Bond Moment 5**.

With the rifle, you can retreat to the bay doors and use snipe rifle scope to search for any remaining threats, or you can jump down to the main floor. Rappel down near an opening where you found the rifle, Crouch and **head left to find an armor vest atop a box 6**.

You need to progress down the hall, dispatching enemies along the way: The high-priority targets are the rocket-launching enemies in the middle of the room—one in plain view in the center and another one in a room accessible only with a Q Spider. You have many options open, but you might want to send **a Q Spider sleeper dart to scout ahead and clear the area of these soldiers 7** as well as any that appear along the sides of the room as doors open.

Sleeper Dart

Using the Network Tap to control the tanks is another option. As soldiers appear as you move forward, retreat to safe cover and use whatever tactics you're most comfortable with—however, **watch out for soldiers with Nano Suits 8**, as they blend in with their environment and may be able to surprise you if you're not vigilant. Whichever tactics you use, **look for an armor vest in the middle of the room atop a box 9**.

TIP

If you suspect enemies with Nano Suits are nearby but are unable to target them, use Thermovision temporarily to track their movements and target them.

When you reach the other end of the room, look for an armor vest and battery atop boxes to the right near a Nanotank 10. From here, send out a Q Spider and look for a sniper on the left side of this area. He'll appear behind a location only accessible by a Q Spider—use a sleeper dart or detonate to get rid of the sniper. **Near where the sniper had been will be another battery on a box 11**.

RED UNDERGROUND: MAP 02

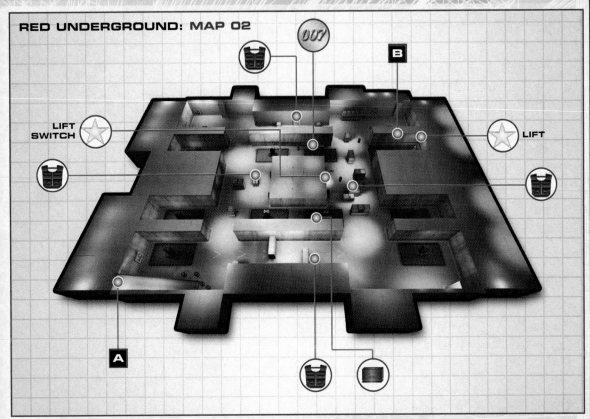

LIFT
SWITCH

LIFT

007

B

A

MISSION 27

SCENE 4
007 **BOND MOMENT**

While in the upper catwalk level's control room, look for a guard standing underneath a platinum spray. Activate the switch in the control room to spray him.

SCENE 5
007 **BOND MOMENT**

Once you have enough battery power, use the Network Tap on a Nanotank, then shoot an enemy with it.

SCENE 6
007 **BOND MOMENT**

Upon opening the final doors near the end of the mission, use a strobe grenade to stun the rocket-launching enemies behind the door.

12

With the batteries recharged, now would be a great time to head downstairs with the Q Spider's sleeper dart function on. **Look for a ramp downstairs blocked by barrels: Go around them with the Q Spider and navigate the lower level 12.** Dispatch enemies along the way and scout ahead.

WARNING

Do not explode the fuel barrels blocking the ramp! Destroying them will allow enemies to run up to the upper level and attack you. Although, let's face it, does that really bother you?

13

14

Instead of using the ramp, look left for a hydraulic lift to walk onto. **Fall to the lower level so you're behind cover 13.** Dispatch any remaining enemies along this lower level, using cover at all times and targeting fuel barrels for maximum ammo efficiency. **Look for an armor vest atop a box 14,** and **a battery underneath a hydraulic lift 15.** Upon reaching the other side of this room, you'll find **a second armor vest atop a box near the lift controls 16,** a third behind a wall of large metal boxes 17, and a fourth atop a box flush with a wall 18 for good measure.

15

16

RED UNDERGROUND: MAP 03

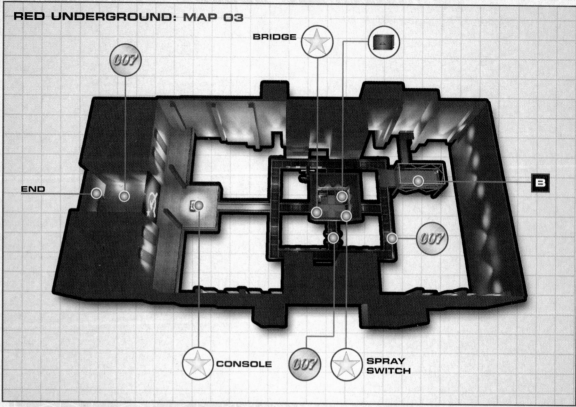

Speaking of the lift control, that's how you'll need to get to the upper level. **Look for the switch by a door** ⑲ —if you want to send a Q Spider up, you can place one on the lift and use this switch to bring him upstairs. Otherwise, **get on the lift and look for a switch to go up yourself** ⑳.

You'll encounter some fire as you head up to the catwalk level, but don't panic. Instead, run into the control room and **look for a green switch to the left** ㉑ —this triggers a platinum spray to dispatch a hapless guard. **Look for a battery on the ground in the control room** ㉒, then take out the remaining guards on the catwalks.

23

5 - 5
Sleeper Dart

007

The goal will be to cause maximum damage with minimal ammo. Some ways to do that include aiming at fuel barrels with a one-shot weapon such as a shotgun, using the rocket launcher (or a network-tapped tank) to target a crowd of enemies (such as those in a group appearing in a doorway), and/or using the Q Spider to dispatch multiple foes before getting destroyed.

It is vital that you do not destroy the fuel barrels blocking the ramp between the main floor and lower level—that way, enemies can't easily follow you downward and gang up on you.

In the control room is a switch ㉓ that lowers a bridge that leads to a console ㉔. Crouch behind the console and press the action button on the switch to open a door, then use **a strobe grenade to stun the rocket-launching enemies behind the door for a Bond Moment ㉕.** Dispatch these guards with hand-to-hand combat, and run to the door behind them to complete the mission.

Also look for items to throw such as hammers on all three levels (these throwable items will be atop consoles and red tool drawers throughout the area). When you reach the control room, complete the platinum spray Bond Moment, then resort to hand-to-hand combat and make a dash for the exit. Also complete the final Bond Moment by using a strobe grenade to get to the exit safely—strobe grenades do not count toward your ammo tally, so use them when in a crowd to escape!

24

007

4 - 5
Sleeper Dart

25

007

EXTRA OBJECTIVE: EARN PLATINUM 007

To earn a platinum (once the objective is unlocked), complete the mission firing 10 rounds or less. This will be an immense challenge, given the quantity (and quality) of enemies you'll be facing.

First off, you'll need to achieve gold, which will require using as much stealth as possible to dispatch the patrols. If you can reach ground level while avoiding detection, you'll be able to score big points for any stealth attacks you can pull off. Using the Q Spider sleeper dart as well as the sleeper dart weapon in lieu of weapons will help boost your score as well. Using hand-to-hand combat, aiming accurately with the sniper rifle, and targeting fuel barrels to dispatch multiple foes will boost ammo accuracy and efficiency. Finally, if you can beat the 6:00 target time for scoring and complete at least five Bond Moments, you'll get a 100,000 point boost to your score (which is doubled at 00 Agent difficulty).

MISSION 27

GOLD TARGET

Score 325,000 points to unlock the Platinum objective.

PLATINUM TARGET

Complete the mission taking 100 points of damage or less.

STARTING WEAPONS

	THERMOVISION
	Q SPIDER
	NANO SUIT
	NETWORK TAP
	GRENADE
	STROBE
	EMP
	SLEEPER DART
	P99 w/Silencer
	SIG 552

ACQUIRED WEAPONS

	AK-74
	AT-420

THE FINAL CARD

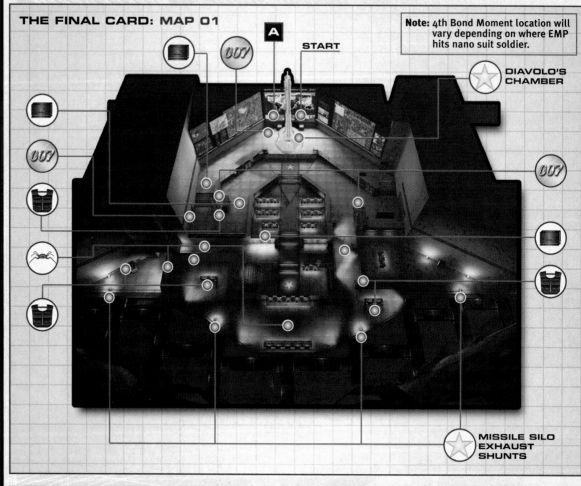

THE FINAL CARD: MAP 01

A START

Note: 4th Bond Moment location will vary depending on where EMP hits nano suit soldier.

DIAVOLO'S CHAMBER

MISSILE SILO EXHAUST SHUNTS

START: MISSION BRIEFING

You've reached Diavolo and Katya, who are ready to launch nuclear missiles tipped with nanotech robot warheads to unleash on the world. You'll have to stop Diavolo from launching the missiles, then make sure you take care of him once and for all. This mission is all about finding "safe zones" to protect yourself from enemy fire while completing mission objective.

OBJECTIVE 1: DEFEAT DIAVOLO

Immediately dispatch the guards that rush you using hand-to-hand combat as the mission begins, then immediately **run left behind the nearest cover point ❶** to take out guards. After you eliminate five or six guards, turrets will drop down from the ceiling.

Picked up battery

30 SIG

MISSION 28

SCENE 1
BOND MOMENT

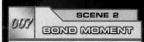

While controlling the turret with the network tap device, destroy the other turret.

SCENE 2
BOND MOMENT

While controlling the turret with the network tap device, dispatch six guards that enter the room – three from underneath Diavolo's chamber, and three from a door to the left of the control room.

OBJECTIVE 2:
NETWORK TAP A TURRET

You'll need to use the network tap to take control of the turrets. **Quickly run down the metal stairs and turn left at the T intersection, picking up a battery along the way on the floor ❷. The best "safe zone" cover point once all nearby enemies are dispatched is behind a low metal wall with stars on it ❸.** Crouch behind the wall (there's a wall on the left and right sides of the room, depending on which turret you prefer to use). Use Bond Sense to target the turret with the network tap. Once in control of the turret, **disable the other the other turret for a Bond Moment ❹. Then immediately look for two sets of three guards rushing out of doorways—one from where you began the mission ❺, another to the left of the turrets ❻.** Dispatch all those enemies with the turret to earn another Bond Moment, then clear out any remaining enemies on the floor. **Once all the threats have been eliminated, shoot at Diavolo's raised chamber ❼** to bid him farewell.

OBJECTIVE 3:
DISABLE THE MISSILE SILO EXHAUST SHUNTS

From behind your safe cover point, you'll see a series of four exhaust shunts ringing the outer edge of the room. Run to the two closest shunts in your area, **pressing the action button to disable each one ❽.** Nearby, you can find two more "safe cover" points behind L-shaped consoles near each shunt—**an armor vest will be behind each console ❾.** Crouch and dispatch enemies from behind these consoles as they approach.

Once these two shunts are disabled and all enemies are subdued, send out the Q Spider on a hunting mission. First off, crouch behind a console, making sure no enemies are nearby to hurt you. **Take the Q Spider down a short set of stairs ❿** to reach a red carpet walkway. Equip the sleeper dart function, head to the lowest level of that red carpet, and **immediately turn right to see enemies guarding the third shunt ⓫.** Take them out with the Sleeper Dart, then switch back to Bond. Follow the Q Spider's path, picking up the Q Spider as well as any ammo lying on the ground along the way.

SCENE 3
BOND MOMENT

Use a Q Spider bomb to enter the room with the fourth missile exhaust shunt, and subdue the guards in that area by using the sleeper dart.

SCENE 4
BOND MOMENT

Use an EMP grenade on an enemy wearing a Nano Suit to make him visible.

Dispatch two guards hiding behind consoles at the bottom of the stairs to find a battery ⑫ (**Note:** You may be able to dispatch these guards with the Q Spider as well, depending on which is closer). When you reach the area where the third shunt is, **look for an armor vest in a corner nearby ⑬**, and then **deactivate the third shunt ⑭**.

Behind that third shunt will be your next "safe cover" point: **A small metal box you can crouch behind ⑮**. From this hiding point, deploy your Q Spider again—this time go straight down the lower level walkway until you reach **a hole in a vent along the left wall ⑯**. Inside is a battery as well as two Q Spider routes. Take the route that branches right first—this leads to the area where the fourth shunt is. It'll be guarded by two soldiers—use the **Q Spider sleeper dart to dispatch them all for a Bond Moment ⑰**.

OBJECTIVE 4:
DISLODGE WRENCH

With the soldiers subdued, return the Q Spider into the hole it came from, and turn right at the end to take the alternate path. This winds down to a dead end, where a wrench has caused the fourth silo exhaust to remain stuck. Detonate the Q Spider to complete the next objective before it even comes up on screen!

OBJECTIVE 5:
ESCAPE THROUGH MAIN ENTRANCE

Run to where your Q Spider had been to disable the fourth and final shunt, picking up ammo along the way. Then find your next "safe cover" location—**either behind a console, where an armor vest is located ⑱** or the wall closest to the door—because enemies will be rushing your position—including some equipped with Nano Suits. Equip your Thermovision to see them, or look carefully for their outlines to appear. The moment they pop into view, **throw an EMP grenade at them to short-circuit their suits ⑲**, then dispatch them. Look out for more guards behind boxes as you head through the doorway—send out a Q Spider quickly to dart them, or use more conventional means to dispatch them from behind cover. Now just fight your way back to the point where you began your mission, dispatching enemies along the route. The optimal path is by taking the long red staircase and turning left—**along this path will be two more batteries and an armor vest ⑳**. Keep your eyes peeled to make sure you haven't forgotten any Nano Suit guards hoping to ambush you, then reach the entrance point to finish this half of the mission.

THE FINAL CARD: MAP 02

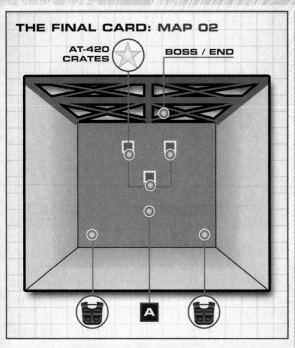

AT-420 CRATES ★   BOSS / END

A

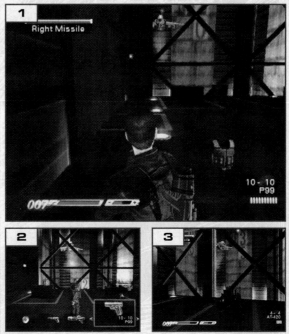

1 Right Missile

10 - 10
P99

007

2

10 - 10
P99

3

4 - 4
AT-420

007

MISSION 28

PART 2 START:
MISSION BRIEFING

You've defeated Diavolo and Katya, and you've stopped them from launching the nano missiles. It's time to escape, but unfortunately you'll find out that Diavolo and Katya are still alive - and they wish to end this feud once and for all!

OBJECTIVE 1:
DESTROY DIAVOLO'S HOVERJET

Diavolo and Katya will be following up your escape shaft in their hoverjet, armed with machine guns and missiles, as well as a Nano Bomb in the belly of the jet. You'll have to take out the hoverjet with a limited supply of AT-420 rocket launchers.

TIP

Smaller arms also work on the hoverjet, but they do far less damage. Stick to the rockets to get the job done quickly. In fact, that's an important life lesson for us all!

Before you begin, make note of **two armor vests—one in each corner of the platform along the back edge ❶**—so you'll know where to run if you get hurt.

If you aren't armed with an AT-420, the crates in the middle of the platform contain 48 shots worth of ammunition. **Shoot the crates or get the AT-420 once the jet damages the crates with their fire ❷.**

This mission may appear intimidating with everything going on at the same time: The moving jet, the rising platform, the metal framework blocking your view—plus all the explosions and enemy fire. However, once you break it down, it isn't as rough as it may appear.

First off, you need to dodge the missiles. **Once you see one streaming your way, immediately roll left or right to avoid ❸.** You don't want to roll forward or backward because the missile may still hit you, and you don't want to be shooting and be locked in place when a missile's headed your way. The worst thing you can do is get hit by a "chain" of missiles—each hitting you in sequence because you couldn't get away from the last one—that's bad news.

MISSION 28

Left Missile

4 - 4
AT-420

Right Missile

3 - 2
AT-420

2 - 4
AT-420

Second, you need to hide from the machine guns. **A hint that the jet will attack with guns: The nose of the jet will dip down below the platform then level out ④.** You can hide behind the metal boxes in the back, but since they get destroyed and are sometimes too far to run to, the **best protection spot is right behind the middle steel beam closest to the jet ⑤.** As long as you're completely behind that beam when the machine guns fire, you won't get hit. As an added bonus, you may be able to get a few shots on the jet as it passes across.

Finally, you need to get away from the edge of the platform **when fire spews from below ⑥.** The flames and any falling debris will hurt you if you're right next to the edge. Run back for safety when you see fire.

However, survival is only half the battle: The other half is how to hit the jet with rockets before you run out of ammo. The biggest key is **to make sure you have a clear shot ⑦:** When locked on, wait a second or two before firing (you'll be able to hear a small beep to know that you're locked) to increase accuracy. It also helps to get as close as you can to the jet—but **don't fire when a steel beam is in your way**

3 rounds AT-420

3 - 5
AT-420

3 - 5
AT-420

⑧, or you'll hurt yourself. A good tactic is to stay up close to the jet—moving back only when there's fire or when you need an armor vest or more ammo—and quickly drift from one side to the other side (a snake-like motion back and forth) until you get a clear shot. Stay near the middle while moving to reach the steel beam for cover when the jet's machine guns kick in.

Target the jet when its cockpit or underside is exposed ⑨: After you hit the jet, lock in and get in another shot before it recovers—you can chain a good string of hits together in this manner. Finally, be selective with your shots. Don't waste ammo trying to hit the jet if it's moving upward or downward rapidly. Wait for the jet's movement to stabilize, then fire. Repeat this process to take out both right and left missiles, and then the Nano Bomb to complete this mission.

EXTRA OBJECTIVE: EARN PLATINUM 007

To earn platinum (once the objective is unlocked), you must complete the mission taking 100 or fewer points of damage. Slow and steady is the key for the first half of the mission: Immediately dispatch foes as you make your way to the "safe zone" cover point—you might want to keep restarting the level until you get to the first safe zone with most of your health intact. Make sure you dispatch all enemies with the turret once you tap into it, then run to disable the two closest shunts before enemies can appear and shoot at you. Immediately take cover again and wait for enemies to approach—it'll feel like you're wasting time, but you don't ever want to venture into the open. The walkthrough points out the safe zones you can use to protect yourself from damage, and make sure to stay behind cover at all times. Send out your Q Spider whenever possible to dispatch foes with the Sleeper Dart.

EVERYTHING OR NOTHING

EVERYTHING OR NOTHING: MAP 01

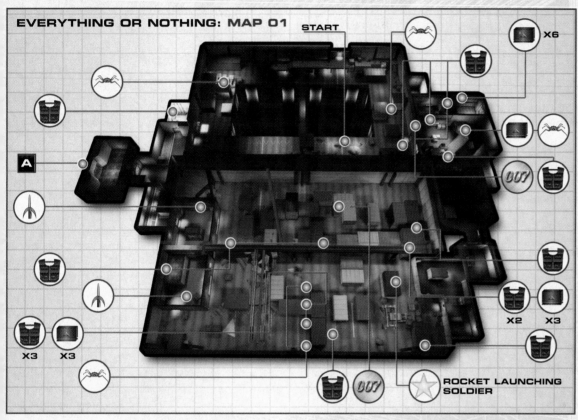

START

A

X6

X2   X3

007

X3   X3

007

ROCKET LAUNCHING
SOLDIER

GOLD TARGET

Score 450,000 points to
unlock the Platinum
objective.

PLATINUM TARGET

Complete the mission in
5:00 or less.

STARTING WEAPONS

	RAPPEL
	THERMOVISION
	Q SPIDER
	NANO SUIT
	NETWORK TAP
	GRENADE
	STROBE
	EMP
	SLEEPER DART
	P99 w/Silencer
	SIG 552

ACQUIRED WEAPONS

	DESERT EAGLE
	DRAGUNOV
	SPAS 12
	AT-420

START: MISSION BRIEFING

It appears that you've finally taken care of Diavolo once
and for all—or have you? Get ready for the final showdown between you and Diavolo as you fight your way
through one of the most intense battles in the game. Your
skills at wall cover and targeting will be put to the test—
as will your ability to find secrets with the Q Spider!

OBJECTIVE 1: FIND THE LAUNCH AREA

You'll find yourself back at the area from which you began
the Dangerous Descent mission. Did you earn the Bond
Moment from Dangerous Descent that unlocked a vault? If
so, you'll be in really good shape. If this dosen't ring a bell,
you might want to replay that level before beginning this one.

When the mission begins, immediately run forward and take cover
behind an orange metal box as enemies stream out from a doorway
ahead. Dispatch them all, and make note of an **armor vest sandwiched between the warehouse wall and a red metal container ❶**.

Picked up Desert Eagle

5 - 19
SIG 552

007

Send a Q Spider out to **look for an opening ❷** that will ultimately lead up some stairs to the starting point of the
Dangerous Descent mission. (Note: If you find yourself
stuck, look for a wooden crate you may need to destroy,
then send a second Q Spider through that now-opened passageway.) Once there, use the path you found for the Bond
Moment in that mission to return to the vault room.

SCENE 1
007 BOND MOMENT

At the start of the mission, send the Q Spider to the room where the vault was located (originally found in the Dangerous Descent mission). Head to a door braced with a metal bracket, then detonate the Q Spider to unlock the door.

SCENE 2
007 BOND MOMENT

Go through the door unlocked by the Q Spider and enter the vault room (but only if you opened the vault via a Bond Moment in the Dangerous Descent mission).

Equip the Q Spider Sleeper Dart to subdue the guard in that room, then **look for a locked metal door with a reinforcing brace** ❸. Detonate the Q Spider to unlock the door and earn a Bond Moment.

Enter the room the enemies originally streamed from, crouch behind cover straight ahead, and dispatch the enemies that appear in this room. To the left is the room unlocked by the Q Spider. **Go inside to find an armor vest next to an AT-420 on a table** ❹, then enter **the vault room to earn a second Bond Moment** ❺. In this room is a cache of weapons, as well as **four armor vests and six batteries** ❻. If you ever get hurt badly, you can backtrack here to recover.

Upon returning to the room, send out a Q Spider **to find a nook underneath the metal ramp where a battery is located** ❼. Go up the ramp to the window, **finding an armor vest in the corner** ❽. You'll see **a sniper rifle resting by a window** ❾. Crouch in front of the window, then equip the sniper rifle to shoot at two enemies on the other side of the warehouse.

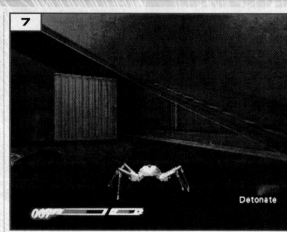

OBJECTIVE 2:
DEFEAT THE MISSILE-LAUNCHER GUARD

Find the metal double-door exit to enter the next room, which is arguably the toughest of the entire game in terms of sheer combat mayhem. Before opening the door, arm yourself with a heavy weapon such as the AT-420—you'll need it to **use a quick shot to dispatch the missile-launching soldier that guards the entrance** ❿. Also make note of **an armor vest to the left of the entrance** ⓫.

Once the guard is eliminated, return to the original objective, which is to get through this large warehouse area to reach the launch pad. Get ready to use wall cover exclusively as you wend your way through the maze of boxes. There are many places

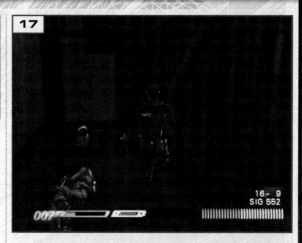

MISSION 29

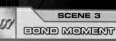

SCENE 3
007 BOND MOMENT

where you can get outflanked, so tread carefully. When you see enemies on the upper balcony, use a long-range weapon such as the missile launcher. Backtrack to any previous armor- vest locations whenever necessary. Finally, if you have a Q Spider to spare, use it to scout ahead and disable any foes you encounter with its Sleeper Dart.

You'll find **an armor vest in the open, to the left of a yellow metal container near the wreckage created by defeating the missile the missile-launcher guard** ⓬.

Near that area is **a red metal container with an open door** ⓭. Go inside it and **use a Q Spider to find two batteries and an armor vest** ⓮.

When you reach the other end, watch out for a sniper and a rocket-launching enemy to pop up on the upper level. Use rockets to dispatch them quickly, then watch for the windows of the building ahead to open, revealing more enemies. This is where it gets nasty, as the guards now have Nano Suits equipped—it's very easy for one of them to sneak up behind you, **so employ your Thermovision** ⓲. You'll find **another armor vest next to green metal container** ⓳ as you look for an entrance to the building ahead.

When navigating through the large warehouse filled with metal freight containers, look for one suspended in the air. When enemies appear underneath, use Bond Sense to shoot the glowing switch that holds the container to crush the enemies below.

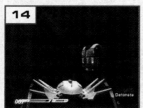

From that point, move forward and prepare for an ambush as **a red metal container opens above you** ⓯. Dispatch those threats and move right to see a squad of guards rushing forth. Look up to find a large red container suspended above the guards. **Use Bond Sense to target the switch holding the container so it crashes down on enemies for a Bond Moment** ⓰.

Proceed forward until you reach the warehouse wall. **Look right to find an armor vest in the corner** ⓱. Then head up the right side of the warehouse—watch out for another ambush point midway through as another red metal container door opens. (**Note:** This creates a shortcut if you ever need to backtrack).

The first entrance option is a rappel point to the right side of the building ahead ⓴. This will help you bypass most of the guards outside. Drop down a hole to find a ledge with an armor vest atop it.

The second entrance option is to fight your way to the left side of the building **to reach the front door** ㉑ or **a second rappel point up to the roof** ㉒. If you take this option, use the Q Spider to navigate the wide-open area to the right of the entrance—along the outside wall is **a small crevice that leads to an open red-metal container** ㉓—inside are two armor vests and a battery.

TIP

If you're on the roof, walk on the thin red support beam that spans the warehouse. **Midway across is an armor vest ㉔**, but don't stop there. Go to the end and fall so you land on top of a red container. **Look for a thin red ledge to land on ㉕:** If you land correctly, you'll open the door of the red container you fell on top of to reveal two armor vests, three batteries, and three AT-420s.

TIP

In the room with the large red blast doors, **you'll see two sets of doors ㉗**. The doors on the left lead to the room in which you disabled the security lasers in the Dangerous Descent mission (it was a Bond Moment). **There'll be an armor vest in this room ㉘.** The doors on the right lead to a Nano Suit–wearing guard, who may surprise you in the worst way. Choose your path accordingly.

Once you're fully armed, enter the building and look for the doors that lead to the next area. Defeat the enemies in here and **open the large red blast doors ㉖** to get to the final part of this mission.

OBJECTIVE 3: DEFEAT DIAVOLO

Now is your final battle with Diavolo, as he prepares missiles for launch. To the right is a barred door that a Q Spider can go under. Behind the door is an armor vest, but you

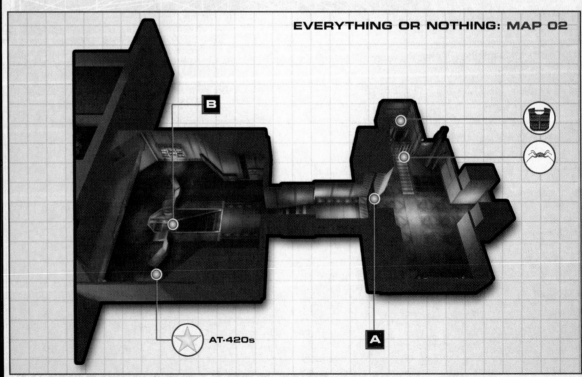

EVERYTHING OR NOTHING: MAP 02

B

AT-420s

A

EVERYTHING OR NOTHING: MAP 03

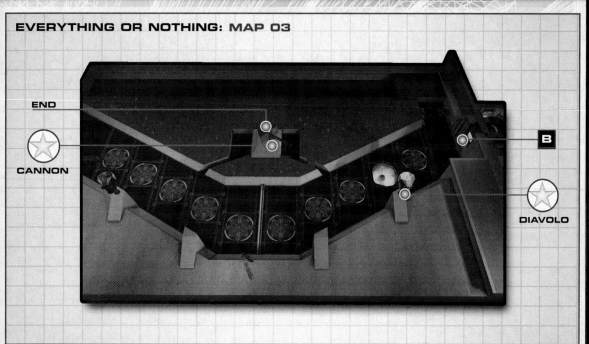

MISSION 29

END

CANNON

B

DIAVOLO

30

31

33

34

don't need to retrieve it if your health meter is already full. To begin, **head through the blast doors and get the AT-420s on the rack to the left ㉙ before heading down the ramp.** Equip an AT-420 and head down to trigger a cinema.

When the battle begins, take a quick shot at Diavolo's perch, then **run forward and roll as he fires salvos at you ㉚.** Make sure you **run past the missile silo hole ㉛** before focusing your attention on Diavolo again. It is crucial to run past the missile silo opening before defeating Diavolo because the missile silo's exhaust flames are deadly. **Shoot at his perch while avoiding his attacks ㉜**—three or so rocket shots will do the trick.

OBJECTIVE 4:
SHOOT DOWN THE ROCKET

Diavolo might be taken care of once and for all, but your job's not over yet. **Quickly look for an opening**

32

in the wall to get to a camera-controlled cannon ㉝. Once equipped, **immediately aim at the launching rocket and take at least three shots ㉞** before it lifts off. If successful, you'll see an ending cinema—and bonus extras—that'll make you glad you experienced Everything or Nothing. Congratulations!

EXTRA OBJECTIVE:
EARN PLATINUM 007

To earn platinum (once the objective is unlocked), you must complete this mission in less than 5:00. Get ready for one of the toughest challenges in the game. Forget the Bond Moments to get to the secret vault and any Q Spider tricks you might have used before. Outside of the possible rappel short-cut (the rappel point to the right of the building on the other end of the large storage warehouse area), you'll have to fight your way through while preserving health and picking up armor vests en route. Picking up the AT-420 hidden in a wooden crate (in the darkened room with the sniper) may help defeat some of the upper-level foes quickly. Otherwise, you'll need pure gameplay skill to pull this off. Good luck!

MULTIPLAYER

MULTIPLAYER

INTRODUCTION: MULTIPLAYER STRATEGY

The multiplayer portion of *Everything or Nothing* comprises a separate storyline that's intertwined with the single-player missions. You get to play as fellow MI6 agents assigned to investigate suspicious nanotechnology production sites and report their findings. Completing the objectives in these missions earns you points that you can use to unlock hidden multiplayer characters, extra levels and other goodies.

CO-OP AND RACE MODES

In Cooperative Mode, **players work together to complete mission objectives ❶**, using firepower and stealth to achieve their goals. Usually you'll travel together, but sometimes you'll have to split up to perform certain tasks—such as one team member operating an elevator while the other team member rides it. In later missions, you'll be equipped with gadgets such as the Nano Suit and the Q Spider to complete objectives.

Cooperative mode is the biggest element of the multiplayer section, and the multiplayer walk-through deals with this portion of the game exclusively. This mode is broken down into chapters that must be completed to unlock individual missions within each chapter.

In Race mode, **two players compete to complete missions in the least time possible ❷**. Team members get time bonuses for dispatching enemies, but are penalized for losing a life. It isn't necessarily a race to the finish line, because at some points you'll have to wait for your teammate to catch up to open a door switch, for example. The key is to take out more enemies than your opponent to subtract time from your total without losing health.

MULTIPLAYER SCREEN

The multiplayer screen is a little different from the single-player screen. The screenshot here will help you interpret the display.

A POWER MODE

This "glowing player" icon pops up after a team member dispatches a certain number of foes using hand-to-hand combat. In Power mode, your hand-to-hand attacks will be more powerful, and you'll suffer less damage from enemies.

B HEALTH METER

The thin blue bar indicates how much health remains. It will begin to flash red if you are running low on health. Note: In missions that use the Nano Suit and Q Spider (and in Tunisia), a battery gauge will appear next to the health meter.

C GPS RADAR

This radar shows where enemies are located, as well as where your team members and objective points might be. A colored arrow will appear along the circle's edge when a team member is out of GPS range.

D WEAPON DISPATCHES

This number indicates how many enemies you dispatched using weapons.

E OTHER DISPATCHES

This number indicates how many enemies you dispatched using stealth, unarmed combat, or other means (such as targeting fuel barrels).

F TIMES DIED

This number indicates how many lives you've used so far.

G LIVES REMAINING

This number indicates how many lives your team has remaining for the mission or chapter.

H WEAPONS AND AMMUNITION

As in the single-player mode, you see the weapon currently armed and how much ammo you have left.

TIPS: GENERAL GAMEPLAY

Being a smart player in the multiplayer environment is crucial to your success. The following tips will allow you to refine your skills.

GENERAL TIP

Unlike Bond, the team members don't have the ability to freeze time and target enemies with Bond Sense. You'll have to do your best to look up and around for targets while playing through a mission.

GENERAL TIP

Two-Person Cover and Advance: It's a classic tactical combat move. **One person advances quickly toward the nearest hiding point ahead while the other one offers cover fire and scans for enemies ❸**. This "leapfrogging" action will help you avoid being ambushed, and let you remain protected as much as possible when exploring new areas.

GENERAL TIP

When an armor vest is found, note its location for later use or save it for the team member with lower health.

GENERAL TIP

The GPS radar is useful but not perfect: Enemies on a level above or below you will show up on radar, so you have to interpret the red blips properly ❹.

GENERAL TIP

The radar sometimes allows you to see enemies behind a door or window before it opens, so take cover and watch that door or window if you suspect an ambush.

GENERAL TIP

To boost your score, use one-shot weapons such as shotguns and the Desert Eagle to boost ammo efficiency. **To boost accuracy, wait for your auto-aim crosshairs to turn red ❺**: This indicates that a foe is in close range, and your shots will be more accurate as a result. Of course, nothing beats the satisfaction of taking down an enemy with a head shot.

GENERAL TIP

To earn more non-weapon dispatches to boost your score, shoot an enemy to stun him, then punch him out.

GENERAL TIP

While playing through a chapter or individual mission, your team has a limited number of lives—if you run out too soon, you won't be able to complete the chapter! Your best bet is to restart the chapter from scratch and try to preserve as many lives as possible—this is most vital for the final Egypt Chapter missions.

GENERAL TIP

Use both halves of the screen: Although it may be confusing, it's vital at times for **one team member to adjust his camera angle so the other team member can see what's going on ❻**. This is useful in stealth missions, when one team member hidden from view wants to know when the coast is clear. The other team member can act as a spotter—and both players can watch that screen to know when to act.

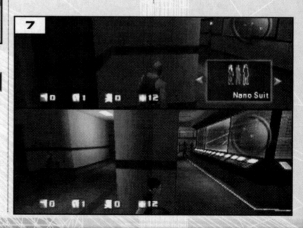

TIPS: COMBAT

Obviously, how well you handle yourself in combat will have a huge impact on your multiplayer success. Here are some bits of advice.

COMBAT TIP

Be warned: Although you cannot auto-aim at another player (except in Scramble mode), your bullets will do damage if they hit a team member.

COMBAT TIP

Powerful one-shot weapons such as the SPAS 12 are great for weapon efficiency and accuracy scoring—use them whenever possible.

COMBAT TIP

Team members can meet to share ammunition . To do so, stand next to each other with the same weapon in hand: The team member needing ammo should press the action button to initiate a request, which the other team member can accept by pressing the action button. You can choose to ignore a request if you wish to be greedy.

COMBAT TIP

Use stealth whenever possible. In some missions, for example, avoiding detection will prevent reinforcements from arriving—and since armor vests are few and far between in these missions, health preservation is a vital part of completing chapters without difficulty.

SCRAMBLE MODE

In Scramble mode, **players compete against each other for the best score** . The scoring parameters can be tailored to emphasize certain objectives, such as using only nonlethal dispatches. The options are as follows.

OPTION	DEFAULT	RANGE	DESCRIPTION
Weapon Dispatch	100	0–1,000	Points earned for using weapon to neutralize foe
Non-Lethal Dispatch	200	0–1,000	Points earned for using nonlethal means to neutralize foe
Stealth Dispatch	500	-1,000–0	Points earned for neutralizing foe stealthily
Player Death	-500	0–1,000	Penalty for being dispatched
Marksmanship	200	0–1,000	Points earned for aiming accuracy
Disarm	300	0–1,000	Points earned for disarming a foe
Multi-Dispatch Bonus	2	1–5	Bonus for taking out multiple enemies with a single shot.
Time Limit	??	1–25	Game time limit
Player Targeting	On	On or Off	Ability for players to shoot each other

ARENA MODE

In Arena mode, two to four players can battle each other, and **the player that scores the most dispatches wins** 🔟. Here's a quick description of each of the extra levels:

CISTERN

LEVEL ICON

This underground arena features switches that trigger lasers, and a carpet bomb of the entire lower and upper levels. You can even run into the large wall fan on the right, although this is seriously hazardous to your health!

TEST LAB

LEVEL ICON

This multitiered arena is a laboratory that features a gas chamber. Inside is an armor vest and an AT-420 rocket launcher. However, there's a switch enemy players can press to trap you inside. Elevators will transport you from level to level, and various switches trigger carpet bombs on the upper and lower levels.

BURN CHAMBER

LEVEL ICON

This arena features Jaws, who randomly wanders the arena looking for players to hurt. He can't be hurt himself, so it's best to stay clear of him. Look for AT-420s to spawn on the right side, and pick up the armor vests on the outside ring—but watch out for switches that trigger bolts of electricity from the ceiling.

OPTION	DEFAULT	RANGE	DESCRIPTION
Time Unlimited	0	1-25	Game time limit
Dispatch Limit	10	0-100	Dispatch total limit (for each player)

007: EVERYTHING OR NOTHING

BRIEFING

In the first chapter of multiplayer cooperative play, you will be sent to an isolated area in Tunisia near the Gulf of Gabes. Your mission is to investigate an individual known only as M. Sappho, and report back to MI6 what you discover.

MISSION OBJECTIVE

Make your way to the town square.

SCORING OBJECTIVES

- Don't lose any lives.
- Dispatch all enemies.
- Score above 70% Team Accuracy.

37+ TOTAL ENEMIES

TUNISIA: CROSSFIRE

TUNISIA: CROSSFIRE

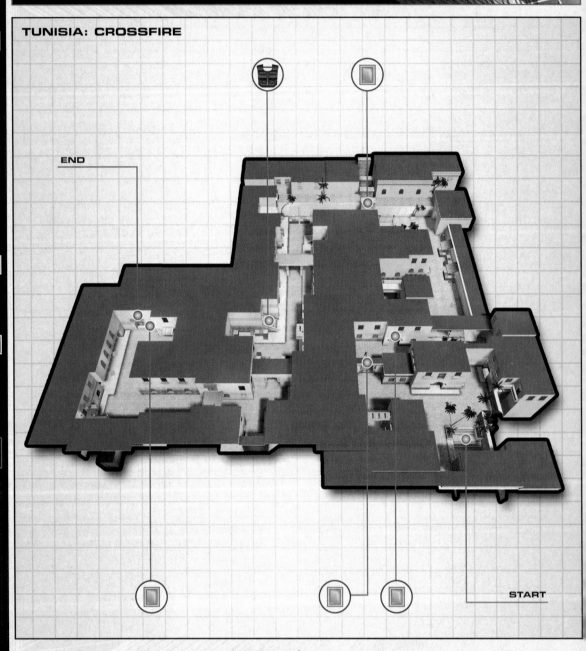

As the mission begins, head left to find a **gate with a switch on either side ①**. Each player must stand in front of a switch and press the action button simultaneously to open the gate. This action will alert the guards, so make sure your weapons are drawn.

After opening the gate, **look left to enter a room with a door switch ②**. One person can go through that door, while the other goes around the building. Time is not an issue, so move slowly and make sure the radar screen is clear of foes—watch out for occasional enemies popping out of doorways and windows. If one surprises you, use hand-to-hand combat to neutralize him quickly.

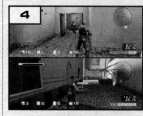

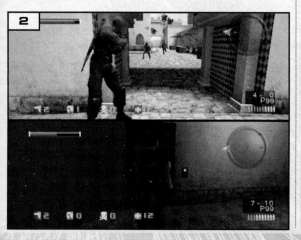

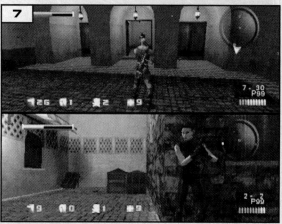

Make your way to a second gate. Quickly dispatch **the rocket-launching soldier beyond the gate** ❸, then open the gate. Before proceeding, have **one person camp out at the doorway behind that gate** ❹. As the other team member crosses through the gate, the door will open to reveal a second soldier armed with an AT-420. Surprise him and take his weapon before he can shoot.

At this point, rocket-launching enemies should be your priority targets. **Go under a long arched bridge with support columns** ❺—they're thin, but you can use them as cover in a pinch. Then move alongside the street, using the various entryways as cover. **Look for an armor vest up a short set of stairs** ❻ along the right side of the street.

After finding the vest, turn right on the street. Watch out for the rocket-launching enemy at the end of the street—take him out quickly. After another right turn, you'll reach the final gate—but not before a sniper pops up from behind. You can surprise him by having **one team member camp out where he is (his position will show up on the radar)** ❼ as the other team member moves toward

the gates. Activate the switches at the same time, then go through the gates to finish the mission.

TUNISIA	TARGET TIME
Crossfire	5:00
Cornered	3:00
Short Fuse	5:00
Last Stand	8:00

ANDAMAN SEA	TARGET TIME
Cliffhanger	4:00
Warzone	3:30
Firefight	7:00
Death Trap	10:00
Core Descent	6:15

EGYPT	TARGET TIME
Flashpoint	8:30
Sabotage	9:00
Knife's Edge	3:00
Inferno	12:00

BRIEFING

In this mission, you must wait and dispatch all the enemies you encounter until M finds the secret entrance to M. Sappho's palace.

MISSION OBJECTIVE

Find the entrance to the secret palace.

SCORING OBJECTIVES

- Don't lose any lives.
- Dispatch all enemies.
- Score above 70% Team Accuracy.

40+ TOTAL ENEMIES

TUNISIA	TARGET TIME
Crossfire	5:00
Cornered	3:00
Short Fuse	5:00
Last Stand	8:00

ANDAMAN SEA	TARGET TIME
Cliffhanger	4:00
Warzone	3:30
Firefight	7:00
Death Trap	10:00
Core Descent	6:15

EGYPT	TARGET TIME
Flashpoint	8:30
Sabotage	9:00
Knife's Edge	3:00
Inferno	12:00

TUNISIA: CORNERED

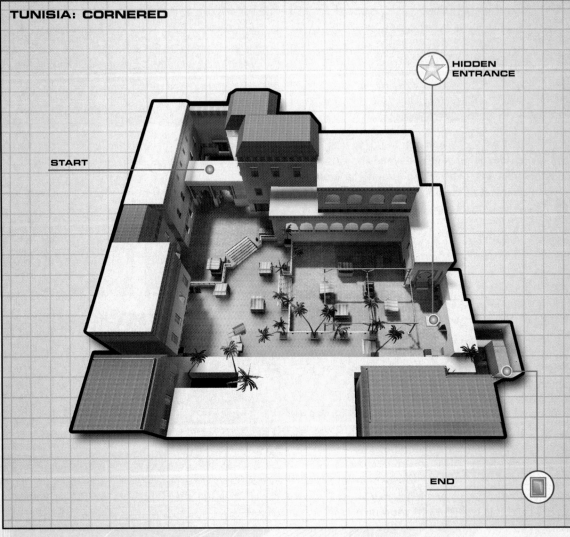

TUNISIA: CORNERED

START

HIDDEN ENTRANCE

END

Get ready for an intense firefight. Dispatch all the enemies in this mission, which will activate the secret entrance to the palace. Use the boxes next to the stairs to **set up an initial area of crossfire ❶** so that each player can scan and protect the path leading up the stairs. After a certain number of enemies are dispatched, beware of an ambush from the closed doors behind the crates near the stairs—this is designed to flush you out, but if you prepare for it, you can dispatch the ambushers quickly.

The top-priority targets after that point are those that appear in windows or terraces—especially the rocket-launchers. If you're having trouble auto-locking onto

targets, make sure you have a long-range weapon such as the AK-74.

Find an entrance at the end of the market area: **Look for a sunken underground staircase ❷**. At the bottom is a double door switch. Press the switches at the same time to complete the mission.

TUNISIA: SHORT FUSE

TUNISIA: SHORT FUSE 01

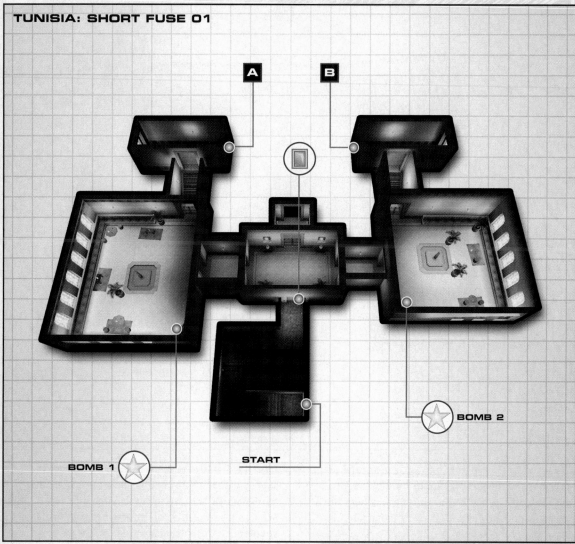

A

B

BOMB 2

BOMB 1

START

BRIEFING

Sappho's henchmen are planning to deploy explosives to eliminate all traces of his operation. You must defuse the explosives before they detonate—so time will be a factor in this mission.

MISSION OBJECTIVE

Defuse all explosives in M. Sapppho's palace.

SCORING OBJECTIVES

• Don't lose any lives.
• Dispatch all enemies.
• Score above 70% Team Accuracy.

60+	TOTAL ENEMIES

At the start of the mission, run up the stairs to find a double switch. Press the switches at the same time to gain access to the palace. You can choose to go left or right, but do not split up. Down each path (left or right) will be several guards around the first bombs to defuse. Dispatch the guards, then have one team member **stand next to the bomb, pressing and holding the action button to defuse it** ❶. You'll see a green light moving up the bomb as it's being defused. Do not let go of the action button, or you'll have to start again.

007 EVERYTHING OR NOTHING

TUNISIA: SHORT FUSE 02

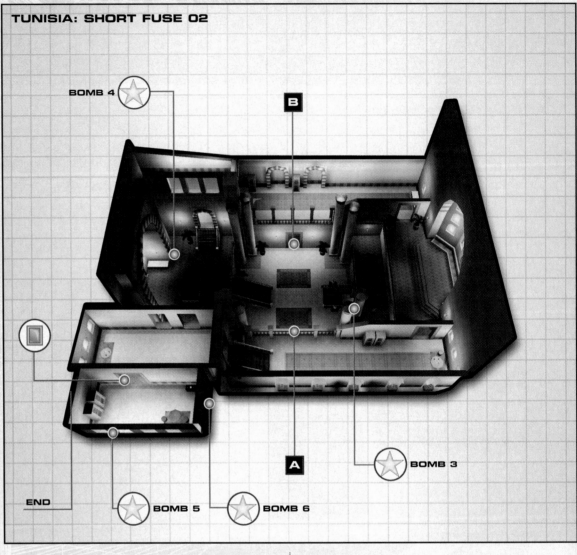

BOMB 4

B

BOMB 3

A

END   BOMB 5   BOMB 6

While the bomb is being defused, **the second team member should stand guard in front of the gate across from the bomb ❷**. Eliminate any henchmen that come down, and protect your teammate from enemy fire.

After the first two bombs are defused, head up the stairs where the gates opened **to reach a large ballroom area ❸**. Look for the third bomb on this level, but first use the available doorway cover **to eliminate the shooters on the balconies above ❹**. Once most of the

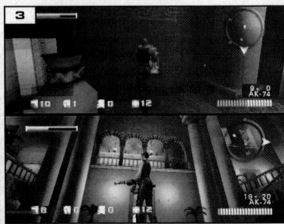

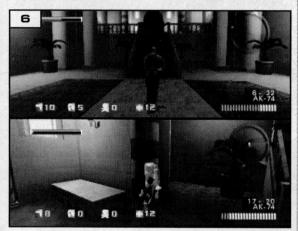

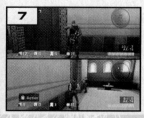

TUNISIA	TARGET TIME
Crossfire	5:00
Cornered	3:00
Short Fuse	5:00
Last Stand	8:00

ANDAMAN SEA	TARGET TIME
Cliffhanger	4:00
Warzone	3:30
Firefight	7:00
Death Trap	10:00
Core Descent	6:15

EGYPT	TARGET TIME
Flashpoint	8:30
Sabotage	9:00
Knife's Edge	3:00
Inferno	12:00

enemies are dispatched, have one team member **run out and defuse the third bomb ⑤** while the other one stands nearby, taking out any enemies firing from above. Go up the stairs across from the **third bomb to find the fourth explosive ⑥**—repeat the process once again. Don't waste too much time, though, or the bombs may detonate. Make sure no team member runs ahead until all four bombs you've encountered so far are defused.

Once the fourth bomb is defused, head right up some stairs and follow the hallway that rings above the ballroom area. Run quickly across the open balcony to avoid a rocket-launching enemy across the ballroom from you. Dispatch any enemies along the route—including the rocket-launching foe—and keep your eyes peeled for the AT-420 he leaves behind. **At the very end of this U-shaped hallway is a double door switch ⑦.** Open the door to reveal the fifth bomb and some guards in the room. Defeat the guards, then have one team member defuse the bomb while **the other stands outside to dispatch the snipers that appear across the way ⑧**—preferably the person with the AT-420 and/or Dragunov sniper rifle. Once the fifth bomb is taken care of,

immediately run down and **take out as many rappellers as possible (using cover such as the row of palm trees where the fourth bomb was) ⑨** before you are notified that you must defuse the sixth bomb. When that occurs, rush back down the U-shaped hallway to where the fourth bomb was. **A gang of henchmen will appear from a cracked wall ⑩.** If you have the AT-420, launch a rocket into that alcove to dispatch enemies quickly.

Look for a newly opened room to the left of the fourth bomb; it contains the sixth and final bomb ⑪. Have one person defuse it while the other takes cover at a doorway nearby to take out any remaining enemies.

WARNING

You will pass the fourth already-defused bomb. Don't confuse it for the sixth bomb.

Once the sixth bomb is defused, dispatch any remaining enemies in the ballroom, then head right from the sixth bomb's location to find a double door switch. Press the switches at the same time to finish the mission.

MULTIPLAYER

BRIEFING

You have made it to Sappho's inner sanctum, and now you must prepare for a final battle against him.

MISSION OBJECTIVE

Defeat M. Sappho.

SCORING OBJECTIVES

- Don't lose any lives.
- Dispatch all enemies.
- Score above 65% Team Accuracy.

62	TOTAL ENEMIES

TUNISIA: LAST STAND

TUNISIA: LAST STAND 01

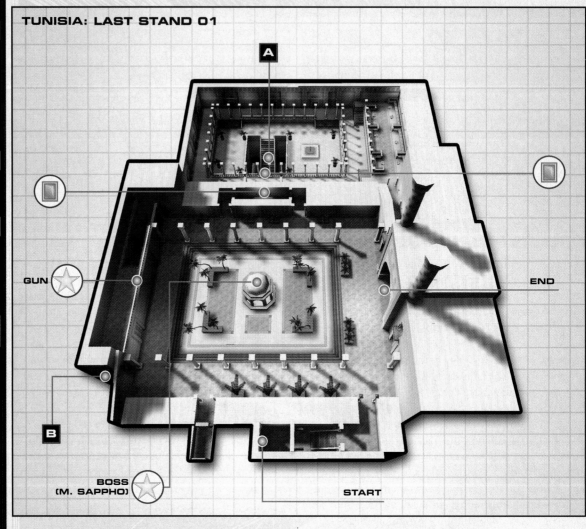

At the start of the mission, use hand-to-hand combat to defeat the first guards you see, then turn a corner. One team member can **crouch and look up and to the right to dispatch a sniper on a balcony in the courtyard ❶**. Your top-priority targets are those on the balcony—but you can focus on them after clearing the courtyard of ground soldiers. You can roll to get to the other side of the courtyard.

Once the courtyard is cleared, look for a double door switch that leads to a second compound. One team member should **charge right from the entrance immediately to engage a rocket-launching solider ❷**. The other team member should clear out any remaining enemies.

In the second courtyard, look for a staircase down that leads to **several more enemies and another double door switch** ❸. Activate it—it leads to an underground factory room. Split up to take the left and right paths separately. Use wall cover to dispatch onrushing enemies, then make your way to a second opening that leads to a similarly shaped room. Use the **boxes in this room as cover** ❹ as you progress down the path. At the end is as set of stairs—watch out for soldiers coming down as you head up.

This route takes you back to the first courtyard area, where you will finally face Sappho. **One team member can man the big gun on the upper level** ❺ while the other one takes care of enemies at ground level. You can use the gun on the rocket-launching soldiers that will appear on the balcony across the courtyard—but save the big gun's ammo for the final battle. Make sure you don't leave any rocket-launchers alive, or they may knock out your gun.

When Sappho appears, try to neutralize as many ground enemies as possible. You can avoid Sappho's salvos by crouching behind the short palm-tree planters around Sappho. Ideally, one team member can draw his gun's attention while the other targets him. With Sappho destroyed, run to the other end of the courtyard to find the mission-exit point.

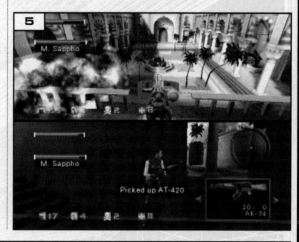

TUNISIA	TARGET TIME
Crossfire	5:00
Cornered	3:00
Short Fuse	5:00
Last Stand	8:00

ANDAMAN SEA	TARGET TIME
Cliffhanger	4:00
Warzone	3:30
Firefight	7:00
Death Trap	10:00
Core Descent	6:15

EGYPT	TARGET TIME
Flashpoint	8:30
Sabotage	9:00
Knife's Edge	3:00
Inferno	12:00

TUNISIA: LAST STAND 02

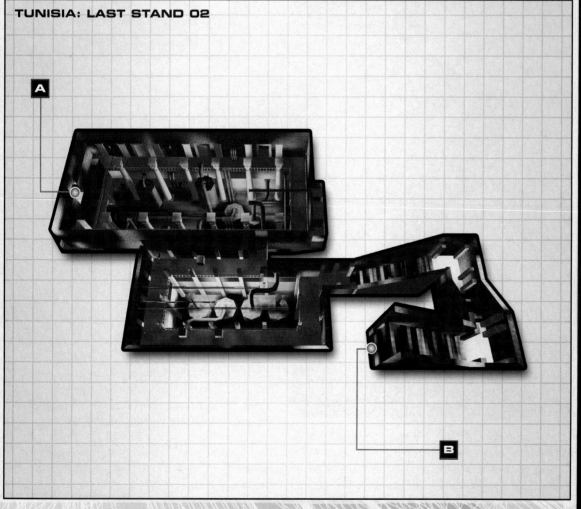

BRIEFING

In the second chapter of multiplayer cooperative play, you will be sent to a secret research facility on an island. MI6 suspects that Dr. Lazarus Beam, an expert in the field of nanolasers, is running the facility. Your mission is to infiltrate the facility and get as much information as possible. Stealth is paramount: Do not alarm the local authorities. If you are caught, it may affect how you have to approach future missions in this chapter.

MISSION OBJECTIVE

Get to the top of the cliff.

SCORING OBJECTIVES

- Don't lose any lives.
- Score above 90% Team Accuracy.
- Don't be seen.

37+ TOTAL ENEMIES

ANDAMAN SEA: CLIFFHANGER

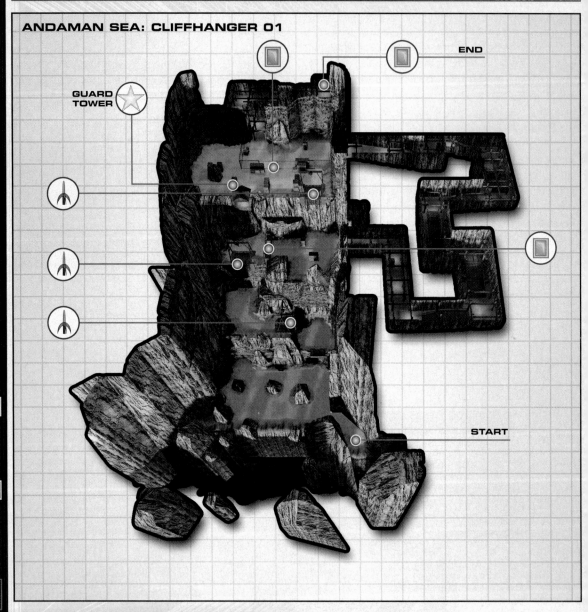

ANDAMAN SEA: CLIFFHANGER 01

GUARD TOWER

END

START

TIP

Having trouble pulling off a stealth takedown? Put your weapon away (press the left punch button while crouching) before performing one.

Both team members should crouch and quickly head toward the nearest patrol guard—one member should use a stealth takedown to neutralize him. Stay to the outside edge of the island so the guards on the second floor do not see you. The other team member should scout into **the mine-entrance tunnel ahead ❶**—if no guards are forthcoming, it'll be safe to go up the stairs. Otherwise, backtrack and hide behind the stones flanking the entrance, and wait for the guard to come out and investigate—stealth-attack him from behind.

Enter the mine shaft. At the top, wait for a guard or guards in the that area to turn around, then perform a stealth takedown.

Look for the **first rappel point up and to the right** ❷; you'll reach a level with two guards with their backs turned. Dispatch them both with stealth takedowns, then rappel upward again. You'll reach a double gate switch—get on either side and open the gate once the guards turn. **Wait until the guards are moving in sync toward the gate** ❸. Dispatch the closest guard once he turns around, then **hide behind a large wall of boxes to the left** ❹ and wait for the other guard to turn his back— then use a stealth takedown on him as well.

At this point, it'll be time to split up: One team member should **look for a rappel point upward while the other (preferably the one better at stealth takedowns) should navigate the mine shaft ahead** ❺.

The team member navigating the mine shaft will have to perform a series of stealth takedowns. They get increasingly difficult because **some enemies at the end will be carrying flashlights** ❻—if the flashlights drop on a hard surface, it'll make a sound that will alert nearby guards. You need to perform stealth takedowns before they walk toward other guards (so any sounds made don't travel far enough for other enemies to hear).

The team member who rappelled to the guard-tower level can wait for the other to show up (you can opt to dispatch the guards nearby as long as you don't get noticed by the one across the gate). **That person can also act as a spotter to let his teammate know when it's OK to advance up the stairs to the top level** ❼. The team member who took the long way up the mine shaft should stealth-attack the guard patrolling the gate. Then, with the coast clear, the team member who rappelled up can stealth-attack the guards near the watch tower, including the sniper in the roof. With the coast clear, open the gate switch, then look for a double-switch door at the end of a stone passageway nearby to finish the mission.

TUNISIA	TARGET TIME
Crossfire	5:00
Cornered	3:00
Short Fuse	5:00
Last Stand	8:00

ANDAMAN SEA	TARGET TIME
Cliffhanger	4:00
Warzone	3:30
Firefight	7:00
Death Trap	10:00
Core Descent	6:15

EGYPT	TARGET TIME
Flashpoint	8:30
Sabotage	9:00
Knife's Edge	3:00
Inferno	12:00

ANDAMAN SEA: WARZONE

BRIEFING

After you make it to the top of the beach, M informs you that another guard tower lies ahead. You'll need to get past all the guards and find the mine entrance. Once again, stealth is a requirement to succeed and complete all scoring objectives.

MISSION OBJECTIVE

Find the mine entrance.

SCORING OBJECTIVES

- Don't lose any lives.
- Score above 90% Team Accuracy.
- Don't be seen.

*6 TOTAL ENEMIES

* More if you're detected

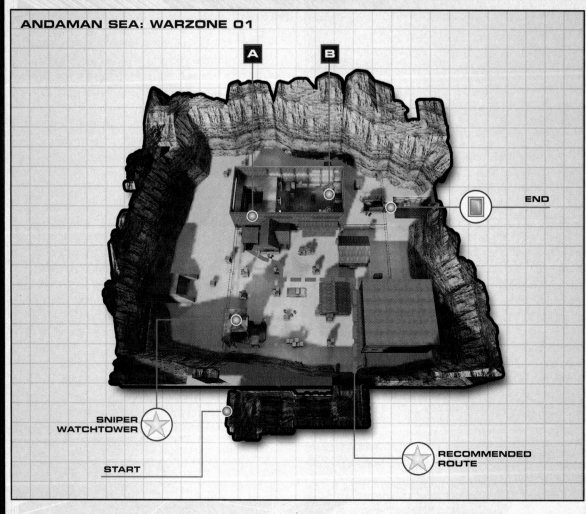

ANDAMAN SEA: WARZONE 01

A

B

END

SNIPER WATCHTOWER

START

RECOMMENDED ROUTE

To get through the courtyard, your team must follow a pattern and cannot hesitate midway through, or you will be spotted. Crouch and head down the mine shaft, dispatching two guards with stealth takedowns. Head straight when entering the courtyard, and **make a left while hugging the outside walls of the barracks to the left ❶**. Creep straight to the right side of the truck parked nearby and **turn right as you approach a stack of boxes ❷**. The instant the guard behind those boxes turns to walk left, go around the boxes behind him to get to the stairs.

Once down the stairs, hug the right wall to ascend with your rappel ❸. Make sure you're deep enough into the room on the right side when you do so the sniper in the watchtower does not see you. Once the first rappeller has gotten up, that team member can act as a spotter to tell when the other is clear.

TIP

You may be spotted by a guard or two en route using this path, but as long as you don't get shot and can reach the second floor before any guards can find you, they will stop looking for you eventually.

ANDAMAN SEA: WARZONE 02

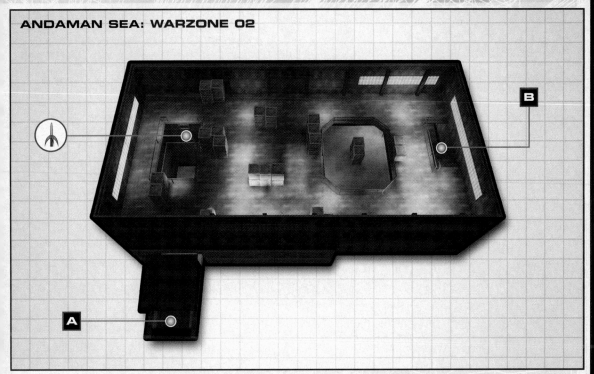

TUNISIA	TARGET TIME
Crossfire	5:00
Cornered	3:00
Short Fuse	5:00
Last Stand	8:00

ANDAMAN SEA	TARGET TIME
Cliffhanger	4:00
Warzone	3:30
Firefight	7:00
Death Trap	10:00
Core Descent	6:15

EGYPT	TARGET TIME
Flashpoint	8:30
Sabotage	9:00
Knife's Edge	3:00
Inferno	12:00

Once on the second floor, take positions to get close to the two guards walking the length of the room. **Your signal to strike is when two enemies are lined up on the same side as the rappel point ④**. It is possible to time it so one team member dispatches the guard on the right first, then the other team member dispatches the one on the left immediately afterward. The person who dispatched the guard on the right should immediately **approach the third guard in the room as he turns his back ⑤**. That guard will be alerted to his missing comrade to the left, and will run to check on his status. It is possible to creep around the large opening in the floor to get behind the third guard and attack with stealth.

With the room clear, **hide behind boxes to monitor the movements of the guard walking behind a fence below ⑥**. Don't bother trying to dispatch him. When that guard heads left down a small incline, that's the signal for both team members to creep downstairs and hide behind a wall of four boxes before he turns to look at the stairs again.

When this guard turns left to walk again, enter the long hallway to the right and stay to the back. When a guard approaches, he will not detect you hiding in the hallway—**in fact, it's possible to hide and creep toward him by hugging the left edge of the wall as he approaches!** ⑦ In any case, when this guard turns around, stealth-attack him before he reaches the corner of the building. If you're successful, just peer right around the corner to make sure the coast is clear, then head down the stairs nearby to reach a double switch that'll finish the mission.

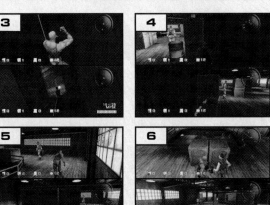

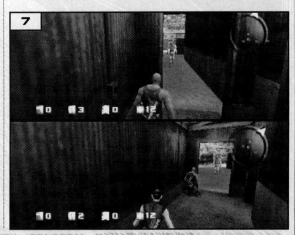

007 EVERYTHING OR NOTHING

MULTIPLAYER

BRIEFING

Intelligence indicates that the entrance to the secret laser facility is located inside a dilapidated mine building ahead. You must scout the building and find a way into the facility. Stealth is not a scoring objective in this mission, but is desirable whenever possible to preserve health.

MISSION OBJECTIVES

- Find the entrance to the laser facility.
- Restore power to elevator 1.
- Restore power to elevator 2.
- Find a way into the control room.

SCORING OBJECTIVES

- Dispatch all enemies.
- Don't lose any lives.
- Score above 55% Team Accuracy.

115 TOTAL ENEMIES

ANDAMAN SEA: FIREFIGHT

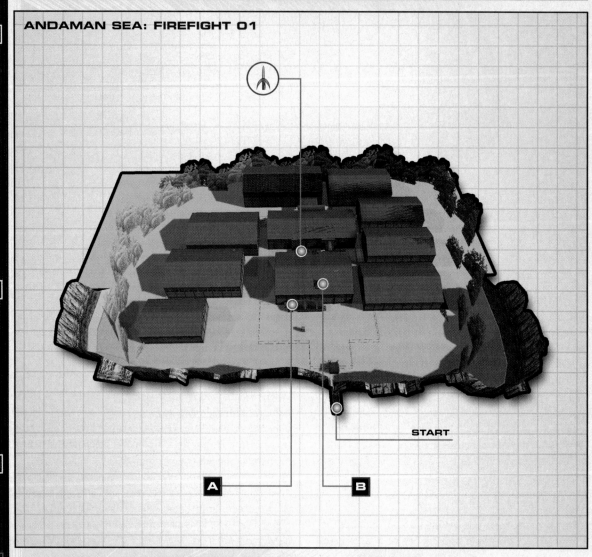

ANDAMAN SEA: FIREFIGHT 01

START

A

B

1

Begin by splitting up: **One person should enter the ground-floor entrance while the other goes around the back ❶.** Each team member should dispatch the first guard he encounters with a stealth takedown. **The team member going around the back of the building will find a rappel point to the roof ❷.** Head up and look for a hole to fall through.

It is possible to perform several more stealth takedowns upon entering the building, but at some point, detection will be very difficult to avoid. The team member on the second floor should take out the guard patrolling the catwalk, then crouch and

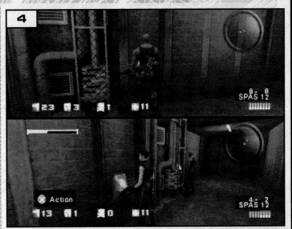

cover behind the windows to **target enemies on the second floor ❸**—the area atop the stairs to the right of the rappel entrance is a prime place to stay once the second-floor area is clear; from there you can take out any enemies that approach the stairway (go downstairs to retrieve ammo and wait for more soldiers to stream in). The person on the first floor should dispatch all nearby threats by finding cover and attacking.

At this point, up to 97 percent of the enemies should be dispatched. Once the area is cleared of enemies, both team members should **head downstairs to find a double switch to activate the elevator power ❹**. You'll notice more red dots as you go

down—that's the signal that an ambush awaits you once those doors are opened. Dispatch the foes that appear (with hand-to-hand combat for points), then fight your way to the staircase. Have each member **take cover behind the two staircase entry points ❺** and proceed to mow down foes as they go down the stairs.

TUNISIA	TARGET TIME
Crossfire	5:00
Cornered	3:00
Short Fuse	5:00
Last Stand	8:00

ANDAMAN SEA	TARGET TIME
Cliffhanger	4:00
Warzone	3:30
Firefight	7:00
Death Trap	10:00
Core Descent	6:15

EGYPT	TARGET TIME
Flashpoint	8:30
Sabotage	9:00
Knife's Edge	3:00
Inferno	12:00

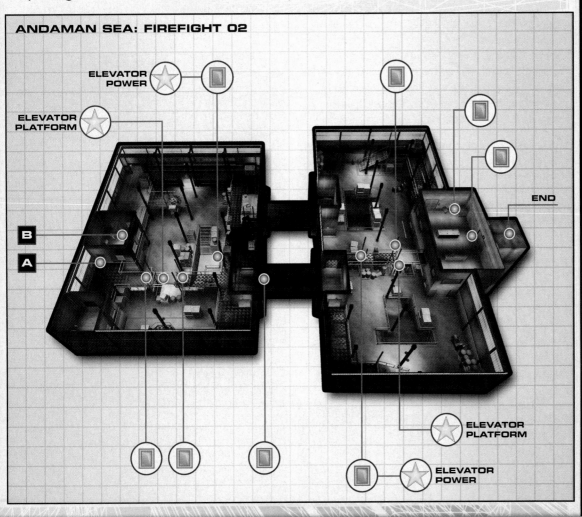

ANDAMAN SEA: FIREFIGHT 02

ELEVATOR POWER

ELEVATOR PLATFORM

END

B

A

ELEVATOR PLATFORM

ELEVATOR POWER

MULTIPLAYER

When all threats are eliminated, collect as much ammo as you can before heading downstairs to the double power switch. Activate the switch and get ready for a serious firefight as the remaining guards in the room rush your position. Look out for a newly opened door, from which guards will stream out. Overrun their position, then take cover inside the room they came from. To advance, **both team members must find cover points so that all entrances to the downstairs area are monitored ❾**—one team member should watch the main stairway entrance while the other monitors a newly opened back route.

Once cleared, **take one team member to the second floor to stand in front of the elevator ledge while the other mans the switch ❿**. This will trigger yet another ambush, so be prepared to retreat behind cover and eliminate this new wave of enemies before crossing the bridge. Once one team member crosses, look for a door switch that will open a path for the team member on the first floor to enter the room—but take cover behind a table immediately. **A final group of enemies will stream out of the elevator ⓫.** Use weapons or the throw the bottles on the table nearby to eliminate these foes, then go in the elevator and activate the double switch inside to finish the mission.

Have one team member (preferably the one with less health) stand on the elevator while the other returns to the second floor to activate it ❻—the activation will trigger the appearance of more enemies on the first floor. The team member at the switch should return to the staircase and dispatch the remaining threats on the first floor, then stand on the elevator. **The team member that already crossed should find the corresponding switch on the other side to activate the elevator ❼.**

WARNING

When you reach the second half of the warehouse, do not jump to the elevator platform. This will damage you seriously.

Look for a double door switch that leads to the second half of the warehouse—try to use stealth takedowns on the first batch of guards you see, then resort to firepower once detected. Head down to the first floor, dispatching any enemies along the way. Look for a stairway down that leads to the second power generator, but don't rush in just yet: Set up a field of fire, with **one team member dispatching guards approaching up the stairs while another covers and stands above the entrance by the railing ❽.**

ANDAMAN SEA: DEATH TRAP

BRIEFING

You have infiltrated the nanolaser facility, and now you must fight your way though it to disable the generators that power those lasers. Since your presence has been detected, stealth is no longer necessary.

MISSION OBJECTIVES

- Disable the first nanolaser generator.
- Disable the second nanolaser generator.

SCORING OBJECTIVES

- Don't lose any lives.
- Dispatch all enemies.
- Score above 50% Team Accuracy.

76	TOTAL ENEMIES

ANDAMAN SEA: DEATH TRAP

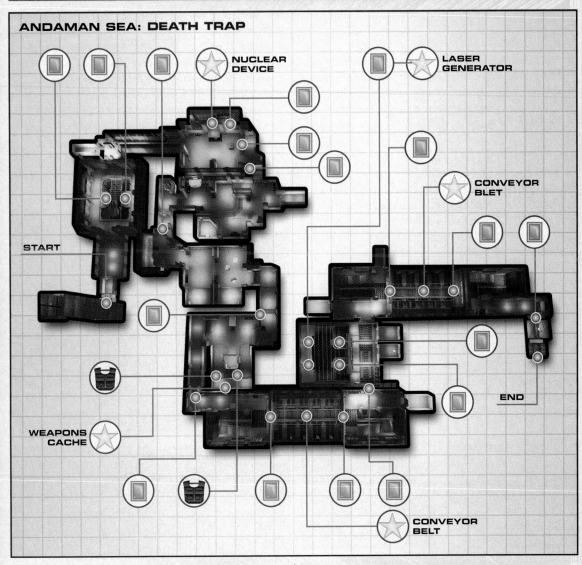

When the mission begins, run for door cover to the first room ahead, and dispatch the enemies on the floor as well as on the balcony. Look for a double switch in the room to activate a laser that will blow open a hole to the next area.

Go down a hallway to reach the next room, which is filled with enemies. Once that area is clear, watch out for a rocket-launching soldier who tries to ambush you from the hallway behind you. Roll to avoid his rockets, and dispatch him with hand-to-hand combat. **Find a switch that activates an elevator lift ❶**. Have one team member get on the lift to find another switch that opens a locked door, and a double door switch that opens the way to the next room.

WARNING

Do not fall into the elevator shaft once the lift is raised. You will lose a life.

The biggest threats in this room will be rocket-launching soldiers—make them your top-priority targets before eliminating the rest of the soldiers. Look for a double door switch that leads to the next room, which will feature enemy soldiers atop a raised balcony to the left. Take them out quickly before moving on.

MULTIPLAYER

TUNISIA	TARGET TIME
Crossfire	5:00
Cornered	3:00
Short Fuse	5:00
Last Stand	8:00

ANDAMAN SEA	TARGET TIME
Cliffhanger	4:00
Warzone	3:30
Firefight	7:00
Death Trap	10:00
Core Descent	6:15

EGYPT	TARGET TIME
Flashpoint	8:30
Sabotage	9:00
Knife's Edge	3:00
Inferno	12:00

The next room will have another rocket-launching soldier who'll dart in, so be careful. **Take cover behind the wall and the gray box nearby** ❷ to clear out the room. Find **a weapons cache featuring two armor vests and some AT-420s** ❸. Grab these items before leaving, because you won't have a chance to backtrack after the next room.

If you're thinking that this mission seems pretty simple, the next room may change your mind: Both team members will have to cross the room on a conveyor belt. **While one team member mans a switch, the other must get on the platform** ❹. Press the switch to alternate the laser pattern so the team member can cross. A good way to get the timing down is to have the team member on the conveyor belt crouch and remain stationary: **When the next laser is at the same level as the head of the crouching team member, press the switch** ❺. The first person who crosses using the conveyor belt will need to shoot at enemies that appear on the other end of the room.

After the conveyor belt room is a chamber containing the two generators you need to disable. One team member will have to press and hold a switch to extend a platform. The second team member will have to press and hold a second switch while on that platform to disable the generator. However, enemies will appear from behind multiple times as you attempt this. **Watch your GPS radar, and when enemies pop up, let go of the switch and neutralize the oncoming enemies** ❻.

Repeat this process for the second generator to initiate a five-minute countdown before the area melts down. The next room will have yet another laser conveyor belt and enemies to dispatch. Repeat the process you performed in the first conveyor belt room, but this time run against the conveyor belt to cross. **Have the team member on the conveyor belt run forward without stopping, then press the switch when the laser is at that team member's waist level** ❼. Once the first man has crossed, an ambush will occur on both ends of the room. Eliminate the foes, then have the second team member cross the conveyor belt in the same fashion. Don't celebrate too soon: A final rocket-launching soldier will appear at the other end—take him out and find a last double door switch that leads to the exit point. If you're efficient, you'll be able to complete the mission with more than three minutes to spare.

ANDAMAN SEA: CORE DESCENT

MULTIPLAYER

ANDAMAN SEA: CORE DESCENT 01

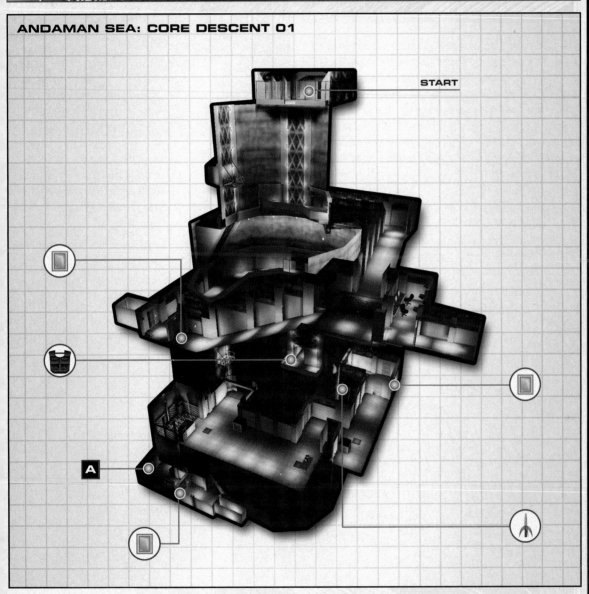

START

A

BRIEFING

With the laser generators destroyed, the final mission in this chapter will require you to escape the facility by rappelling down a large sinkhole—it is heavily guarded, but the guards will not expect you to go down this route. The key is to have one team member target threats along the walls while the other rappels down: Try to avoid having both team members rappelling at the same time.

MISSION OBJECTIVE

Escape from the facility.

SCORING OBJECTIVES

- Don't lose any lives.
- Score above 50% Team Accuracy.
- Dispatch all enemies.

138	TOTAL ENEMIES

Perform a stealth takedown on the very first guard you see, then have one team member rappel while the other targets enemies that pop up along the other openings in the sinkhole. When the enemies are cleared, the second team member can rappel. Go down a hall, dispatching enemies along the way, until you reach a double door switch. Once it's activated, get ready for enemies to appear from behind the hallway as well as beyond the door.

Past that hall is the second rappel point in the sinkhole. Again, have one team member go down while the other targets enemies that appear. This leads to a small corridor with two more enemies and another double door switch. Go down once again—this time both team members can descend at the same time—to dispatch a squad of soldiers. **Look for a small alcove across a walkway spanning the sinkhole to find an armor vest ❶. Then look for a rappel point upward ❷**—a commando will come down as you go up, so dispatch him immediately.

TUNISIA	TARGET TIME
Crossfire	5:00
Cornered	3:00
Short Fuse	5:00
Last Stand	8:00

ANDAMAN SEA	TARGET TIME
Cliffhanger	4:00
Warzone	3:30
Firefight	7:00
Death Trap	10:00
Core Descent	6:15

EGYPT	TARGET TIME
Flashpoint	8:30
Sabotage	9:00
Knife's Edge	3:00
Inferno	12:00

The next area features a double door switch. The room beyond features a large open area with enemy soldiers rushing in. **Take cover on both sides of the room (to the left is a gray metal cabinet, to the right is a wall corner and box) to avoid damage ❸**. Rappel to the lower level, then look back up immediately to see more commandos rappelling after you. **Move away from the rappel landing point and aim up to get a good firing angle on them ❹**.

Upon reaching the next room, you'll encounter enemies behind boxes. Dispatch them, then watch behind you

for enemies sneaking up from the rear. Look to find a rappel point downward. This will lead to enemy fire coming from two levels. **You'll need to find a rappel point back up to reach these enemies ❺**—don't waste ammo trying to hit them from afar.

ANDAMAN SEA: CORE DESCENT 02

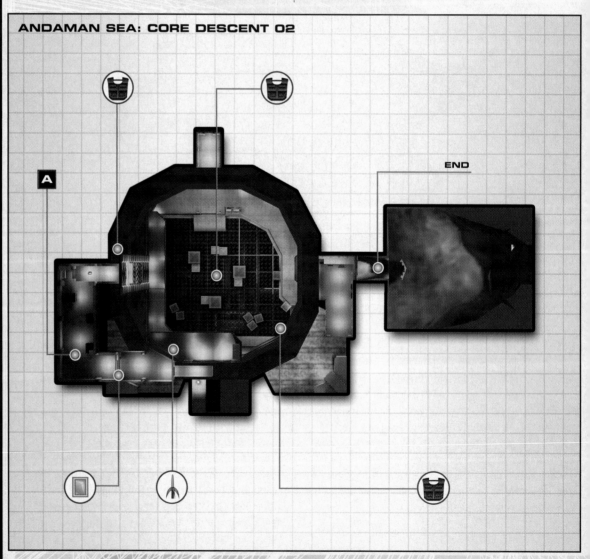

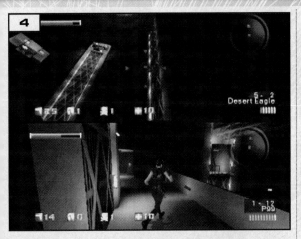

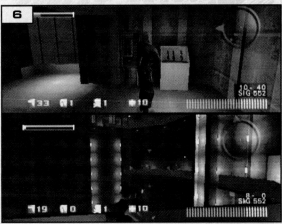

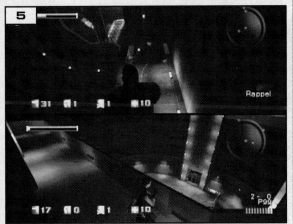

TIP

Looking for ammo? There are small weapons-storage boxes at various points throughout the mission, almost always in plain view 6.

This upper level contains a final rappel point downward, which leads to a chained fence area; multiple enemies will attack. **Take cover behind a nearby electrical generator next to a double switch gate and take out all enemies before opening it 7.** Inside the gate will be two armor vests. However, have only one team member at a time go in the gated area to retrieve it. Once both team members enter, a massive firefight will begin. You'll face overwhelming numbers of both rappellers and attacking guards. **The best point for cover is behind two metal boxes in a corner of the room 8.** It's best to stay together to prevent getting outflanked from either side. Looking up often to target rappellers is essential. Once there's a lull in the action, a team member can venture out to the middle of the room to replenish ammo while the other covers. Also look for a third armor vest in a narrow corridor that some enemies run out from.

Once a certain number of enemies are destroyed, watch out for the wall behind your cover point to break and allow more enemies to appear. One will carry an AT-420—that guard should be your primary target. Steal his weapon and get ready to face the final barrage of enemies—at this point your cover will be compromised by the appearance of foes, so dispatch them to regain your cover location. Once you've dispatched all the enemies, look for a hole on the other side of the fence to complete the mission.

MULTIPLAYER

EGYPT: FLASHPOINT

BRIEFING

Your mission is to infiltrate the nanotech center in Egypt and plant explosive charges within the facility. Avoid alerting the guards. Otherwise, this mission will become extremely difficult because detection will trigger the arrival of reinforcements.

MISSION OBJECTIVES

- Plant a Spider Bomb in Nano Machine 1.
- Plant a Spider Bomb in Nano Machine 2.

SCORING OBJECTIVES

- Don't lose any lives.
- Score two stealth disables on floor 132.
- Above 50% Team Accuracy.
- Score four stealth disables on floor 135.

*30+ TOTAL ENEMIES

* If detected

EGYPT: FLASHPOINT 01

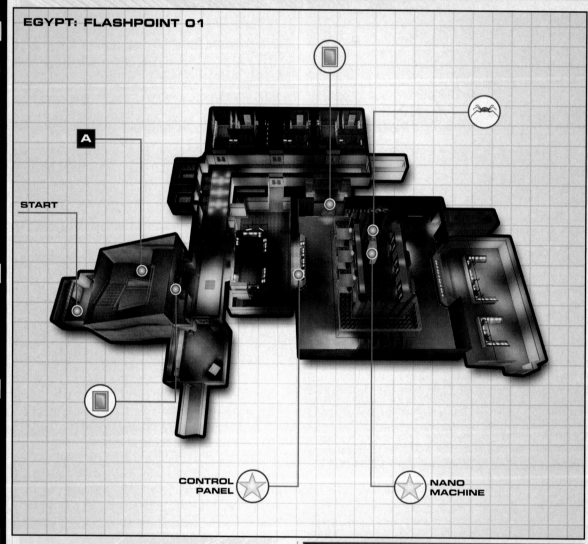

A

START

CONTROL PANEL

NANO MACHINE

Stealth is required for this entire mission—once guards are alerted, expect to take a lot of damage in the resulting firefight (it might be worth restarting the mission from scratch). You'll have to remain crouching for most of the level unless you're sure the coast is clear: Any sounds made by running will alert nearby guards.

When the mission begins, head up the stairs to Level 132—there's a double-switch door there. **Crouch and unlock the door, then look left to see a guard walking away ❶.** Creep behind him and perform a stealth takedown, then move to the corner. You'll see a second guard on patrol—stealth-attack on him as well when his back is turned.

WARNING

To the right of the entrance to Level 132 is a room with a guard inside. You can open the door to see him, but do not get in his line of vision, or he will alert others. For scoring purposes, a team member can choose to stealth-attack this solider—but you can also just leave the room undisturbed.

EGYPT: FLASHPOINT 02

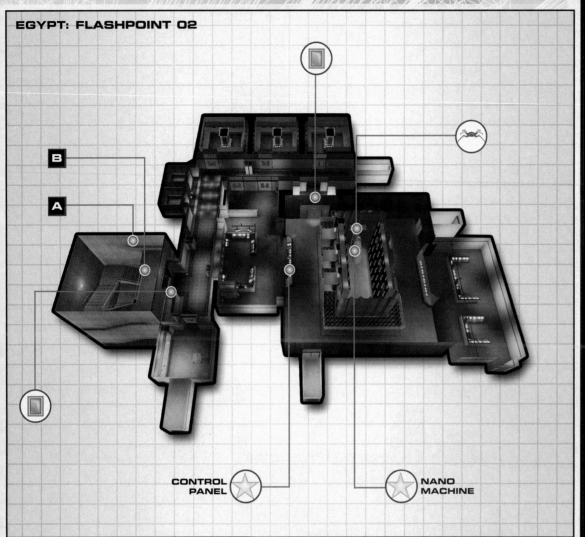

TUNISIA	TARGET TIME
Crossfire	5:00
Cornered	3:00
Short Fuse	5:00
Last Stand	8:00

ANDAMAN SEA	TARGET TIME
Cliffhanger	4:00
Warzone	3:30
Firefight	7:00
Death Trap	10:00
Core Descent	6:15

EGYPT	TARGET TIME
Flashpoint	8:30
Sabotage	9:00
Knife's Edge	3:00
Inferno	12:00

CONTROL PANEL

NANO MACHINE

With the hallway clear, look for second double-switch door. It leads to the first Nano Machine. Open the door. **One player should send out a Q Spider while the other returns to a control panel in front of the machine ❷.** Do not go into the Nano Machine room: Guards will be monitoring the back of the machine from behind a glass partition. Note that if you prematurely explode the Q Spider, nearby guards will hear the sound. However, if your team has been detected, you can go into the room and access the Nano Machine directly.

TIP

You can ignore the three rooms across from the double-switch door: They'll be empty unless you alert the guards.

Send the Q Spider up some yellow metal stairs behind the machine until it reaches the end. At this point, the team member in front of the control panel will have to **press and hold the switches in front of the control panel to lower a bridge so the spider can cross ❸.** This will have to be performed three times—once for each switch on the panel (which corresponds to the bridge directly across). Send the Q Spider into a small hole on the left side of the machine and detonate it to complete the first mission objective.

3

Detonate

Return to the Level 132 entrance and continue up the stairs to Level 134. The layout is similar; however, there are more guards patrolling the hallway in this level. One team member should stealth-attack the guard to the right (a Nano Suit helps). Once done, progress down the hallway, using cover and/or the Nano Suit to stealth-attack foes. Repeat the process as in Level 132 to disable the second Nano Machine.

On Level 135 are more enemies to dispatch. **The first two you see will require a double stealth takedown, in which both team members take out their foes simultaneously ④**. If your team is unable or unwilling to clear out this level of foes with stealth takedowns, you can merely bypass the two guards with your Nano Suit, then enter the first door on the left in that hallway to

find a double-switch door that leads to a friendly encounter and the end of this mission.

EGYPT: FLASHPOINT 03

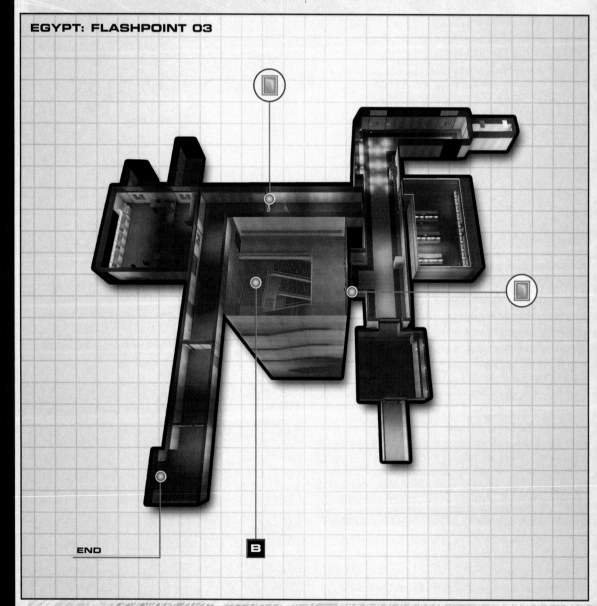

END

B

EGYPT: SABOTAGE

EGYPT: SABOTAGE 01

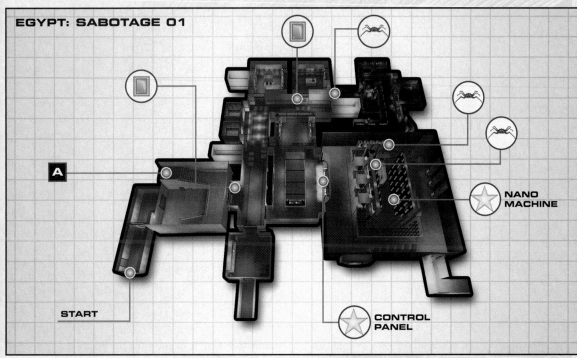

A

NANO MACHINE

CONTROL PANEL

START

BRIEFING

This mission is similar to Flashpoint—stealth is a primary objective. However, it'll be more challenging: This time, you must send your Q Spider on its own into the Nano Machine room—and the increased guard presence will make stealth preservation much more difficult than in the previous mission.

MISSION OBJECTIVES

- Plant a Spider Bomb in Nano Machine 3.
- Plant Spider Bomb in Nano Machine 4.

SCORING OBJECTIVES

- Don't lose any lives.
- Score five stealth disables on floor 136.
- Score above 50% Team Accuracy.
- 6 Stealth Disables on Floor 139

*30+ TOTAL ENEMIES

* If detected

Head up the stairs to reach a double-switch door. Crouch and open the door. The team members will have to work together to quickly stealth-attack two guards simultaneously: **One will be walking into a control room and the other will be standing in a room to the right ❶**—do not delay, or you will be spotted by the guard in the room.

WARNING

Some of the guards on this level carry items that will make noise if dropped. Keep that in mind when stealth-attacking. Any noise made will alert nearby guards, so make sure you're at a safe distance from others beforehand. Double-check your GPS radar if you're unsure.

Next, take cover and watch the guard patterns. You'll see a guard enter and exit the hallway from the control room. Use the Nano Suit to stealth-attack the guard in the hallway so the guards in the control room do not hear you. Then **both team members should creep into the control room and hide behind a counter to see two guards moving in sync ❷**. Your team will need to perform a stealth takedown on both guards simultaneously.

Once done, look for a double door switch in the hallway. **This leads to a room with a Q Spider hole ❸**. Have the other team member return to the control console in front of the Nano Machine.

Send the Q Spider through the hole until it reaches a ramp up to an opening in the Nano Machine room ❹—this leads to a small elevator platform for the spider. There may be guards nearby, so do not send the Q Spider out into full view, or it may be destroyed, and guards will be alerted to your presence.

TUNISIA	TARGET TIME
Crossfire	5:00
Cornered	3:00
Short Fuse	5:00
Last Stand	8:00

ANDAMAN SEA	TARGET TIME
Cliffhanger	4:00
Warzone	3:30
Firefight	7:00
Death Trap	10:00
Core Descent	6:15

EGYPT	TARGET TIME
Flashpoint	8:30
Sabotage	9:00
Knife's Edge	3:00
Inferno	12:00

EGYPT: SABOTAGE 02

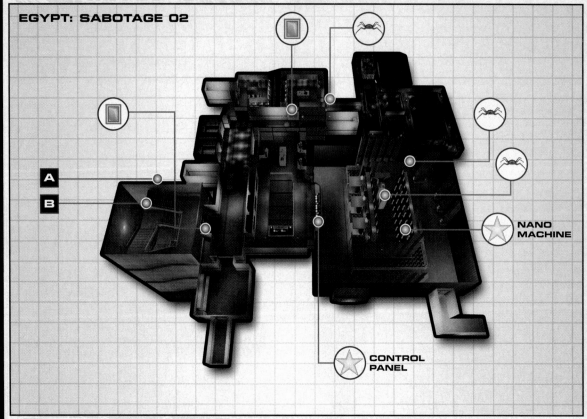

A
B

NANO MACHINE

CONTROL PANEL

When the coast is clear, **the team member behind the control console must press the far-left switch to bring the Q Spider to ground level ⑤**. Then the spider can navigate up the stairs of the Nano Machine and repeat the process from the earlier mission to destroy it.

However, there's a wrinkle: There may be guards patrolling inside the Nano Machine room (they won't trigger the alarm, but they will put up a fight). They will see the team member pressing on the control console if he's not crouching. Since you must stand to lower the bridges on the machine, you have to time your button presses so you aren't spotted by guards. Also take care not to accidentally make the Q Spider fall from the platform, or you'll have to repeat the process without benefit of stealth.

The layout on Level 139 is similar to that of Level 136, but the guards' patrol patterns and numbers will be different, as will the structure of the Q Spider path. Again, you can **begin by using stealth takedowns on the**

guards to the right as you open the door—but this time there will be three guards to the right. Two will **be standing in the room rather than walking ⑥**. You can perform stealth takedowns on all three guards quietly. Once these two are taken care of, monitor the patterns of the remaining guards from behind cover, then stealth-attack them when isolated (or simultaneously when necessary). Make sure no other guards are nearby or in your line of sight when you execute stealth takedowns. Whether you use stealth or brute force (the latter is highly undesirable), you'll need to clear the hallway of guards to open the room with the Q Spider hole.

Once both levels are cleared out, head up to Level 141 to complete this mission.

EGYPT: SABOTAGE 03

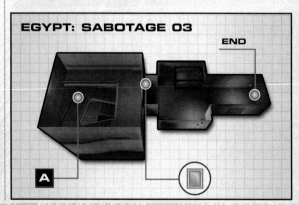

END

A

MULTIPLAYER

EGYPT: KNIFE'S EDGE

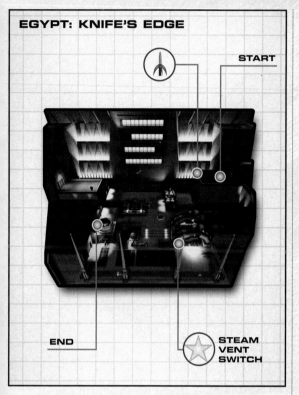

EGYPT: KNIFE'S EDGE

START

END

STEAM
VENT
SWITCH

Once you've cleared out a relative safe zone, one team member should be using **corner wall cover from the roof to target rappelling enemies** . Collect their ammo when you're running low, then retreat to that cover point. **The second team member should set up shop along the outer perimeter of the building** 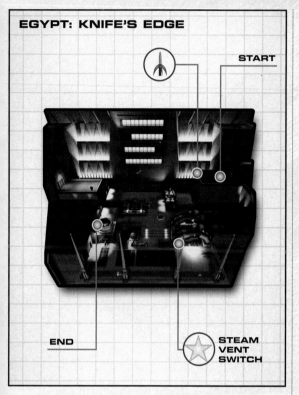, taking cover to shoot at enemies patrolling on foot nearby, as well as setting up a second line of fire to take out rappellers.

Midway through the mission, **watch for the doors along the left side of the area to open** —an ambush that makes the team member along the outer perimeter of the building vulnerable to attack. That player may need to retreat into the tunnel where the steam vent switch was to take cover and regroup.

Once all the enemies in this area are cleared out, look for an opened access door along the wall opposite the mission starting point to complete the mission.

BRIEFING

MI6 efforts to send in a helicopter to extract you have failed because of the heavy security surrounding the facility. While MI6 examines the building's schematics for another way out, you'll have to fend for yourself as a barrage of soldiers look to put your team out of commission. You will remember this area as the start of James Bond's "A Long Way Down" mission in the single-player game. Who knows: If you're lucky you just might meet up with him—but you'll have to survive long enough to find out...

Compared to the previous stealth missions, this one's more straightforward but more intense from a combat standpoint. The first step is to stealth-attack the guard on the roof of this building. Once you've done so, the team member that grabbed the Dragunov sniper rifle on the roof needs to **look across the way to dispatch enemy guards** ❶: Two will be firing a machine gun and the other will be shooting rockets. Find cover behind the vent shaft on the roof and pick them off quickly with the sniper rifle.

Once that's completed, both team members should rappel down. Clear out any immediate threats nearby. Targeting fuel barrels will help, and **activating the steam vent switch underneath the tunnel** ❷ will stun any enemies atop the vent.

MISSION OBJECTIVES

- Wait for evac instructions.
- Escape through the access door.

SCORING OBJECTIVES

- Don't lose any lives.
- Score above 75% Team Accuracy.

	TOTAL ENEMIES
31+	TOTAL ENEMIES

TUNISIA	TARGET TIME
Crossfire	5:00
Cornered	3:00
Short Fuse	5:00
Last Stand	8:00

ANDAMAN SEA	TARGET TIME
Cliffhanger	4:00
Warzone	3:30
Firefight	7:00
Death Trap	10:00
Core Descent	6:15

EGYPT	TARGET TIME
Flashpoint	8:30
Sabotage	9:00
Knife's Edge	3:00
Inferno	12:00

007 EVERYTHING OR NOTHING

MULTIPLAYER

BRIEFING

The good news is that you've found your escape route. The bad news is that it's through a flaming building filled with enemies seeking to neutralize you. These enemies include soldiers with Nano Suits, making your hopes of escape that much more challenging.

MISSION OBJECTIVE

Escape the building before time runs out.

SCORING OBJECTIVES

- Don't lose any lives.
- Score above 65% Team Accuracy.
- Dispatch all enemies.
- Complete the mission within 9:00.

85+	TOTAL ENEMIES

EGYPT: INFERNO

EGYPT: INFERNO 01

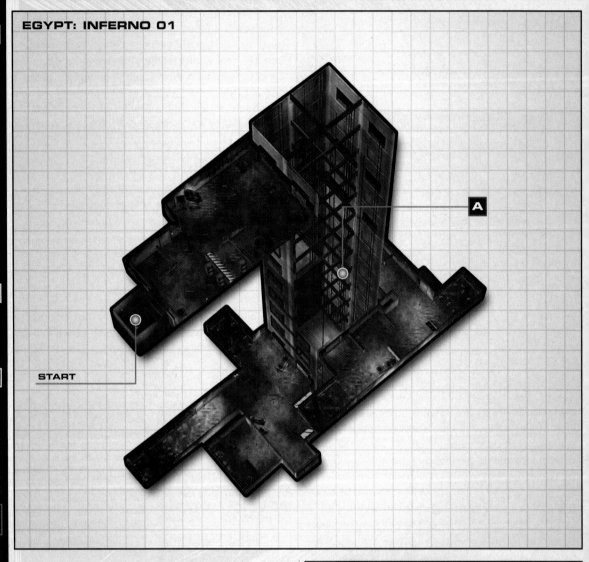

A

START

Your team will have 25 minutes to escape the nanotech facility—and it'll be an intense firefight. Take cover at all times when in combat, and avoid flames at all costs. Whenever you're stuck in what seems to be a dead-end area such as an elevator shaft, you'll need to use your rappel to ascend.

From the first room, rappel down the open elevator shaft. **Watch out for a major explosion that occurs in one of the elevator shafts ❶**—bypass it during a lull to avoid damage.

EGYPT: INFERNO 02

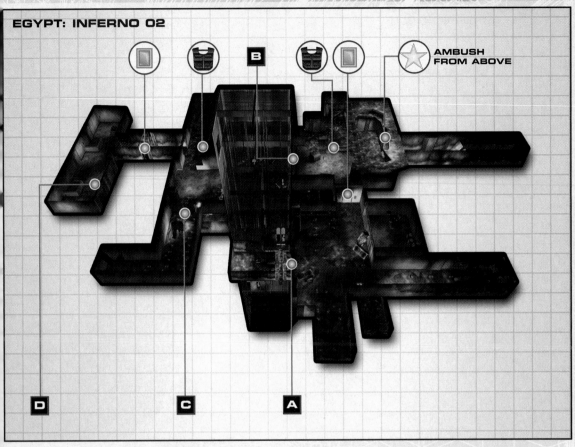

B

AMBUSH
FROM ABOVE

D   C   A

TUNISIA	TARGET TIME
Crossfire	5:00
Cornered	3:00
Short Fuse	5:00
Last Stand	8:00

ANDAMAN SEA	TARGET TIME
Cliffhanger	4:00
Warzone	3:30
Firefight	7:00
Death Trap	10:00
Core Descent	6:15

EGYPT	TARGET TIME
Flashpoint	8:30
Sabotage	9:00
Knife's Edge	3:00
Inferno	12:00

Clear out the room you reach at the bottom of the shaft, then head down another shaft—this time enemies will appear from opened elevator doors. Dispatch them and head to the bottom. More enemies will appear from an opening above your head. Look up to target and dispatch these enemies, then ascend again to another opening.

After the electric arcs is a room featuring a glass wall (behind which you can see a soldier trying to assist a fallen comrade). Dispatch the enemies in this room, then **trigger the double door switch next to the glass wall ❷**. The next room has an armor vest in a corner—but watch out for a hole in the roof nearby **that'll be the site of an ambush of your team ❸**. Enemies will stream out from above, as well as from hidden rooms at ground level, so be prepared.

You will reach elevator shafts blocked by electrical lightning arcs ❹. Stop and wait for a pause in the arcs, then quickly rappel down—it's vital that you not get hit, because these are highly damaging attacks. Once at the bottom, you'll need to rappel up once again.

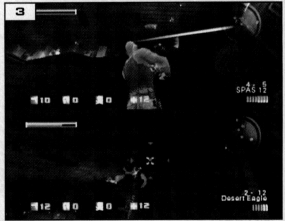

EGYPT: INFERNO 03

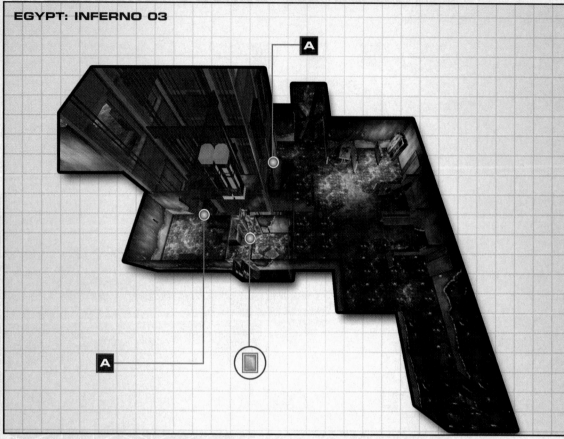

When you reach the next room, immediately crouch and take cover behind the wall in front of you to eliminate soldiers. Once the coast is clear, head right to **find an electrical-arc switch ⑤**. Clear the other end of enemies first, then have one team member hold the switch while the other crosses; repeat on the other side so the second team member can cross.

Go through the blown-open wall, then rappel up two levels to a room **featuring a second electrical-arc switch ⑥** and more enemies—including several deadly rocket-launching foes. Take them out first, then clear the rest of the room. When you trigger the electrical-arc switch, watch out for enemies that pop up—let go of the switch once your teammate crosses through so both of you can fire on these soldiers.

WARNING

To avoid the flames in the elevator shafts, rappel to the left or right edge of the shaft—don't go straight down the middle.

Once past the second electrical-arc switch, look for **two open elevator shafts side by side ⑦**. You'll have a choice: split up or both head either left or right. Rather than split up your firepower, stay together. The best choice is for both team members to go right—the left

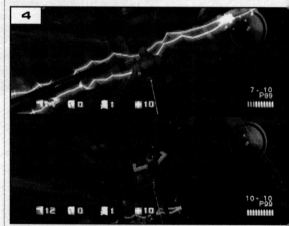

EGYPT: INFERNO 04

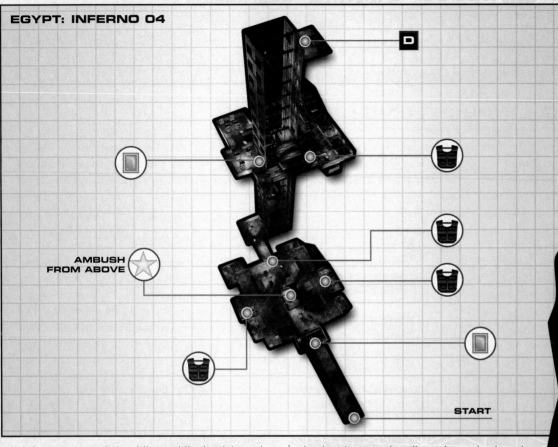

D

AMBUSH FROM ABOVE

START

MULTIPLAYER

path features Nano Suit soldiers, while the right path features conventional soldiers (but more of them). At the bottom of the shaft, each team member should hide behind the elevator doorway and dispatch all enemies in his line of sight.

Proceed down the stairs to find a room with glowing blue lights and a **double door switch that leads to the bottom level 8**. However, don't go through just yet. Pass the door and employ **Thermovision to see the hiding Nano Suit soldiers 9**: They'll be guarding an armor vest that's worth fighting for. Rappel down once

the door is opened to dispatch a rocket launcher (as well as meet a friend).

When you reach the bottom level, get ready to enter a large room filled with Nano Suit soldiers. You'll have to employ Thermovision again to see and attack these enemies. Stay to the outside edges of this large room, because in the middle is a major ambush point: A ring of enemies will fire on you from the upper level if you drift into the middle. You'll be able to **find three armor vests along the outside edge 10**: one as you enter the room and one more on each side.

If you have time, try to knock out the ring of enemies on the upper level (to dispatch all enemies in this mission), but you can avoid them altogether by reaching the large door switch at the end of this room if time's running short. Press and hold the switch to open the blast doors and complete your mission.

TIP

Look for a surprise in one of the elevator shafts near the end of the mission—it'll go by quickly, so keep your eyes peeled!

 7
 8
 9
 10

FOR YOUR EYES ONLY

APPENDIX

EVERYTHING OR NOTHING: SECRETS

Everything or Nothing has plenty of unlockable bonuses and extras for players willing to go above and beyond the call of duty on behalf of James Bond. At the Mission Select screen, you can view a list of "unlocks" that catalog the gadgets, rewards, and cheats you've been rewarded—the ones you haven't yet unlocked will remain darkened so you'll know what you're missing. Consult the appendix for a complete list of the following items and their individual requirements.

REWARDS

Rewards are unlocked depending on how many gold 007s you've earned. They include everything from bonus artwork and alternate character outfits to hidden levels. While viewing a reward, press the action button to activate or deactivate it.

GADGETS

Gadgets are unlocked after you beat certain missions on any difficulty setting. Press the action button to hear Q give you a description of the device.

CHEATS

Cheats are unlocked depending on how many platinum 007s you've earned. Cheats are power-ups and hidden weapons (such as the legendary Golden Gun) that'll make it easier to complete a mission. To activate a cheat once it is unlocked, pause the game during any mission and enter the code listed underneath the cheat. A tone will play to confirm it has been activated. **Check your status after unpausing to see your cheat!** ❶

1

TIP

It's important to note that using a cheat (or cheats) nullifies your score for that mission. Therefore, you cannot use a cheat to unlock the next mission or earn any medals. In addition, cheat codes do not actually work until earned and saved to a memory card or your hard drive, and they do not work in multiplayer game modes.

BONUS MISSIONS: SINGLE PLAYER

The rewards in single-player games include several extra missions. Here's a quick description of each one and how to unlock it.

BONUS MISSION: UNDERWORLD

LEVEL ICON

How to unlock: Earn 11 gold 007 medals.
The optional Underworld mission takes place between The Kiss Kiss Club and Death's Door. In this mission, **Bond navigates the tunnels that connect Yayakov's club with the graveyard** ❷.

2

BONUS MISSION: MI6 COMBAT SIMULATOR

LEVEL ICON

How to unlock: Complete the game at any difficulty level.
The MI6 Combat Simulator is a level-based skill test in the MI6 VR training system. **Survive as many rounds as you can, and defeat all enemies to advance to the next round ❸**. Each new round will spawn a new wave of VR enemies, and their tactics will evolve mission by mission (some enemies can be dispatched only using hand-to-hand combat). There are 50 rounds total, and the fiftieth round will spawn enemies endlessly.

BONUS MISSION: MI6 SURVIVAL TEST

LEVEL ICON

How to unlock: Complete the game at any difficulty level.
The MI6 Survival Test is similar to the Combat Simulator, but the goal is to survive as long as you can ❹. VR enemies will continue to spawn endlessly until your health goes down to zero. You rack up points depending on how many enemies you dispatch.

BONUS MISSION: GALLERY

LEVEL ICON

How to unlock: Get 27 gold 007s.
Earning gold on all missions will unlock the gallery, **a multilevel art museum filled with production assets from the game ❺**. Hung on the walls are concept artworks from all parts of development, and key props from the game are displayed under glass (including Jaws's teeth, Yayakov's metal hand, and so forth). Each chamber is built around statues of the game's main characters. Players are free to wander the gallery and look around to their hearts' content.

TIP

On the MI6 Combat Simulator mission, look for the armor vest atop the area at each level; to grab it, head to the top floor and walk across a very thin walkway.

MULTIPLAYER MODE

There is a separate Unlocks screen in multiplayer mode, which you can access on the level-select screen. It is similar in format to the single player Unlocks menu: Items you've earned are in full color, items you haven't are darkened. Multiplayer rewards include hidden arena levels and bonus characters (from the game as well as from previous Bond movies). (A complete list is in the appendix, and detailed descriptions of the hidden arena levels are in the multiplayer strategy section.) To unlock these rewards, you must play the multiplayer missions and complete objectives successfully. Each successful mission objective will earn you 10 points.

GAME ENDING: SINGLE PLAYER

Beating the final *Everything or Nothing* mission will trigger an **ending cinema featuring Serena and James ❻**. After that, the credits will roll. When they're over, a **special "behind the scenes" video featuring the cast from the game will play (❼ - ❾)**.

Shannon Elizabeth

Willem Dafoe

DATA TABLES

For all you tables-of-data junkies, did you think we forgot you? The following tables offer all the crucial stats for the various areas of the game.

NOTE: The target time for a level is for scoring purposes only; you usually do not have to beat this time to complete a mission.

LEVEL	GOLD PTS. TARGET	PLATINUM REQUIREMENT (OO AGENT)	TARGET TIME*
Ground Zero	75,000	Complete mission taking 500 pts. damage or less	1:30
A Long Way Down	90,000	Complete mission in 3:30 or less	3:00
Train Chase	150,000	Complete mission in 2:10 or less	3:15
An Old Friend	125,000	Complete mission without taking any damage	1:00
Sand Storm	160,000	Destroy general's base in less than 0:45	4:00
Serena St. Germaine	150,000	Reach bottom of fortress in less than 1:55	6:40
Vertigo	150,000	Complete mission in 4:00 or less	4:00
The Ruined Tower	175,000	Fire 10 rounds or less in mission	2:00
Death of an Agent	200,000	Complete mission taking 100 pts. damage or less	2:00
A Show of Force	200,000	Get to extraction point in less than 0:45	5:45
Mardi Gras Mayhem	200,000	Get to van in less than 0:40	8:00
The Kiss Kiss Club	225,000	Complete mission using no ammunition	1:30
Underworld	None	None	2:00
Death's Door	275,000	Complete mission in 3:15 or less	4:30
Battle in the Big Easy	250,000	Get from hideout to compound in less than 0:55	5:00
Faded Splendor	300,000	Complete mission taking 100 pts. damage or less	3:00
The Machinery of Evil	300,000	Fire 10 rounds or less in mission	3:00
The Pontchartrain Bridge	300,000	Complete mission in 3:10 or less	4:15
A Simple Exchange	325,000	Complete mission in 0:40 or less	1:00
Red Line	350,000	Complete mission in 4:50 or less	5:20
Ambushed!	350,000	Complete mission using no ammunition	2:00
The High Road	300,000	After reaching demolished mine entrance, get to mine in less than 1:20	3:45
Diavolo's Plan	375,000	Complete mission in 3:00 or less	6:00
The Platinum War	400,000	From start of mission, neutralize bomb in 2:15 or less	4:40
Dangerous Descent	300,000	Complete mission taking 100 pts. damage or less	6:00
Red Underground	425,000	Fire 10 rounds or less in mission	6:00
The Final Card	325,000	Complete mission taking 100 damage or less	6:00
Everything or Nothing	450,000	Complete mission in 5:00 or less	6:00

CHEAT	HOW TO UNLOCK	DESCRIPTION
Golden Gun	Earn 1 platinum	Equip Golden Gun during mission
Improved Traction	Earn 3 platinums	Better handling for vehicles
Improved Battery	Earn 5 platinums	Extended battery life
Double Ammo	Earn 7 platinums	Double ammo-carrying capacity
Double Damage	Earn 9 platinums	Cause double damage to enemies
Full Ammo	Earn 11 platinums	Have full ammo supply
Cloak	Earn 13 platinums	Enable cloak function for vehicles
Full Battery	Earn 15 platinums	Have full battery power
All Weapons	Earn 17 platinums	Begin mission with all weapons equipped
Unlimited Battery	Earn 19 platinums	Never run out of battery power
Unlimited Ammo	Earn 23 platinums	Never run out of bullets
Slow Motion Driving	Earn 25 platinums	Drive in slow motion
Platinum Gun	Earn 27 platinums	Equip Platinum Gun during mission

007 nightfire

Keith M. Kolmos / Steve Honeywell

Prima Games
A Division of Random House, Inc.

3000 Lava Ridge Court
Roseville, CA 95661
1-800-733-3000
www.primagames.com

Associate Product Manager: Christy L. Curtis
Project Editor: Matt Sumpter
Design and Layout: Simon Olney, Derek Hocking

ISBN: 0-7615-3998-0
Library of Congress Catalog Card Number: 2002114074
Printed in the United States of America

02 03 04 05 GG 10 9 8 7 6 5 4 3 2 1

Contents

Introduction

Welcome to Prima's Official Strategy guide for the latest Bond experience: *007 NightFire*. In this adventure, the Americans have lost a key component to their new Space Weapons Platform, and it is up to NATO to help recover it before it falls into the wrong hands. MI6 believes that noted green industrialist Rafael Drake is behind the plot and have assigned 007 to the task. Drake's company, Phoenix International, works on decommissioning the nuclear weapons arsenal of the world's superpowers and closing old nuclear power plants. Could it be possible that this noted philanthropist is behind the theft of the missing computer chip? Bond will bounce across the globe as he puts the pieces together in an attempt to unravel the plot, and this guide will lead you along.

Bond is back, and he'll be traveling the world. From a castle in Austria...

...to a corporate office building in Japan...

...to a decommissioned nuclear power plant...

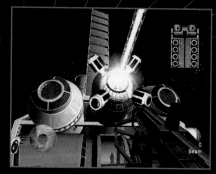

...and even into outer space. *007 NightFire: Prima's Official Strategy Guide* has got you covered.

How to Use This Guide

Although the basic plot is the same, the console and PC versions of the game are drastically different. Don't worry, though; *007 NightFire: Prima's Official Strategy Guide* has the tips and walkthroughs you need to beat both versions of the game.

The next section introduces all of the characters. You'll meet Agent Nightshade, Dominique Paradis, Q, Armitage Rook, and all the rest. We give you a breakdown of all the cool weapons and gadgets you get to use in the game. We cover basic gameplay tips that will help you in your adventures as James Bond; you'll learn how to stun guards and sneak around to accomplish your mission. The walkthroughs are specific to the version of the game you are playing. If you are playing on a gaming console, check out the first walkthrough; there are maps, tips, and strategies for completing the mission. If you are playing on a PC, turn to beyond that, where every part of the PC mission is explained in great detail. Finally, turn to the last section to discover all the multiplayer basics.

Characters

The Good Guys

James Bond

James Bond, also known as 007, is the premier agent for MI6, the British intelligence agency. Known for his quick wit and astounding abilities, Bond is regularly assigned the most difficult situations. He has never let MI6 down. As a OO agent, Bond has a license to kill anyone and anything that stands in the way of completing his assignments.

M

M is the current head of MI6. For security reasons, her identity is known to a select few. You receive most of your mission objectives directly from M, and her guidance will take you through many of your missions. Always pay attention to anything M tells you.

Q

Q is shorthand for "Quartermaster." A gadget guru, Q is legendary in MI6 for the many unique items he has developed for agents. Most of Q's ingenious items are disguised as something else, allowing them to be used in plain view of others. See the next chapter for the latest goodies Q has cooked up for you.

Zoe Nightshade

CIA agent Zoe Nightshade is a rising talent in the American equivalent of MI6. She has been paired with Bond before, and is most noted for her driving skills. Agent Nightshade's assistance will be critical to the success of your first missions.

Dominique Paradis

A French agent, Dominique Paradis is a top undercover agent as well as an expert in small arms and explosives. She has been sent to track down a missing nuclear warhead, and has infiltrated Raphael Drake's organization at the highest level. She has access to extensive information about Drake's network.

Alura McCall

Alura McCall is an Australian agent currently on loan to MI6 for the duration of this crisis. Her assistance will be timely and critical. In addition to her knowledge of security systems, Agent McCall is also an expert with a variety of weapons.

The Bad Guys

Raphael Drake

Raphael Drake's possible involvement in the missing US guidance chip and the bomb in Paris is curious because of his high-profile position as the leader of the Phoenix International Corporation. Upon his purchase of the company, Drake turned it from an environmentally-unsound collective into the world's biggest "regeneration" company, cleaning up toxic sites and decommissioning nuclear facilities. However, this position also gives Drake access to a variety of nuclear facilities.

Armitage Rook

The head of Drake's security force, Armitage Rook is a true physical force. His massive physique is exceeded only by his tremendous will to complete any assignment given to him. He will not be an easy man to eliminate.

Alexander Mayhew

Alexander Mayhew is the head of Phoenix International's Japanese concerns. If Phoenix International is up to something, it's a sure bet that Mayhew knows about it and is fully involved. Any information regarding Phoenix International is likely located somewhere in Mayhew's estate outside Tokyo.

Makiko Hayashi

Better known as "Kiko," Hayashi is a dedicated bodyguard completely devoted to Alexander Mayhew. While she appears slight of build, Kiko is deadly and will stop at nothing to protect her employer.

Weapons and Gadgets

Console and PC

These items are found in both versions of *007: NightFire*.

Weapons - Pistols

Kowloon Type 40

More powerful than the P2K, the Kowloon pistol is the weapon of choice for Phoenix International guards and thugs. It offers a high rate of fire for a handgun and has decent accuracy.

Raptor Magnum

This pistol fires a .357 shell, offering premier stopping power in a handgun. Its loud report draws attention, but its raw power tends to rapidly silence that attention.

Machine Guns

SG5 Commando

The Commando offers a decent rate of fire and good power. Its secondary firing mode enables the attached sight and fires quick and accurate three-shot bursts. This weapon features a distinctive laser sight.

Storm 32

This lightweight machine gun offers the best of all worlds. Its high rate of fire allows for serious stopping power, and its virtually silenced firing allows for stealth. This weapon features a secondary firing mode for short accurate bursts.

Explosives

AT-420 Sentinel

There is no better delivery system for high explosives at long range than this micro-missile launcher. Sporting a four-missile clip, the Sentinel can be fired in both unguided and guided modes.

Flash Grenade (Flashbang)

While this explosive causes no physical damage to the target, it does temporarily blind anyone caught in the blast radius. Using this device requires caution, because it is just as likely to blind you as it is your enemies.

Frag Grenade

A standard hand grenade packed with 5,000 steel balls that rocket out at high velocity when the grenade detonates. This weapon features a standard four-second delay, allowing you to hurl it away before detonation.

Laser Trip Bomb

No other device in your arsenal discourages pursuit like these mines. In standard mode, they create a laser light that detonates if crossed. The secondary fire mode is a proximity mine that detonates when anyone walks within range.

Militek Mark 6 MGL

This weapon is a rapid-fire grenade launcher sporting a six-grenade barrel clip. The fragmentation grenades used with this weapon can be fired with pinpoint accuracy and at long range.

Other Weapons

Frinesi Automatic 12

This combat shotgun holds eight rounds. Excellent at close range, the Frinesi can be fired rapidly both in standard or wide-spread modes, allowing either concentrated or wide-radius damage.

Phoenix Samurai

You will use this weapon any time you are wearing a Phoenix International space suit. Unlike other weapons, it does not use standard ammunition, but runs off a battery. It can fire up to 20 shots rapidly, but then requires time to recharge the battery. Its secondary fire mode creates a burst of energy that uses one-fifth of the battery's power.

Gadgets

Decryptor

Your PDA has been updated to include powerful decrypting software capable of breaking any numeric code. You will find this invaluable for breaking into high-security areas.

Laser Watch

Your wristwatch has a small laser device added to it. This can be used to burn through locks and wires. It is not powerful enough to be an effective weapon.

Micro Camera

While it appears to be a normal cigarette lighter, the micro camera is actually a sophisticated device. It takes pictures quickly and accurately.

Q-Specs

For the PC, your specs have three different modes of viewing. You can select from infrared (IR), X-ray, or nightvision modes. IR mode detects heat, allowing you to see enemies in near or total darkness. Nightvision enhances available light, allowing for distinction in low-light areas. X-ray mode allows for vision through walls, flesh, and clothing. For the console, the Q-Specs offer nightvision and thermographic vision. This device has a short battery, but it self-charges.

Q-Worm

Disguised as a credit card, the Q-Worm is actually a sophisticated computer virus that enables Q to monitor any activity on the computer it is placed on. The Q-Worm also gives you limited access to the target computer's controls.

Phoenix Ronin

Disguised as a normal briefcase, the Ronin is an effective backup weapon. In standard mode, it deploys a high-powered autocannon that fires at any detected motion. It can also be detonated to create a huge explosion in a large radius.

Stunner

Disguised as a simple set of car keys, the stunner emits a powerful electrical jolt that incapacitates its victim. This device must recharge after every use.

Console only

These items are found only in the console version of the game.

Weapons - Pistols

Gold P2K

This upgraded 9mm pistol with a 16 shot clip provides a little more punch. The under the barrel laser sight helps improve your aim. It can be silenced, but it will reduce the range and stopping power of your weapon.

Golden Gun

The Golden Gun only has one round in the chamber, but that's all a man with a Golden Gun needs. One shot equals one bad guy eliminated. Take steady aim as the reload process after each shot will slow you down.

Wolfram PP7

Your standard pistol, the Wolfram PP7 comes with a removable silencer that allows covert firing. This weapon is extremely accurate even at long range, which more than makes up for its relatively low power.

much stopping power. The magazine holds 15 rounds and the weapon can be silenced.

Explosives

AIMS-20

The Advanced Individual Munitions System (AIMS) is two weapons in one. In Rifle mode, the AIMS-20 is equipped with a computerized sight. This weapon has excellent accuracy with its 6x telescopic sight. With 30 rounds in the magazine, this weapon carries real stopping power. As a grenade launcher, the AIMS-20 fires explosive grenades from its six-round magazine. These grenades do a ton of damage and will help clear the way in any firefight. The shells can be fired from long range—when you need to reach out and touch someone.

AT-600 Scorpion

The AT-600 Scorpion rocket launcher can fire four rounds from the magazine at a time. This weapon can fire unguided rounds or remote-guided munitions over a long distance. Bond will use the AT-400 to take out Armitage Rook's helicopter in the very first mission–The Exchange.

Remote Mine

This small anti-personnel device can stick to any surface and can be detonated from a remote distance. This weapon is great for taking out patrolling guards if you can tuck it out of view and eliminate unsuspecting guards from a position of relative safety.

Satchel Charge

Need some cover? Throw a smoke grenade into the room to obscure your opponent's vision—but, it will obscure your vision. The bullets will still be flying, but everyone's accuracy will be severally diminished.

Smoke Grenade

Need some cover? Throw a smoke grenade into the room to obscure your opponent's vision—but, it will obscure your vision. The bullets will still be flying, but everyone's accuracy will be severally diminished.

Other Weapons

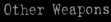
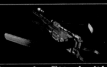

Delta 900X Repeater

This heavy-duty hunting crossbow is made from machined aluminum, reinforced graphite, and magnesium. It can be fitted with a telescopic sight to make it the perfect silent sniping weapon. The weapon does medium damage, but it has a very short range.

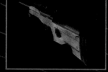

Covert Sniper Rifle

This high-powered sniper rifle is capable of downing an enemy with a single shot. It can be used with our without the free zoom. The Winter Covert Sniper is a bolt-action weapon, which makes for slow recovery between shots. It holds a 10-round clip.

Tactical Sniper Rifle

The Tactical Sniper Rifle is truly a deadly weapon, but its slow reload time can make taking down multiple targets difficult. Use the rifle's telescopic sight with 10x magnification to fire normal and armor piercing rounds.

Gadgets

Korsakov K5

Sometimes non-lethal force is needed when dealing with the enemy goons in NightFire. During the Night Shift mission, gun shots would attract the attention of the other guards. That's when Q Branch saves the day with the Korsakov K5 Dart Gun. Guards will be out for about two minutes.

Shaver

The Shaver Stun Grenade can be used to disrupt enemies and incapacitate them. A great tactic is to toss a stun grenade into a room and then hop outside. Once the Shaver Stun Grenade has detonated, head back into the room and the guards incapacitated from the bang.

PC only

These items are PC specific.

Weapons - Pistols

Wolfram P2K

Your standard pistol, the Wolfram P2K comes with a removable silencer that allows covert firing. This weapon is extremely accurate even at long range, which more than makes up for its relatively low power.

Machine Guns

Munitions Belga PDW90

Light, fast, and accurate, the Belga PDW90 is the true leader in machine guns. The top-mounted clip allows for rapid reloading, and its stopping power is second to none. This weapon holds a 50-round clip.

Phoenix International X6 Annihilator

An experimental weapon designed for use by Phoenix International commandos, the Annihilator is essentially a minigun that spits high-velocity shells at a tremendous rate. It is difficult to fire accurately because of the tremendous kick. Like the Commando, it features a laser sight. The minigun holds a 100-round clip, but takes a long time to reload.

Gadgets

Dart Pen

This fountain pen appears ordinary, but the tip can be fired with high accuracy. When it strikes a target, it injects a sleep toxin that knocks out the victim for a time. This gadget is prized for its ability to take down a target with a single hit and without attracting attention.

Vehicles (Console only)

V-12 Vanquish

The V-12 Vanquish is Bond's preferred choice for getting around town. Loaded with gadgets from Q Branch, such as Q-Missiles, machine guns, Q-Smoke, Q-Pulse, and Q-Charge, the Vanquish is definitely a deadly weapon. On the Deep Descent mission, you will learn that the Vanquish can even double as a submarine!

Armored Snowmobiles

As Bond escapes from the Castle, he will need to fight from the back of an armored snowmobile. This arctic titan packs one heck of a punch with dual rocket launchers and dual machine guns. Let the enemy have it when you are getting out of town in the Alpine Ambush mission.

Security SUV

In the Island Infiltration mission, Bond and McCall do battle from a stolen Phoenix Security armored SUV. This off-road vehicle has a pair of missile launchers and a mounted machine gun turret to take out the enemy.

Ultralight

In Island Infiltration, Bond will get to man the guns while McCall flies this ultralight. The small plane has dual small pulse cannons and dual missile launchers. As you dart through the canyons, you will have to shoot it out with boats in the river, other ultralights in the air, and armored SUVs that patrol the banks of the river.

Offense

Shooting Basics

Anybody can pull the trigger of a weapon. Not everybody can do it efficiently, hitting for maximum effect with minimum ammunition. There are a few tricks that can help you get the most out of your weapons.

Attack with the element of surprise. When your enemies aren't aware of you, your shots are more effective. You'll be able to squeeze off multiple shots before they react. Generally, this means you can drop an enemy before retaliation is possible.

Aim for vital areas. Just as in real life, bullets that hit vital body areas do more damage. An enemy can take a lot of damage to an arm or a leg, but can't handle much to the more vital parts of the body.

Use the right weapon for the job at hand. Each weapon at your disposal has a particular strength and weakness. Pistols, for instance, are extremely accurate, even over long distances. But the P2K and Kowloon lack power, and all three pistols have very small magazines, requiring that you reload frequently. These weapons are great for one-on-one battles but are a poor choice when confronted with large groups. Conversely, the Annihilator minigun causes havoc, but is hard to aim accurately and takes forever to reload. It's great for groups of tough enemies, but almost worthless at range.

TIP

If you have several appropriate weapons on hand, use the same type your enemies are using. This way, you'll be able to collect ammunition after the battle, keeping your own supply of ordnance maximized. Some weapons share ammo types, so know what you are firing!

group of Yakuza, and seeing only five bullets remaining in your Commando. This doesn't mean that you should reload each time an enemy goes down. Simply put, when the smoke clears, make sure your weapon is fully ready for the next combat.

Watch where you aim. An enemy can take a lot of shots to the arms, legs, and midsection. Aim for more vital areas.

Subdue, Don't Slay

At the end of a mission, you get a bonus for every enemy taken out of combat. You get a larger bonus per enemy if you simply disable them instead of eliminating them completely. Using your fists, the stunner, the dart gun, and the dart pen (the dart pen is only in the PC version) will help increase your end-of-mission score dramatically. If you are very sneaky and can get behind enemies, virtually all of them will surrender when you approach them. This gives you a perfect opportunity to knock them unconscious, preventing them from attacking you, and contributing to a higher mission score.

Stunning your opponents gains you a higher score at the end of the mission. Use your fists, the stunner, and the dart pen (on the PC) to subdue your enemies.

Defense

Walk, Don't Run

Running gets you from place to place quickly, but it also makes a lot of noise. If enemies are nearby, running alerts them to your presence, making it more likely they'll spot you and fill you full of holes. You can always walk. While this does reduce your speed by about half, it also cuts the amount of noise you make dramatically. If you are particularly cautious, you can often ignore enemies completely, slipping past without having to take them down.

Crouch

When you crouch, it becomes difficult to move quickly. However, it also makes you tough to see. Whenever there is any sort of cover, be it a desk, a crate, or a low wall, crouching makes you all but immune to taking damage from your enemies.

Crouch to gain some cover. When you need to reload or when you are simply trying to be sneaky, crouch down behind any cover that you can find.

Lean Into It (PC only)

You can often spot action ahead by leaning around corners. When you lean, you are still virtually invisible to your enemies. They won't spot you even if it looks like they are looking at you.

Not only does this allow you to look ahead at where you will be going, but it also gives you the chance to eliminate enemies before they get a chance to shoot at you. Whenever you have the option, lean around corners and obstacles. Use the Q-Specs at the same time, and you can really check out the area ahead.

Other Advice

Choose Your Weapons (PC only)

You can carry up to four different weapons at any one time, which means that you will need to make some choices. In this case, fragmentation grenades, flash grenades, laser tripwires, and Ronin Suitcases do not count as weapons. Everything else does: all three pistols, all four machine guns, the sniper rifle, shotgun, rocket launcher, and grenade launcher.

A good guideline is to carry a pistol (for accuracy), a machine gun (for powerful or grouped enemies), an explosive device (usually the rocket launcher), and any other weapon of your choice.

Also, when offered the chance to pick up a new weapon, look through your current weapons. If you have a weapon that is out of ammunition or virtually so, ditch it in favor of the new weapon. This is especially true of new weapons that are carried by the majority of your enemies, because you will have a ready source of ammunition for them.

Using the Q-Specs

Your Q-Specs are an easily overlooked tool. Used properly, they can be as powerful as any weapon in your arsenal. They can help you pinpoint enemies in the dark, see through walls to scout ahead, or see in near-total darkness.

True, you can't wear them constantly because the battery doesn't last too long. But you should use them before walking into a new area. Lean out and put on the Q-Specs to look ahead. They recharge quickly, allowing you to use them frequently.

They are particularly effective when paired with the sniper rifle, the Commando's secondary firing option, or the P2K.

Your Q-Specs are a great addition to your list of gadgets. You can see enemies through walls...

...or see laser tripwires before you stumble into them.

Strafing

You have been sneaking around, moving through ventilation shafts, and staying one step ahead of the Drake's security forces. Sometimes you have to shoot it out with the enemy.

How can you hit the target if you are moving around? Strafe. Use the controls on your controller or keyboard to move in one direction while you keep the weapon trained on the target. Strafing will be a big help in multiplayer, as eliminating smarter and unpredictable human opponents is a trickier task.

Walking into a firefight and going toe-to-toe with the enemy is never a good idea, so is standing in one spot—it gives your foes too easy of a target. If you can keep moving, you have a good chance of avoiding the hail of bullets and keep Bond alive.

Be Bond

You'll notice that one of your scores at the end of the mission is for Bond moves. We've gone through and detailed all of these special moves in the guide so you can earn the extra points, but being Bond isn't just about accomplishing these moves in the mission. You'll have a lot more fun playing the game, and become much more involved in the world of Bond, if you try to think like Bond does. Don't go charging into the room guns blazing. Look for the ventilation shafts to gain access to the next room and sneak around to accomplish your mission objectives. Be Bond, the best 00 Agent in the world.

Console Walkthrough—Paris Prelude

It's a few minutes before midnight on New Year's Eve and 007 is on the case. French Intelligence Officer Dominique Paradis is being chased through the streets of Paris as she pursues evil-doers who are trying to deliver a bomb to the Eiffel Tower. MI6 has sent its number-one agent, James Bond, to help Dominique and prevent the bomb from going off.

   This mission serves as a quick primer to some of the controls and introduces you to some of the game's basic strategies and tactics. Get ready Bond, the fate of the world is once again in your hands.

Dominique Paradise is being chased through the streets of Paris a few minutes before midnight on New Year's Eve. Never fear, Bond is rushing to the rescue.

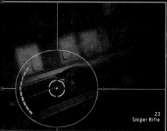

The mission starts with two cars chasing Dominique, guns blazing. Shoot the front tire of the lead car with the sniper rifle. The car spins out of control and takes the second car with it.

The path looks clear until another pursuer joins the chase. Shoot the enemy popping out of the sunroof. A couple of shots into the gas tank explodes the car, eliminating another of Dominique's tormentors.

There isn't anything to shoot for a while as the helicopter swings around to get ahead of Dominique. Take aim for a long-distance shot at another car with your sniper rifle. Shoot at the gas tank to take out this attacker.

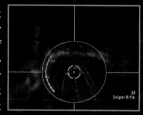

The helicopter swings around again and Dominique's car jumps via a construction ramp. Shoot out the blue clasp holding the ramp in place. The bad guys fall to their doom.

This triggers a cutscene showing Bond picking up Dominique in the helicopter. Q drives Bond's trusted Aston Martin V-12 Vanquish via remote control to their position. Once you control the Vanquish, use the Q-Smoke to take out two pursuers and chase the truck with the bomb.

You race through the streets of Paris in pursuit of the truck carrying the bomb. As targets pop up along the way, use the Vanquish's missiles to take them out. Wait for the targeting icons to turn from white to red before you fire. Along the way, traffic pushes the Vanquish onto side streets and through outdoor cafes. Avoid the pedestrians.

As you race through the streets, watch out for the enemies' fire. Slow down to let enemies pass you by, then engage them with your missiles.

As you approach the bomb-carrying truck, Q activates the Q-Pulse of your Vanquish. Fire the gadget to take out the truck. It veers off into the river, and the crisis is averted. There is plenty of time left for Bond and Dominique to enjoy a glass of champagne at midnight.

The Exchange

Mission Briefing

Good evening, 007. A redesigned piece of missile guidance hardware intended for the orbiting US Space Weapons Platform has been stolen. NATO has advised that recovery is critical—should an unfriendly power "reverse engineer" this device, the platform's global defense capabilities would be compromised. Recent intelligence implicates Rafael Drake in the theft. It's hard to believe, as Drake is a respected "green" industrialist, whose company, Phoenix International, dismantles obsolete atomic reactors and decommissions nuclear arsenals. An allied agent planted in Drake's organization reports that Alexander Mayhew, a British expatriate who heads Phoenix's Japanese branch, is en route to Drake's castle in Austria. The stolen guidance device will change hands tonight, during a formal gathering at the castle. Drake's security teams are hardened men—as a OO Agent, you may have to answer aggression with aggression. Good luck, Bond.

To reach the castle undetected, Bond performs a 30,000 foot HALO (High Altitude Low Opening) parachute drop.

The Americans have lost a critical piece to their new Space Weapons Platform. Recovering it sounds like a perfect job for your favorite OO Agent.

Penetrate the defenses surrounding Drake's castle to recover the device.

Once you land on the small rampart, the cutscene ends and the mission begins. Your first task is to breach the castle's walls and enter the party undetected.

OBJECTIVES

- **Breach castle walls.**
- **Find a way inside to the party.**
- **Rendezvous with undercover agents.**
- **Spy on the secret meeting.**
- **Retrieve guidance chip from "safe room".**
- **Escape with Zoe in gondola.**

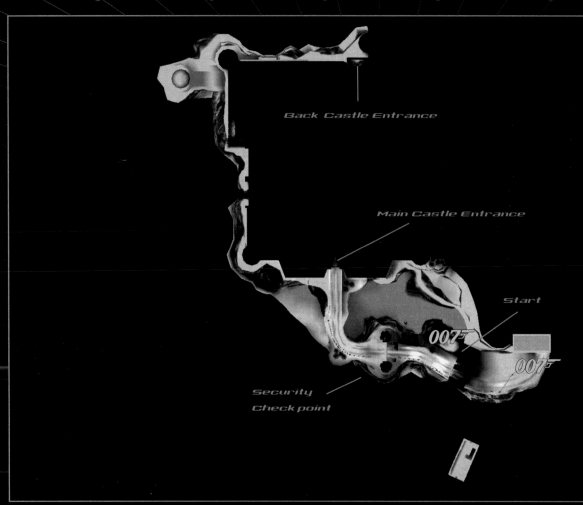

Back Castle Entrance

Main Castle Entrance

Start

007

007

Security
Check point

You gain control
of Bond on this
narrow bridge.
The castle lies just
up the road, but
which is the best
way in?

Or you could shoot
this guard here.
Your silenced
Wolfram PP7 has
enough punch to
take the guard
down with a couple
of shots. Taking
him out gains you
a sniper rifle.

You could take
these stairs that
lead down to
the road.

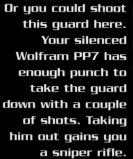

But the best way
to get into the
castle is via the
truck coming down
the road. Wait for
it to a stop, then
jump from atop the
ledge along the
bridge.

The Exchange

TIP

Sneak up on the guards and make them surrender for bonus points. Approach them with your gun out, then puit away when they surrender and knock them out.

Bond Move #1

Jump into the truck. Once you land in the truck, crouch down to prevent the guards from seeing you; ride the whole way to earn the Bond move.

Ride in the back of the truck. The truck stops at a security checkpoint. If you stay crouched down, the guards won't spot you.

Bond Move #2 *Alternate Route*

You can ride the car all the way into the castle and navigate the courtyards into the party. There are armor pickups and a 007 icon for the taking if you go in that way. Be careful; there are guards all over the place, and it is definitely a more arduous road to take. If you decide to go through the main door of the castle and head in through the courtyards, you can make your route a little bit easier. In the guard room, there is an electrical panel with a green wire. Use the laser to cut the green wire only. This will kill the power to the searchlights, giving Bond more shadows to move in as you make your way into the party.

Once you're past the security checkpoint—where the driver told the guards he was delivering wine to the party—wait for the truck to turn right. Jump out of the back of the truck and hurry down the short path. It's possible to ride the truck all the way to the castle and go through the front door, but getting into the party is difficult and you'll forfeit the opportunity for a Bond move.

As you approach the small ledge, a short cutscene is triggered. Everything is going fine until the snow crumbles beneath you, alerting the guards above. Lucky for you the guards don't look in your direction. Once you have control of Bond again, head left along the ledge.

Walk along the castle's outer ledge. There's no point in keeping your gun out—you won't encounter any guards.

As you continue along the castle's exterior, watch your step! One wrong move and Bond will be history.

When you reach this part of the castle, an action icon appears in the screen's upper right. Use the pole to reach the other side of the crevice.

 Once you have gotten past the windows, follow along the edge of the castle until you reach the second crevice. There is no pipe to climb along this time.

Bond Move #3

Lucky for you, Q branch has equipped you with a grapple. Select the grapple and use it to swing from the hook attached to the castle walls.

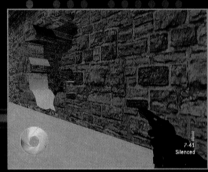

As you round this corner, you approach the next Bond move. You must sneak past three windows. Two guards patrol inside the castle right next to these windows. You have to time your movement just right—if one of the guards inside sees you, he will sound the alarm. Wait at the first window for a while to notice the guards' pattern. Wait for them to walk away from the window, but wait another fraction of a second after they disappear from sight. If you move too soon, the guards will spot you and trip the alarm. If you get past the three windows without being spotted, you earn another Bond move.

Ah-ha! You have found the back way in. If you tripped the alarm at any point along the way, two guards await in this room, so be ready.

Go through the hole in the wall and up the staircase.

Head over to the wall and stay out of the searchlights. If a guard sees you, he will raise the alarm and you will have to shoot your way into the castle.

When you approach the door at the top of the stairs, equip your stunner. This Q-gadget is handy once you open the door.

Once you're through the door, run.

Move over toward the archway on your left. Watch out for the guard who patrols the area on the other side. Wait for him to start walking away from you, then move in. Use the stunner if you want, or ignore him and head to the party.

You need to cover the distance between the doors—a guard is coming up on one of his patrols. Use the stunner to knock the guard out.

CAUTION
On Agent and OO difficulty, watch out for the sniper above this guard.

Blend in with the crowd inside the castle. The guards will notice if you have your gun out.

Head down the stairs to the door at the bottom. When you approach the door, you hear voices. Be on your toes—the castle is crawling with guards.

15

Start

007

Library

Armor

007

Introducing Kiko

Later on in the game, you will formally meet Kiko Hayashi, Mayhew's trusted assistant and bodyguard—but you can run into her here at the party. She's the stunning woman in the red dress in the gallery. Walk up to her and wait for a moment to trigger a quick cutscene of the exchange between Kiko and Bond.

Head back down the stairs and over to the library. There you run into Dominique, the French agent you previously rescued. She has infiltrated Drake's organization and has been getting information about his operations.

Head through the gallery and over to the staircase. You need to enter the library, but you can't until the guards move away from the library door. Climb the staircase and go through the door to trigger a short cutscene. This gets the guards and the rest

Before you leave the room, pick up the armor on the table. You need all the protection you can get for an upcoming firefight.

of the party guests over to the salon so you can enter the library.

Now that the guidance chip has changed hands, you'll have to recover the device from the safe.

When you encounter the first guard, he knows a fight is coming. Once the firefight is over, take all of the ammunition and weapons the guards dropped. The Kowloon Type 40 has a bit more punch than your Wolfram PP7 and can fire in a three-round-burst mode.

TIP

Slide into view, take a couple of quick shots and then slide out of view. Watch your ammunition. The clip in your Wolfram PP7 holds only seven shots. You don't want to reload with guards shooting at you, so retreat behind the door when your clip is about to run out.

Move to the window at the end of the corridor and head outside. Equip your Wolfram PP7 and get ready to take down a couple of bad guys.

Slowly approach the edge and make sure you have a full clip. Wait for your targeting icon to lock on to one of the two guards below. Once you are in range, take three quick shots to put down the first guard. Quickly change aim to eliminate the second guard.

When you approach this door, be ready for another firefight. More guards are on the other side. Use the same tactic as before—retreat behind the door when you need to reload.

Bond Move #4

Once the two guards are eliminated, move over to the high wire and jump up to it. Bond swings down to the ledge where the two guards were standing. This triggers the final Bond move. Congratulations 007.

Climb this staircase and open the door at the top. When you go through the door, you observe the exchange between Mayhew and Drake.

Gondola

007

007 Start

Armor

Safe Room

Armor

When you move through the door, depending how the fire fight went, there might be another guard or two inside.

At the first landing is a door with a security lock. Open the control panel for the lock and use the laser to destroy the circuit. When the circuit board is destroyed, the door opens.

Recover the Deutsche M9K machine guns the two guards were carrying. Slowly approach the edge of the ledge you are standing on. Several guards are below. Take them down with a few quick bursts from the Deutsche M9K.

Picked Up 12x 9mm Rounds

Once the guards are out of the way, jump down onto the awning and from there to the ground. Pick up the ammunition and weapons from the ground and move over to the door.

CAUTION

Stand off to the side when you use the laser.

Ready the Deutsche M9K and take down the two guards inside. Strafe left to shoot, then strafe right to take cover to reload and to avoid the hail of bullets.

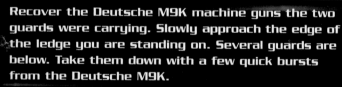

18

Once the guards have been eliminated, use the laser to take out the hinges on the safe. The AT-420 Sentinel rocket launcher and the guidance chip are inside. Take both items.

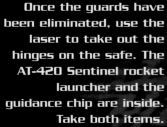

Before you leave the room, take the body armor at the foot of the bed.

With the guidance chip in hand, it's time to meet Agent Nightshade at the gondola and escape. Head back down the stairs and out the door. Enter the gondola building and immediately go down the stairs to the gondola.

NOTE

If your body armor is low, pick some up from in front of the gondola. Be wary—this gives guards time to catch up to you and you'll have another shoot-out on your hands.

Enter the gondola where Agent Nightshade awaits. Once inside, shoot out all of the windows.

When the helicopter appears, use the AT-420 Sentinel to take it out. After you fire the missile, guide it to the target. Normally it takes several shots to bring the helicopter down, but aim for the tail rotors. They are more vulnerable to damage. Agent Nightshade tries to pin down the guards that appear back at the gondola station, but she might need a hand while you work on the helicopters. Fire a missile back at the control station and the explosion takes out any pesky guards.

TIP

Shoot missiles at the helicopter through the skylight; this will give you the best angle and the best protection from the helicopter's machine gun.

After the final shot, the helicopter starts its descent. It looks like Armitage Rook—the burly security guard you ran into at the party and the helicopter pilot—is out of the picture, or is he?

19

Mission Briefing

No lengthy mission briefing is needed for this adventure. You are on the run as you escape the castle where you stole the secret guidance chip. As Bond and Agent Nightshade flee the compound, they come across the guards' motor pool. Several armored snowmobiles here are the perfect way for Bond to escape. In this mission, Agent Nightshade drives while Bond shoots. Listen to Agent Nightshade as she calls out where the enemy attackers are coming from.

As Bond and Agent Nightshade flee the castle, they stumble upon the guards' motorpool, with several armored snowmobiles.

To limit the number of attackers in pursuit, Bond sets the timer on an explosive. Nightshade must start the snowmobile's motor.

Agent Nightshade drives while you man the weapons. Listen to Agent Nightshade, as she announces the direction the attackers come from.

You drive, I'll shoot.

OBJECTIVES
- *Escape from Drake's castle compound.*

As Agent Night-shade starts the engine, several guards attack. Take them out quickly.

More guards appear as you progress.

NOTE
You can run out of ammunition, so don't keep the guns blazing—your accuracy will be low and your score will suffer.

Bond Move #1

During the firefight, the gondola Bond escaped in at the end of the previous mission slides into the scene along the right. Aim at the gondola's top, where it attaches to the suspended cables. This drops the gondola onto the attacking guards below and earns you your first Bond move.

Bond Move #2

Guards come from behind the large fuel tank on the left. Shoot out the fuel tank—aim at the light blue square on the left—it explodes. This earns the level's second Bond move.

Several more guards attack as you and Agent Nightshade attempt to escape. Shoot them or the fuel barrels they are standing next to. Agent Nightshade eventually gets the snowmobile started and you barely escape.

Rotate your JL-7 machine guns to face the direction Agent Nightshade is driving. Ahead on the right is a small encampment of guards. Shoot out the fuel barrels next to them to get rid of them.

Bond Move #3

As you approach the second encampment, shoot at the fuel barrels at the base of the lookout tower. The tower comes tumbling down, earning your third Bond move.

Several snowmobiles are chasing you now. Listen to Agent Nightshade as she tells you what direction they are coming from. Try to shoot at the gunner at the rear, rather than at the driver or at the snowmobile itself. If you can take out the gunner, you can move on to another target.

Bond Move #4

As you deal with the guards on the snowmobiles, Agent Nightshade calls out "They're up ahead." That is your cue. A van is crossing a bridge that has a sewer pipe running underneath it. Shoot out the grate covering the sewer pipe for the fourth Bond move.

Deal with the guards on the ground. Two on the left come out, then two on the right, then one more on the left.

Next comes a game of chicken with a guard on a snowmobile. Fire rockets as he zooms past.

Now it's a straight shot to another cutscene. The guards have blocked the path and Bond has to fight it out.

As you approach the large swinging doors, take out the guards up top first. Their missiles do a ton of damage. Keep the guns on them until they are no longer a threat.

Bond Move #5

You could deal with each guard individually, but here's a simpler way. Switch to the missile launcher and fire a volley into the doors. The explosion removes the obstacle and allows you to progress. But that's not exactly the Bond way. To earn another Bond move, shoot the control panel next to the door before it closes. If you can do this in time, the doors stay open and your snowmobile simply cruises right on through.

Of course, you could shoot the door out with the missile first, to avoid dealing with the guards. If you take too long, the helicopter approaches from behind and one of its stray missiles blows up the doors, but on harder levels this missile blows up Bond.

Once out of the chalet, you have a couple more snowmobiles to deal with. Watch out for the very last one. He's shooting missiles that do a ton of damage. Lucky for you the helicopter gunner winds up hitting his own guys accidentally when he's firing at you.

Once you're past the doors, you have a short ride with the helicopter hot on your heels. Eventually you stumble upon this little chalet. Going around it would be the logical thing—but this is Bond.

After evading the last snowmobile, you trigger the last cutscene. Bond and Agent Nightshade race down a small cave and jump through the pursuing helicopter. Way to go Bond, the second mission is over.

Enemies Vanquished

Mission Briefing

After a long night of rest and relaxation, Bond and Agent Nightshade are ready to leave, but Drake's men have other ideas. It's up to Bond and his trusty Aston Martin V-12 Vanquish to save the day. You have limited time to get to the rendezvous with Q. The local authorities don't take kindly to a high-speed chase running through their town, so watch out for the police. Because you are one of the good guys, you can't shoot at the police. Use your non-lethal weapons to take care of your pursuers and earn some Bond moves.

OBJECTIVES

- Avoid civilian casualties.
- Evade local police using non-lethal means.

As you drive your Vanquish down the streets, watch out for the armored snowmobiles giving chase.

Wait for the targeting icons to turn from white to red before you fire your missiles.

Be careful with your missile usage. There are a limited number of missiles scattered along the roadside.

After you deal with the first police car, a vehicle filled with Drake's goons pulls out in front of you. Put a couple of missiles into the car and move on.

As you approach the first turn, you will see a billboard along the right side of the road. A police officer waits for you there. Don't shoot at him! He's one of the good guys.

Eventually, you come along a bend in the road. Two shooters are on either side of a staircase leading to a row of shops. Take out the shooters with a couple of missiles and drive your Vanquish up the stairs.

Bond Move #1

After the police begin chasing, M lets you know that the Q-Smoke on your V-12 Vanquish have become available. Lay down a cloud of smoke to earn the first Bond move of this mission.

Bond Move #2

Jump your Vanquish over the railing at the end of the row of shops. This slick little move will earn you your second Bond move of the mission. Be careful when your car hits the ground; there are tons of pedestrians, lamps, and benches in the square below.

Two more cars join the pursuit. Hit them with a couple of quick missiles.

When you land in the square, you can drive through the restaurant at the far end. When you emerge on the other side, you rejoin the main road.

Bond Move #3

Another police officer waits for you at this turn. Get ahead of him and use your Q-Smoke to elude pursuit.

Shoot out the cars filled with Drake's goons as you rejoin the road.

You are almost home free when you reach this tunnel. Stick to the middle of the road and get ready to make a sharp turn.

When you see this sign on the road, get over along the right shoulder; there is a crate filled with missiles that you can pick up here.

CAUTION
Keep your speed up! You have to make a jump up ahead.

When you emerge from the end of the tunnel, you see a large police barricade blocking the road. Cut the wheels sharply to head down the side road just in front of the barricade. Pick up the armor waiting for you in the middle of this road. After a few moments, a cutscene triggers and shows you jumping over the bridge.

Eventually, you reach the extraction point. Several helicopters and armored snowmobiles wait for you there. Take them out quickly; time is running out.

Several more armored snowmobiles pop up along your path. Try to conserve your missiles at this point by switching to the Vanquish's machine guns. Keep the car moving from side to side to avoid the enemy's return fire.

As you race around the frozen lake trying to take out the enemy, keep your eyes peeled for armor and missile crates. These will keep you alive as you whittle down the attacking forces.

Watch out for the shooters on top of this bridge. Take them down with a couple of quick missile hits.

When you have eliminated the last attacker, a cutscene shows your escape.

Double Cross

Mission Briefing

Bond, MI6 has been contacted by Alexander Mayhew, Rafael Drake's chief of Asian operations. Mayhew fears that Drake intends to kill him, holding him responsible for their little "setback" in Austria. In exchange for our protection, Mayhew will deliver evidence exposing Drake's master plan, code-named "NightFire"—a scheme that Mayhew insists threatens global security.

MI6 CLASSIFIED
Bond—MI6 has been contacted by Alexander Mayhew, Raphael Drake's

chief of Asian Operations, Mayhew fears that Drake intends to kill him,

In exchange for our protection, Mayhew will deliver evidence exposing

Mayhew wants out, and it is up to Bond to escort him. In this mission, you are introduced to another *NightFire* main character: Kiko Hayashi, Mayhew's bodyguard.

MISSION OBJECTIVES

- Escort Mayhew to bunker.
- Destroy Mayhew's computer.
- Rescue geishas.
- Find door to servants quarters.
- Find dragon safe contents.
- Rescue Mayhew's servants.
- Find door leading to Mayhew.
- Defeat the assassin.

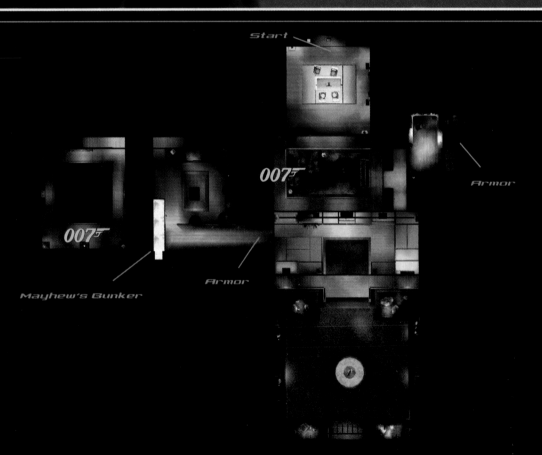

Start

Armor

Armor

Mayhew's Bunker

Turn left and go into the small room. You can use the security cameras to get an idea of where enemies are and what they are doing. Pick up the armor.

 Things start out bad. As you talk to Mayhew, three of Drake's goons come busting through the windows. Shoot the guards quickly. Pick up their weapons; you'll need the extra firepower.

Pick up the ammunition on the table before you leave the starting room.

 Watch out behind you. Two of Drake's goons are approaching. When you eliminate one of them, a smoke grenade goes off, giving you some cover as you take out the second guard.

Keep moving; the smoke obscures the guard's vision, but it will not stop enemy bullets. Once the guards have been cleared out, go back to the console. There are security cameras there. Press the action button to see what they can see and use the manual aim control to move the cameras around. This will help you scout the level.

Once you have eliminated the three guards, follow Mayhew to the next hallway. He tells you that he's not going anywhere until you check out the path ahead.

 As you approach this door, a cutscene plays, telling you the guards are ready for your approach.

Open the door and quickly retreat, firing your weapon along the way. Duck down the hallway for cover as you eliminate the guards on the other side.

After you take care of the first group of guards, Mayhew shouts out that you need to head to the right. Before you move out, though, pick up the weapons and ammunition.

One of the weapons should be the Frinesi Automatic 12, a combat shotgun that proves to be effective at short range. When you round the corner, there should be two more guards. Use the combat shotgun in pump-action mode to take them down.

Mayhew advances down the hallway once the last two guards have been taken down. Race ahead of him and pick up the armor on the other side of the door.

Shoot the guards as they come around the corner. The combat shotgun does a nice job of taking them down.

TIP
Use the Frinesi in pump-action mode; in automatic mode, the gun fires a ton of ammunition quickly and inaccurately.

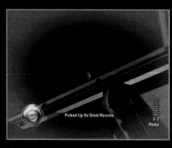

Get rid of the rest of the guards in the next room. Watch out for the one on the balcony above. If you enter the room slowly with your gun aimed at the ceiling, you can pick him off before he can get a shot at you.

Once you take care of the last guard, Mayhew opens the secret door to his underground bunker. This will keep him safe while you clear out the building.

Pick up the armor at the foot of the bed if you need it. Hop on the bed and go into the corner of the room. You can find some ammunition tucked out of the way. You can also use the security cameras in the bunker to see what is going on in the rest of the level. Take a look over by the gong, there is a weapons stash that you could pick up there, including a sniper rifle.

Kitchen

Mayhew's Computer

Dining Room

007

007

Exit to Servant's Quarters

Armor

First Hostage

007

Armor

Start

From the bed you can open up the grate covering the ventilation shaft. Hop into the air ducts and head on up.

You can use the stunner or your silenced PP7 to take out the guard standing beside the rock. Be careful as you sneak around on this level. There is a sniper on top of the viewing pavillion, and his deadly accuracy can end your mission quickly.

Bond Move #1

You can enter the water and take out the guard from underneath the bridge. Be careful, though; he is in view of the other guards, and they can start shooting at you. Pick up the ammunition before you head inside. There's a sniper up on top of the viewing pavilion. This level can be quite tricky, but you're Bond...James Bond.

Stay in the water and go under the bath house.

Bond Move #2

Climb the ladder and enter the bath house. Take out the guards quickly and earn another Bond move.

Pick up the fallen ammunition and grab the body armor over in the corner if you need it.

Go in the direction you saw the servant girl flee. Several guards will shoot at the girl once you appear. Take them out quickly to keep her safe.

Bond Moves #3 and 4

The other geisha girl is in the kitchen. Use the sniper rifle to take out the Yakuza threatening her to earn a Bond move. Shoot out the globe lanterns and use the rope to enter the small house on the other side of the water to earn another Bond move.

Be careful when you enter this door. Guards are in the hallway on the other side, and they will attack when you approach.

Shoot Mayhew's computer to achieve one of your objectives.

Move into the room and take out the guards and free the remaining geisha girl. You can earn bonus points if you can sneak up on these guards and punch them, rather than shoot them.

Before you open this door, equip the flash grenades. Quickly enter the dining room and toss the flashbang into the kitchen. This should stun the three guards there.

Open this door to enter the next portion of the level. Good job, Bond; it's been a tough battle so far, but the mission isn't over yet.

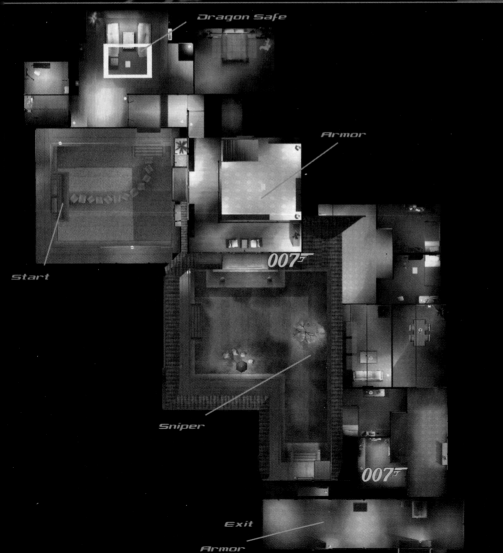

Dragon Safe

Armor

Start

007

Sniper

007

Exit

Armor

Equip one of your handguns as you rush through this doorway. Take out the guard quickly.

33

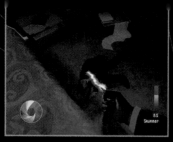

Get rid of the guard in the bedroom and head back to the lounge area. The safe that Mayhew talked about is sitting right there. Feed the key to the dragon to pick up the code key.

Be ready for a firefight when you pick up the code key. The enemy must be monitoring the safe, because several goons come rushing in when you empty the safe.

You hear the voices of the guards as you turn this corner. Get a flash grenade ready and toss it into the room. Shoot the stunned guards when you enter the room.

Climb the stairs and take out the two guards up there. Be careful when you approach the door. A sniper is on the roof across the courtyard.

TIP
Use stun grenades to disorient the hostage takers.

Bond Move #4
There is another Bond Move you can earn here. Use the thermographic lenses and take a look around. There is a secret entrance in the library that will lead you to guards that are holding the final servant hostage.

Head back downstairs and cross over to the doorway on the other side of the courtyard (near where the sniper appeared on the roof). Toss a flash grenade into the room and close the door. The flashbang will stun the guards, making them easy work for you.

Pick up the armor on top of the shelves in front of the open window in that room. Head up the ladder and use the rafters to climb out onto the roof.

Double Cross

Mayhew is dead. Defeat the assassin by moving around the courtyard as you shoot.

NOTE
If you allow the assassin to get in close, that sword will really carve you up.

Bond Move #5

Hop along the roof and shoot out the window and the guard below. This will trigger a Bond move. Hop down and take out the guards below.

Open this door and cross over to the door on the other side of the courtyard. This leads to Mayhew and triggers a short cutscene. Don't rest; the mission isn't quite over.

Night Shift

Mission Briefing

Alex's code key and password should get you into the Phoenix mainframe...but they'll have everything locked down by the time you get there. You've got three new items from Q Branch to aid in your entry to the building: a dart gun to tranquilize the guards; a decryptor to defeat any code-locked doors you encounter; and the Q-Worm, a virus that will help MI6 infiltrate their computer network.

Kiko and Bond ride off in the Vanquish to the headquarters building of Phoenix International.

The cutscene shows Bond sneaking into headquarters by hiding underneath a security van that enters the building.

You get a few new gadgets on this mission: a dart gun, a decryptor, and the Q-Worm.

OBJECTIVES
- **Prevent the security guards from raising the alarm.**
- **Get to the lobby and activate the main elevator.**
- **Take the main elevator to the office floor.**
- **Install Q-Worm on the office computer systems.**
- **Find the security center and unlock exterior door.**

NOTE
Choose your weapon carefully! Use the dart gun, not your trusty PP7. If you shoot your gun at any point in the early parts of this level, the mission will be over. Use stealth.

There is no time to waste. Follow the guard on his patrol through the underground parking area. Pick up the 007 icon here before you head upstairs.

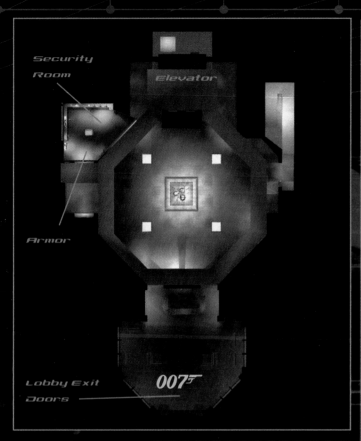

When you get up to the main floor of the Phoenix International headquarters, look out for the guards patrolling the lobby. Remember—this mission is all about stealth.

You are aiming for this room. It is the first-floor security room. Enter the room via this door. Look through the window before you go through the door to make sure there isn't a guard waiting inside.

No need to shoot him. You have a limited supply of tranquilizer darts—don't waste them.

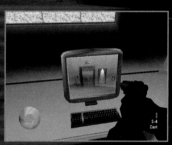

Once inside, you will see a bank of three computers. First go to the one on the right and activate the main elevator. Go to the one on the left to deactivate the laser trip wires on the upper level. Look around the room to find the body armor on the counter. You will need it later in the mission.

Follow the guard until he reaches the elevator area. Walk up to the elevator and press the button. When the elevator arrives, enter and press the button to go up a floor.

With the main tower elevator activated, you can now make a run for it. Don't worry about shooting any more of the guards; if you can swing it, save the ammunition for later on in the level. When you enter the elevator, the next scene of the mission loads.

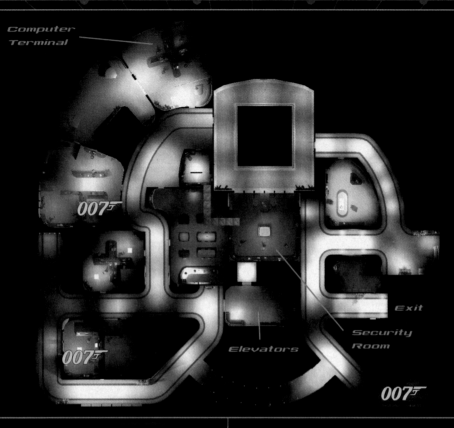

Computer Terminal

007

007

007

Exit

Security Room

Elevators

Mission Status Update
NEW OBJECTIVE

When the elevator reaches your floor, you need to quickly get a sense of your surroundings. Remember, you can't let the guards raise the alarm. Use the dart gun and the stunner to knock out unsuspecting guards.

As you move down the hallway, you pass many closed office doors. Leave them alone; you don't need anything inside. Watch out for the video surveillance system (as noted by the red beam coming out of the rotating camera). If the camera lingers on Bond, the alarm will sound.

As you move out the door, a guard comes out and walks away from you. Don't bother shooting this guard, either; if you take the turn to your right, the guard won't see you at all, and you can save the ammunition.

Your destination is room 70E.

Enter the office and approach the computer with the red glow about it. Accessing this computer will let you load the Q-Worm into most of the network.

Bond Move #1

Exit room 70 E and cross over to the janitor's closet across the hall. You can pull down the vent cover here and grapple up into the ventilation shaft. This will earn you another Bond move and provide easy access to the security center.

The entire time that you have been lurking around the building, that voice has been telling you how much time is left in the laser trip wire system's power-down cycle. If the time counts down to zero before you reach the security center, you must use the IR mode on Q-Specs to see and avoid them.

Equip Q's Decryptor and leave room 70E. Move over to the locked door and point the decryptor at the locked panel. Press the trigger to start getting the combination. Slowly the combination will appear on the screen and the door will unlock.

Use the offices to work your way around the laser trip wire systems if they are active.

Head through the door and follow the security guard around to the other side. There really is no need to tranquilize him, but if you have the ammunition, you can.

This pathway looks clear, right? Wrong. Check it out with you infrared sunglasses. There is a laser trip wire moving along the floor. Jump over it.

Take out this guard as you move past the laser trip wire along the floor.

PRIMA'S OFFICIAL STRATEGY GUIDE

Use the decryptor tool on this door to get into the security center.

Move along the wall to the gap between the ledges and wait for the elevator to come down. Jump on top of the elevator and ride it to the top.

Once inside the security center, move over to the computer terminal. One will unlock the tower exterior, the other will deactivate the laser trip wire system on the upper level. Head for the stairs outside.

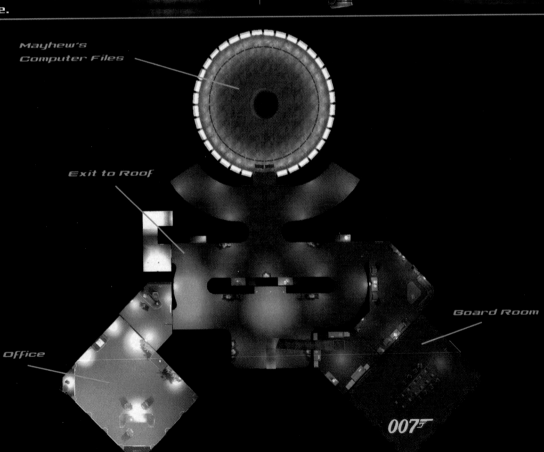

Mayhew's Computer Files

Exit to Roof

Board Room

Office

007

40

PRIMAGAMES.COM

When the elevator reaches the top, find the small ventilation shaft that you can crawl through. Crouch and travel through the shaft to the janitor's closet inside.

Go to the computer and upload the Q-Worm again. Objective complete. Pick up the Scorpion rocket launcher before you go. I wonder what this could be for?

Exit the janitor's closet, through the office, and out into the hall.

Open this door (you got the key from the dragon safe) and activate this console inside. Don't linger in this room. The guards will be rushing upstairs, and the automated sentry guns in this room will activate.

Carefully walk down the hall, sticking to the walls. Video cameras are all over the place. You must use the decryptor to enter the office.

With the guards coming up and the alarm raised, you must go up to the roof. Head for the stairs. When you reach the door, you run into Dominique. She tells you that there is a parachute on the roof. Perfect.

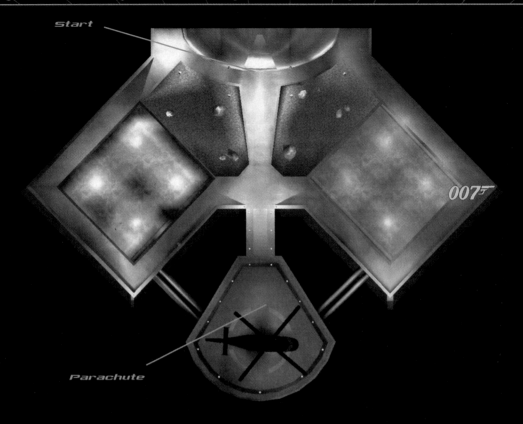

Start

Parachute

A ton of guards are on the roof. You could make a run for it; the second helicopter on the right is unguarded and holds a parachute. But that wouldn't quite be Bond's way, would it?

Bond Move #2

Use the Scorpion to destroy the airborne helicopter for another cool Bond move. Unfortunately, you don't have a lot of ammunition, but these are guided munitions.

With the helicopter in the air destroyed, run toward the helicopter on the ground. Pick up the parachute inside and simply jump off the building. Mission is over. Good job, Bond.

Mission Briefing

MI6 has decrypted the Nightfire files and they don't look good. Bond's job is to sneak into the facility and find out even more evidence of what is going on.

Your job will be to infiltrate this nuclear power plant that Drake is supposed to be decommissioning.

As you move along the roof on your way in, you observe Drake giving an interview to a pretty, young reporter. As soon as she is gone, the snipers come out and the security at the facility is tightened up. Your first order of business will be to take out all those snipers.

MISSION OBJECTIVES

- **Investigate building ST-1.**
- **Photograph the jetpack prototype.**
- **Advance through Warehouse TR-2.**
- **Investigate building ST-3.**
- **Photograph the laser prototype.**
- **Destroy C5 Door with the mounted. laser on catwalk.**

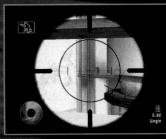

If you want to go far in this mission, you must take out the snipers patrolling the rooftops of the various buildings.

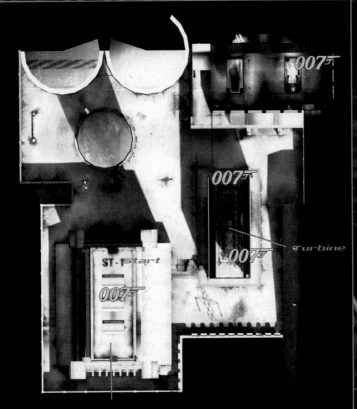

Entrance to ST1

TIP

Before you take your first shot, check out the area and find the guards that need to be taken down. Go for the guards to the right of your starting location first.

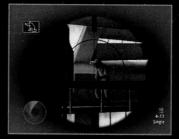

When you drop into the warehouse, stay crouched behind the boxes. There are tons of guards patrolling down there, and you need the cover of the boxes to stay alive.

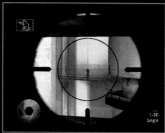

Stay crouched and move to the other side of the ventilation shaft; two more guards are observing the scene from high above. Take out both.

Move back along the building to the ventilation shaft at the rear of the building.

Once you have taken down all the guards, move out from your hiding spot and collect their fallen weapons and ammunition. Your objective is to get to the rocket pack at the end of the warehouse. Get in close and snap a picture to fulfill the task.

With the picture taken, use the security cameras. They have special motion sensors to help you spot the snipers scattered throughout the level. Then head down to the main floor and make your way out of the building via the stairs.

Bond Move #1

Use the laser to take off the hinges holding the cover onto the ventilation shaft. Drop down into the building below to trigger another Bond move. Stay crouched because there are tons of guards down there.

Be careful as you head back outside. There is a shooter in the guard tower around the corner. Take him out with a quick shot and pick up the ammunition.

Look out for the shooter on the other tower before you cross over on the cable. Take him down with a quick shot.

Cross over to the other tower and advance to the cable that will take you over to the warehouse labeled TR-2.

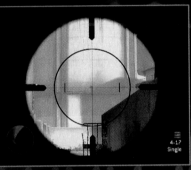

But that isn't the only shooter you need to worry about. A sniper is up high and off into the distance. Take the shot now before you advance, or you will be eliminated.

Goodies

You can use the zipline to cross over to the building with the turbine in it (see the level map). Grapple up to the catwalks and use your laser watch to blast the latch off of the old turbine in the middle to pick up a lot of goodies including some armor, a Ronin suitcase gun, and the crossbow (in the rafters).

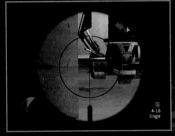

Look out for the two shooters at the forklift. The first one is on the forklift, and the second is hiding behind it. His leg is the only part exposed, but that is enough to take him down.

Use that cable to cross over to the TR-2 warehouse.

Climb up the ladder and walk around the catwalk to where the cable ties the two towers together.

Be careful when you head into the TR-2 warehouse. Several guards are inside, and there isn't an easy way inside.

Take out the guards at the first-floor balcony. Use the fallen beam to head up to the door. When you head outside, a short cutscene plays. The snipers you took out earlier have been found missing. From now on, the guards will be on a higher state of alert.

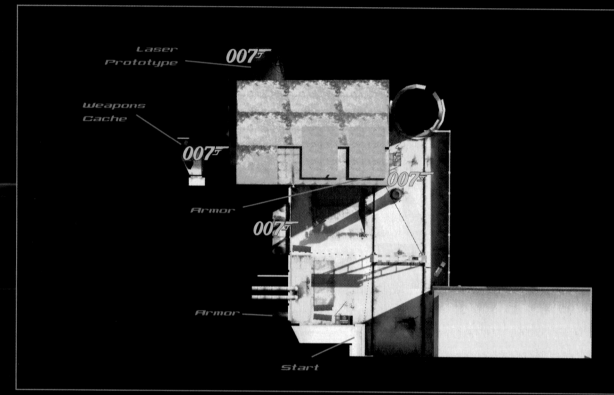

Laser Prototype

Weapons Cache

Armor

Armor

Start

There are several snipers patrolling this area. Quickly take them down. If you take moments to crouch (like when you are reloading) you can survive this encounter.

TIP
You need the get to the crane. To get there fast, use the Q-Grapple from the top of the forklift—the grapple icon shows when you're in range.

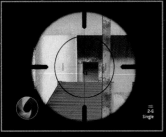

Once the readily apparent snipers are history, move down the ladder and over to this little doorway. There is a guard, some ammunition, and some body armor there.

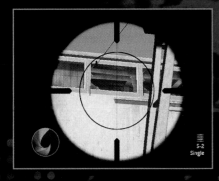

As you move over to the crane, look for snipers shooting from these three windows. Take them down before you start climbing to the top of the crane.

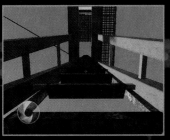

Climb up the crane and crouch down immediately. Several snipers are on top of the building across from the crane. Be quick about it. You don't have very much cover up here on top of the crane. Luckily, you picked up that body armor; you'll need it.

Use the cable to cross over to the other crane. Enter the cab and activate the controls.

This swings the crane over so you can walk over to the doorway that will let you into the final building. You can also jump up to the roof from the crane. This will allow you to pick up the ammo the snipers dropped on the top of the roof, and you can move over to the windowed room from which the snipers attacked you. There is a weapons cache there.

Enter the room to your immediate left. Grab the body armor there.

Bond Move #2

Activate the controls to start the overhead crane moving inside the warehouse. Then use the Q-Grapple to grab onto the hook on the warehouse ceiling. You can now drop onto the crane when it travels beneath you and complete the Bond move. Way to go.

Ride the crane over to the area where the laser prototype sits. You need to photograph it to complete one of your objectives. Be quick about it; there are lots of guards in this warehouse.

Use the laser prototype to cut down the guards. It will overheat if you fire too long. If it gets too hot (watch the red bar on the right side of the screen), you must wait until it cools.

TIP
Use exposive barrels to your advantage—shoot them with the laser.

After you mow down a large group of the guards, use the laser prototype on the door labeled C-5. The metal will superheat and the door will explode.

With the door out of the way, run through the opening. Several guards continue to shoot at you, so you must move quickly.

Picked Up 2x .300 sniper Rounds

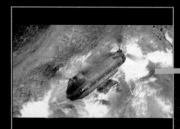 

Once you get down the hall, a short cutscene is triggered. Bond escapes from the power plant with the evidence in hand. MI6 needs to see all this information; Drake definitely is up to no good. As Bond escapes, he is picked up by Mayhew's former bodyguard Kiko Hayashi. Unfortunately, as you are about to learn, she's working for Drake.

Phoenix Fire

Mission Briefing

Kiko brings the subdued Bond back to the headquarters building of Phoenix International. Drake means to kill both Bond and Dominique Paradise. Hidden security cameras caught her helping Bond during the Night Shift mission. Dominique and Bond struggle to break free of their captors and Bond is able to jump free—down to the glass elevator you used to reach the top of the tower in the last mission. Bond must escape the tower to complete this mission, and the task won't be easy. The guards are on high alert, and it will be a shootout all the way.

The subdued Bond is brought back to the headquarters building of Phoenix International.

Bond is able to escape from the clutches of the guards and ends up back at the glass elevator that you used in Night Shift. Unfortunately, Dominique's fate is not as pretty.

OBJECTIVES

- Escape from the tower.
- Gain access to the lower office floor.
- Activate elevator override control in security.
- Escape through the elevator shaft.
- Gain access to the lobby.
- Raise security gate and escape through front entrance.

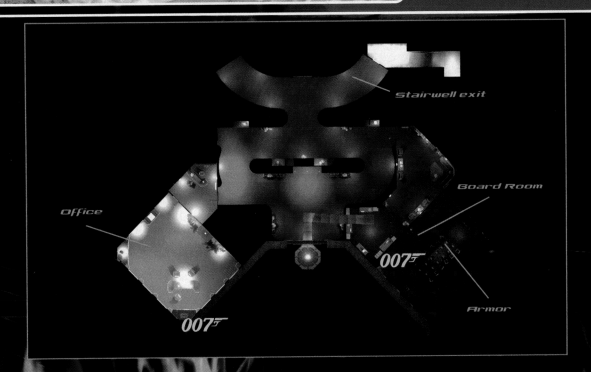

Stairwell exit

Board Room

Office

007

Armor

007

Bond Move #1

There are loads of guards just outside the lobby. Remember how you got into this office level back in the Night Shift mission? There was a ventilation shaft on top of the elevator. Jump through the broken window and out onto the ledge, and use the Q-Grapple to get on top of the elevator. Open the cover on the ventilation shaft and head inside. When you drop into the janitor's closet, the Bond move will be completed.

Get your gun ready and exit the janitor's closet. Guards are all over the place. As you take down each guard, make sure you pick up their weapons. You will need the ammunition on this mission.

Make your way back to the main office. You must get an access code from the computer there. Thankfully, the Q-Worm virus is still in the computer, and it gives up the code quite easily.

Once you have obtained the access code, several guards bust into the room. Use the desk for cover and crouch when you need to reload.

Head over to the stairwell door. The door is locked, but you have the access code. Enter it and head down the stairs.

Be careful when you hit the stairwell. Guards are coming up the stairs. One of the guards you popped earlier should have dropped some fragmentation grenades. Pull one of them out now and chuck it down the stairs. This will take care of the guards lurking around the corner.

When you head down to the landing, make sure you look up. Several guards come repelling down the ropes. Take them out quickly.

Perform the same trick when you come to the next corner. The frag grenades really come in handy.

Keep battling your way down the staircase. Several more guards come down the rope lines, so keep an eye there, too.

As you come around the next bend in the staircase, the area opens up. Several guards wait for you downstairs.

TIP
Use the waist-high wall along the stairs as cover as you take out the guards below.

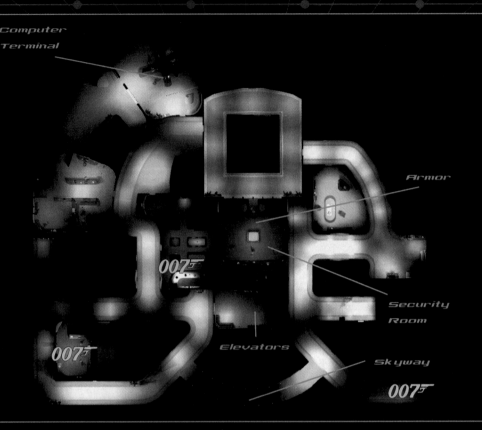

Computer Terminal

Armor

007

Security Room

007

Elevators

Skyway

007

When you open the door, you are back on the mid-office level. Two guards have their backs to you as you come out of the stairwell. Subdue them.

NOTE
Pick up the Ronin Suitcase gun that is clealy visible on the floor at the beginning of the second stage in this level.

You could use your own Ronin suitcase gun and move back around the corner to take out the guards, but deploying the Ronin gun takes time. Toss a couple grenades around the corner instead.

As you round this corner, you stumble into one of these remote-controlled gatling guns.

TIP
Use grenades to stun the suitcase guns and get behind them.

Move back across the office level to room 70E. You installed a Q-Worm virus there in the Night Shift mission. It will give you the access code to the main security room.

TIP

Deploy your own Ronin Suitcase gun and move back around the corner. With remote control mode, you can steer the gun manual via the on board camera. You can also use the gun in automatic mode to take out the guards on its own, but taking control of the gun requires delicate skill.

Head on over to the elevators and go down to the lobby. As you ride down in the elevator, several guards attack you. Take them down quickly.

Go back to the main security room. The access code will get you through the door. Inside you can unlock the elevator and raise the security gate on the skyway via the two computers.

About halfway down to the lobby, two guards up above throw a timed bomb down onto the elevator. Use the laser to disarm the bomb before it goes off.

Before you leave the security center, pick up the body armor and the Scorpion rocket launcher from the table.

After you take out more guards, another guard from above plants another bomb. This time he puts it on the elevator cable. This explosion will drop the elevator all the way down to the lobby, but Bond will survive the fall unhurt.

Bond Move #2

Hmm, a Scorpion rocket launcher. What could that be used for? Head out to the glass-encased walkway between the two towers. A helicopter is circling the building outside. Start firing your Scorpion. After a several hits, the helicopter will be destroyed, and you will earn another Bond move.

You are back in the main lobby of the Phoenix International headquarters building. The security doors are down, so you won't be able to escape right away.

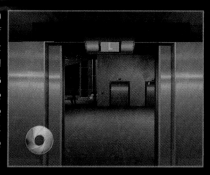

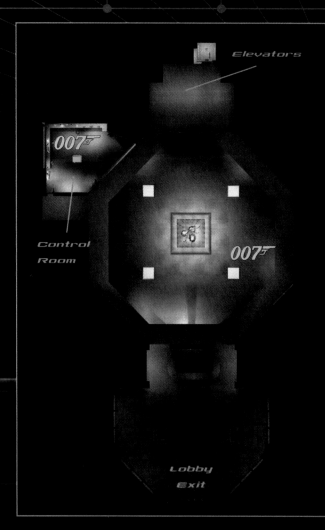

Elevators

007

Control
Room

007

Lobby

Exit

Go to the security room and use the computer to raise the barrier that is locking down the lobby entrance.

Run for the lobby doors. When you reach them, the mission will be over and another cutscene will be triggered. Australian Intelligence Operative Alura McCall has come to Bond's rescue.

Deep Descent

Mission Briefing

Bond and Agent McCall need to infiltrate Drake's island facility. Phoenix International disarms nuclear weapons at this base, and UN weapons inspectors have cleared the facility, but MI6 doesn't believe so. Your trusty V-12 Vanquish doubles as a submarine, and you will use this special feature to get into the base undetected. You must evade all of Drake's island defenses: laser trip wires, magnetic mines, and submarines. This is a difficult mission. One misstep, and it's over. There are no save points along the way. Get used to starting this mission over and over; it takes a lot of skill to complete this mission.

likely harbored at Drake's missile disassembly works in the

It's time to infiltrate Phoenix International's nuclear weapons disarmament facility.

Precisely.

Bond's V-12 Vanquish doubles as a submarine. When you are piloting the submarine, remember that pulling the control stick forward will push your submarine deeper beneath the water, and pulling the control stick backward will pull your submarine toward the surface.

MISSION OBJECTIVES

- **Make it to the beach undetected.**
- **Find alternate way into Drake's Base.**
- **Destroy Communications Node.**
- **Plant charges on missiles.**
- **Follow sub into base.**
- **Plant charges on 3 nuclear subs.**
- **Destroy the attack submarine.**

NEW OBJECTIVE
Find alternate way into Drake's base

OBJECTIVE COMPLETE
Find alternate way into Drake's base

30 Torpedo

After the short cutscene, head inside the sunken ship. This prevents the enemy sub from seeing you. It also allows you to sneak in the back way.

Once you are in control of the V-12 Vanquish submarine, veer off the right. Phoenix International seems to own several nuclear-powered submarines that are patrolling the waters around the facility.

We've got company James. We should get out of the main channel.

An entry to an underwater cavern is inside the sunken ship. Enter the cave, and another short cutscene shows a small submarine that Drake has patrolling the cave. Phoenix International seems to have all the bases covered.

OBJECTIVE COMPLETE
Find alternate way into Drake's base

30 Torpedo

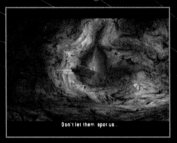

You can't engage the small submarines; they will sound the alarm if you try to attack them. Take the small passage to the right.

Bond Move #1

Switch to the remote torpedoes and shoot a guided torpedo through the spinning fan blades. Once the communications array has been destroyed, you can head back down into the cave. When you attack the enemy submarines, they won't be able to sound the alarm. You will also trigger the first Bond move of this mission.

Bond Move #2

Once back in the main cavern, fire off another remote-controlled torpedo. Steer the guided ordnance deeper into the cavern until you can see the small enemy submarine hovering above the underwater tanks. If you steer the torpedo into the tanks, the explosion will take out the enemy submarine and trigger another Bond move.

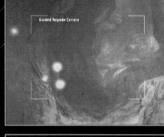

The enemy submarine was guarding the entrance into another section of cave. Fire off another guided torpedo and steer it through the laser trip wires. Follow the lighted cable into the control box to deactivate the detection lasers. Once the laser trip wires are out of the way, prepare to enter the next section of cave.

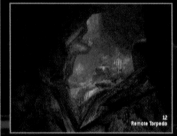

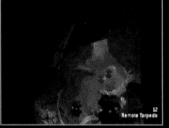

Put the pedal to the metal and hit the cave entrance at full speed. Drake has placed mines that will be drawn to the V-12 Vanquish. It can take several attempts to get through this section of the cave. Negotiating a path through the mines is tricky. Stay high and to the right; it seems to be the easiest path.

CAUTION

Get through there quickly. If the mines get anywhere near you, they will detonate.

Whew. You made it through the first section of mines. Yes, the *first section* of mines. There is another one you must go through in just a little bit.

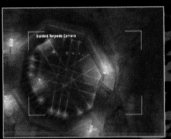

Another cavern entry point is guarded by a set of laser trip wires. Use the remote-controlled torpedo again. This time, the control box is much farther into the cavern. Follow the lighted wire from the trip wire gate all the way to the control box.

TIP
The torpedo picks up speed the longer it travels, so line it up on the control box when it is traveling slowly.

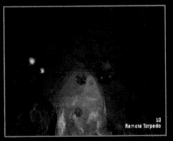

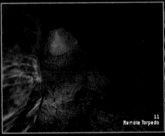

There is another sequence of mines to get past. Again, you must be careful. If you make a mistake here, you must restart at the beginning of the mission.

Once through the last group of mines, you approach yet another cave. The UN inspectors were wrong; Phoenix International has squirreled away nuclear missiles that they supposedly had dismantled.

Switch to the standard torpedoes. A small enemy submarine patrols the area. Wait for the weapon to lock on (the targeting icon changes from white to red). It will take several torpedo shots to bring down the sub.

There are six nuclear missiles. You must place a Q-Charge at each of them, but time is of the essence. Once the first charge is placed, you have only seconds (50 on Hard, 90 on Easy)

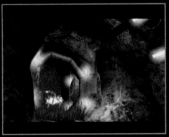

before the explosion occurs. If you haven't placed a charge at each of the six missiles before time expires, the explosion will crush the Vanquish and the mission will be over.

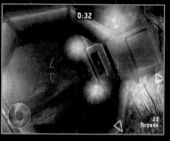

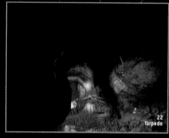

Once you have placed a Q-Charge at each of the missiles, the exit opens. Two more enemy submarines guard the exit, but you can blow right past them.

A short cutscene shows you another small enemy submarine. Rather than fight you, the submarine chooses to flee. Follow the little submarine, because it opens doors for you along the way.

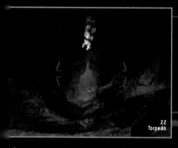

You must stay right on the tail of the submarine. Access doors open as it approaches, but immediately close behind it. If you make one misstep along the path, you will never catch up.

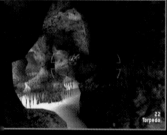

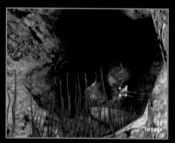

Watch out for this rock formation in the cave. If you follow the path to the right (the way the enemy submarine goes), a rockslide will block your path. Take the path to the left to stay on the enemy submarine's tail.

Watch out for small depth charges that the enemy submarine drops along the way. One or two of these depth charges will not destroy your Vanquish, but several will ruin Bond's day.

Bond Move #3

There is an armor pickup in the tunnel just before you reach the launching point for the small enemy submarines. Shoot the gas cylinders to destroy them in one quick blow to earn a Bond move.

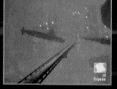

Drake can't be allowed to keep these submarines. Use your remaining Q-Charges on the conning towers of the three submarines.

After you have placed the depth charges on the three nuclear submarines, one of Drake's subs comes back from its patrol. You can either shoot torpedoes to destroy the attack sub, or simply sneak past it using the last docked nuclear submarine as cover. Once you are past the submarine, your Vanquish will drive up onto the beach..

Island Infiltration

Mission Briefing

Bond and Agent McCall have made it safely through the underwater caverns and onto the beach. Now the two secret agents must discover the location of Drake's command center. Lucky for Bond and McCall, an armored SUV is waiting for their use. Drive the SUV around the island and disable the island's defenses.

You've made it onto the beach. Now it is time for Bond and McCall to find the command center and disable the island's defenses.

 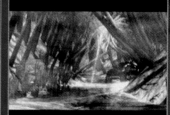

Bond's V-12 Vanquish would stick out a little bit on this island. Lucky for Bond, an armored SUV is ready and waiting. Driving the SUV is a real blast, especially with the onboard missiles.

MISSION OBJECTIVES

- **Dismantle Drake's island defense systems.**
- **Download defense system code from compound.**

You'll drive along the road in your borrowed SUV for quite a way. Bond and McCall approach a fork in the road. Take the right-hand path.

Bond Move #1

You have two options here as you approach the enemy compound. You can go busting through the gate and shoot up the joint, or you can simply come to a halt at the security gate. You're driving one of the security detachment's SUVs, so they will allow you in if you don't act suspiciously. If you come to a halt and get in without shooting, you will earn a Bond move.

On the right side of the compound, a box of missiles lies on the ground. Drive over the box to get a little extra ammunition.

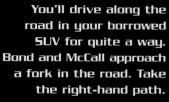

59

Head for the left side of the compound. An armor pack waits on the ground. It will come in handy later.

Drive toward the helipad. As you approach the building on the right, you can steal the security codes that will get you through the island's security checkpoints. Pick up the Bond icon here.

Several other security SUVs pop up, as do a couple of snipers who appear on the overhead bridge. Don't drive at full speed. A slower speed allows your missiles to strike at the enemy from a greater distance. This tactic prevents your SUV from taking too much damage.

Head out of the compound. Crash through the security gate because it doesn't open as you approach it.

Head back to the fork in the road. This time, take the left path.

Use the access code to open the first security fence. The first Sentinel gun tower is right there on the beach. Shoot it with a few missiles to take it down.

NOTE
You can't simply race past this defense; elimination of all the Sentinel guns is one of your mission objectives.

As you work your way up the road, another Sentinel gun is in the town on the left. You can get a lock on it before the Sentinel can shoot at you, so take it out from a distance.

Wait for the bridge to extend. If you reach the river too quickly, the bridge won't be there yet, and your SUV will crash into the river.

You need to take out a couple of snipers up ahead in the town. More vehicles need your attention, too.

Use missiles to get the enemy SUVs out of the way.

There is a missile pick-up and an armor pick-up in the middle of the road. Make sure you pick up these valuable items.

Race across the bridge and through the tunnel to the final conflict of this mission. Two more SUVs and another large Sentinel gun await you. You've been saving some missiles for this last confrontation, right? Take out the enemy quickly and drive around to the back of the circular platform.

As you approach the last security fence, use the access code to extend the bridge that spans the river.

Bond Move #3

As you approach the last security fence, use the access code to extend the bridge. Take a look to the right before you go too far. There is a bush near the bend in the road. Crash into the bush to discover a secret road. This will get you another Bond move and an armor pick-up.

After you have eliminated the Sentinel gun and the last two SUVs, a short cutscene shows Bond and McCall taking off in a small airplane. McCall flies the plane while Bond takes control of the plane's weapons systems. Good job, Bond. You are hot on the trail.

Mission Briefing

Bond and Agent McCall have brought down some of Drake's defenses, but there are still more out there. McCall will fly the plane while Bond mans the controls of the plane's weapons. You have a pulse cannon and missiles to take out the enemy targets. You need to bring down all of the Sentinel guns and other island defenses, like other enemy planes, guard towers, and riverboats.

Keep at it, Bond; you have almost all of their defenses taken out. For the most part, use missiles to take out the enemy.

Don't waste your missiles. Wait for the lock-on icons to turn from white to red before you launch your attack. There is no way to rearm your plane, so you have only the missiles you start with.

The first objective is to take out the bridge; this is the main road into and out of Drake's base. A convoy of trucks rolls along the bridge at the moment. Wait for the lock icon to appear on one of the trucks, then let your missiles fly. The explosion brings down the bridge and fulfills the first objective.

As McCall continues to fly the plane down the canyon, you encounter the first of Drake's defenses. A guard tower appears up ahead. Take it down with a pair of missiles.

Bond and McCall press farther down into the canyon and encounter the first Sentinel gun. These guns will rip your plane to shreds if you don't deal with them quickly, so fire a couple of missiles.

Once the first plane is down, quickly switch back to missiles and fire on the second ultralight.

Another guard tower is ahead. Again, take it out with a pair of missiles.

Bond Move #4

You stumble across another convoy coming up along the left bank of the river. Wait for a truck to get onto the bridge. Target that vehicle, and the explosion will take out the bridge.

As you do battle with the first two ultralights, a third appears. Chase it down the waterfall and let your missiles do the dirty work for you.

Destroy the boats in the cove below at the base of the waterfall. Use either the pulse cannon or missiles.

Two ultralight planes, like the one you are flying, appear in the canyon up ahead. They make a very close pass to your present location. Quickly switch to the pulse cannon and rip into the first ultralight.

There are more ultralights to take down. You will leave this area after two passes.

Once you leave the cove, you approach another guard tower. Bring it down with a couple of missiles.

Switch to guns and let the armored vehicle have it when it appears.

Take out the last Sentinel gun as you advance farther down the river.

Bond Move #6

After a time, several planes fly in from the canyon to the left. Use the guns to take them down quickly. You will earn a Bond move if you can take all three planes out.

Switch back to the big pulse cannon and let the armored vehicle on the right have it.

Holy cow! There is a huge surface-to-air missile (SAM) battery up ahead. Your little ultralight has no chance of standing up against the MEGA SAM site. It takes you down and triggers a quick cutscene showing the ultralight crash. Bond and McCall survive the crash and take over the controls of the MEGA SAM.

Bond Move #5

When the armored vehicle appears, use the pulse cannon to take out the propane tank. The explosion will take out the vehicle and earn you another Bond move.

Bond Move #7 and #8

More planes will attack. This time, they approach from the right and from straight over the waterfall. Switch to guns and rip the enemy planes to shreds. You will earn a Bond move if you can defeat all three planes from the right, and another Bond move if you can take out the planes that come over the waterfall and attack you.

Switch back to the pulse cannon and take out the armored vehicle that approaches on the left.

After a while, McCall will inform you that she has found a weakness in the MEGA SAM. She needs you to cover her while she sets up the destruction of the site. One of Drake's nuclear submarines will pop up in the cove; fire on it with the big pulse cannon and the guns.

Mission Briefing

Bond and McCall have made it deep into the island base of Phoenix International. It is up to Bond to find out exactly what is up and to stop it if possible. This mission has you sneaking around the compound and chasing Kiko Hayashi. Bond owes her one for throwing Dominique off the top of the Phoenix International headquarters building. This mission also has Bond in a final confrontation with Armitage Rook. This is a difficult mission to complete. Good lock, Bond. You'll need it.

Bond and McCall have made it deep into the island base of Phoenix International. After escaping the MEGA SAM, the two run into a small control bunker deep in the jungle. Inside, McCall finds a computer that she can break into while Bond heads into the ventilation shaft.

MISSION OBJECTIVES
- **Investigate Drake's facility undetected.**
- **Follow Kiko to Security Control Center.**
- **Sabotage Base security and escape from room.**
- **Take exit to Delta Sector.**
- **Find the exit to Omega Sector.**
- **Reach Drake's Launch site.**
- **Prevent Kiko from launching into space.**

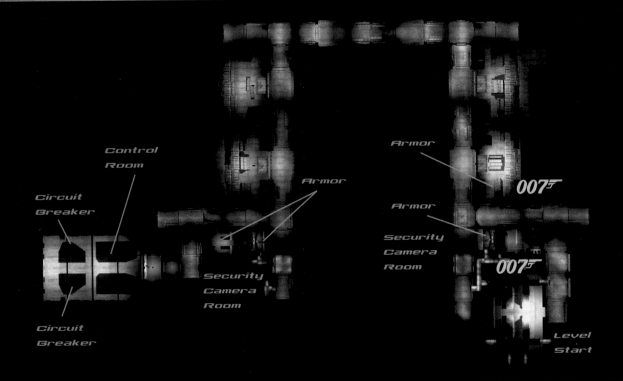

Control Room

Circuit Breaker

Armor

Armor

007

Armor

Security Camera Room

Circuit Breaker

Security Camera Room

007

Level Start

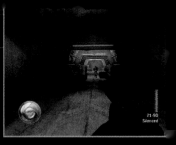

Careful James, those lasers will trigger the alarm.

Travel through the ventilation shaft and drop down into the room below. Take out the guards quickly.

Agent McCall is monitoring Kiko's progress through the level. Follow her directions and keep on Hayashi's tail.

Head down the hall and be ready for a fight. Many guards are in the enemy compound.

Eventually, you catch up with Kiko as she enters the security room. She leaves the room and locks the door behind her.

Bond Move #1

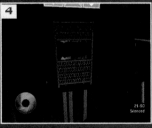

1 **2**

3 **4**

As you travel through the halls, you stumble onto a room with a security camera icon on the door. Open the door, head inside, and use the cameras to scope out the level. There is a body armor pick-up and a circuit breaker in the room. Open the breaker door and use the laser to destroy the three circuit boards. As you walk about the level, you will discover a second camera room. If you also destroy the circuit boards there, you will earn a Bond move.

To get out of the room, you must cause a power overload. Go down to the two circuit breaker boxes and destroy the circuit boards inside.

When you destroy the circuit boards, head back to the computer. The destruction of the circuit boards causes an explosion.

A cutscene plays, showing Armitage Rook unlocking the door. He unleashes his elite guards, the toughest guards you have faced to date. Take out the two guards and move down the hall.

Bond Move #2

Several barrels are scattered throughout the level. When you shoot them, they explode and take out any nearby guards. The first time you take out a guard this way, you trigger a Bond move.

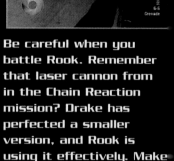

Be careful when you battle Rook. Remember that laser cannon from in the Chain Reaction mission? Drake has perfected a smaller version, and Rook is using it effectively. Make sure you use the cover provided as you take out Rook.

When you have defeated Rook, pick up the laser cannon and use it yourself.

With Rook defeated, head on over to the door to Delta Sector.

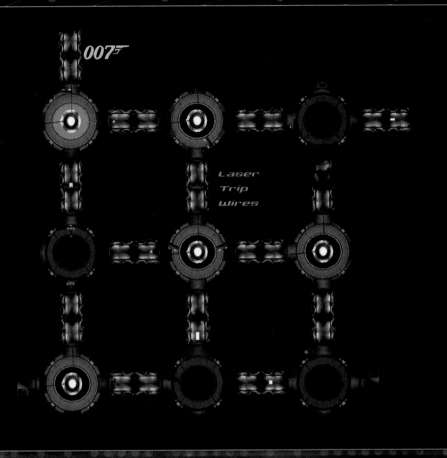

From time to time, you come across these laser tripwires that block your path. Shoot out the control boxes to deactivate them.

You are deeper into the Drake compound.

Keep pressing on as you move from silo to silo. Use the crates for cover. Toss a grenade or two to wipe out the enemies that stand in your path.

NOTE

This section of the level can be confusing if you don't remember one thing: There is only one way into a silo, and only one other way out. So don't worry about getting confused. Press forward, and you will do fine.

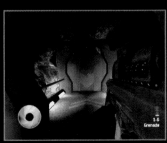

You have made it out of the silos when you make it to this door. Open it and quickly move inside.

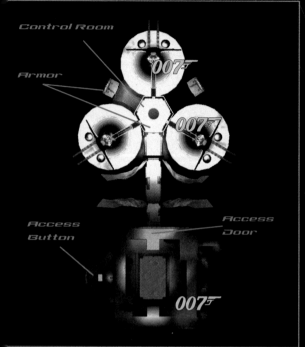

Control Room

Armor

Access Button

Access Door

This is the control facility for Drake's space shuttle launching facility. As you move through the room, you have to listen to Drake pontificate about how his mission is almost complete—and that he will soon rule the world.

Well, you are still alive and will have something to say about that. Head upstairs and press the button to unlock the door that leads to the Space Shuttle.

Head over to the door with the Space Shuttle logo above it. It is now open.

TIP
Remote mines and laser trip bombs make the upcoming battle with ninja easier.

As you advance to the Space Shuttle, a short cutscene triggers. Kiko Hayashi drops the gantry you are walking across.

You are trapped at the base of the Space Shuttle launching pad. A computer voice tells you how long it is until the next Space Shuttle launch. You can't be standing there when the rockets begin to lift off. Head to the control room in the middle (there's body armor here). When it comes time for the launch, the doors will automatically close.

Once the Space Shuttle has taken off, the doors open and several guards come down via the elevator in the center. Take them down. Watch out for the ninja that Kiko deploys to take you out. They are very difficult to eliminate.

The doors open again, and when all the ninja and guards are eliminated, Kiko takes the elevator up. A cutscene shows Bond using his Q-Grapple to head up with the elevator. Kiko is trying to escape on the last Space Shuttle. Bond pulls the same trick Kiko did, dropping the gantry on her before she can make it. Now Bond is free to get on the Space Shuttle and foil Drake's master plan.

Equinox

Mission Briefing

This is it: the final battle. Drake's forces have taken over the US Space Weapons Platform. Drake wants to take out the remaining nuclear arsenals that threaten his island. With his island arsenal and the US Space Platform under his control, Drake would be unstoppable. Bond will have to be on top of his game in order to defeat this evil plan. You must take out the missiles' guidance systems before they launch. You have the laser weapon you stole from Armitage Rook at the end of the last mission. Get ready, Bond; this is the final test.

Bond rides Drake's Space Shuttle up to the US Space Weapons Platform. Drake's special forces have taken over the facility.

Raphael Drake wants to destroy the nuclear arsenals that could threaten his island. The combination of his arsenal and the US Space Weapons Platform would make Drake unstoppable.

Bond is the only one who can stop this evil plot.

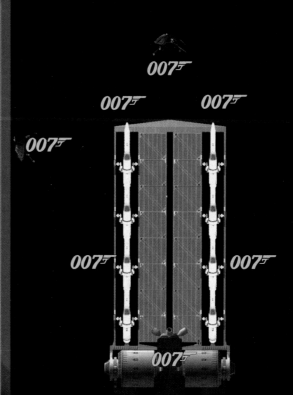

MISSION OBJECTIVES
• **Disable the missiles before they are launched.**
• **Defeat Drake before the laser cannon goes critical.**

the missile's guidance computer. The missiles will launch on a set schedule. Move over to that missile and repeat the above process.

NOTE

There are no Bond moves in this level. It will take all your concentration to knock out the missiles before they launch.

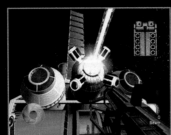

Drake is using the laser as an offensive weapon. He's bouncing the laser off the oribital mirrors toward Bond. Keep moving to avoid the beams and use the audio clues to tell you when to move.

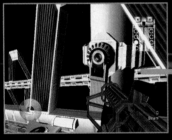

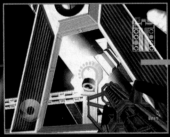

Agent McCall will let you know when the missiles are about to launch. Look out for the blinking green icon on the display in the upper-right corner of the display; this tells you which missile is about to launch. Quickly move over to that missile and wait for it to rotate into position. As the gantry rotates the missile into place, a control board will come into view and the countdown will begin. Hit the missile three times with your laser weapon to disable

NOTE

The green LEDs cycle down as the missile gets closer to launching.

After you disable the second missile, two nukes are rotated into position for a simultaneous launch.

While you wait for the gantry to place the first missile into firing position, take a couple of pot shots at the guards flying about.

TIP

Jump and crouch to dodge the bullets from the laser cannon.

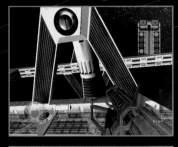

After defeating the two missiles, the remaining three rotate into launch position. You must move as quickly as possible to defeat all three missiles at once.

Once Drake is out and on the loose, he fires on you with a portable rocket launcher. Use careful aim with your laser to take Drake down.

With the missiles defeated, it's just you and all of those guards. Square off with them for a while, but keep moving. You wouldn't want to die now.

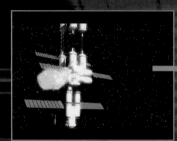

An errant piece of metal comes and crashes through the control room of the US Space Weapons Platform. You will now have to defeat Drake before the space station destroys itself.

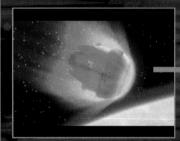

You did it, Bond! Drake has been defeated, and the world is safe once again. You meet up with McCall on the beach of Drake's island base. Time for a little rest and relaxation. Good job, Bond; you've earned it.

Bond Icons

At the conclusion of each mission, your score will be posted on screen. If you've been following this strategy guide, you should be earning Gold Medals each and every time. Want a little bit more Bond action? Head back into the levels and go for a Platinum Medal. To earn a Platinum Medal, you need to collect all of the Bond icons scattered throughout the level. Here is a complete list of the Bond icons and where you can find them.

> ## NOTE
> Players can achieve Gold awards on early levels by playing Operative and Agent, but the later levels require OO Agent difficulty to acheive the more valuable awards.

At the end of the mission, your score is tallied and medals are awarded (if your score is high enough that is). If you have been following this guide, a gold medal should be a shoe in. You can go back into the levels and try for a Platinum medal by executing all of the Bond moves again and collecting the Bond icons scattered throughout the levels.

Paris Prelude

- At the first right hand turn where you attacked the first 2 enemies with Q-Smoke
- In the plaza above where the moving truck backs out, blocking the road
- After the archway that collapses, floating in the air
- After the bridge jump, in the alley into which the Bomb truck went

The Exchange

- In front of the doors that the truck appears from
- In the ravine on top of the broken crate
- At the end of the passage that you star on when you've done the secret route way on exterior
- In the wine cellar behind the destroyable crates
- In front of the fireplace in the banquet hall after Drake's speech
- In the Library after you meet up with Dominique
- Outside the window at the end of the hall after you watch the exchange between Mayhew and Drake
- In the storeroom beneath the cable car

Alpine Ambush

- Destroying the ammo shack on the right of the player after exiting the garage
- Taking out the snowmobile you play chicken with before he passes you
- Taking out the 2 enemies with rocket launchers on the castle walls

Enemies Vanquished

- Between the tables halfway through the village on the left
- Exiting the sunken plaza in the village shortcut
- When you make the jump off the waterfall onto the frozen river
- On the left side of the frozen island along the frozen river
- On the frozen lake behind the leftmost island

Double Cross

- On a walkway in the courtyard next to the meeting room
- Top floor of the display room
- Next to the gong
- On walkway opposite entrance to northern garden
- Behind screen in dining room
- On the balcony opposite where Bond shoots the sniper—look left after crossing the beam
- The unused fuse box room in the servants quarters

Nightshift

- In the garage behind a wall barrier—walk forward from start position
- At the entrance to the building on the ground floor
- At the closed barrier end of the sky bridge
- In the office just before you reach the camera guarding the atrium door
- In the dark dead-end corridor past the level exit
- In the boardroom
- Opposite end of the roof to where the player begins

Chain Reaction

- Top of the forklift
- Inside building with the ronin
- Left catwalk of the hangar
- Behind the generator in tr-2
- In the room where the three snipers shoot the glass windows out
- On the beam on the far end of the moving platform
- In the room to the left of the laser, behind some of the boxes on the second level

Phoenix Fire

- Go through the smashed window in lift, one on the ledge
- In the boardroom
- In the cafeteria, to the left as you go in the door on the floor in front of the vending machines
- At the end of the corridor to the left of the spawn point, on the floor
- In room 70A, at the end of the corridor straight down from elevator to tower 2-C
- In the security control room on the floor to the right of the shutter activation console
- To the left of the shutter door on the lobby floor in front of the row of gold-colored columns

Deep Descent

- In the sunken tanker
- Beside the COM station
- Below a mine just after the 2nd laser grid
- Along the sub chase just before the 3rd door
- In the condom room above where the sub clamps are
- In an alcove in the final hangar up and to the right of the entry.

Island Infiltration

Driving the SUV

- Behind the starting position for the player, by the beach
- Inside the compound beside the large satellite dish
- Inside the volcano to the right of the last Sentinel the player needs to take out

Ultralight

- Destroying the first tower after the bridge, the token appears in the air

Countdown

- In the vent system off first room
- In the first crate room, secret area where you crawl to
- In the second hackable door
- Resting on a box in the last silo just at the end of the level
- In the opposite room to where you go to activate the door
- One under each Shuttle

Equinox

- In the middle of the Giant Lens
- Below the missile second one down from the top to the left
- Below the missile second one down from the top to the right
- At the front end of the platform on the right
- At the front end of the platform on the left
- In front of the center laser relay where the beam travels
- On the right side of the left laser relay

Award Levels

Earning medals will unlock other secrets in the game. Keep playing the levels over and over again until you can earn Platinum medals on each mission. Then you will have all of the secrets unlocked.

Medal Awards

Mission	Bronze	Silver	Gold	Platinum
Paris Prelude	Card, Dominique	Skin, Jaws	Upgrade, Racing Missile	Skin, Renard
The Exchange	Card, Zoe	Skin, Oddjob	Upgrade, Pistol	Skin, Baron Samedi
Alpine Ambush	Card, Military Snowmobile	Scenario, Assassination	Upgrade, Grapple	Skin, Zorin
Enemies Vanquished	Card, Vanquish	Skin, Scarmonga	Upgrade, Micro Camera Scope	Skin, May Day
Double Cross	Card, Mayhew Servant Girl	Scenario, Uplink	Ugrade, Rifle	Skin, Xenia Onatopp
Night Shift	Card, Kiko	Scenario, Team KOH	Upgrade, Pistol	Skin, Christmas Jones
Chain Reaction	Card, Rook	Skin, Wai Lin	Upgrade, Dart Gun	Skin, Goldfinger
Phoenix Fire	Card, Alura	Scenario, Demolition	Upgrade, Pistol	Skin, Drake Suit
Deep Descent	Card, Vanquish Sub	Skin, Nik Nak	Upgrade, Decryptor	Skin, Electra King
Island Infiltration	Card, Ultralight Ultimate Laser	Scenario, Protection	Upgrade, Stunner	Skin, Bond Tuxedo
Countdown	Card, Drake	Mode, Explosive Scenery	Upgrade, Laser	Skin, Pussy Galore
Equinox	Card. Bond	Scenario, Goldeneye Strike	Upgrade, Rifle	Skin, Bond Space

Rendezvous

Infiltrate the Castle

You land outside Drake's castle on one of the towers. Right click to put the silencer on your Walther PPK and drop down to the catwalk below you. When you do, M contacts you and tells you to sneak aboard the incoming supply truck. This will give you an easier way into the castle. To do this, look left and wait for the truck to drive by. Jump over the ledge and onto the truck. This takes you all the way to the front entrance of the castle.

Drop down and turn left to see the truck. Jump on the truck as it passes for your first Bond move.

NOTE
This is a Bond move, and will give you extra points at the end of the mission.

If you decide not to ride the truck, there's more to investigate. The door in front of you leads to a small room containing a radio set. You can't use this, but you can shoot it if you wish. The door behind you when you drop from the tower leads to a set of stairs down to the ground. Walk down and open the door at the bottom. The truck drives past and M tells you that it's too late to use it as a method for getting in. Don't worry about this. Instead, with the silenced Wolfram P2K, pick off the guard standing on the catwalk that the truck drives under. There are a few guards on the ground as well, so you'll have to drill them, too. The guard above you is more dangerous because he has cover, so he should be your first target.

Use your Q-Specs on the infrared setting for best accuracy at the start.

TIP
If you wish, you can target many of the guards from your drop location. Also, be sure to attach the silencer before you start firing.

Continue up the road until you find the supply truck waiting at the gate. There is a guard on either side of it. Your hand grenades are useful here. It's tough to get both with a single explosion. However, you can take out one and drop the other when he reacts to the grenade. When you are ready, walk in front of the truck to continue.

There is a better way in than the front door if you miss the truck. To do this, start the mission the same way, waiting for the supply truck to go by and taking out the guards on and near the tower by your drop location. Get to the ground and go up the road to the catwalk. On your right, there is a locked door leading inside. Use the laser on your wristwatch to destroy the lock and head in. At the top, you can pick up the weapons of the two guards that were here. Go through the door beyond and climb up the ladder to your right, opening the trap door at the top.

If you wish to head for the back door, the laser wristwatch comes in handy.

TIP
There's armor in the room with the ladder.

You can see one of the guards next to the truck at the main gate. Shoot him and look to your left. There's a wire here running from the ledge you are on to the top of a hill. Watch the wire for a few moments. There are a couple of points on the wire where sparks appear at irregular intervals. If you are on the wire and a spark hits you, you'll let go and drop to the ground. When you are ready, jump up to the wire and go hand-over-hand to the other side, watching for the sparks. Drop down to the ground on the far side.

This stealthy hand-over-hand approach leads to the rear of the castle.

Hug the side of the building and start walking around. You will pass your landing spot. The next pair of towers holds a pair of guards who will begin shooting at you as soon as they spot you. A grenade or a barrage of bullets will silence them. Once they are down, continue moving along the side of the castle.

To improve your chances, shoot the spotlight. It'll make you much harder to spot.

A little farther along the path, you come to a place where you must press yourself back against the building and slide along. There are a few guards inside the room, but if you are quick, they will not spot you. Beyond the windows, continue following along the side of the building.

Move quickly along the narrow ledge. If you're spotted, it won't take long for the guards to get rid of you.

Finally, you come to a point with a small balcony above you. You can walk to the far side and jump up. A better way is to do as Q suggests and use your grappling wire to snag onto the hook over the door. Once you drop down from the grapple, you'll move to the next part of the mission.

You can walk around and jump to the ledge, but using the grapple is quicker and a lot cooler.

Infiltrate the Party

Since you have three methods of completing the first mission, there are three possible starting positions for the second. If you jumped onto the back of the truck, you'll start the mission here. The truck will drive through the gate and you come under fire from a pair of guards on the ground below you. Dispatch them quickly and turn around. The truck backs into the building, which holds a third guard. Drop him, collect his weapon, and burn through the locked gate to find some armor plating. From this point forward, completing this mission is the same as going through the main gate. Skip the next paragraph.

If you come in on the truck, expect to draw fire immediately. You can drop to the ground if you wish. This will make you easier to hit, but will improve your aim.

If you walked through the main gate, you'll be on the same level as the two guards. Drill both as quickly as you can and collect their weapons. Enter the door next to where the truck stops and plug the third guard. Get the armor if you need it.

It's a good idea to eliminate this guard even if you don't need the body armor now. You may later, and this clears the way to it.

Leave this area and walk past where you entered. You can go forward or up a couple of stairs to your right. Take the stairs and walk carefully. It's hard to see the guard on the other side of the window in the building. If you can, whack him, then go to the door on the far side of the courtyard.

Inside, there's another guard (there will be two if you failed to drop the guard behind the window). Inside, you find a control panel with large switch. Flip the switch or shoot the panel. This allows you to shut off the power to the entrance to the interior of the castle. At the top of the stairs, there is a bulletproof vest. When you are ready, leave and cross the courtyard to where you entered.

You haven't found the door the switch here controls, but you may as well grant yourself access now.

You are back near where you entered this part of the mission. Go right to find the generator. Move in carefully, because there is a guard on the ledge above you. Shut down the generator to kill all of the spotlights in the area.

With the generator off, you can sneak past the guards in the next courtyard.

NOTE
Shutting off the spotlights instead of destroying them or shooting the guards manning them is a Bond move.

TIP
There's a place to attach your grapple on the ledge. Use it to find the first secret in this mission. On the ledge, you can find some grenades and armor, as well as the weapon of the guard who was here. To get back down to the ground, drop through the hole next to the armor.

Continue forward through the next area. There is a guard at each spotlight on the ledges above you. If you stick close to the wall to your left, you can get past them without having to shoot them. Make your way to the door at the far end of the area and go through it. This leads to a room with a door into the castle on your right and a staircase on your left.

With the spotlights out, you can pass this courtyard without firing a shot.

You don't have to take the stairs, but it's worthwhile. Go all the way to the top, passing the landing on the second floor for now. At the top, you spot a pair of guards, one of whom is armed with a sniper rifle. Plug them both and collect the sniper rifle in case you need it later—it will come in handy at the end of this scene. Go back down the stairs to the second floor landing. If you need it, there's armor to be found as well as a flash grenade. You can't open any of the doors here, so don't worry about them. Instead, return to the main floor.

The sniper rifle is valuable for the end of the mission, and climbing to the top of the tower is worth the effort.

Walk away from the stairs and go straight to the door. The lights should be green—this is the door you activated with the switch near the beginning of the mission. Open the door, but don't go through. Inside there's a host of guards. The first is looking over the balcony on the stairs directly in front of you. Plug him.

You'll notice right away that the spotlights in this area are still working. Turn right and shoot the spotlight here. Use your Q-Specs and switch to IR to spot the guards on this balcony easily. Drop them both, then walk out carefully. Turn around and look up.

The spotlights are still working here. Shooting them makes you a harder target to spot.

There's another spotlight right above you. You can shoot the guards from your current position or you can use a hand grenade. This is a tough throw, though, but much quicker if you are accurate. If you don't want to worry about it, use a gun. IR vision helps with aiming.

TIP
Shoot the large icicle. It will fall and cause the guards to shine the spotlight away from you.

When all the guards are gone, go up the stairs to the glass door. You've made it inside. M tells you that both the deep operative and Agent Nightshade will meet you in the library inside. You strip out of your outer clothes, revealing a tuxedo underneath. You're ready for the party.

NOTE
In addition to losing your camouflage, you also drop all of your weapons and all of your gadgets except your wristwatch.

Note
If you started this mission next to the tower, there will be two guards next to the garden walkway near the line of spotlights.

If you came in the back way, you've got a more interesting path. You start on the second floor of the tower. Go to the top and claim the sniper rifle. From here, you can pick off a number of the guards manning the spotlights, which will make your path to the generator much easier. You can't prevent the guards from turning on the lights, but you can prevent the guards from being there in the first place.

Go to the ground floor and outside. Take care of the guard above the door and run forward to the generator. This controls the spotlights, which you've already dealt with. You should take out the guard on the ledge above you and claim the items there if for no other reason than to find the secret area. However, since the guard at each spotlight is gone, you will not get credit for the Bond moment by turning off this generator.

From here, your path is similar to the others. You can take out the three guards near the front entrance and proceed to silence those around the fountain and protecting the switch controlling the door to the interior. With this switch taken care of, retrace your steps to where you started, finishing the scene as on the other two paths.

Remember to unlock the door to the interior, or you won't be able to move on.

The Party

Regardless of how you completed the first two parts of this mission, you start the third section in the same place: a hallway inside Drake's house. Your task this time is to rendezvous with Agent Zoe Nightshade and the deep cover operative while maintaining your cover. This means no fighting, which is good, because you are currently armed only with your fists and your wristwatch.

Drake's goons line the hallways inside the house. Fortunately, you don't have to deal with them yet.

Walk past the guard to the door at the end of the hall. This opens up to a balcony. You arrive here just in time to hear Drake's speech regarding the events of the night—a fund for refugees. After Drake's short speech, the guests retire to the salon. Drake tells his associate to play hostess while he attends to business.

When the cinematic ends, you are told to collect your gadgets from the waiter, who is a plant. Head down the stairs, ignoring the guards for now. At the bottom of the stairs in the gallery, approach the waiter and speak with him. You decline a drink, but you happily take your collection of items. Once you are

done with the waiter, you will have your cigarette lighter camera, the dart pen, and the stunner in addition to your wristwatch.

The waiter holds your gadgets. Getting these is critical to completing the mission.

Once you have collected the items, you are told that Alexander Mayhew's bodyguard is in attendance. You must photograph the four woman guests in the gallery. Once you do, the pictures will be uploaded to MI6 immediately. Set to work with the lighter camera and get snapshots of all four women. You will need to get fairly close to them to get a good enough shot. Once all four pictures are taken, you can put away the camera.

MI6 doesn't know which of the four women is Mayhew's bodyguard, so you'll need a picture of each.

NOTE
For a little fun, try putting on the Q-Specs and switching to x-ray mode. While the male guests appear as skeletons, the female guests reveal their lingerie. Just what you'd expect from 007.

Armitage Rook who was guarding the doorway upstairs has walked away at this point, allowing you to get through the door. Do so and follow the path to the door at the end. This opens to reveal the library, where you are supposed to make contact with Nightshade.

Once you have all the pictures, the path to the library opens.

The dart pen works quickly. Hit the goons and move and be sure to collect their guns.

Before Nightshade arrives, you meet the deep cover agent, Dominique Paradis from French intelligence. As you reacquaint yourself with her, Agent Nightshade of the C.I.A. arrives. Nightshade tells you that Mayhew has arrived with the guidance device. Dominique tells you that Drake has retired to the conference room, probably to take possession of the item. You've got to get there and photograph the meeting. If you can get it, you need the device itself. The women leave, Dominique to return to the party and Nightshade to create a distraction for you.

Climb to the top of the stairs in the library and walk to the door. As you leave, M tells you that she wants you at the meeting between Drake and Mayhew. You aren't to endanger any civilians, but you can take out any of Drake's men you encounter. Equip your dart pen and walk to the door on your right.

As you open the next door, M contacts you again. She tells you that agent Paradise has informed MI6 that Drake placed some files in his safe. She doesn't know what they are, but they are likely of interest. The safe is behind a painting in the red gallery, which happens to be the room you've just entered.

If you wish to find the safe, open fire on the goon on the floor below you. Jump the railing and get to the ground below. The painting in question is the one to the left of the fireplace. Open it and use the wristwatch on the safe beyond. Inside, you find some grenades and the papers M was talking about. When you are done, climb the stairs at the far end of the room and go to the door and the hallway beyond. If you don't wish to open the safe, you can simply walk across the beams to the far end of the room and go through the door.

Your dart pen will come in handy until you run out of ammunition. By then, you'll have acquired other weapons.

When you open the door, you spot a goon at the far end of the room. Silence him with a dart, then take out anyone else who investigates. There are a number of guards here, and it's likely you'll run out of darts before you drop them all. Collect a pistol or two and use it to fight back, grabbing more ammunition when you can. Leave through the door at the far end of the room and continue through the next hallway.

TIP
Opening the safe is the second secret in the first mission.

Follow the short hallway to the next door and enter it. When you do, you'll see the meeting between Mayhew and Drake. Mayhew gives the stolen missile guidance module to Drake, who asks about something like NightFire. As Mayhew is answering, two of Drake's thugs enter with Nightshade between them. She's been caught. Drake tells his men to take her to the cable car station.

Now you've got a fight on your hands. Use the balcony as cover and drop a few of the guards below you. They'll retaliate, and one will hurl a flash grenade at you. To avoid being caught in the blast, run back into the hallway. Your own grenades are useful here. A few of the goons will charge up at you, coming through the door opposite where you entered. Plug them and get their weapons, then leave, going down the stairs they came up. This will take you to the conference room below.

The balcony is a good place for a few rounds and a few grenades. Watch the door to your right.

Remove any remaining thugs. The only exit from the room is through the bookcase, which has opened to reveal a secret passage. Slip through and move carefully, since there's a final thug at the bottom of the stairs around the corner. Hit him and go through, down the next set of stairs. This will take you to the final scene in this mission.

The Cable Car

You start the final part of the first mission on the staircase where you ended the last scene. Continue to the bottom and turn to your right. Slide left and plug the goon waiting for you. If you need it, you can burn through the lock to find a

bulletproof vest as well as some smoke grenades.

When you are ready, walk toward the last goon you flattened and again turn to the right. Slide left again to find the second thug. He ducks behind the crates in the back corner, so time your shots when he appears and split him. Walk forward, but look to your left.

There are four enemies by the gondola, at least at the beginning of this scene.

You should notice a couple of downed guards that you didn't slay. These are the two who dragged Nightshade here, and it looks like she's managed to take care of them. Walk down the short staircase and flip the large switch. This turns on the cable car, which will allow you to escape.

Once the cable car is turned on, you'll be able to make your escape.

Walk toward the second goon you took out. This time, turn left and slide right. There's a third thug down by the cable car. Like the last one, he ducks behind crates to avoid your shots. A couple of solid hits to the head will silence him. Go down the stairs, again turning to the left.

The final goon is on the other side of the cable car. Shoot him, then turn around. In a crate you find a huge weapon. This is a missile launcher, and you'll want it in a minute or two. Get it, then jump onto the cable car. Nightshade has located the guidance module and has it with her. When you are ready, hit the green switch to start the cable car moving.

Don't pass up the rocket launcher! You'll definitely want this for the trouble ahead.

You and Nightshade zoom away, but just as it appears you've made it out safely, the cable car stops. Two thugs appear back in the station, and you hear the sound of an approaching helicopter from the right. Split the goons with your pistol—it's the most accurate weapon you have. If you are quick, you can nail both before the helicopter gets too close.

You need to eliminate Drake's men before you turn your attentions on the helicopter.

With these two down, switch to the rocket launcher. As the helicopter approaches, fire a rocket or two. It will fly under the car and back, with guards inside peppering the inside of the cable car with bullets on every pass.

There are more guards inside you'll need to knock out. You can use any weapon you've got, but the rocket launcher is the most effective one you have. By right-clicking on the mouse, you can control the missile to some extent, which will help your overall accuracy.

The rocket launcher might not be incredibly accurate, but it is very powerful, and even near hits will get rid of the guys shooting at you.

Once all three shooters are down, the helicopter itself will go up in smoke. You and Nightshade climb to the roof of the car and slide down the cable while the helicopter goes out of control, taking out the cable car behind you. You've managed to survive this far, but you've still got to get off the mountain.

Using the targeted mode of firing can help your rocket launcher accuracy.

CAUTION
The guided rockets have a limited life span when fired.

Austria Ambush

Airfield

Bond and Agent Zoe Nightshade have reached an airfield. While it offers a way off the mountain, it's also heavily guarded. Being spotted by anyone ends the mission in failure—you must accomplish your objectives without attracting any attention whatsoever. You decide to send Nightshade to handle the alarms while you take care of the guard and spotlight towers.

When the mission starts, Agent Nightshade is crouched behind you. Turn and move behind her, and wait for her to move. She runs forward to the nearby building. Do the same and wait. After a few moments, Nightshade tells you that you need to take care of the spotlights.

Move when Zoe does. You're safe from view against this building.

Walk around the back of the building. As you turn the corner to the left, you spot someone manning a spotlight on the back corner. If you hug the building, you can sneak past him. You can also silence him with the dart pen or take him out with a silenced pistol shot or two.

It's easy to miss this guard on the corner of the building, but taking him out here means you won't have to later.

TIP

Once the guard is down, look for a grapple point on the radio tower directly above where he was standing. Use this to reach the roof and collect grenades and ammunition. Drop off the grapple as soon as you are over the roof or the fall will damage you. Don't touch the other guard here, or the alarm sounds. This is another secret.

Go around the next corner to the generator box. Burn through the lock with your wristwatch, open it up, and flip the switch. This shuts down all of the spotlights around the airfield. Retrace your steps to Nightshade and sit tight. Nothing will happen until you get there.

Open the generator to shut off the lights. This allows Zoe to sneak inside the security office.

When you do, Nightshade makes a break for it. She runs for the door, but as she approaches, she hears a guard. Nightshade ducks out of the way, and when the coast is clear, she enters the building. Nightshade is now inside, but you've got your own problems. The guard who has just appeared speaks with the one standing nearby, telling him to look at the spotlight generator. He walks toward you.

Pull back a bit. Let this guard come around the corner and out of the line of sight of the other guards. When he has, take him down and get his security badge. You need this to get into the next building.

Knock out the guard going to check on the generator. This clears the way to the tower.

Use the offices across the hall to avoid the camera and the guard.

Go back to where you began the scene and look up at the aircraft control tower. A guard stands on the corner of it. Drop him with a couple of pistol shots or a carefully fired dart. Once he is down, wait for the second tower guard to make his rounds and nail him as well. This makes things easier later in the mission.

This is a tough shot, but you need to silence these guards eventually, and now is better than later.

Go up the short staircase to your left and through the door labeled Control Tower Administration. As you enter, Nightshade contacts you, telling you that she hasn't yet succeeded in shutting off the cameras. Be careful while moving through this building. You have a problem right away. At the first intersection, right in front of you, there's a guard to your left and a camera on the right.

Wait for the guard to get a drink from the water fountain, and run forward to the door ahead and to the left. Duck inside and wait for him to walk by. There's nothing in here, but it makes a convenient place to sit for a moment. When the camera has panned away, cross the hall to the administrator's office. Open the desk drawer to

NOTE
Finding the Kowloon gives you credit for locating a secret.

Go back to the hallway and move directly under the camera. You're safe from detection here, at least for the time being. Let the camera pan back to where you entered. Use this opportunity to move through the door on your right. You are now in the administration offices. You can move through several rooms here without having to worry about the cameras.

The second room here leads back to the hallway. Wait for the patrolling guard to walk past and keep your eye on the camera outside. When the guard walks away and the camera has panned off, go out the door and run across the hall toward the server room. Turn around and duck into the utility closet area. Again, wait for the camera to pan away before moving.

When you are behind the guard, you don't have to worry about getting rid of him.

TIP
Inside the utility closet is the third secret: an ammunition bag holding frag and flash grenades as well as 9mm ammo.

Continue down the hallway and duck into the accounting office. There isn't anything here, but it's a convenient place to stop. Turn around and look into the hall. The lounge across and to your right has a camera in the back. Wait for it to pan all the way left, then run under it. Once there, let it pan back to the right. Head for the stairs at the back of the area.

The stairs up are your next target. Wait for the camera above you to pan away before you run for them.

The good news is: While you are upstairs, you don't need to worry about cameras. The bad news is that there are two guards inside the room, and you need to get inside. Use the dart pen or the silenced Wolfram to quell both. Get the bulletproof vest from the table if you need it. More importantly, snag the level 2 security pass. When you have this, leave the room. Back in the hallway, go down the stairs to your right.

Once the guard is out of the way, get the armor and the pass. The armor is optional, but the security pass is a must.

There is a camera at the bottom of the stairs to your right. Let it pan off, then run under it. When it moves back to the stairs, go to the door, access the control pad, and leave. This takes you to a long staircase leading up to the control tower. Start walking.

It's a long staircase to the top. The good news is that there's no one here.

Near the top of the stairs, you find a door labeled "catwalk access." Go outside to collect the sniper rifles from the guards you dropped earlier. Go back in and wait for Agent Nightshade to contact you. When she tells you that she's managed to shut off the cameras, you can move. Go up the last of the stairs and into the control tower. There are three guards here, so split them all and collect the additional sniper rifle lying nearby. Load up your Wolfram and systematically shoot all of the monitors in the control tower to disable it completely.

Get rid of all of the monitors to trigger the next part of the mission.

When the last monitor goes up in smoke, you see a brief cutscene in which Nightshade bursts out of the security office, pursued by guards. When you regain control, run down to the catwalk and equip the sniper rifle. Nightshade needs you to protect her, but first you have to protect yourself. Take out any guards standing on top of the buildings in the area, because they concentrate their fire on you. Once they are out of the way, start picking off enemies on the ground.

Agent Nightshade's safety depends on your accuracy with the sniper rifle. Shoot and move quickly to get them all.

Don't worry too much about Nightshade. She moves around on the ground while you handle the bad guys. Try to keep track of where she is. When she makes a break for the gate, look down. Two enemies appear directly beneath you. Pick them off, and Nightshade's path to the building below is clear.

Once Nightshade is gone, run down the stairs to the bottom of the tower. Retrace your steps to the outside, fighting through the guards as you go. You can't enter the door Nightshade did, but back on the ground, a guard opens a door for you near the loading dock. Take him out and take that door to continue.

NOTE
An alternate entrance to the main warehouse is located on the far right side of the building. Find the door marked "Main Warehouse Administration." It leads to the back offices.

TIP
If you jump and crouch onto the crates by the second truck, you can jump into the back of the truck. Burn the lock off the crate to collect another Kowloon pistol and some ammunition. This is a secret.

Once inside, collect the bulletproof vest and go through the door marked Main Warehouse. When you do, you are attacked by a huge number of guards. Fight your way through them into the warehouse, and cautiously start moving. The red barrels explode once they take enough damage.

The main warehouse is filled with enemies. Take them one or two at a time to avoid being overwhelmed.

TIP
If your armor is still okay, consider taking the bulletproof vest after you take out the first few guards.

Start moving through the warehouse carefully. Look between stacks of crates for additional guards. The small administration offices contain several guards. Explore both fully. In the one on the left, find crates of ammunition and weapons and a good amount of armor plating. When you are done, return to the warehouse.

If you can take out enemies before they are aware of you, this will be easier.

Back in the warehouse, move down the narrow aisle between the crates. You emerge in an open area with some large pipes on your left. Crawl through the pipes once the area is clear. A few more goons are on the far side. Slaughter them with extreme prejudice and take a look around. Take the door and go through the next room to return to the outside. While you are here, Nightshade contacts you and tells you that she is in the primary hangar. Your job is to check out the secondary hangar.

The pipes offer a little cover. Act quickly to take down the guards because your mobility is limited.

Use the scope with the sniper rifle to ensure accuracy.

TIP

Use crouch-jumps to get on the crates and then the freight cars. Proceed to the administration offices and walk along the roof to the fenced area at the back, where you find armor, grenades, and ammunition. You've tallied another secret!

That's easier said than done. The outside is crawling with thugs. Use grenades to suppress them and take them down with any weapons except the sniper rifle. You need this later. If you have a lot of ammunition, you can use it. It's not fast, but it is efficient and effective.

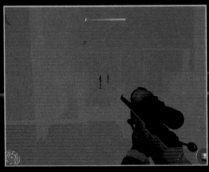

X-ray mode on the Q-Specs gives you an idea of what to expect before you open the door.

Your goal is the maintenance garage, on the other side of the compound. Make your way over, carefully picking off any enemies in your way. The Q-Specs are extremely effective here, both on X-ray and IR modes. Once you get to the mainte-nance office, rearm yourself and collect the bullet-proof vest. When you are ready, step into the secondary hangar, on the other side of this small room. Ready your sniper rifle before you leave.

Be observant. It doesn't look like much, but that's an enemy peeking over the crate in front of you.

When you step outside, Nightshade joins you. You've found Drake's private plane. While Agent Nightshade gets the plane out onto the runway, cover her from the radar tower. Start by taking out the guards on the radar tower. When they are down, run there and climb up to the first level.

TIP

If you climb to the tower's second level, you can use the machinery for cover.

Enemies appear on the tarmac behind where you climb up. They also come out the door by Nightshade. Switch your view back and forth. While you can't safely target the barrels near Nightshade, the ones on the tarmac are fair game, and can help you silence groups of enemies at a time.

Keep moving the scope to find and eliminate all the foes.

It takes Nightshade a few minutes to get the plane ready to leave. Once she starts taxiing away, climb down to the ground and run out to meet her. You don't have much time, so don't hesitate. Run out to the tarmac and run next to the plane. You hop onboard and fly away to Switzerland. The guidance chip is back in your hands, at least for now.

Once the area is clear, board the plane and go.

Uninvited Guests

Escort

> **NOTE**
>
> Unlike most missions, here you can travel between the different scenes frequently. The following walkthrough suggests one path through that allows you to find all of the secrets and claim all of the Bond moves.

MI6 has determined that Rafael Drake plans to eliminate Alexander Mayhew, the head of his Asian operation. Drake blames Mayhew for the security breach in Austria and is now cleaning house. Mayhew has agreed to give up important information regarding Project: NightFire on one condition: you must be the one to bring him in. He's currently holed up in his Japanese estate with his bodyguard, Kiko Haiyashi.

It should be a simple pick-up and extraction, but you haven't arrived alone. Moments after you arrive, Drake's men appear to eliminate Mayhew. You've got to get him to his security bunker in one piece.

When the mission begins, expect to be attacked.

You don't have much time to react. As soon as you regain control, a thug appears in the hallway just beyond the glass door. Take him out and get his weapon, a Commando. When he drops, Mayhew runs through the broken window to the left. Follow him and use your X-ray Q-Specs to look through the door he's standing by.

Another goon is inside. With luck, he'll have his back to you and you can take him out quickly and efficiently. Grab his weapon and again let Mayhew show you where to go. He moves to the doorway and stops. When you are ready, go through.

Attacking from surprise has benefits here. If you can sneak up behind this guy, you can knock him unconscious.

> **TIP**
>
> There is a door on the side wall opposite where you entered. Go inside to find Mayhew's security area. Through a door at the back, grab a Commando and a clip as well as some armor. Doing this brings an extra guard to attack you when you try to leave this area.

Look right. Three more thugs are in here, and you should have the drop on them. Take out at least one before you draw any fire. Slide over to the left side of the room for easier firing angles at the remaining goons, especially if you eliminate the closest one first. When the room is clear, Mayhew again runs in and heads to the door at the back. Follow him. Collect the ammunition first, and make sure your weapon is fully loaded.

Several Yakuza goons wait for you in this large gallery. You need to clear the path for Mayhew to enter the room.

Crouch and move in carefully, not going past the wall to your right into the main room. Sit tight here and wait for the guy on the balcony to walk past. Nail him with a few silenced pistol shots to prevent him from tossing grenades your way later. Arm the Commando and lean around the right corner. Plant the two thugs on the ground level before ducking back. There's one more on the top floor. Move in carefully and nail him.

The main gallery holds more thugs as well as the secret entrance to Mayhew's bunker.

With the four goons in this area dealt with, Mayhew enters the room and runs to a painting. Go in yourself and collect all of the ammunition you can find. The picture hides the entrance to Mayhew's bunker. When you have collected all of the ammunition in the area, return to Mayhew and leave.

Once all of the Yakuza have been dealt with, Mayhew retreats to his bunker.

Mayhew's Bunker and the Bathhouse

Mayhew tells you that what you need is locked in his bedroom safe. He gives you a small white marble and tells you to "feed the dragon" to open the safe. Mayhew also asks you to wipe the hard drive on his computer so that Drake can't use the data stored there. Finally, Mayhew begs you to look out for his servants and rescue them if possible.

Collect the weapons and ammunition near Mayhew, then go down the winding hallway to the storage locker. Burn the lock and take the weapons inside. The grenades will be particularly useful in the upcoming areas. Trigger the switch next to the ladder and climb up to the top. This puts you behind the bathhouse.

Check out the locker before climbing the ladder. You find valuable items inside—and rack up another secret.

Equip the sniper rifle and look over toward the bridge. Pick off the four guards one by one. When they are gone, cross the bridge and look toward the door into the building on the opposite side. A fifth guard is here. Again, a sniper shot clears the way.

The sniper rifle is invaluable for clearing the path to the bathhouse.

Walk forward from the bridge, off the path, and into the water. Walk up to the building and crouch. Find a tunnel directly in front of you. Swim through until you spot the ladder in the distance. Climb up the ladder and go through the trapdoor at the top. You've entered the back of the bathhouse, directly behind the hostage and the man holding her.

More ammunition and goodies are inside this locked chest. Even better, you can open it without alerting the nearby guards. It's another secret.

A quick shot frees the hostage and puts you a little closer to completing your mission.

Sneak up to the nearby case and burn the lock to find another Commando, armor, and a flash grenade. Drop the guard to rescue the hostage, who thanks you properly. The two exits from this room both lead to the same area, but if you go right, you'll be spotted. Go left and toss a flash grenade into the next room to stun the goons. Drop both, then go left through the next two doors. This takes you back outside to a position near the viewing platform.

A well-placed grenade helps clear this room and open the way to the viewing platform.

NOTE

There are two additional paths to the viewing pavilion. You can drop back to the tunnel behind the bathhouse and continue to the left to the end. Or, if you go right past the two guards, you return to the area behind the bathhouse. Cross the bridge and walk around to the large wooden gate to reach the viewing platform.

The Viewing Pavilion

NOTE

Leaving through the house is the easiest path in to this part of the mission. If you decide to go through the tunnel, you start below the house. If you come via the gate, you're distant from the viewing platform, but in a good position to snipe.

Equip your sniper rifle and put on the Q-Specs set to infrared vision. Goons walk the grounds outside the viewing pavilion. Start shooting. Pick off a few from your beginning location, and move a bit to find the rest. Half a dozen thugs roam outside the house. If you are quick, you shouldn't draw any fire from them.

While you don't need the IR vision, it helps your aim tremendously.

The viewing pavilion is the building sitting over the water. Walk around until you have a good view inside. A goon holds a woman hostage. Once again, use the sniper rifle and drop the thug. This frees the hostage.

One more shot, and the hostage is free.

Now you have an issue—there doesn't seem to be a good way back into the house without backtracking all the way through the bathhouse. You can do this if you wish, but there is a more

elegant solution. Shoot the two red lanterns on the wire between the shore and the viewing platform. Climb up the rocks under the wire and go hand-over-hand to the platform. Be careful of the two areas where the lanterns were; they spark occasionally. If you are hanging on to an area that sparks, you drop into the water. This solution not only saves you the trouble of backtracking, it awards you with a Bond move.

Destroy the hanging lanterns to clear the wire.

Once that's done, clamber across to the platform itself.

Check out the viewing platform if you wish, but there's nothing there save the ammunition from the thugs you killed. Walk down the long hallway to the door at the end. Put on the Q-Specs and switch to X-ray vision, and you can see three guards in the room beyond. Puncture them and enter the room. Look left toward the next door.

The Q-Specs help you shoot accurately through the paper walls.

Approach the door and again don the Q-Specs. A goon stands directly on the other side, and if you look carefully, you can see another in the kitchen a little way back. Hit both and move out carefully. Enter the kitchen and look into the pantry on your left. Drill the thug here, then return to the hallway and look left. Follow the hallway around to the door at the far end. Go through the very small courtyard to the next door. This takes you back inside the main house.

One more Yakuza bullyboy to go and the kitchen will be clear.

NOTE

Technically, walking back into the main house takes you back to the first scene in this mission. However, for the sake of clarity, it will be considered a part of the third scene.

You are now back inside the room where you first met Mayhew. Walk forward through the glass door and outside. Follow the same path you did with Mayhew until you come to the large wooden door. Stop here.

The carport is just outside this large double door.

Open the door to find three goons outside, the one in the middle standing over the third hostage. Drop all three to free the girl. Then collect the ammunition and return to the house. The sniper rifle works well here simply because it quickly eliminates foes.

With the third hostage rescued, you've got only two more to save.

Retrace your steps back to the room you started the mission in. The door to the right of the mural leads to the final scene and the last two hostages. Go through it when you are ready.

The Library

You are in a hallway that leads left. Open the door on your right. You see a guard directly in front of you, but if you are quick, he won't see you. Plug him and walk out into the garden area. Go around the walkway to your right and drill the second goon. This clears this area. Continue around the path to the stairs and get to the ground.

Once again the Q-Specs come in handy.

Walk forward and look up to see a grapple point. Use it to reach the second floor of the library and claim another Bond move. Arm yourself and enter. Some thugs are inside, mostly on the balcony level with you. Be careful when you look down into the library, because the fourth hostage is here, and stray bullets will end your mission.

The grapple point gets you inside on the top floor of the library, which is easier and safer than the path through the house.

Walk down the stairs and curl around. Go through the library and look left. Shoot the passing guard, then investigate the bookcase to the right. A red book with a Phoenix logo sticks out just a little. Activate it to open a secret area filled with armor and ammunition, both of which you likely need.

Activate the red book to open a secret panel loaded with weapons and armor.

Leave the secret area and go out the door to your right. In the hall beyond, exit through the double door back to the garden. Walk straight across to the door on the other side. As you do, notice the open windows on the roof. These windows are your next goal.

At the door, put on the Q-Specs with X-ray vision activated and shoot the two thugs right by the door. Once they are down, enter and look slightly right to spot the staircase. Drop the goon guarding it and walk forward carefully. Another one is in the room to your left, and one above him on the balcony. Slay both and take the stairs.

Using X-ray mode on the Q-Specs helps you eliminate goons without putting yourself at risk.

There is a single room at the top of the stairs. Destroy the guard inside and get the body armor if you need it (you shouldn't). Climb on the items under the windows, then crouch-jump to reach the roof. Walk over to the skylights and look down. Swat the two guards standing over the hostage. You now have saved all of the hostages. Only Mayhew's computer and the information you came for remain.

You've got the drop on the guards standing over the fifth and final hostage.

TIP

Open the closet in the room with the guard and the body armor (for another secret). There's a locked chest inside. Burn off the lock to find a silenced MP9, two clips, and a frag grenade.

NOTE

Dropping in via the balcony is this mission's final Bond move.

Crouch and crawl through the skylight. Drop onto the beam below you, then drop to the ground. Walk out the door and look left. Pin the goon at the end of the hall, then turn around. Two more thugs are behind you. A grenade can take them both if you are careful. Otherwise, mop them up with anything other than the sniper rifle, because you'll need this soon.

Walk left down the hall toward the first guard you shot here. The rightmost of the two rooms to the left contains another guard. Take him out so he doesn't appear behind you. Walk to the door at the end of the hall. Open it and silence the thug standing over the computer. Continue firing to destroy the computer. This fulfills another objective.

Shoot through the thug and take out the computer to fulfill another mission objective.

Enter the room and go to the door on your left. This takes you back into the library. Walk to the back and go right through the narrow doorway. This leads you to Mayhew's bedroom. Be on your guard, because there are tons of enemies here.

Go past the door on your left to the room beyond. You can step in carefully, but three enemies lurk here. Walk in and slide left to hit the guy standing in the bathroom. Once he drops, turn and face the main room. Whack the two thugs in here, then proceed into the room itself. Approach the single door out.

A quick shot helps reduce the odds in the area outside Mayhew's bedroom.

This door leads to Mayhew's bedroom, with four goons inside. Use the Q-Specs to scout the area and plug a couple of bad guys before you enter the room. The easiest guy to hit is the one standing at the back of the room. Defeat him, and two should come to the door without opening it, making them easy targets. The fourth enemy is inside to the left, near the dragon statue.

Drop the first thug and two more come to investigate. This sets up a couple of easy shots.

Enter the room when all of the guards are handled. Other than the dragon statue, the only thing of note is the dressing area to the right, which holds body armor. Activate the dragon to open the safe above it. Get the information you came for. This completes all of your objectives. Return to Mayhew's bunker to leave.

Once the safe is open and the access card collected, return to the bunker.

The simplest way is to leave Mayhew's bedroom the way you entered, through the library. Go through and past the ruined computer, out into the hallway. Walk to the far end and go through the door. In the next hall, again walk to the end and go out the door on the far side.

NOTE

Technically, you have returned to the first scene, and entering Mayhew's bunker returns you to the second scene.

Walk forward again and go to the painting on the left wall. Activate the door into the bunker and descend. Follow the hall around until you reach Mayhew. When you approach him, the scene ends.

The Assassin

Mayhew asks about Kiko, but you never saw her upstairs and you don't have time to worry about her now. The two of you prepare to leave the estate—you have everything you came for, so there's no reason to hang around. You tell Mayhew to wait so you can make sure the area is clear. He doesn't listen to you, much to his peril. As he steps out into the carpark, an assassin jumps down from the roof and slices the man fatally across the back. Mayhew lies dying, and you've now got a nasty fight on your hands.

The assassin is tough to defeat, partly because he's physically strong and partly because he is fast and has a number of devastating attacks. Your best weapon here is the sniper rifle because it does the most damage and can be fired accurately, if not quickly.

The ninja moves quickly. While the sniper rifle doesn't have a good rate of fire, it is powerful enough to handle the ninja with just a few shots.

The ninja assassin, when he has range, attacks with withering weapon fire. Keep moving to avoid his shots. If he wants to close the gap quickly, the assassin can move with blinding speed, rushing forward and swinging his katana to deadly effect. For truly deadly attacks, the ninja can also move from point to point instantly, again attacking with his katana. He also favors flash grenades, using your temporary blindness to move in for the strike.

You're the safest with the ninja far away and without a weapon drawn. Strike as often as possible then.

Your best defense is to keep moving quickly, sliding left and right to avoid the ninja's shots and katana swings. If he vanishes, start moving and don't stop until he reappears. Keep firing. You must hit him multiple times with the sniper rifle to finish him off, but you should be able to do it in short order, even if you take a lot of damage in the process.

Try not to let the ninja get any closer than this.

Once the assassin is defeated, approach Mayhew and speak with him. He tells you that the access card you retrieved allows you to gain access to the NightFire information at Phoenix International. To ensure his own safety, Mayhew didn't keep the material you need at his house (not that this plan did him any good). Just as Mayhew dies, Kiko appears. It's no longer safe for her, so you take her with you to Tokyo, and Phoenix International's building.

Getting In

You and Kiko drive to Tokyo and the headquarters of Phoenix International. Armed with the access card and Mayhew's password, you have everything you need. However, Kiko tells you that chances are good that the entire building has been locked down because of the security breach.

As you drive, Q calls and tells you about a few of your more interesting items. The magnetic grapples allow you to climb sheer glass or metal surfaces; the decryptor, disguised as a PDA, can grant you access to areas locked with numeric keypads; the Q-Worm is a computer program that allows MI6 to monitor any computer on which it is installed. With these gadgets, the mission ahead should be interesting, to say the least.

As you begin, M tells you to avoid killing the security guards because they are innocent civilians. You also need to avoid detection. This means you must use non-lethal methods to eliminate security guards. Your fists, dart pen, and stunner will be extremely useful. Start by approaching the guard walking in front of you. You don't have many darts, so don't waste one here. Instead, use either the stunner or your fists.

You need the dart pen to take out the guards near the elevators.

TIP

If you approach the two downed guards and go right, you find a Phoenix van. Investigate it to locate three flash grenades and get credit for finding a secret.

Now you need to be especially stealthy. Walk past the two guards you just dropped and spot the door with the yellow sign next to it. You must get to that door, and if possible, avoid using another dart. Creep forward; there's a technician working. Open the door, go through, and climb the stairs to the next floor. When you open the door, you move on to the next scene.

Knock the security guard out to prevent him from sounding the alarm.

If you are quick and stealthy, you can get by the last two guards without attacking.

Continue forward around the corner to your right. Hug the wall and creep up until you can hear the conversation between the two guards standing nearby. When they finish talking, back up and move behind the green car until you see both. Take out your dart pen and peg them both. There's no good way around them, and you need to make these shots from range. If they spot you, they will raise the alarm.

The Lobby

You need to get to the top of the building, but the main elevators are offline. To activate them, you must find a security pass and access the security office to turn the elevators on. Once this is done, you can use the elevators freely.

Two guards are walking away from you to your left. Follow them and listen to their conversation. One of the guards mentions that he left a security card on the front desk. Once you hear this, approach the pair and knock them senseless. Try not to use valuable darts here.

Once again, conserve your darts. Use your fists to disable these two guards.

The next part is a little tricky. Go back toward where you started and take the other path toward the front desk. As you approach a large, open area, you are notified to use your Q-Specs on X-ray mode to pass the one-way glass to your right. A better way is to look up on the balcony. Use your grapple to swing up and claim a Bond move. Silence the two guards on this balcony, walk to the far side, and drop back down to the ground.

The grapple is handy for bypassing the security area on the ground floor.

TIP

On the overlook at the far end of the balcony, find a Kowloon and a clip for it. You've grabbed another secret.

Again, you have two possible paths, one left and one right. The left path is better. Walk until the area in front of you opens up into the main lobby. Two guards are here, one behind the desk and one near the front door. The guard behind the desk is sleeping, so don't worry about him. Take out the guard by the door with a well-placed dart, and crouch down.

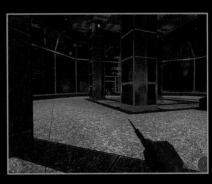

If you are careful, the guard behind the desk won't spot you.

Go over to the main desk. When you get to the desk, stand up and take the access card. Return the way you came, back to the last open area with the one-way glass. Hug the right wall back to where you started, and again take the path to the right from your starting location. The first door on the right opens to the security area, and you now have a pass to get in.

This door leads to the security office. Once inside, you can turn on the elevators.

Duck inside, and be ready for the single guard here. Once he is out of the way, approach the red glowing panel in the back of the room. Using your decryptor (as recommended by Q), unscramble it and turn the elevators back on.

CAUTION

Guards knocked out by Bond will eventually wake up. Be quick in this level or cautious when returning to the elevator area. The guards may have regained consciousness and try to sound the alarm.

Use the decryptor to activate the elevators. When this is done, it's time to move on.

All that remains now is leaving. Go back to the hallway and go left to your starting location. The elevators are now online. As you approach the elevators, Q contacts you. He tells you that there are invisible tripwires in the offices above. You have to use your Q-Specs to see them. Call an elevator down, and when it arrives, step in to be carried to the next scene.

Dodging Security

Move quickly when this scene starts. Move to the round desk and duck down, because a guard is walking nearby. Peek out to make sure he's walked away, then look around the corner. Once the guard is moving along and the camera has panned off, run left down the hallway.

Again, be cautious, because there's another guard here. This one is more problematic, though, because you need to get through him. Knock him out or stun him and run past. The rounded corridor to your left leads nowhere, so avoid it. Instead, continue down the hallway in front of you.

Move slowly to take out this security guard without raising the alarm.

Lean out around the corner to the right. If you look with the Q-Specs, you see a trio of laser tripwires across the hallway, so that path is out.

To avoid them, go through the door to the left. Follow this series of offices around to the right and back to the hallway. Be careful of the guard and camera in the hall. You know you're at the right place when Q contacts you and tells you to be wary of the cameras.

If you trail behind the guard, you don't have much to worry about until you encounter the cameras.

TIP

If you don't want to keep putting the Q-Specs on, look at the walls. Any time you see a column of small, black squares, you've found a laser tripwire location.

The way around this guard and camera is simple: the door across the hall that leads into the server room. While in the server room, wait for the guard to walk past to the right, then duck out and curl around to the left. Run down the hall to the first door on your right, which is labeled as the kitchen. There's a camera here, too, but don't worry about it. It's right across from the door. If it's not pointing directly at you, you can cross the room and stand under it.

Hide in the server room to the left and wait for the guard to walk away to continue.

When the kitchen camera pans left, run across the room to the door at the far end. Go through and run directly under the camera across from you in the hallway. You can't get through the double doors here, but you can enter the small door that was to your left as you exited. This is where you need to go. There is ammo for your Dart Pen through the second door on the left.

Follow this darkened room around to the back and right to another hallway. The administration computer is in the office in front of you. Enter and use the Q-Worm. Now MI6 can monitor this system remotely. That's one down, one to go. Backtrack all the way to the last camera, being wary of the guard to the right out in the hallway.

Use the Q-Worm to link this computer to MI6 head-quarters.

The next part is quite tricky. Run under the camera again, heading down the hallway. This leads to an atrium with a couple of guards. You can take out the guards if you wish, but there's a better way. Equip your grapple and use it to haul yourself up to the hooks holding the massive artwork. Use the grapple again to move from the first sculpture to the second, then drop down and continue forward. Not only does this allow you to avoid the guards, you also get credit for a Bond move.

The hanging sculptures are the best way through the atrium.

Your next goal is just a few feet down the next hallway. It's the first door on the right. Hide inside before the guard spots you. Go through this office to the next hallway. Another guard is here, but at least it's camera free. Silence the security guard and go through the door labeled "Accounting Exec." The second computer is here. Install the Q-Worm and leave.

One more Q-Worm installation and you can move on.

Out the door, take the first left. The door at the end of the hall is the security office. Gain entrance via your access card and quiet the man inside. Use the decryptor on the red panel. This shuts off the laser tripwires for about 30 seconds, giving you ample time to escape. To leave, go out of the security office and go right. The first door on your left leads to the stairs. Access the door, and you move to the next scene.

Use fists or the stunner on the final security guard to gain access to the panel.

Elevators

You've made it deeper inside Phoenix International, but you still have farther to go. Here, your job is to plant the Q-Worm into the elevator control computer. Stay undetected and avoid slaying any innocents. You may be low on darts, which means you need to rely on your fists and your stunner to continue. Fortunately, this level has no cameras.

In front of you are a set of windows with a worker behind them. Go to the left of the windows and through the door. Stun or knock out the worker and continue across the room to the door at the far side. Go through it to the room beyond.

This worker goes down easily. Knock him out quickly and there's no chance of the alarm sounding.

> **TIP**
>
> If you go right at the windows, you find a storeroom at the end. Burn the lock off the locker here to find a Commando, armor, a flash grenade, and both 9mm and Kowloon ammo. It's another secret!

Now you have your work cut out for you. A number of workers are in here, and any one can set off the alarm. Walk out onto the catwalk and turn left. Peg the guy standing outside the central area with a dart, then drop to the ground. Knock out the two workers on the floor, and proceed up the stairs at the far end of the room.

> **TIP**
>
> If Bond disables the fuse box, the worker and security guard will eventually make their way to the fuse box. Bond can avoid knocking out either of the two if he waits for them to pass by after he downloads the Q-Worm.

You have to be fast and accurate to silence all the workers in this large room.

At the top of the stairs, go through the door. Turn left immediately and use your wristwatch on the lock. When the fuse box opens, pop a shot into the controls to knock out the lights in the area. Not only does this make you difficult to see,

it gives you credit for another Bond move. Turn around and walk down the hallway, turning left at the first opportunity. Walk toward the red light.

Make your exit simpler—shut off the lights by opening this fuse box.

Go through the door at the end of this area and disable the worker, then head for the door at the opposite end of the room. This leads to the control area. Knock out the last worker here and use the Q-Worm on the computer. Leave the way you entered.

When you return to the hallway beyond, you hear the penthouse elevator come online, then immediately shut itself off again. M tells you that Drake is likely hiding something. Find another way to Mayhew's office. Take care of the guard in the hallway and go left to the next door. Your Q-Specs set to night vision will help tremendously here.

What would you do without the Q-Specs?

At the end of the hallway, go left. One last worker is on this level. Knock him out and walk to the doorway across from where you entered. This leads out to the roof, where you can find another way up to the penthouse and Mayhew's office. Once you open the door, you move on to the next scene.

Once you go through this door, you're on a lower roof.

Climbing

When you set foot outside, your new objective becomes clear. You have to use the magnetic grapples to reach Mayhew's office. Switch to a weapon and take out the thug walking around the area. Collect his weapon. As you continue walking, Q contacts you and tells you a little about the grapples. They've never been tested on a wet surface, but you have no choice. Walk to the large open semicircle (which is where the penthouse elevator travels), and you don the grapples automatically.

The only way to the top of the sheer glass and steel wall is to trust in Q's magnetic grapples.

Now comes perhaps the most interesting part of this mission. You must climb up five stories while avoiding detection. You'll face two types of enemies. The first are typical security guards who raise the alarm if they spot you. The second are more serious. These armed thugs will shoot out the windows, causing your grapples to fail and sending you plummeting to your death.

The first floor is easy. Slide a few windows to your left and climb up. The single security guard here stands in place near the alarm on the right, so just get out of his line of sight to pass him.

The first window is easy. Just move left and the guard won't see you.

The next floor is quite a bit trickier. The security guard on this floor walks a steady beat around the office. Move all the way over to the right and watch him. You'll be tempted to move a lot earlier than you should. His path takes him to the alarm, then back. He turns suddenly to face you, moves up to the window, then saunters to your left. Once again, he turns suddenly to look right at you. When he turns back to the elevators from here, you are clear to move.

Past the first window, move back to the right. Fortunately, you aren't on a time limit here.

Now you are up to the third level. This one is more difficult, because this time, you have three guards to deal with. One stands to the far left and looks straight ahead. The second follows a path similar to the guard on the floor below. The third is the one to keep your eye on. He carries a Commando. Wait for him to approach the corner directly above you. When he walks away, assuming the second guard is off to your left, climb past.

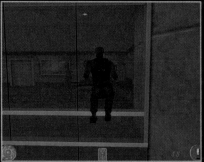

The armed guards are more serious because they'll kill you if they catch sight of you.

The next floor holds two armed thugs. They seem to walk randomly, which makes this floor appear much harder than it really is. To get past, wait for both to walk away to the left, then climb quickly past them. The one closer to you appears to turn around to see you, but he's angled toward the wall and won't catch sight of you.

For the final floor, you simply have to be patient. Wait until both guards are far to your left and climb up past them. Continue all the way to the top. Once you are past this floor, you reach Mayhew's office.

Mayhew gave himself a fairly impressive office.

Wait until the right moment to move. Go too soon, and it's a long fall to the ground.

Mayhew's Office

This one is the simplest area in this mission. There's no opposition until you get everything you've come for. Walk down the hallway to the left to the first door you come to. This leads to Mayhew's secretary. Walk through to Mayhew's office. There's nothing to worry about yet.

The door opens to a small room with a thick metal security door on the other side. Use your decryptor to hack the panel on the left. This opens the security door, revealing the path to the central computer terminal.

Use the decryptor to hack the panel and gain access to the computer beyond.

There's no reason to worry at this point. You're perfectly safe.

Walk forward on the bridge that appears in front of you. The terminal rises up from the center of the floor. Access it, and you've got the NightFire data MI6 wanted. You can leave now. Of course, you will face some opposition.

Go to Mayhew's desk and upload the Q-Worm. When you have done this, leave through the door you entered and go back to the hallway. Head left around the curving hall. When you come to a set of large double doors with the Phoenix International logo, M tells you it's likely that the NightFire information is here. Walk up to the door and access it with Mayhew's password.

When you turn around, you spot the opposition in the room you just left. Flash grenades are helpful: throw them, then duck around the side of the metal door to avoid being caught in the blast. Gun down all four thugs here and return to the area outside the central terminal. Hug the left wall, because more goons are here. Another flash grenade can help, as can leaning out to the right to throw it.

Once you have accessed the computer, Yakuza thugs arrive to block your escape.

Once the goons have been defeated, M contacts you again, congratulating you for recovering the NightFire data. She asks that you plant bugs in the conference room and in the penthouse above. Planting the bug in the conference room is easy. Walk around the corner where all the goons were and go through the door. Cross the room to the next door and walk up to the table. You plant the bug automatically. You find a gun under the table, but put it back for later use.

There's the conference room. Walk to the table to plant both a bug and a pistol for later use.

You can leave now. Exit the area and go through the door to your left. This leads up to the penthouse. When you leave, you are met by Dominique. She tells you that this entire mission has been an elaborate trap. Drake couldn't open Mayhew's safe without the password. Now that you've got the files, Drake plans to stop you. The stairs here lead to the helipad and the penthouse. Head up to complete your mission.

Take care of a couple more Yakuza before you leave.

The Penthouse

This mission starts easily. Walk past the Zen garden to the doorway into the penthouse. The door opens automatically for you. Even better, no one is firing at you, and there are no cameras to worry about.

Once you have bugged the penthouse, you can leave. At least that's the plan.

Inside, walk to the numeric keypad on the wall. You probably need some armor after the last fight, and a little ammunition wouldn't hurt, either. Use your decryptor on the numeric pad. This opens a small arsenal in the wall, giving you access to weapons, ammunition, and most importantly, armor. Get everything you need. Also note that you can't reach another part of the arsenal yet. You'll get to that eventually.

Hack the panel to open part of an arsenal.

Now walk to the center of the penthouse to the desk. Go around to the other side and walk up to it. This bugs the desk automatically. You have a few seconds to move now, so get away from the desk. Move back to the arsenal.

The desk you need to bug sits in roughly the center of the room.

An attack helicopter arrives on the scene. Its first action is to destroy part of the dome and desk in the middle of the penthouse. You can now access the outside. Equip the Commando if you haven't already and start unloading onto the chopper.

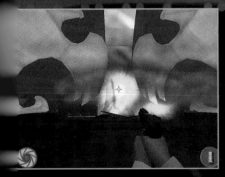

The battle helicopter attacks. This is the toughest fight you've faced so far.

The chopper mainly attacks with machine gun fire, but as you inflict more damage, it starts retaliating with rockets. Some of those rockets go inside the penthouse. The one to watch for is the rocket that targets the arsenal. This destroys the metal gate at the back, giving you access to the armor, and more importantly, the rocket launcher beyond.

Unload as much ordnance into the chopper as you can.

A stray rocket shot grants you access to a rocket launcher.

Switch to the rocket launcher and start firing. You need three or four solid hits on the chopper to take it down. It's tough to get unguided shots to hit, but using guided shots leaves you vulnerable. Stand in one of the doorways and fire out, guiding the missiles into the helicopter.

Guided missiles have the best chance of connecting for damage.

With enough damage, the helicopter starts smoking and begins to crash directly on top of you. You run forward and leap off the building, pulling a drag chute behind you to soften the fall. Kiko is nowhere to be found, so you hitch a ride with passing motorists. The NightFire data is still safe.

Hidden Agenda

Astronaut Training

The NightFire data you uploaded to MI6 contains some troubling information. It appears that a great deal of construction is going on at an abandoned nuclear power facility near Tokyo—a facility that was being dismantled by none other than Phoenix International. Your job is to check it out.

Once you are in, you see an adversary, Rook, the head of Drake's security. Rook survived his helicopter crash into the gondola back in Austria, and he's planning a warm welcome for you. Now, in addition to restoring power to the service elevator and gaining access to the astronaut training facility, you've got to find Rook and take him down.

Crawling through vents might not seem like much fun, but it's the best way to get from place to place at the start.

You start in an air vent looking down on a power facility. The area is crawling with guards, so you must find a good way in. The nearby grates can't be opened, but there is a path leading up to your left. Put on the Q-Specs and switch to nightvision. Crawl up the vent and go right at the top to the next grating.

TIP

From the start of the mission, Bond can look through the vent into the main area and eliminate three guards (one wandering guard, a guard in the control room to the right, and guard in the turbine room).

You can fumble in the dark if you wish, but the Q-Specs make travel through the vents much easier.

If you wish, you can cut through the lock on this vent and drop down to the ground. However, the number of guards in the area makes this plan foolish. Instead, put the silencer on your pistol and nail any guards you see. Crawl over the vent and turn around. If you target the red barrels and shoot them a couple of times, the resulting explosion knocks out a couple more guards. When you are done, turn around and keep crawling.

Dropping down into the middle of the room is hazardous. Don't try this unless you are very accurate, and have cleared much of the room.

Put the Q-Specs back on. Around the corner to the right, you see a drop ahead and a path to the left. Take the left path; this gives you a chance to drop a few more guards before you go to the ground. You pass two more grates. When you've taken out all the guards you can, go back to the intersection, turn left, and drop to the lower vents.

Cutting through the vents allows for more accurate shooting. You can crawl over open vents without dropping down.

TIP

You can drop down to the top of the generators at the last grating. This allows you to crawl hand-over-hand along a wire (a Bond move) to a hidden area containing a rocket launcher (a secret). However, because there are still a lot of guards around and you are armed only with a pistol, doing this is extremely difficult.

Crawl forward again, all the way to the end of the path. Cut through the lock on the vent here and drop down. You're in a small storeroom. Not only is it empty of enemies, but it's also got a loaded Storm 32. Grab this and get to the door. Open it carefully; a couple of very active guards are in the next room.

The back storeroom is the safest place to leave the vents. There are no guards here, and there's a Storm 32 stashed here.

Before you step out, turn left and slide right. The first guard stands right here, and he's looking right at you. If you are quick, you can neutralize him before he gets a shot or a noise off. The second guard is around to the right. He likes to hide behind the machinery here, which makes him a little harder to eliminate. Your best bet is to try to stun him with a flash grenade, then knock him out while he stumbles around. Go to the next door when ready.

A couple of enemies are in the room outside the storeroom, but they aren't tough.

The next room is empty, but it leads back to the main area. As soon as you step out, you draw fire from three places. First, and most dangerous, is the small room on the other side of the area. Second is in the control room to your immediate right. Third is from the floor below you. Once you start taking fire, back up and wait for the guards on the ground to approach. Knock them over, and don't forget about the red barrels on the back wall; shooting these takes out a bunch of enemies indirectly.

Use the barrels to remove guards and create a distraction.

The guy in the room to your immediate right can be handled easily as well. Let him shoot through the glass, then you shoot through him. Suppress the guard across the room with fire as you run for the lower ground. Collect the weapons here for some ammunition and make your way across the room to the stairs on the other side. Climb up and go through the door at the top.

Don't walk in too far; a guard is around the bend to the left. Blind him with a flash grenade, then go around the corner and take him out. Walk past the corridor to your right, take out the hazmat guard, and go to the door ahead and to the right. Carefully open it and back off; two more guards are inside. Knock out both before entering the room.

Flash grenades are useful for distracting guards. If you can prevent the guards from firing accurately, you can knock them out without much resistance.

At the back of this room is a switch that controls the elevators. Flip it, then back out. In the hallway, take the first left and follow the corridor around to the next door. You open it on two more guards, both of whom must be silenced before you continue. Walk through to the next door and into the control room. The guard here should already be out, so you can collect his weapon in peace. Jump onto the console and crawl through the broken window. Take the open door on your left; it's where you first entered the generator room.

Fast reactions are necessary for getting through the guards without taking much damage in return.

TIP
Next to the control console is a grating in the floor. Burn through the lock and drop down. At the end of the vent, burn through another lock to find body armor. Crawl back through the vent when you have it. This is a secret.

Follow the path through the next room to the service elevator, which you've activated. Take it down to the next floor. You may wish to crouch, because two guards wait for you below, and they start shooting as soon as they spot you. Knock off both and walk out. Look left and follow the hallway, but don't go around the corner.

Be careful when you take the elevator. Crouching in the back helps you get the drop on the guards waiting for you at the bottom.

Turn and slide over, then lean out. You should see a single guard standing here. Ventilate him and walk forward once he drops. Activate the panel on the door next to him and walk to the next corner. Again, turn and lean out. Snuff the guard standing in front of you and walk into the room. When you do, you discover good news and bad news. The good news is that you've found the astronaut training area. The bad news is that you can't enter; the path is flooded at the moment. You must activate the turbines to drain the airlock to continue. Return to the elevator.

The astronaut training area is lightly guarded. Once this enemy is gone, you'll have free rein of the place.

The security door across from the elevator is now open. Go in and collect the hand grenades from the floor. Burn through the lock on the fence at the back of the room and flip the switch inside. This disengages the locks on the rooms that control the turbines. Walk out and turn left. Destroy the barrels with explosives, then take the stairs to the top, and you arrive back where you got into the elevator. Around the corner to the left are two guards. Return to the large generator room.

The controls you must access are behind the locked gate.

From the stairs, you see a door immediately in front of you. The switch you flipped below allows access to this room and a similar one on the other side of the generator area. Enter, drop the guards at the top of the stairs, and activate the switch on the back control panel. When you are done here, go back to the generator room and walk across to the other side. There are more guards here. Again, enter and activate the switch to turn on the turbines. As you leave, you are alerted that you've turned on both turbines and that the airlock has drained. Backtrack downstairs and return to the astronaut training room. You must take the stairs, because the elevator no longer works properly.

The door at the bottom of the stairs is now accessible. There's a similar door on the other side of the generator room.

TIP

In the second turbine room, there may still be a guard here. If you didn't knock this guy out when you first game to the generator area, he's still here, and he's plenty mad.

You'll drop all of your weapons and items in exchange for a Phoenix Samurai. Walk down the steps and into the airlock to move to the next scene and your showdown with Rook.

The path to the astronaut training area is clear. Grab a suit and get ready for an interesting time in simulated weightlessness.

Showdown

Things start simply here, but they become complicated quickly. Walk forward and activate the switch near the airlock door. The room floods with water, and the airlock opens. It's the only path you can follow at the moment, so swim through the pipes to the next door. Activate the switch and back off immediately.

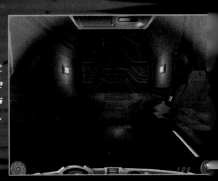

Don't worry about the flooding. You're protected, thanks to the space suit.

The problem is that there are four enemies in the next room. Two are on a platform down and to the right, one is above the first two, and one is on your level to the immediate right. Knock out all four, and try to avoid taking any damage; there's no way to restore armor in this scene. The best way to handle them is to have only one at a time who can see you, and keep his fire suppressed by hitting him.

It's almost impossible to drop the four guards without taking a little damage here, but you can't afford to take much.

When all four enemies are cooling, swim into the vertical corridor and look up. There's another airlock door above you. Swim up and open it to reveal the tunnel beyond. Swim down, but be careful; when you spot a row of three laser tripwires, stop.

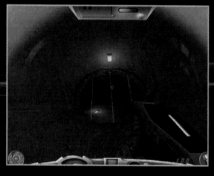

Don't attempt to cross the laser tripwires. They don't just hurt you; they kill you instantly.

These laser tripwires are instantly fatal if you touch them. The first set is pretty simple. Watch it for a few moments. It cycles between being on and off regularly, which makes it easy to bypass. What makes it a little tougher is that you're facing a downward orientation. If you aren't careful, you'll fall into the lasers.

Move down the tunnel to the next set of lasers. This one is a little more complicated. It cycles through three sets of on and off phases. The lasers turn on for about four seconds, then go off; on again for about four seconds and off; and finally on for about six seconds, then off. The time to go is after the first four-second on cycle, because this gives you the biggest window to get through. Continue and swim over the large fan in the tunnel to reach the third laser tripwire set.

The areas between the laser tripwires are thankfully clear. You can move without worry until you reach the next set.

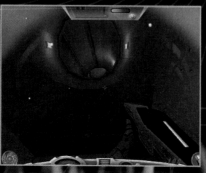

The third set of lasers again has three cycles, two of about two seconds and one of about seven. Wait for the seven-second cycle. The lasers shut off briefly, then turn on again. This is when to go—immediately following the short cycle that comes after the long one.

The final set of lasers is the most difficult, because its cycles are a little harder to judge. The three cycles are short, medium, and long. Your best chance to get through is immediately following the shortest on cycle. Once you are through this set of lasers, all you have to worry about is Rook. Walk into the airlock and activate the switch. You won't have the benefit of being able to swim anymore, so you must rely on your space suit's capabilities. Walk forward and flip the switch to the next airlock.

Past the last set of tripwires, you can take a short rest before confronting Rook.

Now it's finally time for the showdown with Rook. This is a tough battle for you, because Rook has all of the advantages. Although you are affected by gravity, Rook has flight capabilities and can go anywhere. Losing altitude is serious for you, because you must jump from platform to platform to gain height, and this movement is slow and leaves you vulnerable to attacks.

Rook has freedom to move as he wishes. Try not to let him get too far above you.

The biggest worry is Rook's rapid approaches. If he gets close to you, he'll backhand you. This does a substantial amount of damage, so you must avoid it at all costs. Take a few shots as he approaches, then back off.

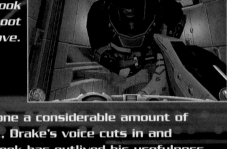

When Rook charges, shoot and move.

Once you've done a considerable amount of damage to Rook, Drake's voice cuts in and suggests that Rook has outlived his usefulness. The grating at the bottom of the shaft opens, and the ceiling begins to descend. Plug Rook a few more times, and he'll drop to the floor, where the massive fan blades do him in.

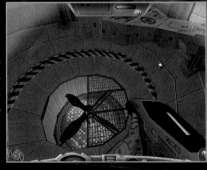

Drake opens the floor, revealing the dangerous fan blades at the bottom.

With the demise of Rook, you crawl through an access tunnel and reach the roof. You're met by Kiko, who takes you onboard a helicopter. Unfortunately, while in flight, Kiko reveals her true colors; she tranquilizes you and takes you back to Drake.

High Treason

Elevator Action

Facing outward, there are two goons to your right and one to the left at the beginning. The ones on the right are more trouble, because one is armed with a rocket launcher. Knock them down quickly so they can't continue to fire on you once the elevator starts descending again.

The sniper rifle is a good choice for much of this mission, but it's most important at the end. Conserve it until you really need it.

Essentially, this is the mission, at least for a little while: The elevator drops a few floors at a time. Each time it descends, you are attacked by enemies from both sides, both at long range and from the windows just next to the elevator. Keep switching your view from side to side, and when the elevator descends, attempt to pick off additional enemies along the way. The guys armed with rocket launchers are your biggest problem, simply because they can cause so much damage at once.

Quick, accurate shooting is the key to surviving this ordeal. If you can hit them before they start shooting, you can prevent taking damage.

As you get close to the roof below, start looking there for enemies to appear. When the elevator stops a floor or two above the roof, you have a long battle. Again, keep switching your view from right to left, making sure you check above, too. The sniper rifle is useful here, but you probably don't have a lot of ammunition for it. Keep your eyes on your ammunition, because you are extremely vulnerable when you have to reload.

Although the scope on the sniper rifle is useful for targeting, you have a much smaller field of vision when using it.

Eventually, the elevator drops one last time, stopping just below the roof area. Face away from the building and wait for the glass in the walkway to shatter. Use the Q-Grapple on the hook to swing over to the building for a Bond move. Flatten the guard while the elevator finally gives up the ghost and falls the remaining 40 stories to the ground.

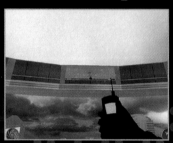

Use the Q-Grapple to get off the elevator. If you take too long, you'll reach the ground very quickly.

Destroy the Servers

You're on familiar ground this time; you traveled through this area during the infiltration mission. You've got to do it again, but this time you must destroy at least 10 of the servers to further destroy Phoenix International's operations, and with luck, to slow down their plans for NightFire.

Facing away from the ruined elevator, you can go either right or left. The left path leads to a pair of dead-ends, so ignore it. Go right, and when the hall splits right and left, go right again. Crouch-jump over the desk and collect the ammunition—and especially the armor behind it. Jump back and retrace your steps, taking the right path instead of the left.

Ammo and armor are just what the doctor ordered. Jump the desk to claim them.

Essentially, you are following the same path you did in the third part of the infiltration mission. The laser alarms are deactivated, so you don't have to worry about them, and because Drake's men know you are here, you don't have to worry about the cameras, either. You do have to worry about his goons, though. You find the first set to the right once you go through the doorway near the locked-down gate. There are three to handle here. Using the scope with the Commando gives you a good chance of eliminating them quickly, with a minimum of damage. When all are lying still, collect their weapons and move to the next door.

The scope on the Commando helps you shoot accurately. Do this before the enemies are aware of you, and you can conserve a lot of ammunition.

You emerge in the hallway by the server room, but you don't have any explosives to use to destroy them. You must find either a rocket launcher or grenades to take them out. Bypass the room for now and move on to the kitchen, but be careful here; the goons have left an active Ronin Suitcase to take you down. To destroy it, you'll need about two full clips with the Commando. Slide out, fire a few rounds, and duck back before it can target you. Once it's gone, open the door and slide in facing left. Swat the thug by the door at the far end and explore the area. Armor is on one of the tables. Even better, you also find a Ronin Suitcase you can take with you! Get it and move through the next door.

Once the Ronin is gone, the kitchen is much easier to handle.

This places you outside the administration offices. The hallway is clear, but the room behind the door is not. Open it and move out of the way, leaning in to pick off enemies when you can. They'll set up a fairly steady stream of fire, so pick your shots with caution. There are three here. When you've handled all of them, go through the room and into the administration offices.

Shoot by surprise when you can. Many guards aren't aware of your presence until you start firing or walk in front of them.

Once again, things get interesting. Go into the office to your left (you planted the Q-Worm here earlier). When you do, a pair of enemies open the main doors into the area. One has a rocket launcher, which he fires immediately. The rocket veers off and blasts a hole in the wall behind the desk. Nail both thugs and collect their weapons, then check out the new area that's been opened. Although you want the rocket launcher, you must move quickly—stepping into the hallway will attract the attention of goons on the far side of the lowered gate.

Both enemies here are dangerous. The guy with the rocket launcher is a bigger problem, so take him out first.

Three more thugs are in the newly opened conference room. They fire and back away when they spot you, retreating into the hallway behind them. Move in with care and grab the grenades and rockets on the conference room table. More are in the locked case. When you have a stash of them, return to the server room.

If you don't get rid of the thugs quickly, they will retreat to the hallway.

It takes a few grenades to fully destroy the servers. You don't need to take out all of them, but you must destroy 10. Put your grenades between racks of servers to take out as many as possible at a time. Three or four grenades should do it. When told that you've destroyed enough, return to the conference room.

A single grenade can take out several servers at once. It's the most efficient way to get rid of them.

You now have a problem—the security gates are up, and there's no way to get to the stairwell. Worse, your access card no longer works. Return to the atrium outside the conference room and shoot through the black plate-glass window. Jump inside and flip the gate control switch. This raises the gates in the area.

Go down the hallway and open the door on your right. Several enemies are inside. Deal with them quickly and move through the room to the far side. There's one last bad guy in the accounting executive's office at the end of this path. Be sure to collect the ammo bag from this room.

The key to getting out lies in the security office.

Return to the accounting executive's office and approach the front door of security. Turn left and lean right to peg the final thug on this level. Once he is down, collect the armor and ammunition near him and access the door to the stairs. You're moving on again.

One last guard stands between you and the stairs.

The Stairwell

Your escape has taken an interesting turn. The stairs appear to be the best way to the ground, but there's plenty of opposition between you and the ground floor. In fact, some guys shoot at you as soon as this scene begins. Swing your view right and peg the two above you. Continue up the stairs to the top to find a little armor and a couple of flash grenades. When you have these, go down the stairs to the 38th floor and go through the now opened door.

Things start right away in this scene. Turn and fire immediately.

Walk toward the window and shoot it to destroy it. Near the window, turn left and lean right. You should see a thug behind a second plate-glass window. Blast through the window and blast him before moving in.

A pistol is a good choice here. It's quick, powerful, and is easy to aim.

In the next room, you can go either straight or to the left. It doesn't matter which way you go, because both paths lead to the same place. There are five goons in the room to the left and the room beyond the hallway in front of you. The left path is a little easier, because you can usually swat two thugs before they even see you. In the room at the back, you find a little armor and a sleeve of rockets. Get both and return to the stairs.

Begin walking down the stairs, but take your time; it's a good idea to lean out every now and then to scout the area below you. There's a thug waiting for you on the 35th floor and another on the 34th. Smack both and continue your slow descent.

Hitting the bad guys from far above allows you to clear the way without taking much in the way of return fire.

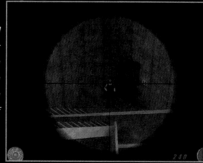

As you approach the 34th floor, the door on 33 opens. There are two thugs here, one armed with a Commando and one with a shotgun. Split both. You can safely walk onto the 33rd floor, because the security gates are down on both sides of you. Collect the ammunition and move on.

If you can make the throw, a grenade or two can be useful for clearing the guys on the 33rd floor.

You aren't attacked again until you approach the 29th floor. When you step on the landing on 30, the door on 29 opens and you start drawing fire. Nail the guy here and descend. As you do, four more thugs come out and attack. Take them all, using whichever weapon you prefer. The Commando with the scope is an excellent choice because of its accuracy. There are five enemies total, including the one who opens the door.

It's a good idea to explore 29 for some useful items.

When all five are gone, explore the floor. In a back room, you can find another ammo bag and a single piece of armor. Check under the desks to find another Ronin Suitcase for a secret. When you're done, return to the stairs.

Your next encounters come on 26 and 25. Each has a single thug standing by the door, neither of whom should be a problem for you. Beyond them, you're clear until you can spot the two guys waiting for you on the 19th floor. Peg them and continue on. As you do, a new wrinkle is added. The next few sets of stairs are destroyed by a timed explosion. Grab the ammunition from the guys on 19 and hug the left wall down to the 18th floor. Beyond this, the stairs are gone, so you'll have to move into the offices whether you want to or not.

Placed explosives destroy the next few levels of stairs. You don't have a choice here; you've got to go onto floor 18.

On the 18th, you can go left or straight. Going straight puts you in the unenviable position of being between two groups of enemies, so left is a better choice. Walk around until you find a door you can open. Beyond it is a suit of body armor and an ammo bag. Get what you need, then carefully open the door here. You're behind two thugs, which makes them easy to dispose.

When you have surprise, don't waste it. Two quick bursts clear this room.

Past them, you return to the hallway, exactly where you would have been if you'd gone straight from the stairs. Open the door across the hall and take out the guy behind the window in the room beyond. Continue into the room and swat his accomplice to the right. Walk forward through this room, collecting any ammunition you need before heading out the door from the room these last two were in.

The hallway is empty, at least at first. As you come around the corner, an explosion knocks you around a bit. Outside, an enemy with a rocket launcher fires at you from above. Drop him quickly and walk to the massive hole in the floor. It's the only way to go down to the 17th floor, so take it.

Don't let this guy get off a second rocket!

As soon as you land, you attract the attention of a guy beyond some glass in front of you. Aerate him and move forward. He has a couple of friends in the room with him, so watch out for them, too. A few well-placed bullets will make the area quiet again. Move in by jumping through the broken window and take their ammunition.

This area is tough if you aren't accurate. Move too slowly, and you'll be pincushioned by the goons behind the glass.

Things don't get any better when you open the next door. Another series of thugs attacks as you step into the hallway. There are two in this room. When you've silenced them, jump through the window and run in. Collect the armor and rockets on the floor where you enter for a secret. Go past the window to your right and immediately back up.

When you have the chance for careful shots, take them. You need a lot of ammunition on this level, so exploit any chance you have to conserve a little.

The reason for this is that across the way are three more enemies. One is armed with a sniper rifle, and it's he who breaks the window. The other two are sporting rocket launchers, and they aren't shy about using them. Lean out and take them down, then go through the door to the hallway. Go from room to room all the way to the back, where the body of the guy with the sniper rifle is cooling. There may be one more guy armed with a Commando here.

The last area is tough because of the heavy weapons. Quick, careful shooting is the best way through.

While you are here, you hear an announcement that a maintenance crew is needed in the stairwell. Shoot out the intact window that leads back to the hall and jump through. The door in front of you leads back to the stairs. You're almost out now, so go in and start descending again. As soon as you do, turn right and aim up to the door on 18. A final goon appears here. Drop him quickly and turn back to the stairs. You're clear for a bit now, so go down to the landing on the 13th floor and stop. Take a breather if you need one, because this is the last chance you have for some time.

Turn around and start backward down the stairs to 12. A few steps down, the doors on 13 burst open, and you are assaulted by a three-member team. These guys are very tough and will take a lot of punishment before being planted. Your best strategy is to snipe and run, letting them come down to you so that you can pick them apart as they approach.

This is a nasty fight, but when it's over, you can collect three P90s. This is the weapon of choice for the rest of the mission.

TIP

If your timing is good, toss a grenade onto 13 and run. When the doors open, the enemies will be caught in the blast. The rocket launcher is also a good weapon choice here.

At this point, you can run for the exit, which is the door on 7. If you'd rather go all the way to the bottom, you must contend with a pair of goons with rocket launchers. Move down from 13, looking over the side of the stairs at every landing. You should spot these guys easily. With the sniper rifle, you should have no trouble getting rid of them. What's your prize for doing this? You get a locked area containing body armor and a rockets. When you are done, return to 7 and leave.

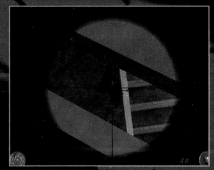

If you fire from several floors up, the guys with the rocket launchers are no trouble.

NOTE

The rocket launcher goons are on floor 2 and the ground floor. The armor and rockets are on B3. This is a secret.

More Servers

If you thought the last few sections were tough, you're really in for a shock. They were a snap compared with what awaits you on the 7th floor. Drake has pulled out all the stops, sending in a crack strike team to stop you. They've put up devastating laser trip mines all over the floor. Worse, the strike team is still here and gunning for you.

Watch for the tripwires. Crossing one will damage you severely.

Walk left in the hallway until you spot the first laser wire. You can jump over this one or destroy it with a gun or a grenade. As long as you take out the explosive mounted on the wall or bypass it completely, you won't have any trouble. Beyond, the doorway is slightly ajar. If you open it, you'll trip a mine and take damage regardless of whether you move out of the way or not. Handle this one by rolling a grenade through the door and backing up as far as you can.

You can snap off a few shots before taking care of the tripwires.

Now the fun starts. Open the door and back up. There are three initial enemies. Skewer the first and move to the door. Slide through slowly, leaning out to your right to peg two more enemies. Back into the hallway annd use the sniper rifle to destroy the end of the laser tripwire, clearing the path into the room.

Once the first group of guards is out of the way, you've got a little breathing room, at least until you are about halfway through the room.

Move in toward the back of the room, but be ready for a tactical withdrawal. Two of the filing cabinets tip over, revealing two more enemies to deal with. Fill both with lead and go to the door on the far end of the room. Because there are a lot of bodies in here now, you may want to ditch a weapon in favor of the P0W90s these guys tend to favor (if you haven't already).

The next room is even nastier. There are three laser tripwires just inside the room. They're tough to get, but you need to shoot the ends to clear the path. Worse, as soon as you step in, enemies appear in the distant room across the hall and a Ronin Suitcase begins shooting in your general direction. Duck behind cover and lean out to deal with the Ronin and the enemies before you worry about the tripwires. When the path is

clear, go in and destroy the four servers on the right wall. As with the third part of this mission, you must get rid of 10 servers before you leave.

You don't have a lot of time for careful aiming once the battle starts. Any shots you can get off before the firefight starts will help.

The Yakuza are tough because they fire from a long way away. Use the most accurate weapon in your inventory, which is probably the sniper rifle.

Check around the room for more grenades and an armor shard. In another nearby cubicle, there's more ammo, two rocket sleeves, and even more armor. There are also two servers in this room. Destroy both before going to the door.

Use rockets on the servers. Shoot the glass first, then fire away. There are plenty of rockets to stock up on, which makes them the best choice.

Step out into the hallway. There's only one way to go, and that's to the right, into the central atrium. Walk around to the opposite side. As you do, the gates in front and behind you close. It's a trap! You can hear a number of Yakuza goons equipping rocket launchers. Get a good weapon ready and prepare for the attack.

The gate drops in front of you. This is not a good sign.

TIP
The Ronin you picked up in the kitchen earlier or from the 28th floor of the last level comes in handy here. It will handle several of the rocket launcher Yakuza and should take out the special forces as well. Additionally, since there is plenty of ammunition in the area, you may want to use the rocket launcher to eliminate your enemies.

Most of them will appear on the balcony above you. A good sniping weapon, either the Commando or the sniper rifle, is the best choice here. Tag each one and move out slowly while looking both on the floor above and below you. Some will reappear in locations you've already cleared. Slow and steady is best approach here until you have to move out into the atrium.

The Commando is a great weapon choice here because it is powerful and accurate, and you probably still have plenty of ammunition for it.

Run over to the side you came from. This will bring a trio of special forces out of the meeting room. Take them down, then enter the meeting room. You find a wealth of ammunition, grenades, and a badly-needed suit of body armor. Get everything, including the explosive devices, before returning to the hallway. The gates have gone up, so you can move off down the hall to the right. Pop the thug here and keep going.

Because they're much more accurate with their weapons, the special forces are more dangerous than the Yakuza with rocket launchers.

The next room has a few more tripwires and some goons behind a glass wall. Drop the goons, then look at the tripwires. You should notice that a couple are connected to servers. Destroy the tripwires, and you take out the servers, too. Hit all four servers in this room to complete your objective. Destroy the tripwires in the next room; you must get an extreme angle to hit their end points. Go through the window.

Walk to the next door and out into the hall. To your left are the ammo pack and body armor. Get them if you wish, but the area is trapped with three proximity mines, so back off quickly. When ready, go through the only door you can open, which is directly across from the one you just came through. The explosion alerts a few guards, so be aware.

Shoot the explosives before you claim the armor and ammunition.

Opening the door triggers another ambush of special forces guys, two in this room and two in the room beyond. Snipe at them from cover when you can. The closest two can be drawn into the hallway and easily dispatched, while the distant two require some precision shooting. Once the area is quiet, move through the two rooms to the back. Smash through the window and enter the hall.

The path looks clear, but it can't be this simple, can it? There's armor, grenades, and rockets in the hallway. It looks open until you spot the proximity mine at the end of the hallway. Shoot it or run past it to the right. Walk into the open elevator to reach the next scene.

Watch for planted explosives. Otherwise, the path to the elevator is wide open.

The Parking Garage

Your task this time is to destroy all the vans in the parking garage. This is easier said than done, considering there's one van driving through the parking garage and firing at you. Hit it when you can, but spend the bulk of your concentration at first on the special forces guys in the area. Go right from the elevators and plunk the two standing on the small platform.

You must destroy the white vans. Rockets and grenades are the best method.

The good thing about this platform is that it provides a little armor and gives you some protection from the guards and the roving van. From this position, slug anything that comes your way before you move out. At this point, start taking shots at the van when it drives past. Use one of your machine guns. When you have spare moments, use rockets to target the stationary vans.

NOTE
There's an ammo box on the platform that dishes out ammo and grenades every minute.

Snap off shots at the roving van when you can, but don't become preoccupied with it.

Destroying a van brings out more enemies from the elevators, either the ones you came from or the ones at the back of the parking garage. When the coast is clear, move out and to the back, shooting any vans you spot and taking out all of the enemies in your path. More armor is in the two back corners. You can also get rockets and grenades here.

You shouldn't need to aim your rockets too carefully. Anything that hits near a stationary van will take it out.

Make your way around the garage a little bit at a time. Keep your ears open for the sound of an elevator arriving, because each time one does, another enemy appears. The sniper rifle is a good friend in this area, especially if you can target the enemies as soon as the elevator arrives and drop them before they fire.

Even when you are taking out vans, the enemies on foot should be your main priority.

Eventually, you'll have taken out six of the white vans. If you haven't already handled the combat van at this point, it's time to concentrate on it. When all the vans have been destroyed, you are told to make for the stairs. These are near the platform you ran to at the beginning of the level. Head there now and plug the guy who runs out from the door to attack you.

A few more enemies are between you and the end of this scene.

You should realize by this time that it's not going to be that easy. Chuck a flash grenade through the door and lean in to drop the next guard. There are two more on the first landing from the stairs. Nail both and move in cautiously. There is a final enemy standing by the door to the lobby. When he is gone, the path is clear to the final part of this mission.

Lobby Escape

When you make to the lobby, the place looks empty. Of course, that's far too good to be true. Walk out and left toward the front door, taking the right path for now. As you near it, a group of enemies appear and start shooting. A tactical withdrawal with a lot of covering fire is a very good idea. Back up and shoot, taking out anyone you can as you pull back to the elevators.

Pull back and keep firing. Anyone you can drop quickly will keep you safe.

If you still have a Ronin, this is the perfect time to use it. Toss it onto the ground in front of the door to the security area. It will probably be destroyed eventually, but it will do a nice job of taking out a few enemies for you, especially in the early going.

The Ronin will help fend off enemies and clear the area around the security office.

With the initial group of enemies eliminated, creep forward and look out into the lobby. Use the sniper rifle (if you have a little ammunition for it) and scout the distance, picking off anyone still standing. Check the main part of the lobby, too.

There's a huge stone sculpture hanging in the lobby to your immediate left. Equip your rocket launcher and target one of the posts holding up the sign. Blowing up the sign causes a lot of destruction, takes out some guards, and also gives you credit for a final Bond move.

With a crash, Phoenix International's expensive lobby art comes tumbling down.

Shoot only those standing in your way. Ignore everything else on your way to the exit.

With the sign destroyed, turn and face the large black window. This leads to the security area, and you've lost your access pass. Shoot the window until it breaks out. Three guards are behind it, all waiting for you to attempt to break through. Take them out, and don't worry too much about taking a lot of damage from them. Two suits of body armor are inside.

Flip the switch and get ready to run.

Once the guards are down, approach the front lobby to lower the security gates, then check the security area for a switch that controls the gates. It's currently active, so you must switch it off. When you do, prepare for some trouble; enemies break through the door into the security area. This is another good time for the Ronin Suitcase if you still have one or didn't use it earlier.

When the gates are up, there's no time to fight it out. Jump back through the window to the lobby, turn right, and run as fast as you can. Don't worry about the fire you draw from the enemies behind you or from the balcony. Run down the stairs and blast your way through the two enemies in front of you. As soon as you set foot in the area at the front of the building, you're extracted by Australian Intelligence Operative Alura McCall—loaned to MI6 for the current crisis—who swoops in to rescue you. It's time to make Drake pay for Dominique's death.

Island Getaway

Infiltration

You've managed to escape Drake's clutches, but that's the only good news. Whatever technology Drake has acquired, he's using it to jam MI6's satellite. No one knows what he's doing on his island, which means it's up to you to shut down the jamming technology.

You wash up on the beach. It's a long road in to save Alura.

There's only one way to go on the beach, and that's left. Stay close to the water until you reach the large rock arch, then go around it to the left through the water. You may wish to use the Q-Specs on the IR setting to scout ahead. There's a guard patrolling the beach and another on the porch of the hut. Take them both out.

Shoot from range to avoid taking a lot of damage in this first battle.

Run straight for the house. A couple of nasty gun turrets that will shred you if you come too close are on the beach. Slide up along the side of the house nearest where you started and peek around the back. Drop the guard standing here, then open the door. Two more guards are inside. Soften them up with grenades, then take them down.

A few grenades and a burst of fire, and the cabin is safe.

Duck inside the cabin and look around. There's a computer terminal you can access by using the Q-Worm. Do so, and you'll shut off the turrets on the beach outside. Go out the back and walk around to the front of the cabin.

Use the Q-Worm to shut off the turrets. This will significantly aid your ability to survive.

Put the Q-Specs back on, switch to nightvision, and crawl under the hut. You should see a pistol lying on the ground. This is a Kowloon, and it's worth grabbing. Crawl back out and cross the water. Go up the ramp here.

The Kowloon is hard to spot, but it's under here.

Use the Q-Specs in IR mode to scout the area. Five enemy guards are on the ramp hiding behind vegetation. You must fight your way through all of them. This will take you to the large stone arch. Walk around it carefully, keeping your view trained to the left.

The Q-Specs are invaluable for spotting enemies on the long ramp.

There are two guards protecting the initial approach to the inner compound.

Two last guards protect the entrance to the cave in front of you. There's no good way to spot them from a distance, and you don't have a weapon with a scope. Your best option is to charge, firing the P0W90 as you go. This should take out at least one, and the second will likely retreat into the cave if he's not silenced outright.

It appears at first as if you've reached a dead end, but there's an area below you. You can either climb down the ladder in the small platform or you can jump off the cliff into the water, which is faster and makes you harder to spot. Either way, get to the lower platform and use the Q-Specs to scout ahead. You should see a couple of guards in the area in front of you.

There's nothing to do but charge here. Fire as you go, eliminating whomever you can.

Two guards are visible at the end of the causeway.

If there's still a guard around, use a flash grenade to blind him before running into the cave. Take him down and walk forward. After a few moments, you progress to the next scene.

The best way to handle these guards is to snipe at the one on the left until he moves. When he starts running, switch your aim to the red barrels and destroy them. The explosion should eliminate both guards, or at least wound both seriously. Run to the end of the causeway and use your wrist-watch to pop the lock on the fence. Go in and check the lockers. The fourth locker in the second group has a little armor, which you probably need.

One guard stands between you and the exit.

Some valuable items are behind this fence. You don't have to enter, but it's a good idea.

The Compound

The tunnel in front of you curves to the right. Move slowly forward, leaning out to the left every few steps. You come to a corner eventually, and there's a pair of guards in the area beyond. Take out the one on the platform first, then slide left and drop the second. Collect both of their weapons if you need the ammunition.

Go back outside the fence area and walk to the left. Two more guards are on the far side of the large green generator, so lean around and drop them, either with gunfire or grenades. Move slowly to the next fenced area. Two more guards are inside. You can probably get one before they notice you, but the other will come out shooting.

These two guards wait for you on the far side of the generator. To avoid taking unnecessary damage, take them down before they spot you.

Walk through the gate and look around. There's some ammunition for your Wolfram P2K on a shelf with a little more ammunition. When you have these items, head toward the tunnel but don't enter. Instead, turn around and look up. You should see a hook above. Use the Q-Grapple to swing up to it and jump onto the pipes. Crawl across them to the tunnel, then inch forward to look over the next area.

NOTE
Using the Q-Grapple to surprise the next group of guards is your first Bond move in this mission.

Use the Q-Grapple. Not only does this make the next fight easier, you get credit for a Bond move.

Move in carefully, because this is a lot more effective if you aren't seen. Crawl forward until you have a clear shot on the red barrels on the ground by the fence. Shoot them to take out a couple of the guards. Continue along the pipes, taking out anyone you spot. There are about half a dozen total enemies in the area, split equally between those inside the fenced area below you and those out in the main area.

Use the pipes as cover for as long as possible.

When you have no more targets, drop down to the ground and go through the gate. Clear the area of any remaining goons. There are two fenced areas in addition the one you came from here. Check out the one on the left first.

The doorway is blocked, but there is a way inside. Use the boxes on the left side to climb over the fence—you'll need to jump-crouch to get on the boxes. Inside, you find body armor, a Raptor Magnum, and ammunition for the Raptor. Leave by jumping on the boxes when you are ready.

Use these boxes to get inside the blocked area.

NOTE
Finding the entrance to this blocked fence is a secret.

Go to the other fenced area and use your wristwatch on the lock. There's ammunition for your other pistols and a little more armor, which you won't need. When you are ready, go through the tunnel to the beginning of the next scene.

Use your wristwatch to open this fenced area. It's not required, but there's a bit of ammunition inside.

The Gantry

This scene is fairly combat-intensive, but you can skip a battle right at the start. Walk forward and to the left into the next cavern. You can see a pair of enemies working on a generator in front of you. Don't worry about shooting them. Instead, go left to the ladder and climb up to the platform above.

The locker room area is loaded with special forces enemies.

Use the ladder to climb to the platform. If you're careful, you can avoid fighting the first two enemies.

Walk to the table and grab the items on it. A wire is strung over to the platform on the opposite side of the room. Jump on the table and leap up to the wire. Go hand-over-hand, watching out for the spark point directly over the two enemies. Get all the way to the opposite side and drop down, avoiding a fight and getting credit for the second Bond move.

The benefits of clearing the locker room are twofold. First, you prevent a huge group of enemies from trailing you. Second, the area is loaded with ammunition and armor. Check the back group of lockers for extra armor, and don't pass up the Ronin Suitcase on the sink. You can also find a Storm 32 on the sink, which you can take by throwing away another weapon (like the Kowloon).

Go out to the next room and peek in. Once again, the room is riddled with guards. Take out the three on the ground and move in. There's a set of stairs at the back. As you climb, one guard appears in front of you and another on the catwalk behind you. Take out the one behind you first, because you can duck back down the stairs for cover from the other one.

Use the wire to cross over the first two guards and skip unnecessary combat with their backup.

Enter the hallway beyond. There are two open doorways around the corner. The first leads to a locker room filled with enemy special forces. Although this is a tough fight, you must clear the area, or you'll have this whole crew at your back. More arrive from next door after the fighting begins. There are about half a dozen in the room, many hiding behind lockers to stay out of your view. Flash grenades are helpful. Lean into the room and snap off shots before dodging away.

More guards appear when you first attempt to leave the room.

Go up the stairs and stand under the wire. Jump up and grab on and go across to the platform on the far side, and claim another secret. Inside the room to your right is a sniper rifle and ammunition. Toss the Raptor and get this. Go back outside and drop down to the ground below.

Go hand-over-hand to the far platform for another secret and a great weapon.

Turn around. The locked area behind you is labeled "Demolitions." This seems like a logical place for explosives. Burn through the lock and go in immediately, switching back to a weapon. Two more guards appear on the stairs above you as soon as you open this door. Hit them both, then grab the items. There's armor and explosives on the table.

Get the items from the table. With the explosives in your possession, you can complete the rest of this scene.

Go back up the stairs and lean into the next hallway. Remove the final guard in the area and approach the numeric keypad. Use your decryptor to unlock the room. When the door opens, eliminate the two guards in the small area below you. Toss one of your weapons and grab the rocket launcher, then turn around and go back to the hallway. Go left and start up the spiral staircase.

You can skip this room if you wish, but the rocket launcher is worth fighting for.

CAUTION

Do not shoot the astronaut! If he dies, the mission ends in failure!

At the top, go through the open doorway and into the next corridor. You can go straight or to the right. Turn right and slide left. Lean out and peg the guard standing behind the forklift, then turn left and walk straight ahead. Follow this hallway through the next enemy until it opens into a large area with a rocket platform in the middle.

Drake has his own private rocket. This can't be good.

Look right and drop the two enemies standing near you. Walk forward and turn left. On a control platform, there's a third guard. Shoot him, then look down into the water. The place to plant your explosives is there. Dive in and swim all the way down to the small structure. Swim through the door and place the explosives on the red generator. Swim out the other side and up to the surface.

Place your explosives here. This happens automatically when you swim next to the generator.

There's a small building across from you. Use the ladder to reach its platform and go inside. There are two astronauts above to your left and two special forces guys below and to the right. Plug the special forces and get the body armor and ammunition near them. Go up the stairs by the astronauts and use the computer terminal. Plant the Q-Worm to fulfill another mission objective.

Place the Q-Worm into the launch computer to confound Drake's plans.

Go outside again and turn right. On the platform to your right, you should see a guard patrolling. Peg him and dive into the water. Swim over to the platform he was on and climb up. Go through the doorway and nail the next guard, who is a little tough to see; he's behind the fence. Keep going in the hallway beyond and take out the next guard. When the hallway goes right and immediately left again, there are two final guards to dispatch.

You'll surprise the last two guards, which makes eradicating them simple.

Continue down the hallway. You pass the body of a guard you removed earlier. Go right when you have the opportunity and follow the corridor to the end. You return to the open space with the rocket gantry. If you didn't notice before, the gantry is moving up and down. Walk over to it, and when it reaches its lowest point, jump onto the platform.

You need to use the moving gantry as a way to climb to the top.

Walk around to the far side of the platform and jump to the ledge when the gantry reaches the top of its movement. Climb the ladder to your left all the way to the top and step off. Use the sniper rifle to plug the three enemies on the ramp above you.

Drop the last three guards.

Spot the grapple point at the top platform and use your Q-Grapple to get up there. Walk around to the door around to the right on the far side of the platform. Walk through, and you'll move to the next scene. When you do, you trigger the explosives on the gantry, destroying it and the rocket completely.

You're finally done with this scene.

Rescuing Alura

You enter a huge cavern at the beginning of this scene. Three enemies are on the ground in front of you. Lean out and drop them one after the other. Once these three are quiet, you have a second to look around.

You should be able to take out the two guards on the ground without drawing much fire.

What you see is a large ramp leading all the way around the interior of the cavern. As in the last scene, there's a gantry in the center of the area, although this time there isn't a rocket. Go over to the bottom of the ramp and start walking up.

As you do, you draw fire from the small structure about a third of the way to the top. The enemies inside only have a shot at you for a few feet before they can't spot you through the window, so run up the ramp as fast as you can. At the structure, open the door and pin the four men inside. There's some Raptor ammunition and body armor inside.

Don't miss the suit of body armor on the table in the back.

Leave and continue up the ramp. Cross the bridge and stop. Turn left to look at the central tower. You should see a grapple point for your Q-Grapple just above your current position. Swing over to the tower and climb up the ladder. The guards in the second building won't see you. At the top of the ladder, step off carefully to the right.

Using the Q-Grapple allows you to skip combat in the second building.

You as soon as you start moving, the guards in the third building—directly across from you—start firing. Nail them through the window, then walk around the platform and jump back to the outside ramp. When you land, you get credit for a Bond move, thanks to skipping combat at the second building.

Two guards in this structure spot you. Silence both and continue.

Enter the third structure and look around. You find Alura here, but before you release her, get all the items from the back room, including the grenade launcher. Use the decryptor to open through the lock. You tell Alura that Drake hasn't been decommissioning the nuclear arms, but transporting them. Alura leaves the cell and grabs her sniper rifle. She'll be following you for the rest of this mission.

Rescuing Alura gives you a little backup for the rest of this mission.

You are essentially at the top of the ramp here. Follow the tunnel outside. When you are in the open air, start moving a little more carefully. Three enemies hide in the foliage ahead. Use the Q-Specs to spot them and the sniper rifle to drop them before you are spotted.

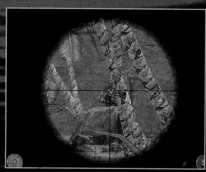

Your break from combat is short. You must fight your way to the next scene.

Past these three bodies, you see a bridge. Move quickly here, because when you set foot on the bridge, a squad of five enemies appears. Step onto the bridge and back up immediately. Two of the five appear and charge the bridge. Take them out with the sniper rifle, then start walking across. Get your Ronin Suitcase ready.

When you spot the next guard, toss it down and activate it. It should handle the next three, or at least make them easier for you to deal with.

Let the Ronin do some work for you.

Walk forward, using the Q-Specs in IR mode to check the ledge in the distance. Use the sniper rifle to hit anyone you spot. Continue forward until you see a pair of enemies on a ledge below you. Back up and use the grenade launcher to silence them. When they are gone, jump down to the lower ledge and continue walking forward.

The grenade launcher is made for situations like this.

As you approach the next bridge, use the scope on the sniper rifle to look ahead. another squad of enemies is on the far side of the bridge. If you have any ammunition in the sniper rifle, use it now to peg as many as you can. When ready, cross the bridge and be prepared for a nasty firefight.

It doesn't get any easier the farther in you go.

Past the first group of three, there's a set of four more. Explosives are the way to go here. A well-placed rocket or two, or a few hits from the grenade launcher, should quiet down the area in a hurry. Creep forward until you see the entrance to the cave. Snap shots off on the two men standing in front of it, and you've cleared the way. Enter the cave and walk forward to complete the scene.

Just two more guards block your path.

The ECMs

Walk out of the caves until you see the buildings in front of you. When you spot them, you tell Alura that these are probably the source of the satellite jamming. You need to get inside to shut off the electronic countermeasures (ECMs) that prevent MI6 from spying on Drake. Drop down to the ground by using the ledges below you to avoid taking damage.

> ### TIP
> Use the sniper rifle to eliminate two of the guards at the first ECM building. There is a guard patrolling the catwalk and another inside the building.

The first ECM is in the building below the radio tower.

Use the vegetation as cover and approach the building. Look under the radio tower to spot a grapple point for your Q-Grapple. Swing up to the tower and grab the ammunition for the grenade launcher. Drop down to the roof and go through the door.

Use the Q-Grapple to avoid going through the front door. This is the final Bond move in this mission.

Creep down the stairs. Two guards are on the far side of the central terminal and one is outside on the walkway. Try to get all three, although dropping the one outside is tough. When the area is clear, walk around the console and flip the switch on the ECM. This takes care of the first one.

One ECM down, one to go.

Look down into the basement of the building and try to knock out the two guys here before continuing. There's nothing down here to pick up, and you can't open either of the two doors. There is, however, a trapdoor in the floor. Open it and drop into the basement hallway. Go to the end and climb the ladder on the far side. Open the hatch at the top and eliminate the two guards inside. On the top platform are grenades and some armor.

Use the secret passage to clear the next building.

Go outside and walk around the structure. You can see the entrance to a large cave in front of you. Use the sniper rifle and pick off the two men guarding the entrance, then walk forward. Inside,

there's another building to your left. Nail the guard through the window and go in. Flip the switch to activate the gate.

This switch controls the gate into the main compound.

Walk to the gate, but hug the left wall. Lean out and use the sniper rifle to pick off the guards. Walk forward and use the door you spot on the left. Go through the corridors until you reach a room with a door straight ahead and one to the left. Take the left door and go through the next hall. The final door opens back to the outside.

Three quick shots clear the path for you.

Look left and plug the guard. Walk forward until you see the next ECM building; it looks exactly like the first, without the grapple point. Run forward to the door on the bottom floor. You will be spotted, but don't worry.

The second ECM building is close. You must get inside as quickly as possible.

There are five enemies inside this building: three in the basement, one by the ECM, and one at the top of the stairs to the roof. Move in, going floor-by-floor, silencing everyone. When the area is clear, go to the middle floor and open one of the doors to the walkway. Peek outside and drop the final guard. When you are ready, shut off the second ECM.

There's plenty to fight in this building. Move slowly, so you fight only one or two at a time.

When you shut off the ECM, you contact M and tell her about Drake's plans. M congratulates you for allowing MI6 to begin spying on the island. At the same time, a half-track appears outside and three more enemies jump out. Use the sniper rifle to pick off the first two, then get to the ground. Go around the truck and nail the third; you can't see him from the ECM building.

The three guards from the half-track are no problem if you are aware of them.

If you wish, investigate the building near the half-track. There's a single guard inside, and you can grab a Raptor and some ammunition—not a bad idea if you've emptied your rocket launcher.

> **NOTE**
> The other building in this area contains two guards, rockets, and flash grenades.

Walk toward the gate behind the half-track. It's locked, and you can't get through. Use the door to the left and investigate the lockers for a little armor as you pass. Walk to the door at the end to complete this scene.

A little armor is just what you need right now.

Destroy the Bridge

This scene is just what you needed: something simple. Walk left to the outside. If you continue forward, you reach a dead end. Look right and drop down to the ledge below you. Continue dropping down from ledge to ledge until you are on the ground below. Walk toward the bridge.

There's no one shooting at you here. It's a rather nice change of pace.

When you near the bridge, Alura contacts you. She's found a jeep you can use to escape. She tells you to meet her at the bridge. To provide a distraction, you are instructed to plant explosives on the bridge supports. Fortunately, you've got three; you found four earlier and only used one.

Drop into the water and swim toward the bridge. When you reach the first support, jump up, walk to it, and plant a bomb. Repeat this with the other two supports. Don't worry about taking any fire from above.

Plant the three explosives, and your mission is done.

When the third support is bombed, Alura drives in, and you detonate the bridge. The two of you have eliminated resistance, and you're clear to move on. It's time to shut down Drake's missile operation.

Zero Minus

The Warehouse

Bond and Alura drive off to another part of the island. Drake's missiles must be put out of commission as soon as possible. Alura tells you that the power generators controlling the security system appear to be the same ones as in the caves. While she works on shutting down the power, you decide to scout ahead.

Walk down the path in front of you, sticking to the vegetation on the left side of the road. The path opens up, revealing another cave entrance in front of you, a small compound on your left, and a set of elevated train tracks on the extreme left. Inch forward and ice the two guards in the compound, then claim their weapons.

One guard walks the perimeter while the other is situated inside the closest building.

Go to the elevated track. There's a locked ladder here. Stand to the outside of the lock and burn it off with the wristwatch. Climb the ladder and walk forward on the tracks.

This is the back entrance to the interior. Using this allows you to skip a lot of very difficult combat.

NOTE
You encounter squads of commandos throughout this mission. In each case, there is a nearby barracks with a few lockers you can access. You will always find armor, a weapon, and ammunition for the weapon in these lockers.

Go forward under the tracks until you come out into a large warehouse area. A number of white-suited guards are in the area. Snipe them, and one of them triggers the alarm. This brings out a group of four extremely powerful commandos. Use the

sniper rifle to peg all four, and take out the others with lesser weaponry.

These commandos are the toughest enemies you've faced up to this point.

TIP
If you can clear the six white-suited guards without anyone raising the alarm, the commandos will not attack.

When the warehouse is silent, drop to the lower level. Stay on the right side and enter the room at the back. This is the commando barracks. Burn the locks off the two lockers and get the armor. Toss away the Wolfram P2K and take the Raptor. Outside, be sure to pick up some miniguns.

Since you've taken out the commandos, you may as well search the lockers for hidden items.

Go to the machinery at the back of the warehouse and flip the switch. This moves the crane out of the way, giving you a clear shot at the grapple point. Use the Q-Grapple to swing up to the catwalk, then jump up to the wire and go hand-over-hand to the far side. Entering the central compound this way is the first and only Bond move in this mission.

Flip this switch to move the crane. The grapple point is ahead and to the left.

NOTE
If you don't wish to go this way, take the door under the catwalks. This leads you to a hallway, through another quartet of commandos. You emerge on the bottom floor of the last warehouse.

Walk to the end and use the decryptor on the numeric keypad. This opens the door in front of you and takes you to a catwalk suspended over a pair of missile assemblies. There's a guard on either side of this room on the floor. Nail them both and walk across to the far side.

Pull out your cellphone. When you approach the door, it opens automatically. Crouch down and look up. Use the Q-Grapple on the hook above you to reach the high catwalk. You are out of sight from the guards below. Walk to the end of this catwalk. If you like, you can pick up the rocket launcher here.

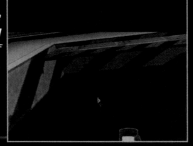

Using the Q-Grapple here is a secret, and it saves you a ton of combat.

Jump over the railing onto the pipe. Walk to the far end of the warehouse and look to your left. There's a grapple point and a vent. Jump down and use the wristwatch to burn the lock off the vent. Crouch and enter it.

The vent is the only way to keep going.

NOTE

If you don't use the Q-Grapple right away, you must fight your way through the warehouse. There are a number of guards, and when the alarm is sounded, four more commandos appear directly across from you. When the room is quiet, use the Q-Grapple on the grapple point by the vent on the far side of the warehouse.

Move carefully through the vents. There are guards here who can see you if they look directly at you. Walk all the way to the end of the vents. When you reach a vent in the floor, step onto it. It breaks under your weight, depositing you in a conference room. Walk up the stairs and to the waiting elevator. Activate it to move on.

Get to the elevator to complete this scene.

NOTE

Don't worry if you are spotted crawling through the vents. If your armor is in bad shape, there is a suit of body armor past the guard in the security office by the elevator.

Scorched Earth

The elevator arrives in a quiet hallway. You are instructed to obtain photographic evidence of the missile assembly. Walk out of the elevator to the door directly across from you. The blueprints are on the table. Snap a picture, and your mission objectives change. Now your job is to disable the missiles.

The first part of your mission couldn't be easier.

Walk back into the hallway and take out the guard walks in the security office. Watch out for another guard. Get the access card the first guard drops. Use the card on the door on the right.

You don't have to enter the security office, but if you have lost armor, it's a good idea.

The warehouse in front of you is crawling with guards who start shooting almost immediately. Slide off to the side and lean in, using the Q-Specs on IR mode to spot them. There are six who can see the door, including two on the catwalks above you. Clear them out and head for the small locked fence straight ahead. There's a bit of armor inside.

You can't bull your way into the warehouse. This takes stealth and a clear head.

Next to the fence is a door. Go through and get the armor from the open locker if you need it. Flip the lever behind the locker to move the crane above the catwalk. There is a grapple point on the crane; Q-Grapple up to the catwalk. Go forward until it opens up to the left. From here, switch to your sniper rifle and use the Q-Specs on IR mode. Pick off any guards you spot on the catwalk and the ground below.

Clear as much of the area as you can before you venture forward.

Continue to move in a few feet at a time, switch back to IR, and peg anyone you see. You should be able to take out all of the guards, including the one all the way around the corner to the right, without drawing any return fire. Climb down the ladder and walk to the train.

NOTE

Drop down from the catwalk or jump up on the conveyor belt to get to the fenced area in the left corner of the warehouse. There's armor and a shotgun with ammo stashed there.

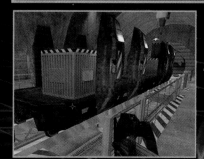

You use the train to reach the end of the scene.

Step onto the train, which begins moving immediately. Walk forward next to one of the crates and crouch. As the train moves through the tunnel, guards appear on both sides. By crouching, you prevent the guards on the left side of the tunnel from seeing you. Fire at the enemies you see; otherwise, stay put until the train comes to a stop.

Expect to take a little damage on this trip. Suppressing fire will stop the guards from doing much to you.

TIP

If you can, target the barrels on the various platforms. The explosions damage the guards and stop them from firing at you.

When the train stops, run onto the platform. Dust the two guards in front of you and any behind you who have spotted you. When the area is quiet again, go to the door and access it with your card or the decryptor. Be careful not to let anyone trigger the alarm, or a group of four commandos will emerge directly across from the door with the numeric keypad.

If the commandos come out, use your minigun to split them quickly. Get the body armor in one of the lockers.

In the hallway, you can investigate the door on your right for some ammunition if you need it. Otherwise, go to the door directly in front of you. This is the command center of Drake's operation. Alura contacts you and suggests that you override the controls on the missiles. If you can fire the missiles with the bay doors closed, it will cause tremendous damage to the base.

Conveniently enough, there's a computer terminal you can access in the launch control room.

Access the computer and use the Q-Worm to override the controls. Turn around and press the button on the console. This launches the first missile, which explodes almost immediately after takeoff. The building starts to shake apart, but there's nothing you can do right now. Walk around to the back of the room and wait for the elevator to open. When it does, step inside and activate the controls.

Once again, you take an elevator to the next scene.

The Inner Sanctum

You have very little time to do anything at the start of this mission. Equip your Annihilator and face the exit to the elevator. As you descend, a guard in a security booth immediately takes aim. Drop him with the minigun and run forward, jumping through the broken window or standing to the right side of the corridor. The alarm sounds, and a group of commandos appear from around the corner. Handle them as best you can and get the armor from their lockers when you are done.

There's no way to avoid tripping the alarm this time. Take out the commandos from cover, or you'll be shredded.

The only way to go from here is to follow the hallway around the corner into the situation room. There's a guard on the catwalk above you, and a couple of security cameras. Getting through without being spotted is tough, mainly because you can't stop under the cameras. If the alarm sounds, more guards and a group of four commandos appear. Getting through without raising the alarm is naturally preferable.

Watch for the cameras on the sides of the situation room. You will also need to silence the guard on the catwalk.

Walk to the door at the end of the hall and use the decryptor to open it. It reveals a small room with a wood-paneled door on the other side. Go through into Drake's inner sanctum. Alura contacts you and tells you that Drake is heading for the Space Shuttle bay.

Drake's office is nice, but you don't have time to look through his library.

Walk up the stairs and out the doorway at the top. This takes you to a winding staircase leading down. It's almost impossible to get through here without being spotted by the camera, so be prepared for the pair of commandos about halfway down the stairs. When they are eliminated, continue to the bottom and walk to the door.

Hit the commandos when they run out of their office.

The next part is tough. Open the door and go through. A guard will see you immediately, and he'll go sound the alarm. Let him. You want the commandos to come out right away. Once the alarm is sounding, silence the guard and his companion on the upper floor of this elevator platform.

Let the alarm sound. By bringing out the commandos now, you can snipe at them from above.

Move around on the platform. You should spot two guards two levels below you, one on each side. Peg them both so that they can't bother you when you get down there. Walk onto the central platform, which starts to descend. Jump off to the catwalk one floor down and deal with the commandos. This is tough, but it's worth it. In their barracks, you find body armor, rockets, and laser trip mines.

Fighting the commandos is tough, but it pays off this time.

Walk out of the barracks and go right. Move to the place where there is no railing and carefully drop down. When you start falling, move right so that you land on the ledge below you; this prevents you from taking any damage in the fall. Walk carefully toward the warehouse and be aware that four more commandos here are looking for you.

IR vision helps you spot your new adversaries.

In truth, there are four sets of four commandos in the warehouse, with each new group appearing once you've dealt with the previous. This means that it's going to take some time to actually penetrate the warehouse itself.

You must move in if for no other reason than to continually furnish yourself with additional ammunition. Watch the platforms above you and try to take it one enemy at a time.

CAUTION

The warehouse is also strung with laser trip wire explosives. Watch out for them, and attempt to lead commandos through the mines. They will trigger them, wounding themselves badly.

Continue to use IR to scout ahead. This is the easiest way to spot the camouflaged commandos.

As you are able, sneak into the four barracks and check out the lockers. You won't find anything truly noteworthy until you reach the final barracks, which is the second one on the left. Here you get a suit of body armor. The right-hand locker takes some time to burn through, but it's worth it. Here you get a lovely poster of Kiko and a Ronin Suitcase.

The poster is nice, but the Ronin is the real prize.

Walk to the door at the end of the warehouse and use the decryptor to open it. Inside, you find four elevators, one of which is out of service. Crouch and crawl inside. Climb up through the open panel to the top of the elevator. If you look up, you should spot a grapple point for your Q-Grapple. Use it to climb.

You will use the Q-Grapple repeatedly in the elevator shaft.

Once you land on the beam, slide all the way left and turn around. Look up to see another grapple point. You may also catch sight of the two guards in the shaft above you. Grapple up to the next ledge and use the Annihilator to drop the guards. From here, use the Q-Grapple again to climb up to the platforms where the guards are. Collect their weapons and climb the ladder.

There's a short fight in the elevator shaft. This is tricky because it's hard to get a clear shot.

Walk to the darkest corner and look up. You see a final hook. Use the grapple and crawl forward to the opening. This takes you to the final scene in this mission.

Finally, you're done climbing.

Lift-Off

You don't have much space to maneuver at first here. Three guards face your exit point in the first room you come to, which means you must fight them either by charging or by hitting them from the small confines of the top of the elevator shaft. You can probably take out one or two with explosives and get the third by charging. Grab the armor and ammo from the right corner.

The grenade launcher is a great help in removing these three guards.

Walk to the locked door and use the decryptor to open it. You step out into a series of gantries located around a central hub. As you walk toward the hub, you see Drake run past on your left. He jumps into a waiting Space Shuttle and blasts off. At the same time, Kiko pulls the gantry back from your location, dumping you on the ground below.

Drake runs to a waiting Space Shuttle. It looks like your final confrontation with him won't be here.

Now things get really tough. You've got a wide-open area and there are a number of commandos all looking to stop you. You'll have to fight them (the grenade launcher helps) until the 20 second warning is announced. The door to the rooms will open. After a few moments, another Space Shuttle blasts off. Anything not standing in a barracks at that point is instantly vaporized. Use this opportunity to open the locker and grab armor and ammunition. After the white flashes, you appear outside the room and have to fight ninjas.

It's hard to see into the blast pit, so don't worry about it too much. If you stay in a bunker, you'll be okay.

The commandos have been handled, but you've got another problem. Kiko has unleashed a number of her ninjas, much like the one you fought way back in Japan. The problem is that these guys are almost impossible to eliminate. So, the same idea holds here. Stay to the bunkers, defend yourself as necessary, and wait for the next launch, which will finish them off.

The Ronin is a good choice for keeping the ninjas off your back.

Now your task is to prevent Kiko from boarding a Space Shuttle. Run to the central pillar and go inside. Activate the elevator and take it to the top.

Kiko was in here a moment before. It's the fastest way to get to her.

You arrive in the middle of a circular control room. Directly in front of you, you see Kiko walking calmly toward Shuttle 3. Follow her. The door closes in front of you, which means you can't pursue her. You can do the next best thing, though; flip the switch behind her. This drops the gantry, sending the nefarious Kiko into the blast pit. You make your own way onto the Space Shuttle. Kiko gets exactly what she deserves, and you get blasted off to your final showdown with Drake.

You can't catch Kiko, but you can still stop her.

you can't get to it in time. You'll have to find another way.

Fortunately, there is a way for you to get to the top catwalk. Jump onto the canisters to the left and get to the top of the platform against the back wall. From here, jump over to the other platform. On it, you find a station to recharge the jump jets in your space suit. Do so and use the jump jets to blast your way up to the top catwalk.

This filling station gives you the necessary juice to rise to the occasion.

Go through the door and into the next hall. As you move forward, a guy in a spacesuit runs in front of you. Blast him, then move to the door and look left. Drop the guy waiting for you here. Run in toward the left and eliminate the third guy, then turn around. Go forward, following the sign

Knock out the two astronauts on the distant platform before jumping down.

Walk around to all four terminals and activate them. This allows you to disengage the rocket assemblies. Each time you activate a panel, another panel, on the rocket, opens. Jump up to the open panel on one of the rockets. You need a powered jump to do this. Look around. There are astronauts in the control rooms around you. Take shots at them to suppress their fire while you disable the rockets.

> ## NOTE
> After activating all four of the panels, stay on the platform and pick off the astronaut guards that are high above you.

If you are out of jump jet fuel, drop all the way to the ground and use the filling station.

Silence the astronauts before shutting down the launches.

To disable each rocket, you must activate the two side levers, then press the central button. This takes a little time, because the levers move slowly, and you must wait until the first has stopped moving before pulling the second. Jump from rocket to rocket and shut down all four.

Drake fires an EMP shot that is devastating if it hits you directly. If the shot hits an area near you, watch out for splash damage.

Pull the two levers, then press the central button to shut down the rockets.

When all four rockets have been disengaged, the self-destruct sequence of the Space Weapons Platform begins. You don't have a lot of time now. Drop to the central platform and look for the open doorway across from you. Jump over to it and run down the hallway. Jump to the next ladder, climb it, and go to the door at the far end of the next hall. Press the button to open the door and reach the final showdown.

Drake is waiting for you behind this door.

When the door opens, you are confronted by Drake. Charge forward and go either right or left. He has a pair of goons with him, and you must deal with them first. Get rid of both, then turn your attention on Drake.

Nail the two astronauts before you start in on Drake.

Continue attacking Drake to keep him off balance. He tends to bob and weave a lot, making him difficult to get a fix on. He also likes to charge and backhand you. When he starts to fly directly toward you, slide away to the side and keep up the pressure with your laser.

This is not unlike your battle with Rook, but this time you don't have to worry about going vertical.

When Drake has taken sufficient damage, doors in the small side corridors open and additional astronauts come out to attack. As with the start of this battle, you are best off taking them out first, then returning to attack Drake.

Two astronauts are down each side corridor. There are also refueling stations for your jump jets here.

Keep up the pressure on Drake, and he will drop eventually. Once he does, you have 20 seconds to activate the escape pod. It's at the end of the short corridor to the right of where you first entered.

Finally, Drake takes enough damage to get exactly what he deserves.

Run to the end of the hall and press the button to enter the escape pod. Once inside, you blast back to Earth while the space platform explodes behind you. Back home, you meet up again with Alura McCall. M congratulates you for a job well done. Once again, 007 has made the world safe.

Multiplayer Tips and Strategies

You can have tons of fun competing in the missions that make up the *NightFire* story line. But you can also have a lot of fun competing in the multiplayer games included in *007 NightFire*. On the console you can compete with up to four different human opponents in split-screen mode and against up to ten computer-controlled bots. You can find out with these exciting matches.

007 NightFire has tons of multiplayer options.

On the console, take on up to four other human opponents in split screen mode.

Sniping

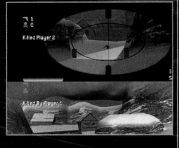

One of the more popular tactics in multiplayer games is sniping. You pick up one of the sniper rifles and hide out, picking off targets from a distance. In the Assassins game, this is an excellent strategy.

But it has some very serious drawbacks. It is easy to get tunnel vision as you look through that scope. The other players can sneak up from behind or from your flanks. If you try to snipe people,

make sure you can back up into a corner. That way, people won't be able to sneak up from behind.

Big Weapons

While playing the regular missions of the game, your choice of weapons is quite limited. That is not the case in the multiplayer maps. Weapons and ammunition are everywhere: everything from the basic Wolfram PP7 to the laser rifle. Be careful with the big weapons—they are great for delivering a lot of ammunition to the target, but their size can hamstring you. The AT-600 Scorpion is a great weapon for taking down the helicopter in the Phoenix Fire mission, and it can do a lot of damage in the multiplayer maps, but it takes a long time to reload and it has a slow rate of fire. Try to stick with weapons like the SG5 Commando, the Storm 32, or the Deutsche M9K. These weapons deliver a good punch and don't take forever to reload.

AT-420 Sentinel

The Sentinel guided missile is an awesome weapon in the multiplayer game. The weapon has a guided missile that you can steer to the target with on the camera embedded in the nose of the missile. You can squirrel yourself away in the corner, in a well-protected spot, and fire missiles out into the arenal—guiding them to your target. There is only one little hitch with this strategy. While you are guiding the missile, you can't see what is going on right in front of you. If an enemy can see the missile launch, they can follow the smoke trail back to your location and take you out with a couple of quick shots as you sit defenseless.

143

Weapon Turrets

There are several other weapons you can use in the level, like the laser prototype. While you are using these massive weapons, you can deal a lot of damage out to the enemy. While you are manning these guns, you are a stationary target. If the enemy can sneak up from behind you, you will get taken out quickly. Keep your eyes open, and don't become fixated on using these powerful weapons

Know the Levels

This is the best bit of advice to get. You must know the levels you are playing on. Play a bunch of games in which your sole goal is to get the lay of the land. When you are locked in an intense firefight against other human opponents, you don't have time to think about where you need to turn to get some cover; you have to *know* exactly where to go.

Console Multiplayer Tips and Strategies

The Scenarios

Arena

This scenario is a deathmatch involving free-for-all combat and using weapons that spawn around the mission area.

Team Arena

This scenario employs the same rules as Arena, except that agents are grouped into two teams. The combined score of every individual on the team results in the overall team score.

Console Multiplayer Tips and Strategies

Capture the Flag

Two bases are situated on every multiplayer level with a single flag on each one. Obtain points by stealing the enemy's flag and returning it to your own base. If a flag carrier is shot, the flag is dropped. If an enemy then touches the dropped flag, it is returned to its base. If neither side collects the flag after a short interval, it returns to its base automatically.

Uplink

Three satellite dishes are situated around the level. To activate the uplink, simply walk into the satellite dish to change it into your team's color. Your score consists of the length of time each satellite is your color, and the more satellites that are your color simultaneously, the higher your score goes.

Top Agent

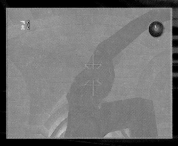

You have a predetermined number of lives (the number set in the Options menu before play begins). After you've used all your lives, you are out of the game. The last agent standing is the winner.

Demolition

MI6 must destroy a designated target site within a set time limit. The defending team must prevent the attackers from destroying the site. The most effective means of destroying a target is by planting a satchel charge on it. Each attacking team is equipped with a single satchel charge at the start of each round.

Protection

MI6 must protect its target object.

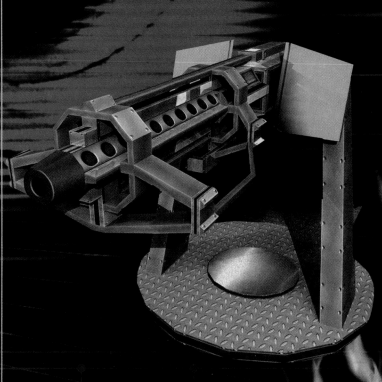

PRIMA'S OFFICIAL STRATEGY GUIDE

Industrial Espionage

The level contains a single disc of blueprints, which each team must collect and return to its base to get a new weapon or gadget for that team, and a new set of blueprints spawns into the level. Rival teams can steal pickups from their spawn points or by shooting the opposing team and looting their bodies. The final set of blueprints wins the game.

GoldenEye Strike

The goal of this level is to obtain the two halves of the GoldenEye controls. When combined, the controls can be used to trigger an orbital weapons strike on the enemy team. Teams compete to obtain both halves. A player carrying one of the halves will drop it if shot. Normal shots do not count toward the score; only those caused by the orbital weapon do. Halves spawn in random locations, except in Sub Pen.

Assassination

This is a team game in which an assassin comprises one team and the remaining players comprise the target team. One player on the target team is designated as the assassin's target. When the target is assassinated, another player is randomly selected as the next target. When the assassin is shot, another player is chosen at random to replace him. The assassin receives five points for shooting the target. The player who shoots the assassin receives three kills. If the assassin manages to shoot the target in the back, it is a one-hit kill.

King of the Hill

On each map is a single power field. You earn points by occupying the field, and the player with the highest score wins.

Team King of the Hill

Same as the nonteam version, except a player's

points earned by remaining in the power field go to the team's score.

The Maps

146

PRIMAGAMES.COM

Sky Rail

This extra-large map is a lot of fun. Use the cable car for a tactical advantage at this deserted ski

The Sky Rail map has tons of places to do combat. The structures at the top and bottom of the hill allow for some classic inside duels. Hanging out on the upper levels of the buildings and shooting down on your opponents is a great strategy.

The long open areas allow for powerful sniping opportunities. Be careful when you are looking through the scope; enemies can sneak up on you.

resort. There are tons of places for a sniper to hide in this level, so watch your back.

Fort Knox

This is another great map for the sneaky player. The multiple levels make it very difficult to root

Do battle in the world's most secure location—America's Fort Knox Gold Depository. Keep on the move, as there are lots of areas for your enemy to hide.

Use the stationary guns scattered throughout the level to do some awesome damage. The one problem with these guns as you are standing in one spot, making for a pretty inviting target.

out each and every enemy. Don't stay in one spot for long. There are multiple ways up and down through this extra-large map, so there is always the chance that someone will sneak up behind you.

Snow Blind

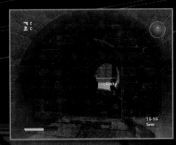 

You are back at Drake's castle, doing battle with your enemies in and out of the various courtyards.

Like the Fort Knox level, there are stationary guns as well. Use them wisely.

Expect a cold reception in this extensive maze of medieval tunnels and courtyards. Be sure you pick up the goodies along the way; there are tons of pickups scattered throughout the courtyards of this level. This extra-large map also offers tons of spots to hide.

Phoenix Base

The Phoenix Base has an interesting structure in the center of the map. Watch out for enemies up there on the high ground.

Or, take the high ground yourself. Watch out; you don't have much cover up there.

Phoenix Base is one of the smaller maps in *007 NightFire*. You will do battle in Drake's submarine pen. The action is tight and furious, and there isn't much room to hide. Go for the missiles in the center of the room to really create some chaos. Conversely, watch for players going for those missiles and pick them off while they are out in the open.

Atlantis

The Atlantis map provides a lot of intense action in and around the hallways.

This underwater base is a feeding frenzy of multi-player action. Run up and down the hallways on this multilevel map. The hallways confine the action. Don't get caught between two other players when you are running down the halls; being caught in a crossfire is always a bad idea.

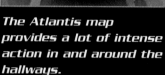

TIP

Mini-vehicles are on every level except Ravine. You can control tanks remotely and attack other combatants. When using mini-vehicles, you can't see what's going on around you while you are guiding the vehicle to other parts of the level.

Missile Silo

The Missile Silo provides a lot of vertical action. Watch out for enemies all around you.

Seize the high ground and pick off the enemies as they scurry beneath you.

You and your fellow combatants battle on four floors of this old missile silo. Use the pillars to provide cover from your opponent's gunshots.

Sub Pen

Not only do you fight out in this submarine pen, but you will fight it out with other secret agents inside the submarine itself. Ferreting out all of the agents on this level can be tricky, so make sure you look in every nook and cranny. Use the elevators to move between the levels quickly.

In the Sub Pen, you do battle around Drake's nuclear submarine—outside the submarine...

...and inside the submarine. Ferreting out all of enemies can be difficult, as the submarine provides a defensible position.

Ravine

This is a great map for snipers. The long distance between the two cliffs makes for some great long-range shots. Ride the cable cars that run between the two cliffs to get from one side to the other. Keep moving to stay alive and avoid the other snipers.

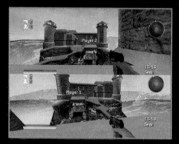 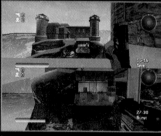

The large ravine will separate the players at the beginning of the level. A good sniper can be very effective on this level.

Aside from using the land bridge, if you want to cross to the other side, you will have to ride the cable cars. Crouch for cover as you move from one side to the other.

PC Multiplayer Tips and Strategies

Game Types

Combat Training

Combat Training is essentially a free-for-all. You are pitted against every other player in the game, who is pitted against everyone else as well. In general, these games go for a certain amount of time or until one player has chalked up a specified number of kills.

Team Combat Training

Similar to Combat Training, this places all of the agents on one of two teams. The teams then compete to wipe each other out. All of the standard rules of Combat Training games apply. These games generally go until one team has scored a specified number of kills or until time runs out. The "Friendly Fire" option allows you to hurt and be hurt by your teammates. Eliminating a team member removes one kill from your team's total. The teams are M16 and Pheonix.

Capture the Flag

In these games, the number of kills you or your teams scores is immaterial. Instead, the goal is to infiltrate the enemy base and grab their flag. Once you do, the flag must be returned to your base to score a point. The maps for these games are set up symmetrically, with each side given the same positions and weapons. Games generally are played to a predetermined number of flag captures.

The Maps

Austria

The Austria map is essentially the same as the second part of your first mission: the exterior and a small piece of the interior of Drake's castle in Austria. There are a few notable differences, not the least of which is the prevalence of grapple points, allowing you to zoom from ground level to a higher floor quickly.

Don't miss the Ronin on the top of this catwalk. You can get there with the grapple or by a ladder on each side.

The most significant differences are the number of areas that have been opened, allowing for a relatively circular map. On the ground, the doorway behind the truck is open, leading to the interior of the building leading up to the tower. The tower itself is open at the top, allowing access to the roof, and to the rocket launcher on the catwalk area.

You can now leave the tower after collecting the sniper rifle. The platform below and to the right holds the rocket launcher.

The second floor of the tower also leads to the catwalks outside and the rocket launcher. You can also go from here to the second floor of the nearby buildings, leading down to where you unlocked the doors in the single-player mission.

Casino

This area is based on the Casino in *The World is Not Enough*. Casino feels very much like new territory because it is new territory. This is a relatively small map and has a claustrophobic feel. In truth, you can get from anywhere to just about anywhere else in a matter of a few seconds. Balconies have convenient staircases, and even the smallest room has multiple exits.

It's easy to get from the ground floor to the second floor on the casino map.

Most of the weapons, armor, and ammunition on this map are hidden on or behind the various counters and gaming tables located throughout. None of these are safe to approach because every one of them is the focal point for a staircase, passageway, or door.

NOTE

There's a secret room behind a bookcase. The room contains a Ronin briefcase. Use your Q-Specs in X-Ray mode to find it.

If you can get to the body armor on this small, secluded balcony, you'll have a safe haven for a few moments.

The secret to this level is to start moving and keep moving. No place is safe for very long, and any position that overlooks another is vulnerable. If you like to sit still and snipe, this is not the map for you. If, however, you thrive on running wild and attacking anything you come across, this one may be your favorite.

Caviar

This area is based on the Zukousky caviar warehouse in *The World is Not Enough*. It is also only playable for Combat Training and Team Combat Training. Unlike Casino, Caviar is wide open, featuring huge areas outside and some relatively secluded areas that are perfect for sniping. The presence of the red barrels is not as dangerous as you might at first think—they aren't explosive, so don't waste your ammunition on them.

The water on this level makes for an interesting addition. In addition to swimming up to your enemies, you also have the added danger of drowning.

It's the warehouse areas of this map that make it particularly interesting. Of note is the crusher, located directly below the catwalk holding the rocket launcher. On the opposite side of the warehouse, a switch controls the floor here. When pressed, the floor drops away, sending the offending enemy into the crusher below—a nasty price to pay for grabbing the rocket launcher. Needless to say, being eliminated in this way is embarrassing.

Get the rocket launcher with caution. If there's anyone on the opposite catwalk, don't take the chance.

This is a large map, and it's easy to get lost. Your best strategy is to keep moving and look for weapons. There are plenty of places to hide under stairwells or behind crates if you feel like sitting still and going the sniper route. The size of this map makes it perfect for large combats between two large teams.

TIP

There is a small tunnel in the "crusher" that you can use to escape the death trap if you fall in.

Fort Knox

This area is based on the Fort Knox in *Goldfinger*. Of all the maps, Fort Knox has the best visibility, thanks to the good lighting and the presence of thousands of bars of shiny gold. You have free reign inside the vaults as well as some of the exterior areas of the Fort.

The exterior of Fort Knox is uncompli-cated and easy to spot targets in.

While the outside is entertaining because it is so open and offers a few bunkers to hole up in, it's the interior of the Fort that deserves most of your attention. All of the good weapons are here, and almost all of them are placed next to several clips of ammunition.

You find the best weapons inside. Naturally, this is where most of your enemies will be, too.

The interior of the Fort can be confusing. There are multiple levels of gold storage, all linked to a large central area with a series of staircases allowing access to each floor. If you have time, move quickly with the grapple, but this leaves you open to attack.

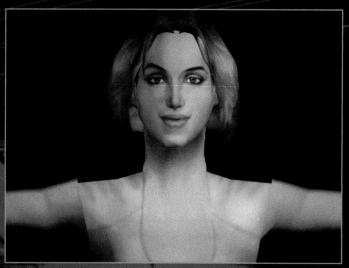

Don't let yourself get cornered. Keep moving and go outside for a break when you need it. Armor is hard to find, and is generally located in the gold storage areas on the ground floor.

Island

It's not what you might think at first. The Island map is essentially the interior of a missile base. It features long, straight corridors set up as firing alleys with very little cover. Accuracy is critical on this map, because you don't have many places to hide.

Gun duels like this one are common on the Island map.

Weapons and armor on this level are generally located on top of the red barrels. These are spread around the level almost everywhere, meaning that almost anyone you spot will be well-armed. Accurate weapons like the sniper rifle and those that do a lot of damage like the rocket launcher are good choices.

> ### TIP
> There is a trap door near the two generators that drop you into a room with a Ronin briefcase, rocket ammo, armor plate, and a PDW90 (Combat Training map only).

The accurate and powerful Raptor is also a good weapon choice for this map.

While much of the terrain on this map features enclosed tunnels, there are open areas. As with all maps that feature some vertical areas, be on the lookout for grapple points to allow for quick access to areas above you. This map is all about being accurate and doing as much damage as you can, as quickly as you can. Having a height advantage and using the element of surprise can help improve your chances.

> ## NOTE
> The Caputure the Flag map for this area is very different from the Combat Training map.

Japan

This map is based loosely on the Japan mission, although it covers a much smaller amount of territory. You can roam through most of the areas of the first single-player Japan mission as well as through a small part of Mayhew's bunker in the basement. It's a small map, which makes it perfect for smaller groups.

Tight quarters make this map perfect for rapid-fire weapons like the PDW90.

The main differences here are where the original single-player map moved into new areas. The ladder at the end of Mayhew's bunker now leads to the carpark area outside. Similarly, the small secret area off where you started now takes you to the area outside the normal entrance to the bunker.

> ## NOTE
> The Caputure the Flag map for this area is very different from the Combat Training map.

Sneak up on your enemies by using the ladder in the bunker. The carpark is a frequent gathering place, making this a good place to surprise a few folks.

Except for a couple of loft areas and the bunker, Japan is two-dimensional, which means you don't have the grapple. This is a very small map with a lot of tight areas. The presence of paper walls means your Q-Specs will be more useful here than on most maps. Use them on x-ray mode to get the jump on enemies fighting it out on the other side of the flimsy barriers.

Jungle

The Jungle map is similar to the fifth part of the Island Getaway single-player mission. The action takes place around the first ECM bunker and some of the landscape in the area. The basement of the ECM building contains a ladder down to a tunnel leading to a nearby warehouse, which is a good location for sniping. This is a tougher map than the others listed so far, and you start with both a P2K and a shotgun.

This is a dark mission, so be sure to use the Q-Specs on IR mode to spot your foes.

The real prize on this map is the Annihilator, which is located at the top of the ECM building. You can reach this from a ladder both along the side of the building and from the lower roof. Going via the lower roof is safer, because it leaves you vulnerable for a much shorter period of time.

The Annihilator is the true prize on this level. With it, you can really tear through the bad guys.

Near the Annihilator, you can climb a huge radio tower for the ultimate sniping position. From this vantage point, you can look down on the entire exterior area of the map, pegging anyone who runs past. This is an exposed point, however, so be careful while you are up here.

Maintenance

This map is a combination of the fourth and fifth parts of the Phoenix Rising mission, consisting of the maintenance area of the building as well as part of the roof. The roof area is interesting because with presence of the elevator. Here, by grappling up, you can claim a battery that allows you to use your Q-Specs constantly. The battery functions even after you've been eliminated.

> ### NOTE
> This area is only playable for Combat Training and Team Combat Training.

Getting the permanent battery should be one of your first goals on this map.

The reason the battery is so important is that the interior of the level is very dark. Having the nightvision aspect of the Q-Specs available to you at all times is extremely helpful in spotting your enemies before they spot you.

> ### TIP
> Using the Q-Specs on nightvision mode helps a great deal when running through the maintenance part of this map.

This is a medium-sized map, good for small groups or two-on-two teams. Once you've collected the permanent battery, the only other thing to get outside is the sniper rifle, which is of limited usefulness on such a small, tight map. Spend your time inside, using nightvision to get the drop on your foes.

Office

This level is based on the interior of the Phoenix International building, but there are a few changes here that you might not be used to. One of the biggest is a small balcony area that overlooks part of the hallway. It's worth investigating both for the position it offers and for the suit of body armor located here.

This balcony is new, and the body armor makes it worth investigating.

The conference room near the central atrium holds a true prize: an Annihilator. This is the premier weapon on this map because it features fairly close quarters despite its size. Pick this up whenever you have the chance.

The Annihilator is a great weapon for this map because you'll often be close to your foes.

While there is a lot of territory on this map, there isn't much up and down. It's a pretty flat area with the exception of the balcony already mentioned and a similar one on the other side. Movement is critical, because there aren't many good sniping positions. Keep moving, using the balconies and crossing hallways as paths to get from one end to the other rapidly.

TIP

The P0W90, rocket launcher, and grenade launcher are desireable weapons for use in multiplayer mode.

Power

This map is based very loosely on the first part of the Hidden Agenda mission which leads up to the astronaut area in the single-player game. The terrain is similar, at least, and some of the rooms have the same feel to them. There are several areas of narrow corridors and small rooms mixed with open areas where anything goes.

There are some open areas on this map, perfect for mixing it up. If you like enclosed spaces, those are here, too.

In the center of the map on the lowest level, there is an Annihilator. Other weapons are dispersed throughout the map, often appearing on the red barrels that dot the area. Weapons can be risky to pick up, because most are out in the open (especially the Annihilator), which means they are easily targeted by other players.

The Annihilator is out in the open. It's worth the risk to claim it.

Unlike the previous couple of maps, this one contains a lot of vertical areas with staircases leading up two or three floors. You will have to watch above and below in addition to your own level as you move. Sniping is risky here. While there are some excellent positions that offer a good field of fire, these are generally exposed and leave you vulnerable to anyone passing into the area.

NOTE
This area is only playable for Combat Training and Team Combat Training.

Romania

Romania is set up specifically for Capture the Flag games and cannot be played in Combat Training or Combat Training Teams games. This is a huge, symmetrical map with each of the two sides having the same flag area and safe areas behind the flag.

Your flag is centered in a small depression. The enemy flag area will look exactly like this.

The key, of course, is getting the enemy flag. Once a team member has it, you will have to guard his retreat until he makes it all the way back to your base. He'll be a target for all enemy fire, which also means you should be prepared to pick up his burden and carry the flag yourself if it becomes necessary.

Once someone on your team has the flag, be prepared to help him get it home.

The middle of the map is the most interesting. In the center, there is a rocket launcher, which is by far the deadliest weapon on this level. Because enemies tend to bunch up when assaulting your position, this is the weapon of choice when you can get it. Sniper rifles on balconies overlook the center area, a good place for accurate shooters to help guard the middle.

Tower

Like Romania, this map is only playable in Capture the Flag games. This time, your flag is in a small enclosure of breakable glass. It takes a concerted effort to break in, and it's tough going to capture the enemy flag.

Your flag is well-protected in its bunker. Of course, the enemy flag is in just as good of a position.

Unlike the Romania map, you don't start near a whole slew of weapons. You will need to search around your area to collect the various weapons that you'll need to either protect your flag or go after the enemy's. Most of the weapons are in the area surrounding your spawn point. Grab a few before taking up a defensive position or assaulting the other guys.

NOTE

The glass around the spawn room is bulletproof.

Use the grapple just outside the spawn point to grab the Ronin. This is the best base defense you have.

Keep in mind that there are multiple paths to each side of the map. Any path you discover on your end is present on the enemy side as well. This means that even in defense, you can't stay too static. You will need to move around to guard the various possible entrances to your base.

157

BEAT THE WORLD,
One Level At A Time

With so many levels to conquer, **you need a plan.** Information about what's coming, what's here, what's now; tips and strategies from the inside, cheats direct from the source...

That's **EAGAMES.com,** where you'll find the latest demos, movies you just can't get anywhere else, screenshots direct from the game makers, and official information about every available EA GAMES title. All in one place, only at *eagames.com*

EA GAMES

Challenge Everything™

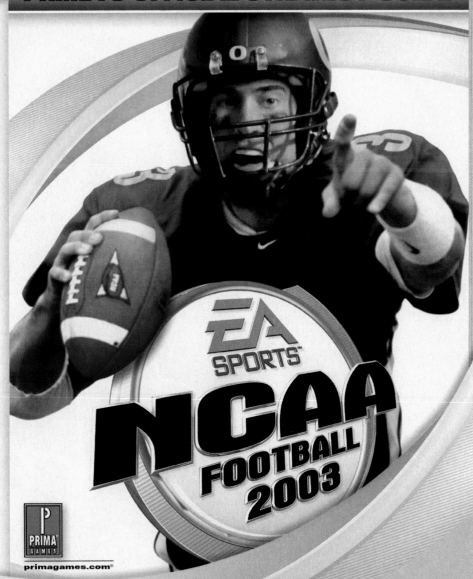

NOW AVAILABLE FROM
PRIMA GAMES!

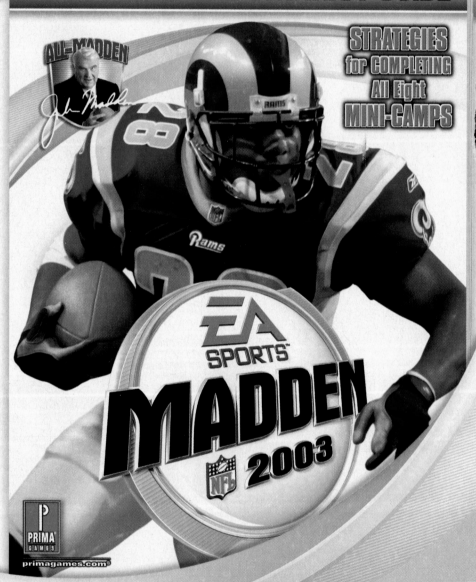

PRIMA'S OFFICIAL STRATEGY GUIDE

ALL-MADDEN

STRATEGIES for COMPLETING All Eight MINI-CAMPS

EA SPORTS™
MADDEN NFL 2003

PRIMA GAMES
primagames.com®

Complete coverage of every NFL team

Strategies for using Franchise mode

Detailed offensive and defensive tutorials

Separate draft lists by position for every player

Madden challenge checklist with all Madden cards revealed!